Africa and Its Explorers

Motives, Methods, and Impact

edited by Robert I. Rotberg

Cambridge, Massachusetts, 1970
Harvard University Press

For Fiona, Nicola, and Rebecca
and other intrepid explorers
on new frontiers

Acknowledgments

The editor wishes especially to acknowledge the unstinting cooperation of the contributors to this volume. He is deeply indebted to James Duffy for advice and criticism, and to the Misses Stephanie Jones, Emily Barclay, and Susan Elliott for significant assistance with the proofs and index. Throughout the many months that elapsed between the gestation of this volume in 1965 and its completion, the editor also received critical administrative and bibliographical assistance from Mrs. Jane F. Tatlock. The debts of the individual authors are acknowledged, where appropriate, in the notes to each chapter.

R. I. R.
Cambridge
16 February 1970

Contents

Illustrations

Maps

(drawn by Richard Sanderson)

Introduction

by Robert I. Rotberg

The explorers who provide the reason for this collective study were all men who, by any European-derived standards, played a significant part in the opening-up of Africa to the Western world. Each added in his own way to the excitement of Africa's discovery; each undertook at least one major journey that stirred the hearts of armchair followers in Europe. Their different adventures were followed avidly by a public obsessed—as today's is with exploits in space—with the drama and glory of the conquest of the mysterious dark continent. All received the medals and plaudits of the world's leading geographical societies, the praise of statesmen, and international recognition of a most gratifying kind. Celebrities of a romantic, evangelical age, they were much sought after in metropolitan society, and were heroes to several generations of men and boys. That the explorers were operating on a critically important and interesting frontier there could be little doubt.

The men whose experiences are analyzed in the present collection include, with but few exceptions, the most important explorers ever to have traversed the interior of tropical Africa. There were others of stature, and the geographical achievements of James Bruce, Mungo Park, Johann Ludwig Burckhardt, Hugh Clapperton, Dixon Denham, Richard Lander, Gaspard Mollien, René Caillié, Paul Belloni du Chaillu, and Alexandre Serpa Pinto conceivably equaled some of the exploits examined here, but only the saga of Mungo Park's strenuous trek to the Niger River and his subsequent death downstream, or Richard Lander's comparatively straightforward journey down the Niger River, ever fully captured the imagination of their contemporaries. In short, although the present collection does not pretend to be either representative (explorers came from unusually diverse backgrounds) or inclusive, it discusses a number of the most interesting and renowned.

Although all but two of the nine explorers to whom the following chapters are devoted were British by birth, their moods and actions fit no convenient, all-encompassing pattern. David Livingstone for the first time focused the attention of the West upon the sufferings of the peoples of Africa; unlike Bruce and Park, his predecessors, he stimulated an overwhelming evangelical and commercial interest in the hitherto uninvestigated interior of Africa. By his words as much as his deeds—three major sorties into and across central Africa between 1851 and 1873—he encouraged the subsequent initiatives of nearly all of the other explorers scrutinized herein. Obsessed by the human condition and geographical puzzle of tropical Africa, he towers above the others by sheer force of personality. Richard Burton lacked few talents and made the most of each. He was a polymath who observed everything through an intensely personal prism, his lush prose making in some senses a more lasting impact than did his actual geographical discoveries. But he led a memorable and controversial expedition to Lake Tanganyika after having previously traversed Somalia and Muslim Ethiopia; later he entered Dahomey and the Cameroonian coastlands. John Speke, Burton's erstwhile companion, surmised that the Victoria Nyanza was the main source of the White Nile and went on, in 1861–62, to demonstrate the accuracy of his prediction. Samuel White Baker, a colorful hunter of determined mien, completed most of the outline of the route of the White Nile when he reached the shores of Lake Albert in 1864. Henry Morton Stanley, the ruthlessly ambitious journalist turned explorer, initially succored Livingstone in 1871 and wrote the first of his racy narratives (the second related his adventures with British troops in the Gold Coast and Ethiopia), and subsequently circumnavigated Victoria Nyanza, visited Buganda, followed the Congo River from its upper tributaries to its mouth, and tried to relieve a beleaguered Emin Pasha. Verney Lovett Cameron sought to find Livingstone in 1873, and, instead, became the first European in modern times to traverse the African continent from east to west. Of the two Germans, Heinrich Barth was the first European fully to explore the Western and Central Sudans geographically, politically, and intellectually. Gerhard Rohlfs, a prototype of the many Europeans who entered Africa somewhat after the sands of ignorance had largely been etched by earlier endeavor, heroically trekked across the Atlas Mountains of Morocco, the sub-Saharan wastes of Chad, the oases of Cyrenaica, and portions of Ethiopia just before and during the height of Europe's hectic scramble for African outposts. Joseph Thomson, a young Scot, pioneered a route to lakes Nyasa and Tanganyika in 1879–80, traversed Masailand in 1883–84, visited the Central Sudan, climbed in southern Morocco, and ventured into trans-Zambezia on the eve of its annexation. Collectively, the exploits of these nine men, whose activities spanned the years between 1849 and 1891, reflect the range of approaches to and the processes of the exploration of tropical Africa.

We know quite clearly and fully in what ways these explorers individually and as a group advanced the sum of Europe's cartographical knowledge. Fragments of their published output and portions of their contemporary lectures still form the stuff of anthologies, their thirty-seven full-length works have provided the basis of a thriving reprint industry, and, if the general reader may know little about Africa, he at least recognizes the names of its three or four outstanding European explorers. By and large, however, our understanding of the historical contribution of explorers in general, and the ones discussed in this book in particular, is still only partial. No modern secondary literature serves a comparative purpose, and Burton alone has been the subject of a penetrating modern biography. The career of Rohlfs is almost totally unknown, especially to the English-reading audience. Baker, Speke, and Stanley are more often stereotyped than understood. Barth's reputation has recently been revived, if only in part, and Thomson is remembered more for his waterfall and his gazelle than for his explorations. Livingstone, the subject of innumerable biographies, paradoxically remains both the best known name and the most elusive personality. The essays in this book attempt to reassess the accomplishments of the nine explorers in the light of modern scholarship and to place their actions in an African rather than a European context.

Without the benefit of a wide and penetrating range of psychoanalytically relevant data, detailed autobiographical statements, revealing biographies, the candid reminiscences of associates or relatives, or, at least, a wealth of circumstantial evidence, it is probably impossible to reach any irrefutable conclusions about the underlying motivations and deep-seated drives of these explorers. A recent study of West African explorers—men like Barth, Thomas Edward Bowdich, Caillié, Clapperton, Denham, Lander, Mollien, Joseph Simon Gallieni, Louis Gaston Binger, and Thomas Winterbottom—called them obsessives who were driven equally by curiosity, humanitarianism (i.e., they favored the conversion of Africans to the European model), the need to open up trade routes, and concern for fostering the political and economic expansion of Europe. None, writes the author, sought—unlike Stanley, Thomson, and Speke—to make a career or money from their exploits.[1] These are generalizations which would fit a few, but certainly not all, of the explorers discussed in the present book. For the most part, the major explorers were possessed of unusually complex personalities, the explication of which defies any easy categorization. Several drove themselves relentlessly, even unto death, being mesmerized by immediate psychic rewards, the quest of grandeur, and the possibility of self-redemption. For others a single foray into the unknown proved ample, or possibly sufficient, to satisfy less obsessive compulsions. Several sought the immediate and intangible rewards of adventure; a few explored in order to pursue the more tangible ends of geographical and scientific discovery; and some simply tramped across Africa in order to escape the tentacles of Europe's dominant class system. Nearly all were hopelessly romantic. No single explanation suffices, not even in an individual instance. It is perfectly clear, however, that only in the case of David Livingstone was exploration meant to serve African as well as European ends. These were not necessarily goals to which Africans would have

1. Hubert Deschamps, *L'Europe découvre l'Afrique: Afrique Occidentale, 1794–1900* (Paris, 1967), 240–243. There is no psychoanalytic literature on African explorers in general, but Fawn Brodie's *The Devil Drives* (London, 1967) is a pioneering examination of Richard Burton's psyche.

aspired, but he presumed that they would welcome European contributions to the cessation of the slave trade and the opening-up of a range of hitherto unknown cultural opportunities. Foremost, in his eyes, the heart of Africa had been brutally slashed by vicious slave raids; those who dwelt therein suffered, and at least some part of Livingstone was intent on bringing about relief. But even Livingstone was not unaware of the ultimate rewards of recognition and fame which could accrue to discoverers of the putative unknown. Nor was he unimpressed with the importance of accumulating knowledge about the peoples and features of Africa; his works testify to a catholicity of scientific taste and skill which overshadowed nearly all of his fellow explorers. Then, too, Livingstone relentlessly sought his destiny—speaking both religiously and psychoanalytically—beyond a distant frontier. In this last regard he is the archetype of them all.

Except conceivably for the more prosaic Cameron, and the markedly materialistic Baker, the explorers discussed hereinafter, and explorers as a class, traveled in search of themselves. Most were in that sense egocentric: in order to open up the heart of a continent a man had, in addition to his other skills, to be imbued with a certitude of vision, an abundance of self-confidence, and a heightened awareness of the proportions of his deed. Stanley grasped these dimensions fully, and probably was the one who exploited them in the most conscious fashion. Burton took Africa as his playground but, uniquely, placed it within a larger, global framework of his own creation. Thomson and Speke were less swashbuckling than Stanley or Burton, but they, too, moved with a not unworthy sense of creativity. Their motives, and those of the others, derived from the same common source of human purposefulness that nourished the mid-Victorian evangelical reformers, systematic thinkers, and, indeed, captains of industry. In the case of the explorers, however, their deeds and their drives were unambivalently acclaimed by a welcoming public which was stirred and uplifted by the real or imagined drama of their seeming valor, derring-do, and idealism.

Given the absence of any overwhelming interest in Africans

for their own sake, it is hardly surprising that the explorers, Barth and Livingstone excepted, evinced such disdain for everything African. They were not alone in this regard and to some extent reflected in their writings, if not in their perceptions, the Social Darwinism of an age distinctly conscious of its own civilization. Their first concern, however, was exploration, not comparative ethnology; here, after all, the rewards were tangible and obvious. Only Barth, a scholar before he became an explorer, steeped himself in the histories of the populations among whom he wandered. Burton and Livingstone were interested in human development as well as in geographical conquests (in Burton's case perhaps more so), but this concern was rare and idiosyncratic. Much of the travel literature of the nineteenth century thus contains only perfunctory descriptions of African life. Only the works of Livingstone, Barth, and Burton, and Livingstone's posthumously published journals, contain a wealth of ethnologically valuable matter, Burton's accounts being sullied for the present generation by blatant displays of prejudice. It is true that Speke provides a lavish description of the Gandan court, Baker paints a picture of the Nyoro monarch Kamurasi, Thomson gives a glimpse of the Chagga chief Mangi Rindi (Mandara), and the writings of the others are not completely devoid of human interest and concern. But for the most part this concern is *en passant*, some of it is inaccurate, distorted, unfairly selected, or misleading, and the conspectus of their own interests that is conveyed by the whole of their publications (a quantitative examination of the subjects treated by explorers would prove exceptionally valuable) is distinctly the opposite of the warm feeling for Africans that has been attributed to them. There is a prurient interest, of course, which is exemplified by Burton's discourses, and there is a degree of patronizing attention, but overall, their interest in the essence of Africa is exiguous (Barth and Livingstone again strikingly excepted). Africans often appear as objects being manipulated rather than subjects worthy of the identification of the nineteenth-century reader.

All of the writers but Barth and Livingstone appear to have been infected to a greater or lesser degree with the microbes of prejudice. Burton's scorn is well-known, the others imitating his mode in print, and presumably acting in a similar manner merely to a lesser degree. Even Thomson, whose reputation as a humane, gentle explorer—the very antithesis of Stanley and Baker in his methods—was widespread, spoke and wrote disparagingly of Africans. Yet could we have expected a more enlightened performance? Nearly all of these men were explorers first, geographers second, natural scientists third, and humanists last. They reflected the emotional responses of their age and, in some cases (Stanley, Cameron, and Thomson), were more concerned to "do a job" great or small, than to spend (or "waste") valuable time examining the lives and behavior of peoples who, in the eyes of their generation, were mere "heathen." In this respect they echoed the sentiments of the tenth-century Arab traveler Ibn Hawqal, who excused his failure to describe the peoples of the Western Sudan: "Naturally loving wisdom, ingenuity, religion, justice, and regular government, how could I notice such people as these, or magnify them by inserting an account of their countries?" Then, too, our analysis of the motives and responses of the nineteenth-century explorers depends largely on the evidence of their printed accounts, the composition of which may have been influenced by the narrow expectations of a Victorian readership.

Each of these essays seeks, within the limitations posed by the lack of evidence, to examine the ways in which particular explorers coped with Africans and Africa, their methods, and their behavior among and toward Africans.[2] Only one obvious conclusion emerges: as explorers they depended on the guidance of Africans and Arabs. They followed oft-tramped paths to predetermined, locally well-known objectives, and "made"

2. The evidential question is important. Although many of the subjects of the following chapters wrote one or more books, and we possess a few of their original diaries and journals, the extent of the revealing correspondence of the explorers is not great. In order to assess motives and methods, the contributors to this volume have of necessity had to read between the lines of the explorers' writings, argue inductively from a variety of disparate and often unsatisfactory published sources, and try to gauge African responses and involvements on the basis of a careful rereading of the extant indigenous and foreign accounts.

discoveries which were, nearly always, mere confirmations of information available in the interior if not in coastal entrepôts. A few deductions were essential, and the explorers could, as Africans usually could not, place their own particular discoveries (the linking of Victoria Nyanza with the land of the Pharaohs is an obvious example) into a larger whole. The explorers, as practical geographers, therefore pushed back the frontiers of ignorance and added empirically to the store of world knowledge at a time when only firsthand observation by literate men could satisfy the curious. They thus performed a vital intellectual and disseminating role even if they cannot be said, in any narrow sense, to have explored Africa unaided or to have made fresh discoveries—of a synthetic kind—of their own.

This small but important sample of explorers shows that very few ever really traveled anywhere alone. Only Rohlfs, Barth, and, toward the very end, Livingstone can be said to have ambled by themselves; the others were led and instructed in the arts of travel by the Africans who headed and helped to organize their journeys. Africans could speak indigenous languages, follow the long-existing and anyway well-marked trails with ease, and cope with life in the bush; in general they were completely at home in what the explorers naturally viewed as a hostile environment. Nearly all of the explorers were sustained by a walking commissariat, depended upon supplies carried by a retinue of porters, and were protected by a small knot of soldiers. It is true, as Deschamps avers, that an ability to improvise was essential, and that the explorers had in most circumstances to be diplomatic (to be discreet and to flatter),[3] but only Barth and Rohlfs were forced to live off the land or (like Stanley) by their own wits. Even Livingstone was dependent upon African companions. And Thomson would probably not have attained innermost Africa without the assistance of Chuma, who had traveled with Livingstone. Indeed, in the annals of East African exploration a number of African names recur. These were the men who guided not one, but several explorers. They were the professionals, and

3. Deschamps, *L'Europe découvre*, 250.

the explorers could rely upon the efforts and experience of the best of this group.

Of the explorers whose methods are discussed, Stanley and Burton were the most ruthless and, for the era of white penetration, the most typical. Stanley brooked no opposition and justified any means to accomplish desired or desirable ends. Corporal punishment won obedience from his followers and the diligent employment of superior firepower cowed any overt displays of African opposition. Others, although they occasionally resorted to arms in order to force their own way, were less aggressive. Some, like Thomson, were temperamentally unsuited to violence; others, the majority, were practical men who realized that the use of violent means could well redound to their own detriment. And few were as well endowed financially or bolstered militarily as Stanley. For the most part the explorers did what they were told, were powerless to prevent their own exploitation by local monarchs, and were compelled to bend principle according to the whims of the persons and groups to whom they were beholden. They negotiated more than they coerced, and only in rare instances were they the swashbucklers that they portrayed themselves to be.

The authors of the following essays were asked to assess the impact of their subject upon African society. Again, the evidence is limited to the writings of the men concerned, extrapolations therefrom, a scattering of indigenous orally communicated contemporary reports, and a very few African written judgments. As such, in most cases it proved far too limited for any confident conclusions to be reached. The overall impression, however, is of a startling lack of contemporary impact. If the explorers were in many cases oblivious of the Africans by whom they were surrounded, Africans appear to have been even less aware of the portentous nature of the explorations and of the peregrinations of the explorers. This is not to say that the *kabaka* of Buganda and the *omukama* of Bunyoro were unaware of the existence of Speke, Baker, and Stanley; rather, these men, and even Livingstone, were customarily regarded in a light similar to that in which the court of Imperial China examined envoys from the West. The explorers were worthy bearers of tribute and, conceivably, representatives of powerful monarchs, but, with one or two exceptions, they created no sensations and were received with (sometimes impolite) curiosity and affection of a kind usually reserved for visiting men of commerce. The less powerful were occasionally mistreated, robbed, and bullied. All were made to experience the sense of their inferiority. In their African setting, the explorers seem to have made no discernible impact; they altered the lives of Africans little and introduced nothing more than the notion of a Western world beyond (most Africans already had far-flung commercial contacts), and, if this is a test, the visits of only a few are remembered in the relevant oral traditions.

What then did the explorers contribute to the sum of Africa's history? There is no gainsaying that the discovery of Africa played a much more striking role for the expansion of Europe than it immediately altered the evolution of the internal history of most parts of Africa. Ultimately, however, increasing the sum of Europe's knowledge of the interior of Africa, its physical features, drainage patterns, and geographical complexity—which was the explorers' immediate contribution—made these areas accessible to evangelical, colonial, and martial penetration by whites of a number of nationalities. Certainly explorers, as a class, logically had to pave the way for others, some missionaries admittedly doubling as explorers, and, in a very real sense, exploration was and had to be the handmaiden of imperialism. But it was not the mere fact of geographical discovery that led inexorably to colonial rule and there may be less of a necessary causal connection between the two than is often supposed. The travels of Burton, Cameron, Rohlfs, and Barth quickened no imperial pulse; Speke's may have, and Stanley and Thomson were, but only at the end, in the employ of European expansionists. Causally, Livingstone's judgments and moral fervor probably mattered more than did his geographical and scientific insights. He dramatized the suffering of Africans, emphasized the demoralization of their lives because of the slave trade, and urged Britons to take up the "white man's burden." The burden—the civilizing mission—obviously played a large part in justifying the outthrust of imperialism and ensuring its widespread support in Europe. And to that extent, begging the question whether colonial rule was or was not beneficial, it can be said that explorers as a group encouraged the twaining of Africa's destiny with the West.

But not even the efforts of Livingstone or Stanley ensured it. The onset of colonial rule might have come about irrespective of the explorers—for strategic, economic, and political reasons quite divorced from the outcome of discovery. Commercially they were even less important, most of Africa having already been exposed to mercantile forays by the traders of the continent. Ultimately, explorers must be seen as disseminators of information and intellectual middlemen, as precursors but not progenitors of imperialism. Africans may logically and rightfully choose to adopt a purely chauvinistic point of view, to ignore the extent to which the explorers contributed to Africa's own self-awareness and to label their contribution minor. But nothing can obscure the inherent drama of the explorers' affairs with Africa.

Heinrich Barth:
An Exercise in Empathy

by Anthony Kirk-Greene

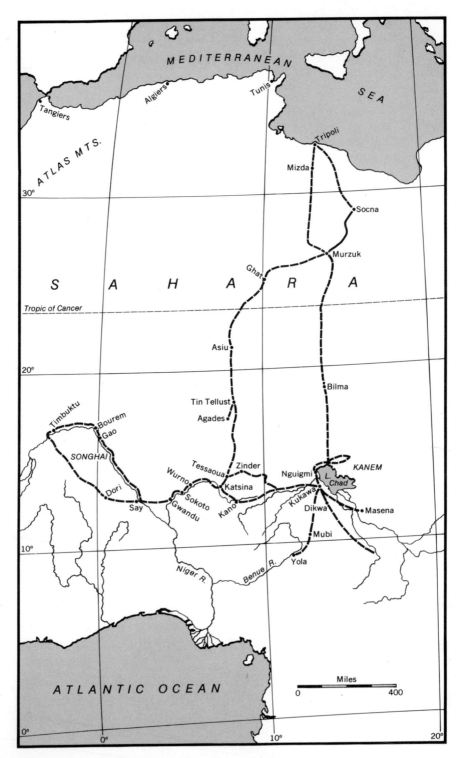

The travels of Heinrich Barth in Central Africa

If memories are proverbially short the world over, in Africa physical and personal reminders are exposed to a much greater risk of rapid deterioration and oblivion than they are in more temperate climates. Letters and memoirs are prone to devastation by the elements and the insect world. Barth records the fate of one of his letters where, "in consequence of the violent rains through which [the messenger] had had to make his way, and the many rivers and swamps which he had to cross, the whole envelope of the letter . . . had been destroyed, so that [the addressee], receiving only the English letter and not knowing what to do with this hieroglyphic, at length returned it to the bearer, who had since used it as a charm." [1] More solid personal belongings are also vulnerable, as Barth again had reason to know: on his way to Timbuktu, white ants played havoc with his clothes and baggage,[2] and a fire in Gwandu town destroyed all the books he had left in a friend's safekeeping. Souvenirs and presents are less well cared for in the typical African residential situation, so they have a harder struggle for survival: Rabeh's sack of Kukawa in 1893 effectively ended any chance of Barth's plentiful presents to the Shehu of Bornu being subsequently discovered in the royal storehouse.[3]

So rapid has been the pace of change in the past century that even personal memories, tokens of friendship, and tales of

1. Entry in journal for 17 August 1854 (*Travels and Discoveries in North and Central Africa* [London, 1857–58], V, 327).
2. 4 February 1853 (*Travels and Discoveries*, IV, 97).
3. In any case, where, one might legitimately ask in reverse parenthesis, are the "four chests" of seventy-seven assorted Bornuese items presented by the Shehu of Bornu to Queen Victoria and duly received at Buckingham Palace in June 1853? One of the first researchers to uncover this correspondence in the Foreign Office archives was P. A. Benton, whose *Notes on Some Languages of the Western Sudan*, containing much of relevance to Barth, has been republished in *The Languages and Peoples of Bornu* (London, 1968), intro. by A. H. M. Kirk-Greene.

reminiscence have been so telescoped that many have been virtually obliterated. In Africa, indeed, it is often hard to point and say, save in a highly figurative sense, "this is what he did." Such a fall into forgottenness, not deliberate but involuntary and inevitable, may have been the subsequent fate of many of the great travelers to Africa during the pioneering period of the nineteenth century, however well remembered— or, in some instances, recently revived—their exploits are in Europe. An added impetus toward this kind of early oblivion is the "initial" character of any voyage of discovery, often resulting locally in the subsequent overlooking of him who blazed the trail. In the context of nineteenth-century Africa this was accentuated by the immediate follow-up of much more impressive and lasting phenomena, such as the expansion of commercial activities, the onward march of evangelistic enterprise, and the imposition of chartered company or crown government. This is by no means the same thing as saying that the impact they made or the esteem and affection in which they were held at the time were nugatory. The contrary was nearly always the case; but even the most dazzling of reputations in Africa may last no longer than does the desert-rose, the centerpiece of renown at the time but its brilliance forgotten as the season of its blossom passes.

What effect, if any, did Heinrich Barth have on the people of Nigeria and the course and direction of their life? What did he set out to achieve? How did he put his aims into effect? What was his method of operation? How did he approach people? Given his interaction with the people, can it be claimed that Barth had any identifiable effect on the course of Nigerian life? Of these considerations, the second is the major one: what do we know of Barth's *modus operandi* in the field situation?

The genesis of the expedition lay in James Richardson's concept of "a political and commercial expedition to some of the most important kingdoms of Central Africa,"[4] envisaged

4. James Richardson, *Narrative of a Mission to Central Africa* (London, 1853), I, 1.

after his return from an earlier mission to the Sahara. Its goal was to be twofold: principally (and in keeping with the spirit of mid-nineteenth-century England), the abolition of the slave trade; and, secondarily, the promotion of trade by way of the desert. When Barth was invited to join as the expedition's scientist (on the nomination of Chevalier Bunsen, the German ambassador at the Court of St. James, who was anxious to ensure his country's representation in the mission and had, as soon as the proposed expedition was brought to his attention by the German cartographer August Petermann, then working at the London Observatory, asked Professor Karl Ritter of the University of Berlin to recommend a good scientist), he modified these aims by insisting that "the exploration of Central Africa" must be the principal object of the mission. He had already spent four years traveling around the Mediterranean on scientific research, including the North African littoral from Algiers across to the Nile valley; he had learned to speak Arabic competently and had familiarized himself with Arab society "where the camel is man's daily companion, and the culture of the date tree his chief occupation";[5] he was master of five European languages; and he had not forgotten how at Kaf (Gafsa), in Tunisia, a Hausa slave had said to him: "Please God, you shall go and visit Kano." Although he was in later years content to believe that providence had led him to Africa, as otherwise his interests would have remained in Asia Minor and "it is scarcely probable that I should ever have entered upon this African career,"[6] the offer of sponsorship by the German ambassador promised an opportunity for scientific observation in an unknown land, too golden a chance to let slide by. Yet, meticulous and far-reaching scholar that he was, Barth was not going to remain content with the minor role of simply recording meteorological observations. Hence his insistence on the scope for genuine geographical exploration. Indeed, within a matter of weeks he had formed the idea of a trans-African expedition, branching from Lake Chad (which now became a stage rather than a terminal objective) either east to

5. Excerpts from the preface to *Travels and Discoveries*, I, vii.
6. Preface to the German edition of *Travels and Discoveries* (Gotha, 1857–58).

the Nile or southeast to Mombasa and Zanzibar.[7] In a subsequent dispatch,[8] permission was given for the mission to travel westwards as far as Timbuktu.

However, when drawing up the final headings of the agreement, Lord Palmerston at the Foreign Office was careful to emphasize that, in addition to the political and scientific objectives of the expedition, the British Government still attached considerable weight to the matter of trade treaties. Barth's own interpretation of the priorities of his commission can best be seen in the finale to his narrative: "I . . . not only made known the whole of that vast region . . . but I succeeded also in establishing friendly relations with all the most powerful chiefs . . . I have the satisfaction to feel that I have opened to the view of the scientific public of Europe a most extensive tract of the secluded African world, and not only made it tolerably known, but rendered the opening of a regular intercourse between Europeans and those regions possible." [9]

Barth and Adolf Overweg (the geologist nominated by Ritter when it had seemed that Barth could not join the expedition— then retained as its third member) crossed to Tunis at the end of 1849; James Richardson did not join them until the following March. The expedition left Tripoli in April and spent the month of October in Agades. Early in 1851, the three members decided to separate and planned to meet up again in Kukawa, the capital of Bornu on the western shore of Lake Chad. Barth went south to Katsina and Kano, before turning eastward toward Bornu, which he reached in April. Overweg, coming through Zinder, arrived a month later, but Richardson died in northern Bornu without seeing his companions again. Using Kukawa as a base, Barth and Overweg spent the next eighteen months in a series of explorations, south to Adamawa and the river Benue, round Lake Chad to Kanem, and southeast to Mandara and Bagirmi. Overweg died in September

7. See R. M. Prothero, letter in *West Africa* (London), 31 January 1959. He suggests that the proposal for the expedition to cross Africa and return to Europe via Mombasa originally came from Karl Ritter.
8. Palmerston to Richardson, 7 October 1851.
9. Excerpt from the final paragraphs of *Travels and Discoveries*, V, 452–454.

er).[14] The fact that Hourst recalls how warmly
youths whom Barth had befriended in Tim-
rs earlier, Zen en Abidin and Kungu, had in-
heir erstwhile benefactor,[15] strongly suggests
sive questioning during the early years of the
might have opened up more memories. Experi-
rn Nigeria confirms that a man who made his
h did would still be remembered a generation
lly when he was virtually the only European
nger," to have lived among the people for months
n no physical or human reminders, only Barth's
, corroborated by the instructive glimpses of Barth
revealed in the vernacular narrative of his servant
ffers any substantial evidence. Fortunately this is
g source.

ho have had experience of living in Africa outside
conurbations will be able to sense how Barth needed
to the vital issue of living with his hosts. A consider-
ow he did it can best be handled on two levels: Barth's
ole and canons of public conduct; and his personal

s still possible to identify German officials who administered the
sixty years ago, or legends about which District Officer left his glass
village shrine to watch over the querulous tribes while he was away
nother who rode so hard that he was dubbed "iron pants." But these
ts, their bearers being in and of the alien government, have perhaps
rpetuated by their successors of the same ilk, providing amusement
rytelling prestige to such as Government messengers and Emirs' repre-
ves gossiping about heroes of the past under whom they had
and suffered. A new postcolonial administration may bring their oft-
xploits to an end. Once the reproductive setting is lacking, memory fal-
nd fades. Such, it seems, was more often than not the case with the lone
rer, who, being no part of an administrative framework deliberately im-
ing on the lives of the people, lacked the built-in fame-perpetuating
hinery.

5. Lieut. Emile Hourst traveled from Dakar to Timbuktu and then down
Niger as far as the Bight of Biafra in 1895–96. His book, which was trans-
ed into English under the title of *French Enterprise in Africa* (London,
98) by Mrs. A. Bell, is full of tributes to Barth. Hourst pretended to be Barth's
phew: "I was thus able to emerge safely from every situation" (Introduction,
ii).

16. "Tafiya da rai na Dorugu," in J. F. Schön, *Magana Hausa* (London,
885). An edited translation of Hausa autobiographical pieces, including this
xtract, by Paul Newman and Anthony Kirk-Greene, is presently in hand.

1852. Barth marched west through Zinder, Kano, and Sokoto, to Timbuktu, where he was held a virtual prisoner for six months. When he was given permission to leave, he trekked back to Kukawa, which he reached at the end of 1854, just before his compatriot Eduard Vogel arrived with two British sappers to reinforce the expedition. Vogel went on to Bauchi (he was later killed in Wadai), and Barth, after further delays, left Kukawa in May and, taking the Bilma route across the Sahara, reached England in September 1855. He spent the next three years writing up his narrative, but he became involved in several personal quarrels and failed to secure the professorial appointment for which he had hoped. He died in 1865, at the early age of forty-four. His five years' work in the Western and Central Sudans have remained one of the greatest achievements in the geographical and exploratory annals of this part of Africa.

The results of the mission can be summarized. As regards commercial treaties, Barth succeeded in persuading Bornu, Sokoto, and Gwandu (but not Adamawa or Kano) to sign. As the result of a swing in international alliances, roundly condemned by Barth as "a sham," nothing came of these treaties. Barth took this as both a personal affront and a virtual denial of his mission, and felt that he and his sub-Saharan potentates had been let down by the British Government. As regards exploration, although Barth was obliged by circumstances to travel westward from Lake Chad instead of southeastward to the Indian Ocean, he did open up the cultural history of the Western and Central Sudans to Europe's scholarship, and his geographical discoveries make a truly impressive catalogue. He was, for instance, the first European to enter Yola and describe in detail the Fulani kingdom of Adamawa, while his analysis of the complex river systems of the Chad basin disproved the earlier theory that the Benue flowed into Lake Chad. Indeed, Barth's personal observation of the upper reaches of this river and his accurate estimate of its lower course (subsequently confirmed by Baikie in the *Pleïad*) down to its confluence with the Niger must rank among the great geographical achievements of the century in Africa. He considered that last far-flung outpost of the Sokoto empire to be "a country [that] is certainly one of the finest of Central Africa," prophetically adding, "I cherish the well-founded conviction that along this natural highroad [Benue] European influence and commerce will penetrate into the very heart of the continent." [10] Small wonder that, as one biographer has claimed, "in terms of exploration no single man ever equalled Heinrich Barth." [11]

It was, above all, Barth who made Europe aware of the sophisticated governmental system that had developed in the post-*jihad* Hausa-Fulani and Bornu emirates, thereby supplementing the work of his eminent predecessors Dixon Denham, Hugh Clapperton, and Walter Oudney, who thirty years earlier had brought back an account of the rise of Usuman dan Fodio and Shehu el Kanemi's new empires in the Central Sudan. As the centennial year of Barth's death approached, there was renewed praise for his other scholarly achievements while on the expedition. Their general tenor finds a neat and handsome summary in the refined assessment of a leading Africanist who has seen Barth as the supreme Nigerian scholar, constructing the frame of reference within which all subsequent historical work has been done and inspired by his temperament and training to pose historical questions of a kind never asked by a European before: "he never described the contemporary situation of the various African communities through which he travelled without attempting to relate it to the past; so that his work, unlike almost all preceding European studies, is a work of exploration in a double sense—in time as well as space." [12]

Central to an understanding of the effect Barth had on the Nigerian people is an appreciation of how he handled his relations with them. In order to marshal the data, however, it is essential to realize the severe limitations inherent in the problem of source material available. With personal reminiscence in Nigeria no longer available, it is only from the clues given in his journals that one can to some extent piece together the picture of how Barth lived during his travels and the im-

10. 18 June 1851 (*Travels and Discoveries*).
11. René Lecler, *World Without Mercy* (London, 1954).
12. Thomas Hodgkin, *Nigerian Perspectives* (London, 1960), 15–16.

pression hi
quaint
must p
diaries a
and Vogel,
of Barth as

It must no
influence a
abundance ne
suggests that
ministrators w
years after his v
Barth—so little t
effort they made.
burial sites of Rich
earlier: experience i
the only European to
Ngurutuwa, "the plac
of Lake Chad, should
was not so, for it took th
inquiry to discover Overw
had not been located by
is true, found the family
Bashir, whom Barth had de
liberal and just man," [13] in
grettably, made little effort to
seems, even at the turn of the
ingly little recollection of the cu
well-known as Abd el Karim; y
bered Clapperton has been when
the Sarkin Musulmi, or Mungo
about his fate, and how several o
1900–1910 era in Northern Nigeria
their Hausa nicknames of *mai-jin*
ostrich" (George Abadie); *mai farin*
one" (Sir John Alder Burdon); *'kubel*
ing" (Harry S. Goldsmith); *dan Hausa*

(Sir Hanns Visch
the two Fulani
buktu forty yea
quired about t
that more inte
colonial period
ence of North
mark as Bar
later, especia
or *bako*, "str
on end. Wit
own journal
the man as
Dorugu,[16]
a rewardin
Those w
the main
to adjust
ation of
official

14. It
Kamerur
eye on a
and of
sobriqu
been p
and st
sentati
served
told e
ters
expl
ping
ma

th
la
18
n

13. April 1851 (*Travels and Discoveries*, II, 295).

"a country [that] is certainly one of the finest of Central Africa," prophetically adding, "I cherish the well-founded conviction that along this natural highroad [Benue] European influence and commerce will penetrate into the very heart of the continent." [10] Small wonder that, as one biographer has claimed, "in terms of exploration no single man ever equalled Heinrich Barth." [11]

It was, above all, Barth who made Europe aware of the sophisticated governmental system that had developed in the post-*jihad* Hausa-Fulani and Bornu emirates, thereby supplementing the work of his eminent predecessors Dixon Denham, Hugh Clapperton, and Walter Oudney, who thirty years earlier had brought back an account of the rise of Usuman dan Fodio and Shehu el Kanemi's new empires in the Central Sudan. As the centennial year of Barth's death approached, there was renewed praise for his other scholarly achievements while on the expedition. Their general tenor finds a neat and handsome summary in the refined assessment of a leading Africanist who has seen Barth as the supreme Nigerian scholar, constructing the frame of reference within which all subsequent historical work has been done and inspired by his temperament and training to pose historical questions of a kind never asked by a European before: "he never described the contemporary situation of the various African communities through which he travelled without attempting to relate it to the past; so that his work, unlike almost all preceding European studies, is a work of exploration in a double sense—in time as well as space." [12]

Central to an understanding of the effect Barth had on the Nigerian people is an appreciation of how he handled his relations with them. In order to marshal the data, however, it is essential to realize the severe limitations inherent in the problem of source material available. With personal reminiscence in Nigeria no longer available, it is only from the clues given in his journals that one can to some extent piece together the picture of how Barth lived during his travels and the im-

10. 18 June 1851 (*Travels and Discoveries*).
11. René Lecler, *World Without Mercy* (London, 1954).
12. Thomas Hodgkin, *Nigerian Perspectives* (London, 1960), 15–16.

1852. Barth marched west through Zinder, Kano, and Sokoto, to Timbuktu, where he was held a virtual prisoner for six months. When he was given permission to leave, he trekked back to Kukawa, which he reached at the end of 1854, just before his compatriot Eduard Vogel arrived with two British sappers to reinforce the expedition. Vogel went on to Bauchi (he was later killed in Wadai), and Barth, after further delays, left Kukawa in May and, taking the Bilma route across the Sahara, reached England in September 1855. He spent the next three years writing up his narrative, but he became involved in several personal quarrels and failed to secure the professorial appointment for which he had hoped. He died in 1865, at the early age of forty-four. His five years' work in the Western and Central Sudans have remained one of the greatest achievements in the geographical and exploratory annals of this part of Africa.

The results of the mission can be summarized. As regards commercial treaties, Barth succeeded in persuading Bornu, Sokoto, and Gwandu (but not Adamawa or Kano) to sign. As the result of a swing in international alliances, roundly condemned by Barth as "a sham," nothing came of these treaties. Barth took this as both a personal affront and a virtual denial of his mission, and felt that he and his sub-Saharan potentates had been let down by the British Government. As regards exploration, although Barth was obliged by circumstances to travel westward from Lake Chad instead of southeastward to the Indian Ocean, he did open up the cultural history of the Western and Central Sudans to Europe's scholarship, and his geographical discoveries make a truly impressive catalogue. He was, for instance, the first European to enter Yola and describe in detail the Fulani kingdom of Adamawa, while his analysis of the complex river systems of the Chad basin disproved the earlier theory that the Benue flowed into Lake Chad. Indeed, Barth's personal observation of the upper reaches of this river and his accurate estimate of its lower course (subsequently confirmed by Baikie in the *Pleïad*) down to its confluence with the Niger must rank among the great geographical achievements of the century in Africa. He considered that last far-flung outpost of the Sokoto empire to be pression his way of life may have made on his Nigerian acquaintances. Among the material lost on the expedition we must particularly regret the absence of the corroborative diaries and scientific journals of his companions Overweg and Vogel, through whose eyes we could have caught glimpses of Barth as they saw him in action.

It must not be asserted that, if we can find no trace of Barth's influence a hundred years after, we would have found it in abundance nearer the time of his sojourn in Nigeria. Evidence suggests that this was by no means true. The first British administrators who penetrated into the same region only fifty years after his visit, found very little in the way of memories of Barth—so little that at times one is apt to be impatient of the effort they made. Witness the difficulty in the location of the burial sites of Richardson and Overweg, dead but a generation earlier: experience in Africa and the Orient would suggest that the only European to have been buried in a petty hamlet like Ngurutuwa, "the place of the hippopotami," or on the shores of Lake Chad, should have been relatively easy to trace. It was not so, for it took the Government several years of patient inquiry to discover Overweg's grave, and Richardson's remains had not been located by 1911! The British Administration, it is true, found the family of the former *waziri* of Bornu, Haj Bashir, whom Barth had described as "a most excellent, kind, liberal and just man," [13] in disgrace, and so, judiciously if regrettably, made little effort to revive links and memories. There seems, even at the turn of the century, to have been surprisingly little recollection of the curious European, widely and so well-known as Abd el Karim; yet consider how well-remembered Clapperton has been when Barth talked about him with the Sarkin Musulmi, or Mungo Park when Lander inquired about his fate, and how several of the administrators of the 1900–1910 era in Northern Nigeria are still recalled today by their Hausa nicknames of *mai-jimina*, "the owner of the ostrich" (George Abadie); *mai farin kai*, "the white-headed one" (Sir John Alder Burdon); *'kubelazhin*, "Mr. Goodmorning" (Harry S. Goldsmith); *dan Hausa*, "a real Hausaman"

13. April 1851 (*Travels and Discoveries*, II, 295).

(Sir Hanns Vischer).[14] The fact that Hourst recalls how warmly the two Fulani youths whom Barth had befriended in Timbuktu forty years earlier, Zen en Abidin and Kungu, had inquired about their erstwhile benefactor,[15] strongly suggests that more intensive questioning during the early years of the colonial period might have opened up more memories. Experience of Northern Nigeria confirms that a man who made his mark as Barth did would still be remembered a generation later, especially when he was virtually the only European or *bako*, "stranger," to have lived among the people for months on end. With no physical or human reminders, only Barth's own journal, corroborated by the instructive glimpses of Barth the man as revealed in the vernacular narrative of his servant Dorugu,[16] offers any substantial evidence. Fortunately this is a rewarding source.

Those who have had experience of living in Africa outside the main conurbations will be able to sense how Barth needed to adjust to the vital issue of living with his hosts. A consideration of how he did it can best be handled on two levels: Barth's official role and canons of public conduct; and his personal

14. It is still possible to identify German officials who administered the Kamerun sixty years ago, or legends about which District Officer left his glass eye on a village shrine to watch over the querulous tribes while he was away and of another who rode so hard that he was dubbed "iron pants." But these sobriquets, their bearers being in and of the alien government, have perhaps been perpetuated by their successors of the same ilk, providing amusement and storytelling prestige to such as Government messengers and Emirs' representatives gossiping about heroes of the past under whom they had served and suffered. A new postcolonial administration may bring their oft-told exploits to an end. Once the reproductive setting is lacking, memory falters and fades. Such, it seems, was more often than not the case with the lone explorer, who, being no part of an administrative framework deliberately impinging on the lives of the people, lacked the built-in fame-perpetuating machinery.

15. Lieut. Emile Hourst traveled from Dakar to Timbuktu and then down the Niger as far as the Bight of Biafra in 1895–96. His book, which was translated into English under the title of *French Enterprise in Africa* (London, 1898) by Mrs. A. Bell, is full of tributes to Barth. Hourst pretended to be Barth's nephew: "I was thus able to emerge safely from every situation" (Introduction, viii).

16. "Tafiya da rai na Dorugu," in J. F. Schön, *Magana Hausa* (London, 1885). An edited translation of Hausa autobiographical pieces, including this extract, by Paul Newman and Anthony Kirk-Greene, is presently in hand.

code of behavior and the manner in which he adapted his pattern of life to being wholly dependent upon, and an integral part of, an African community. For both these areas the Hausa of Northern Nigeria have a recognized terminology: the first concerns his *sarauta*, or office; the second reflects his *hali* or *tsabi'a*, his own nature and personality, as expressed by his *fara'a* or outward geniality.

It may be said of Barth's official approach to Africans that he was in some ways the precursor of the imperial consular or chartered company agent. He was armed with official letters of introduction which were tantamount to being his insignia of office, and after Richardson's death he was empowered—first by default and later by appointment—to act on behalf of Her Majesty the Queen. To enable him to carry out these functions originally allocated to Richardson, no effort had been spared to equip the expedition with the most important credentials of the day in diplomatic Africa: official presents. There are many diary references to these along the lines of the characteristically shrewd comment of the Emir of Kano, who observed, Barth recalled, that "though I had suffered so severely from extortion, yet I seemed to have still ample presents for him." [17] Without presents, not only was there no chance of an audience, there was no hope of even minimal success for the mission, for until one had greeted the chief in customary fashion, no other courtier or district fief-holder would dare to lift a finger to help the traveler. Barth learned this diplomatic lesson the hard way. At Yola, a journey of a month or more from the court of Sokoto, the Lamido, or Fulani chief, had recourse to a classic international subterfuge in order to legitimize his intention of expelling Barth from forbidden Adamawa. "I received," Barth wrote, "a formal visit from Mode Abd-Allahi, the foreign secretary, and [a] friend. . . . Having moistened their organs with a cup of coffee, they acquitted themselves of their message in the following terms: 'The sultan . . . had ordered them . . . to beg me to accept his most respectful regards, and to inform me that he was nothing but a slave of the Sultan of Sokoto, and that I was a far greater man than him-

17. 18 February 1851 (*Travels and Discoveries*, II, 106).

self. As such a man had never before come to his country, he was afraid of his liege lord, and begged me to retrace my steps whither I had come; but if in course of time I should return with a letter from Sokoto, he would receive me with open arms, would converse with me about all our science, and about our instruments, without reserve, and would shew me the whole country.'" In vain did Barth argue that, far from being a slave of Sokoto, the Lamido was famous as being virtually the sole independent governor of a huge province; and when he produced his would-be trump card, that he had sojourned several weeks at the court of the Emirs of Katsina and Kano without any representations being made to their sovereign lord at Sokoto, on whom they were demonstrably dependent, the messengers replied inscrutably, "Oh! but the relations of Katsena and Kano are entirely different from those of this province. These are large and busy thoroughfares for all the world, while Adamawᴐ is a distant territory in the remotest corner of the earth, and still a fresh unconsolidated conquest." [18]

At Katsina, Barth accurately sized up the presents–passport formula in his quoting the Emir's comment that he "would be a fool if he were to let me pass out of his hands. . . . Though it certainly was not a very brilliant present, yet, considering that I did not want anything from him, it was quite enough; but the fact was that he wanted something more from me, and therefore it was not sufficient." [19] Hence the deliberate care with which Barth always sorted out his presents before any audience and recorded them in his journal. Refusal to observe the rules of the game of gifts could mean that one might be detained at the chief's pleasure: unable to move on, as Barth discovered to his discomfort at Yola in 1851, or even back, as he learned with even greater frustration when he was about to take his final leave from Kukawa in 1855.

In considering Barth's unofficial role, as expressed in his personality and way of life, one reaches the kernel of his success. For here is the revelation of how, and how well, he interacted with the local people. Despite his poor opinion of Richardson (which was mutual) and his impatient criticism

18. 24 June 1851 (*Travels and Discoveries*, II, 496 ff.).
19. 23 January 1851 (*Travels and Discoveries*, II, 51).

of his German compatriot Overweg, both of whom he was wont
to describe in terms trenchant enough to suggest that, if death
had not broken up the caravan, clashes of personality (almost
equaling in intensity the poisoned malice of the Denham-
Clapperton expedition to Bornu a generation earlier[20]) might
well have done so, Barth's diary entries take on a very different
tone when he is talking about his African companions. There
is little of the stereotyped Western impatience with the African's "lack of intelligence" and "unreliability." Instead, many
references and anecdotes imply an understanding of and
affection for the people among whom he lived. (Set against
the attitudinal backcloth of the 1850s, undue attention need
not be paid to the contemporarily accepted tone of paternalism that marks his passing references to "those simple people.")

So completely has the circle turned, it could be argued that
Barth, in his position vis-à-vis the African, was a prototype of
many Europeans in the post-independence situation. Now, no
less than then, the only satisfactory and lasting way to make
one's mark in Africa, given average ability in a declared profession, is to know and mix with Africans on terms of equal
give-and-take.

So it was with Barth. There was little weight attached to his
position as the leader of something as nebulous as a mission
to Central Africa. After all, he alone *was* the mission; and in
the emirate context of Northern Nigeria, a person of standing
has since time immemorial been measured in terms of his suite
of courtiers or their inanimate equivalent in conspicuous
consumption. Barth was in very much the same position as
many a "weekend" traveler to Africa. He wanted, nay urgently
needed, to get to know Africa. He was wise enough to realize
that the only way to do this was to get to know Africans. But
how was he to set about it? He had no airport or luxury hotel
bar at which to strike up an acquaintance; he had no government representative to take him along and introduce him to
the Emir; he had no letters of introduction to compatriots in
high places or affiliated to local firms or institutions; nobody

20. See E. W. Bovill (ed.), *Missions to the Niger* (Cambridge, 1966), II,
64–75.

on the "old boy network" nor a consul with whom to get in touch. He had nothing but his own personality. The conclusion is inescapable that it was through personality alone, not through any trappings of office or authority in latent support, that Barth was able to gain the admiration of, access to, and acceptance by his hosts.

Barth learned a hundred years ago what so many Europeans have yet to learn: to succeed in Africa requires something far more important than being hyperefficient and hard-working in one's job. Competence may be assumed, else one would not be there; it is the way one goes about that job that counts most. This assessment of the social situation is as valid for 1850 as it is for today. The comparison of the factors inherent in the social context of Nigeria then and now is both germane and enlightening. For it is clear to the reader of Barth's diaries that he had, or acquired from his travels, many of the valued personal commodities needed in the repertoire of today's successful worker in Africa—qualities like patience, friendliness, understanding, and accessibility. Not all of these virtues were shared by the *colons* and officials of yesteryear. Yet they provide the quintessential explanation of Barth's smooth interaction with Africans.

Despite his outward character of being (at least as far as Europeans were concerned) "proud, priggish and prickly," [21] Barth possessed one rare characteristic in generous measure. It was the quality of empathy: multidimensional empathy, allowing full scope both horizontally (displaying a genuine and trusted interest in every facet of the peoples' culture) and vertically (allowing this interest to range widely over society). Empathy implies not only a liking, a harmony; it also requires a readiness to see the other's point of view. It may call for diverse channels of expression in order to be convincing, or even apparent, to the other party—hence the horizontal matrix. It may best be demonstrated by showing an interest, real and sustained, in other peoples' way of life, without forming value prejudgments or erecting barriers of ethnocentric comparison. Barth practiced this precept, for he at once perceived

21. A. H. M. Kirk-Greene, *Barth's Travels in Nigeria* (London, 1962), 44.

how "these poor creatures . . . seeing, probably for the first time, that a stranger took a real interest in them, were extremely delighted," or again, how "these simple people were greatly amused when they saw me take so much interest in them." [22]

Such a capacity for instantaneous and self-communicating empathy was the strongest point in Barth's array of personal qualities on which he had to call so ceaselessly in his years "alone" in Africa. This was his *hali* or *tsabi'a*, his inner self, as seen by others. Barth was not slow to realize the vital importance of such a behavioral reflex: "These tribes cannot but look upon the white stranger, who suddenly appears before them as if he were fallen from the sky, and regard him with the most profound suspicion, before they become convinced that this wonderful being has the same human feeling as themselves and similar, if not the same, principles of action, notwithstanding the total difference of his color, his appearance, his manner of living, and his unintelligible and apparently absurd and foolish activity." [23] When empathy assumes its outward form of a continuously happy and happy-making disposition, it is recognized in Hausa psychology as *fara'a*. This *fara'a*, or outward reflection of a happy temperament (the inner *tsabi'a*), was the foundation of other attributes which caused Barth to be admired by his African hosts and helped in establishing a good rapport with them.

Barth was a scholar, "inspired by an insatiable craving for knowledge" and gifted "with a mastery and brilliance that none has yet repeated." [24] In an Islamic society like that of Kano, Kukawa, and Sokoto, learning commands the highest respect and the title of *malam*, "the learned one," is a coveted address. As befits a scholar, he had with him his "small library," carried even on his most hazardous travels. He could argue religion with Muslim friends keen to convert him (one recalls how Muhammadu Bello's keen mind had embarrassed Clapperton on such matters), or slavery and agricultural

22. 12 June 1851 (*Travels and Discoveries*, II, 428, 384).
23. Preface to the German edition of *Travels and Discoveries*.
24. E. W. Bovill, "Henry Barth," *Journal of the African Society*, XXV (1926), 311–320; Basil Davidson, *Old Africa Rediscovered* (London, 1959), 22.

schemes with the *waziri* of Bornu.[25] Above all, and so important that it goes into a separate category of learning, Barth was a linguist, and showed a genuine and capable eagerness to learn something about the local languages wherever he went.[26] He compiled over forty comparative word lists and his journal is full of indications of the techniques he used to gather these materials. He did himself untold good by his willingness to provide medicine, sometimes extending to extreme requests such as a medicine "to increase conjugal vigour"[27] or to cure a blind horse. Where practical matters calling for the skills of a handyman were concerned, Barth yielded to his companion Overweg—somewhat grudgingly, it seems, for he notes how his friend "lost a great deal of time in repairing, or rather trying to repair, their watches and things,"[28] and was clearly disgruntled by his own consequent nickname Abd el Karim *faidansa bago*, indicating his helplessness in such practical matters.

Barth's recreation in that precious hour of coolness before the sudden sunset of the tropics was reminiscent of the alien administrator in his outstation: he took an evening walk and chatted with all he met on his way; perhaps climbed a hillock to sketch, listen to legends, take down a few linguistic and historical notes; and purposefully went out of his way to talk with and learn about the people and so become accepted by them. This invaluable approach and unparalleled way of gaining local knowledge and confidence is fetchingly epitomized in a vignette drawn by Barth at Humbutudi: "I then determined to ascend the rock.... After I had finished taking angles I sat down on this magnificent rocky throne, and several of the natives having followed me, I wrote from their dictation

25. Dixon Denham, Hugh Clapperton, and Walter Oudney, *Narrative of Travels and Discoveries in Northern and Central Africa* (London, 1826), 81–83; Barth, *Travels and Discoveries*, II, 290–297.

26. For a detailed review of this feature, see Kirk-Greene, *Barth's Travels*, 60–64.

27. Hausa: *maganin alguwa*, quoted by Barth—29 January 1851 (*Travels and Discoveries*, II, 66).

28. 6 August 1851 (*Travels and Discoveries*, III, 21).

a short vocabulary of their language. . . . The rock became continually more and more animated."[29]

If one item of the African traveler's basic personal equipment is the smile of ready friendliness, the second, a complementary one, is a firm refusal ever to show surprise at the customs of others. Even if one is shocked, he must not reveal it: in few other ways is the arrogance of ethnocentricity so strongly displayed. Barth knew both these lessons by heart. He appears to have learned that in such situations it is possible to have a foot in both worlds, enjoying the new one without giving up the old.

As a lone traveler, Barth may have had certain advantages. It has been a common complaint in Africa and the Orient that the advent of European womenfolk—and this is especially true in the dominantly man's world of Islam—destroyed the easy relations that had begun to mature.[30] In the early days of the "palm-oil ruffian" and the puny handful of bachelor administrators, there was less question of keeping up one's position. Sir Hugh Clifford has made this clear in his Malayan sketches;[31] in E. M. Forster's brilliant assessment of the colonial society, he found it was possible to keep in with Indians and Englishmen, but "he who would also keep in with Englishwomen must drop the Indians. . . . Intercourse, yes. Courtesy, by all means. Intimacy, never, never."[32]

Sexual patterns are a challenge to the unmarried in Africa, no matter what their background. Barth found himself either being offered female companionship or mystifying his hosts who did "not understand how a man can live without a partner."[33] In Hausa society the unmarried male was not only a danger but also a freak, so that traditionally the title *karuwa* was used to describe the single male as well as in its normal

29. 12 June 1851 (*Travels and Discoveries*, II, 385).

30. One African administrator turned novelist has talked of Africans and Europeans working together "in a harmony the Colony had not known since the rosy days before white women had joined their men" (Ian Brook, *Jimmy Riddle* [London, 1961], 222).

31. For example, in *A Freelance of Today* (New York, 1903).

32. E. M. Forster, *A Passage to India* (London, 1924), 51, 141.

33. 23 October 1850 (*Travels and Discoveries*, I, 447).

sense of "prostitute."[34] A century later, Barth might have
been misunderstood rather than applauded for conforming
with the social grade of his hosts, and especially for his wide,
indiscriminate, and genuine circle of friends. Yet it was
precisely this approach that won him local respect and acceptance, without which he might not only have failed to gain
entrée for his mission but quite possibly might even have lost
his life in Timbuktu, where for six months he was unable to
leave the city for fear of assassination and relied solely on
the loyal friendship of Shaykh el Bakay to save his life.[35]

To achieve this acceptance Barth was obliged to bring into
play more weapons from his social armory than one would
need today. He lived as an African. First and foremost, he
spoke only African languages for four years, removed from
any single speaker of his native German or his second language, English. He never employed an interpreter as such,
but determined to be as self-reliant as he could. At the outset,
he had Arabic at his command and a general awareness of
Berber syntactic structure. From the liberated Central Sudanese who attached themselves to the southward-bound caravan he began to pick up Hausa and Kanuri so rapidly that, by
the time that they reached Agades, he was able to converse
with the Sultan independent of any go-between. "The easy
character and the rich development of the Hausa idiom" soon
won Barth's attention. He set his heart on specializing in it and

34. "Hausa classify any adult who has no spouse as a wastrel or prostitute
(karuwa), irrespective of sex" (M. G. Smith, Government in Zazzau [London,
1960], 255). Though the breadth of this term karuwa is not always accepted
by modern Hausa, I have certainly come across this terminology in tax lists in
the remote parts of Hausaland to embrace single persons of both sexes.

35. It may also be argued that Barth did not have the Westernized, usually
non-Muslim, elite with which to contend. One day a study will be made of how,
sadly, nearly always the typical European official could not like or even tolerate
the Western-educated "native." Had he been left with the educated Islamic
gentlemen like the emirs and malamai, or the illiterate peasant so respected
by the District Commissioner, or the Punjabi Mussalman jawan so beloved of
his British officer in the old Indian Army, there would have been less bitterness in imperial personal relations; though not necessarily any closer relationship. The Muslim, like the proverbial Englishman, likes to look on his house
as his castle and does not welcome intrusion or change; entry is by invitation
only, and on the host's terms: zuciyar mutum birninsa, as the Hausa put it,
"the heart of a man is his citadel, and it is not open to all and sundry."

was later to reckon that given another six months he would have become "fully master of the language with all its finest peculiarities."[36] Additionally, he learned some Fulfulde (Fulani) and Songhai, and was constantly at work on compiling vocabularies of the congeries of unrecorded languages that is such a feature of the Chad-Mandara geographical area.

Barth normally wore what he described as a half-Sudanic, half-Arab garb. This consisted of a black Sudan *riga* or tobe, worn over a white one, with a white burnous on top. Earlier he had preferred a *tailelt,* the "speckle-colored" gown and narrow-ankled pants favored by the Tuareg. When approaching Timbuktu he was "obliged to assume the character of an Arab." He also sported a pair of richly ornamented Ghadamsi shoes, "which formed my greatest finery." He went to the extent of staining his skin with indigo so as to give himself the protection of "an appearance more suited to the country." In doing so, he was following the practice of his predecessors in adopting a would-be Muslim disguise. Barth was even prepared to brave the hostile reaction of mid-nineteenth-century European evangelism and observe the outward forms of Islam. Later he regretted his refusal to repeat the *fatiha* when invited to join his Muslim friends in prayer, pointing out that, "although many Christians will object to repeat [sic] the prayer of another creed, yet the use of a prayer of so general import as the introductory chapter to the Koran ought to be permitted every solitary traveller in these regions, in order to form a sort of conciliatory link."[37]

The European in Africa, unlike his counterpart in India, has by and large eschewed the local cuisine. But Barth, deprived of today's supermarket canned or frozen provisions or yesterday's "chop-boxes," stocked for twelve months by Messrs. Fortnum and Mason, lived off the country. For breakfast, he found *zummita* "a cool and refreshing paste," and recom-

36. Quotations from his preface to *Sammlung und Bearbeitung Central-Africanischer Vokabularien* (Berlin, 1862–1866).

37. 2 August 1853 (*Travels and Discoveries*, IV, 316); 10 October 1850 (*Travels and Discoveries*, IV, 398); 9 October 1850 (*Travels and Discoveries*, I, 395); 24 June 1851 (*Travels and Discoveries*, II, 496). See also the apologia in his preface to *Travels and Discoveries*, I, xviii–xix.

mended a kind of thin pancake known as *senasin,* prepared from sorghum, as the best food for European travelers. Cakes made from the fruit of the *magaria* tree might also be "safely eaten in small quantities even by a European to allay his hunger for a while till he can obtain something more substantial." [38]

That the flat-roofed *soro* kind of house, or even the typical Hausa compound, can be made into a comfortable home was discovered by many early European residents in Nigeria, and is one still sought after by those bored with standard Ministry of Works designs. Barth's sketch of the celebrated "English House" at Kukawa indicates how he, too, quickly made himself very much at home.

One of the aids to assessing the impact of Barth on Nigeria is an understanding of the conditions of travel at the time. The modern traveler's concern with visas, vaccinations, and tape-recorders is far from Barth's precision-planned order of march when in unknown country or his tip that "I will mention here, for the use of future travellers, that I always wore not only my azimuth but even my chronometer in my belt, and found this an excellent precaution against accidents of any kind." [39] For transportation, he tried a donkey and a bullock, but in the end opted for horses and camels. One of the latter, Bu-Sefi, carried him from the Mediterranean to Lake Chad, while among his several horses his favorite was the spirited "Blast of the Desert." Nobody, I suggest, who has not undertaken a genuine tour in bush, away from the main road on foot or in the saddle, cut off from the normal creature comforts (however minimal) of civilization, left entirely to his own company, and obliged to carry his home with him in its totality, can begin to have any valid idea of how the Heinrich Barths of this world had to live.

A quotation from Barth's unpublished correspondence gives a few sidelights on his way of life. Writing from Wurno, in Sokoto, he noted, "my little party is provided with straw hats, which are excellent but only when worn over the *shashia* and

38. 15 July 1850 (*Travels and Discoveries,* I, 522); 29 December 1850 (*Travels and Discoveries,* I, 503).
39. 26 February 1850 (*Travels and Discoveries,* I, 85 note).

a large turban. My health is excellent, being kept up with coffee, in which, thank God, I am still able to indulge; tamarind water is also a capital beverage. Without comparison, a thousand times better than lemonade. When I feel a little sick, I add to the tamarind an onion, a strong dose of black pepper and, when I can procure it, a little honey—this forming the most useful medicinal drink in these countries and one that cannot be too much recommended to travellers." [40]

In summary, perhaps the kind of man in the best position to have some conception of the life in Africa of the lone worker is the upcountry administrator, the geologist, the bushwhacking surveyor. In their way of life alone is the European enabled in some measure to put himself, as it were, in Barth's tent or saddle, and begin to appreciate what was involved in traveling in Africa, and, even more important, how such persons had to adjust to local circumstances and practice integration.

What of the expression of his personal philosophy? The supreme illustration of Barth's empathy in his ways of getting on with (the homely phrase is here the most effective) Africans under conditions, let it be remembered, so strikingly different from anything we can imagine today, was his priceless commodity of being ever-ready to extend his spontaneous friendliness to all Africans. It is, today as yesterday, the easy establishment of happy relations with passing acquaintances as well as the founding of more lasting friendships that is one of the rewards of the traveller using his *fara'a*, his instant amiability, as a passport to West Africa's heart-gay society. Time and time again a portrait of affectionate empathy is found in the pages of Barth's narrative. Consider his genuine anxiety over the visit from one of the sons of the Emir of Zaria, "suffering dreadfully from stricture or some other obstruction," and his happier experience with the eldest son of the Emir of Kano, "a handsome, modest and intelligent youth of about eighteen years of age . . . [who] was delighted with the performance of my musical-box. I gave him an English clasp-knife, and we parted the best of friends, greatly pleased with

40. These Barth letters are in the British Museum, Add. MSS 32117 E., 15–63.

each other." [41] Such *fara'a* extended upward to men of dignity and substance, such as the Sultan of Sokoto or the scholarly *waziri* of Bornu, with whom Barth indulged in many hours of intellectual conversation, or that "specimen of an African dandy," the Sarkin Turawa of Gazawa, near Maradi,[42] or noble Arab merchants like the one he rode and picnicked with on the journey between Kano and Gumel. "Here we sat tranquilly down near the market-place, in the shade of some beautiful tamarind-trees, and indulged in the luxuries which my gentleman-like companion could afford. I was astonished, as well as ashamed at the comfort which my African friend displayed, ordering one of the female attendants of his *sirriya* to bring into his presence a basket which seemed to be under the special protection of the latter, and drawing forth from it a variety of well-baked pastry, which he spread on a napkin before us, while another of the attendants was boiling the coffee." Barth's *fara'a* also extended downwards, to stalwart servants such as his camel-drivers, his "faithful Tebu lad" Mohammed, and the Shuwa who accompanied him to Bagirmi, and "the two very handsome and amiable young Fulbe" who implored him to become a Muslim convert and whose friendship relieved the gloom of his unhappy experience of being expelled from Yola.[43] Fifty years later Hourst met two other Fulani whom Barth had befriended in Timbuktu, who spoke with feeling of their beloved Abd el Karim, while the liberated Abbega, a Marghi youth of seventeen, and Dorogu, a fifteen-year-old Hausa boy, returned to Europe with Barth.[44] (Later they were both to make their mark in Northern Nigerian history.) In Barth's pages the characters come very much alive, for even trivial acquaintances are described with sensitivity.

41. March 1851 (*Travels and Discoveries*, II, 112, 113).

42. 31 March 1853 (*Travels and Discoveries*, IV, 132–141); April 1851 (*Travels and Discoveries*, II, 290 ff.); 18 January 1855 (*Travels and Discoveries*, V, 33).

43. 12 March 1851 (*Travels and Discoveries*, II, 160); 16 June 1850 (*Travels and Discoveries*, I, 134, 149, 175, *passim*); 2 March 1851 (*Travels and Discoveries*, II, 114); 5 March 1852 (*Travels and Discoveries*, III, 263); 24 June 1851 (*Travels and Discoveries*, II, 495).

44. For a detailed account, see A. H. M. Kirk-Greene, "Abbega and Durogu," *West African Review* (September 1956), 865–869, and the autobiography of Abbega's grandson, *Mai Maina*, published in Hausa (Zaria, 1958).

Related to this genuine affection for the Nigerians he met is the way in which Barth treated and kept his personal servants. Mohammed el Gatroni, "our best and most steady servant,"[45] remained with Barth throughout those five arduous years in the Western and Central Sudans. He took countless numbers into his service for specific journeys or to learn the rudiments of another language. The list of dramatis personae in Barth's travels is a long one, but study of it provides an index to the extent he interacted with his fellow-creatures.

All of the valuable qualities of Barth's relations with the people among whom he lived, in cultural (and all the habitual assumptions inherent in that concept) solitude for four and a half years are in the final analysis simply elements making up this supreme alchemy: empathy, the gift of easy friendship with Africans of all ranks. If one had to construct the ideal traveler to Africa, half a dozen essential elements would immediately be listed. Of them Barth had all but one. He was unashamedly an individualist. He was highly competent in what he professed to be. He was self-contained and self-reliant without being an introvert. He was intellectually gifted and ceaselessly curious. He was prepared to display his outgoing, natural liking for people. He was generous, a virtue highly prized by Hausa society. Above all else, he was adaptable—flexibility being perhaps the supreme attribute in the visitor to Africa—and content to dispense with the yardstick of ethnocentric standards. The only basic ingredient for African service that Barth lacked was a ready sense of humor, though now and again his journal does betray an endearing willingness to tell a story against himself.

Finally, what of the survival of Barth's impact on Nigeria? It would make a happy conclusion to this search for the secret of Barth's cornerstone success in promoting a happy interaction with Africans not through any *sarauta* or office but solely through his personality (where anticipation of benefit was part of the customary respect for office, Barth must have disappointed his would-be courtiers, for he had little to give in return beyond himself), if we could but demonstrate that

45. 11 July 1850 (*Travels and Discoveries*, I, 209). See also *Travels and Discoveries*, V, 443–444.

Heinrich Barth had some apocalyptic effect on the development of the Western and Central Sudans and on the evolution of the Northern Nigerian modus vivendi. Unfortunately there is nothing to substantiate such a claim. Now and again it is, of course, possible for a person to become part of the local lore, good or bad. In Nigeria, as in so many African countries, several of the early administrators, having the advantage of being utterly strange, awesome of aspect, and but a handful in number, can still be recalled as an historical referent and here and there have taken on legendary characteristics. Yet the Central and Western Sudans recognize no Barth mystique or messianism, no incorporation of Abd el Karim into local folklore; nor is 1851 a personal climacteric reference point in Nigerian history. If we insist on the final proof by posing the question of whether the people of Northern Nigeria would be any different today if Barth had not lived there, the answer must, regrettably to some but convincingly to all, be an utterly negative one. The same test applied to one or two political figures (Lord Lugard, Sir Donald Cameron) and to the occasional merchant tycoon (Sir George Goldie, John Holt) or missionary (Walter Miller, Mary Slessor) would result in a positive answer by virtue of the fact that they were in a position to, and did, influence the mainstream of historical direction. Even the most fanatical of Barth's devotees would hesitate to advance any such claims on his behalf. The fact that in Europe the impact of his travels and discoveries became of the highest significance and from that end played some part in shaping the destiny of the Western and Central Sudans through external political developments is nothing more than another answer to another question. Of Barth's effect on the internal way of life, on the Nigerian personality, as it were, no suggestion of this nature can be seriously put forward.

Nor is it by any means certain that Barth would have wanted or welcomed such a posthumous claim to immortality. It must remain doubtful whether a man of his insight ever suffered from any delusions of Victorian grandeur that he was spearheading a moral crusade or preluding a civilizing mission which would leave its stamp upon the "benighted African." A scholar before anything else, he would, I suspect, have preferred the memorial of his African endeavor to be what in fact it is: the 3,500 pages of his encyclopaedic, authoritative, and immortal *Travels and Discoveries in North and Central Africa.*

Such, then, has been the lot of Heinrich Barth: his reputation recently restored in Europe, in Africa his memory is no more than European-inspired. In his time he was widely known throughout the Western and Central Sudans by a host of nicknames: "The Man Who Spent a Day in the Unsafe Wilderness," "The Needle Prince," "The Man Who Goes Through Fire," "The Father of Three" (from his habit of wearing stockings, thin leather slippers, and thick overshoes simultaneously[46]), and officially as Abd el Karim, "The Merciful One." Yet none has survived; nobody in Africa can identify him outside the *cognoscenti.* Barth has in no form been carried over in the folk-history of the peoples of Nigeria where he spent the greatest of his days and at the time was known from Lake Chad a thousand miles across to Timbuktu.

This need cause no great surprise. Some of the major reasons for such oblivion have already been set out. The totality of assessment revealed in this volume may well suggest that the great African explorers of the last century are, in the nature of things, more poignantly remembered in Europe for what they did in Africa than by the inhabitants of the countries where they undertook their mission. In some cases there are occasional links, glimpses of remembrance and echoes of the past, but by and large the memories have been sharper at the "European" end rather than the "African" one. Today, to put it in blunt terms, only the Western-educated student of African history can say exactly who Barth was.

Even if there is nothing that we can identify as definitely attributable to Barth in the sociological make-up of Northern Nigeria today, he was still the most remarkable traveler of his age in West Africa. If the theme of this book and the bias of this chapter have caused us to rethink his successful methods, it is not too far-fetched to suggest that we can learn much from

46. 19 July 1852 (*Travels and Discoveries*, III, 420).

Barth's interaction with Africans. Its lesson provides the key to succeeding in our own personal relations. Willing integration rather than irrevocable assimilation was his way, inspired perhaps by the counsel of the poet Ubayid Ibn Al-Abras: "Render help in whatever country you are and never say 'I am a stranger here.'" Barth, an uncomfortable companion on his travels, and a friendless, oversensitive soul in Europe, liked Africans for the best of all possible reasons: because he liked Africans.

David Livingstone:
Exploration for Christianity

by Norman Robert Bennett

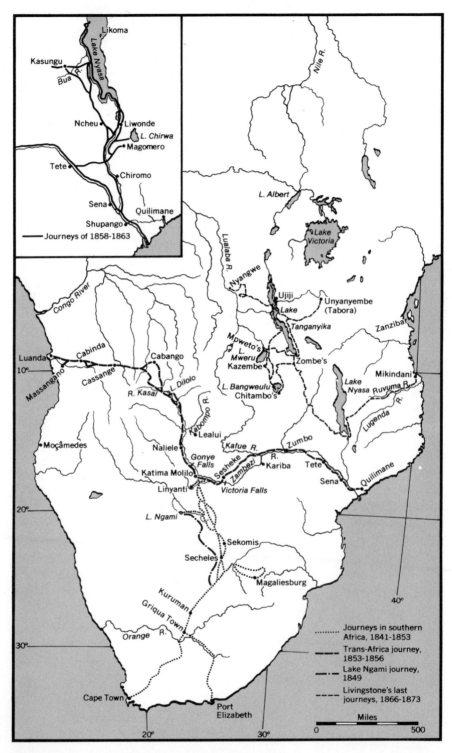

The four journeys of David Livingstone

Inset labels:
Likoma
Kasungu
Bua R.
Lake Nyasa
Ncheu
Liwonde
L. Chirwa
Magomero
Tete
Chiromo
Sena
Quilimane
Shupango
Journeys of 1858-1863

Main map labels:
Nile R.
Congo River
Lualaba R.
Nyangwe
L. Albert
Lake Victoria
Ujiji
Lake
Unyanyembe (Tabora)
Luanda
Cabinda
Cabango
Mpweto's
L. Mweru
Kazembe
Zombe's
Tanganyika
Zanzibar
Massangano
Cassange
10°
L. Dilolo
R. Kasai
L. Bangweulu
Chitambo's
Lake Nyasa
Mikindani
Ruvuma R.
Lugenda R.
Moçâmedes
Kabompo R.
Lealui
Naliele
Kafue R.
Zumbo
Gonye Falls
Sesheke
Zambezi R.
Kariba
Tete
Katima Molilo
Sena
Quilimane
Linyanti
Victoria Falls
L. Ngami
20°
Sekomis
Scheles
Magaliesburg
Kuruman
Griqua Town
40°
Orange R.
30°
Cape Town
Port Elizabeth
Miles
0   500

Legend:
.... Journeys in southern Africa, 1841-1853
——— Trans-Africa journey, 1853-1856
—·—· Lake Ngami journey, 1849
– – – Livingstone's last journeys, 1866-1873

20°   30°

David Livingstone was dominated by the conviction that he had a divinely appointed and directed task in Africa: "I cannot and will not attribute any of the public attention which has been awakened to my own wisdom or ability. The Great Power being my helper, I shall always say that my success is all owing to His favour. I have been the channel of the Divine Power."[1] Livingstone first came to Africa as an ordinary missionary, with medical training, but the slow and frustrating work of convincing Africans of the validity of the belief systems of European Christianity never really absorbed him. It was far more important to spread the word of his god, and by so doing his travels became for him the principal means of insuring the eventual triumph of Christianity in Africa. These travels took place when most of the African interior was unknown to Europeans; when joined with the drama of Livingstone's particular methods of travel, they were to captivate the popular and official minds of the Europe and America of his day and to make him the most famous and revered African explorer and missionary of the nineteenth century.

Arriving at Kuruman in southern Africa in 1841 in the service of the London Missionary Society, the twenty-seven-year-old missionary soon developed his own views toward proselytism and the proper missionary posture. Asserting, "I would never build on another man's foundation. I shall preach the gospel beyond every other man's line of things," Livingstone began to search for his own particular mission field.[2] In the process he discovered that he delighted in travel, and that he had particular personal qualifications for African exploration. "I can," he said in 1848, "bear what other Europeans would consider hunger and thirst without any incon-

1. J. P. R. Wallis (ed.), *The Zambezi Expedition of David Livingstone, 1858–1863* (London, 1956), I, 108.
2. I. Schapera (ed.), *David Livingstone: Family Letters, 1841–1856* (London, 1959), I, 31.

venience."[3] The European world first heard of this determined young missionary with the report of his arrival, in the company of William Cotton Oswell and others, at Lake Ngami in 1849. It was a minor exploration, but it was a beginning for Livingstone and stimulated additional plans for further investigations to the north. The Lake Ngami discovery also marked the European world's recognition of Livingstone: he received from the Royal Geographical Society one-half of the 1850 British royal grant for geographical discovery.

The sequels to this success were Livingstone's first major explorations—in many ways the most successful of his career —which culminated in the magnificent trans-African venture from 1853 to 1856. Setting forth from Cape Town in 1852, he traveled north via Kuruman to Linyanti and on to the Kololo people, a group he considered eminently suitable for evangelization. But the overland route across southern Africa was difficult, particularly because of the antimissionary activities of the Afrikaners, who had attacked his African friends and destroyed his home at Kolobeng during his absence in 1852. Thus Livingstone began a search for a more suitable route to Kololo country from the Atlantic coast. After exploring part of the course of the upper Zambezi River, he proceeded westward through previously unexplored territory to Portuguese Angola, reaching Luanda in May 1854. Not satisfied with traversing this difficult route, he returned to Linyanti, from there striking out eastward to reach Portuguese Moçambique, and ending his journey at Quelimane on the Indian Ocean in May 1856. En route he was shown the Victoria Falls (which he named) by Sekeletu, chief of the Kololo.

The news of this outstanding individual feat of human endurance established Livingstone's reputation with most of the British public. Geographers and cartographers regarded his careful observations of this hitherto unmapped part of Africa as a major contribution to knowledge. Missionaries could not but be interested in the reports of previously un-

3. I. Schapera (ed.), *Livingstone's Missionary Correspondence, 1841–1856* (Berkeley, 1961), 122–123.

known African peoples living in what were pictured as useful territories, and, more importantly, of the new routes to reach them. Humanitarians, stirred by fresh information on the ravages of the slave trade (Livingstone's introduction to the horrors of that trade resulted from this expedition) reacted similarly. The commercial and manufacturing world, absorbing his listings of significant new markets and resources, and basking in his dictum that "no permanent elevation of a people can be effected without commerce,"[4] swelled the numbers of those interested. And, for all of those who had no special concern with Africa there was the absorbing account of a resolute European explorer, with his African followers, conquering the difficulties of travel in an unknown area. As set forth in *Missionary Travels and Researches in South Africa*— "I had always found that the art of successful travel consisted in taking as few 'impediments' as possible, and not forgetting to carry my wits about me"[5]—Livingstone's account soon became a best seller; with over 70,000 copies sold,[6] it became one of the most widely read books of African travel and adventure.

Returning to Britain from Quelimane in 1856, Livingstone found himself a national hero. But, despite the honors and adulation emanating from royalty, municipalities, missionary and geographical societies, and the general public, his essential outlook upon life did not change. He rather mirrored one of the statements of his journey: "It was annoying to feel myself so helpless, for I never liked to see a man, either sick or well, giving in effeminately."[7] Livingstone continued to regard himself as a divinely appointed agent for Africa's betterment—did not his success prove it?—without allowing the hero worship of the public to change his outwardly simple, even prosaic, personality. This reaction only increased his following.

4. David Livingstone, *Missionary Travels and Researches in South Africa* (New York, 1868), 248.
5. *Ibid.*, 250.
6. James I. MacNair, *Livingstone's Travels* (London, 1954), xi.
7. Livingstone, *Travels*, 388.

Livingstone had no intention of remaining long in Britain. Aided by the manifestations of public support, he soon gained the fullest backing for his new scheme for Africa's redemption. This second major African venture, supported financially by the Foreign Office, which in addition awarded him consular rank, was designed to build upon the knowledge gained from the 1853–1856 explorations by opening a route from the mouth of the Zambezi for the establishment of a missionary and commercial presence ("Those two pioneers of civilization —Christianity and commerce—should ever be inseparable"[8]) among the Kololo of the central African interior. Livingstone's paramount missionary aims thus remained the guiding principle, even though he was no longer in the service of the London Missionary Society. He had rather hastily resigned after receiving a somewhat inept letter which appeared to question the missionary value of his travels, referring to his plans as "only remotely connected with the spread of the Gospel."[9] The breach with the Society's directors was quickly healed, but Livingstone, made financially independent from the royalties of *Missionary Travels* and from public subscriptions, decided to remain an independent agent.

The specific instructions for the new expedition, given by the Foreign Office but written by Livingstone himself, called for the explorer and his companions quickly to pass the unhealthy coastal regions of the Zambezi in order to establish a station at the Portuguese up-river post at Tete. Then the rapids of Kebrabasa, heard of but not seen by Livingstone during the earlier trip, were to be investigated to determine if vessels could pass when the Zambezi ran high. Next, the expedition would establish a base at the confluence of the Zambezi and Kafue rivers which would serve as a "civilizing center" and as the starting point for the remaining explorations designed to report on the water network of the Zambezi up to its source. To help accomplish these tasks Livingstone had the services

8. William Monk (ed.), *Dr. Livingstone's Cambridge Lectures* (London, 1858), 21.

9. George Seaver, *David Livingstone: His Life and Letters* (New York, 1957), 269.

of six European companions—Norman Bedingfield, Richard Thornton, John (later Sir John) Kirk, Charles Livingstone (his brother), Thomas Baines, and George Rae—and a steamer.

But despite its impressive organization, the expedition proved the least successful for Livingstone personally. He showed himself an ineffective leader of a large expedition, unable to communicate with his immediate subordinates, and unable to react quickly and realistically when the original goals of the expedition were checked by the impassable Kebrabasa Rapids. Despite the dismissal of several of his British staff, and the discovered unnavigability of the Zambezi, Livingstone accomplished significant work. When progress up the Zambezi was proved impossible, he paddled up the Shire River, reaching Lake Nyasa (now Malawi) in 1859, thus opening to Europe a region for future successful colonization. In addition, two explorations up the Ruvuma River, one of the few large rivers north of the Zambezi, proved it of no immediate use for the penetration of the African interior. Nevertheless, when the Foreign Office recalled the expedition in 1863, Livingstone, because of his failure to prove the Zambezi navigable and because of the failure of the Universities' Mission to Central Africa (founded as a result of Livingstone's dramatic Cambridge speech in 1857) settlement in the region, left Africa a disappointed man.

Once again in Britain, after a stirring voyage in the small vessel of the Zambezi expedition from Zanzibar to Bombay, Livingstone lingered to compose his public exploration report, the *Narrative of an Expedition to the Zambesi and Its Tributaries*. But, inevitably, his sense of mission for Africa drew him on to a new venture. At the suggestion of his influential friend and patron, Sir Roderick Murchison of the Royal Geographical Society, Livingstone readily agreed to undertake an exploration of the central African watershed which had been left unresolved despite the findings and hypotheses of Richard F. Burton, John H. Speke, and Samuel W. Baker, and, more specifically, to solve the problem of the location of the ultimate sources of the Nile. Through the intercession of Murchison, both the British Government and the Royal

Geographical Society gave generous financial support to the new venture, including another consular appointment for Livingstone from the Foreign Office.[10] Reacting against his bitter experiences with European subordinates on the Zambezi, Livingstone set out in 1866 with only African and Indian followers. The subsequent years of travel, lasting until his death in 1873, can be considered the most important single expedition undertaken by a European in nineteenth-century Africa. Its geographical results were significant, but its effects upon future European reactions to involvement in Africa were paramount.

Livingstone left the East African coast at Mikindani, north of the Ruvuma, marching inland with the initial aim to disprove or prove a connection between Lakes Nyasa and Tanganyika. He immediately began, however, to demonstrate that lack of leadership which would endure until his death. He could not effectively direct the Indian troops delegated to accompany the expedition; they were probably suffering from the health problems common to all new arrivals in nineteenth-century Africa, but Livingstone appears to have made no allowance for their human weaknesses. Eventually all of the Indians left the expedition. One of their principal tasks had been to care for the several buffaloes and camels brought along by Livingstone to test their susceptibility to the East African environment. The animals soon died, Livingstone ascribing the deaths to mistreatment by the Indian handlers, rather than to the bites of the clearly present tsetse fly, a fact which did nothing to counter Indian dissatisfaction. A final major desertion came when a group of porters from Anjouan (then called Johanna) Island in the Comoros left because of their fear of nearby Ngoni raiders. Livingstone, fearless as always, was prepared to disregard the Ngoni threat—few Europeans were killed, after all, by nineteenth-century Africans—but his Comoroan followers were justifiably more anxious. Upon their return to Zanzibar, the Anjouan men invented a tale to justify their arrival, asserting that a Ngoni attack on their cara-

10. See the new material on this expedition in Roy C. Bridges, "The Sponsorship and Financing of Livingstone's Last Journey," *African Historical Studies*, I (1968), 79–104.

van had resulted in Livingstone's death. This story, and the subsequent effort to disprove it, added greatly to the drama which was enhanced in Europe as a result of Livingstone's quest for the source of the Nile.

Meantime, Livingstone, prevented from passing across northern Lake Nyasa because of the hostility of Arab slave traders, turned south to reach his goals by walking around the lake. But if he could ignore the diminution of his followers, his reactions to another disappearance were more ominous. On the journey northward one of his African carriers deserted, carrying a load which included the medical supplies. Livingstone wrote in his journal, "I felt as if I had now received the sentence of death,"[11] a premonition which proved correct. By not returning to the coast to replace the medicines so necessary for the treatment of malaria, dysentery, and other ills then facing every African traveler, Livingstone was allowing his once strong constitution—already weakened from his previous expeditions—to degenerate to a degree which would render later medications futile. The choice was clear to him, however: to give up his plans momentarily and return for medicines, or to press on in the hope that a speedy resolution of the problems of the Nile would make the loss irrelevant. For Livingstone there could only be one answer: he went on.

Continuing north from the Lake Nyasa region, Livingstone's reduced band passed through areas later incorporated into Zambia and the Congo (Kinshasa). There he received timely assistance from Arab slave and ivory hunters from Zanzibar and the east coast of Africa. With this aid, the missionary-explorer managed to attain the upper reaches of the Congo River system and to reach Lakes Mweru and Bangweulu. Then, hampered by illness and lack of supplies, Livingstone set off on the long journey northwards to Ujiji, the important port town serving the Arabs on the eastern coast of Lake Tanganyika. His hopes of adequate reprovisioning were disappointed; nevertheless the weakening explorer left for the unknown territories to the west of Lake Tanganyika which were just being opened to significant outside penetration by Arab traders

11. Horace Waller (ed.), *The Last Journals of David Livingstone* (London, 1874), I, 177.

and raiders. After extreme suffering and constant difficulties with many of his remaining followers, Livingstone reached his ultimate destination, the Arab center of Nyangwe on the eastern bank of the Congo River. But he was not allowed to answer the question of whether the great river before him was the Nile or the Congo, the latter unknown except for its outlet and immediate hinterland on the Atlantic coast. Arab hostility, plus his own poor health, blocked further progress, and following a brutal Arab massacre of Africans in the Nyangwe marketplace, Livingstone, much broken in mind and body, returned to Ujiji.

Arriving in a very weakened state at the lakeside town, and finding little of his hoped-for new supplies, Livingstone would have been in a perilous situation but for the totally unexpected arrival of a well-provisioned caravan led by the resolute Welsh-American reporter Henry M. Stanley, sent by James Gordon Bennett's *New York Herald* to interview, and reprovision if necessary, the long-absent missionary. Their meeting, as reported by Stanley, was one of the most striking of the century, and further riveted the attention of Europe upon the African continent. Once revitalized by the fresh provisions and medicines, Livingstone refused Stanley's well-meant suggestions that he should return home in order to recuperate before finishing his explorations. Instead, the two men traveled together to northern Lake Tanganyika in order to ascertain if the Ruzizi River flowed into or from the lake, a problem left unresolved by Burton and Speke. Their discovery of the river's inward flow disproved Baker's contention that Lake Tanganyika was an extension of Lake Albert, and thus a part of the Nile system. Livingstone then accompanied Stanley to the Nyamwezi chiefdom of Unyanyembe (near present-day Tabora), whence the reporter returned alone to Zanzibar. Stanley left Livingstone all of the supplies of his caravan not absolutely necessary for his return trip; arriving with his usual dispatch in Zanzibar, he sent back additional men and supplies to Unyanyembe. Thus, when the missionary left the Nyamwezi center on his final explorations, he was abundantly provisioned.

These renewed explorations took Livingstone, whose health

continued to degenerate as he progressed onward, to the regions near Lake Bangweulu, where in 1873 he died. The dramatic return of his remains to the East African coast, with his followers, Susi, James L. Chuma, Jacob Wainwright, and others, added even more luster to the Livingstone saga, which was fittingly climaxed by a ceremonial burial in Westminster Abbey.

There is little difficulty in determining what led Livingstone on through a lifetime of African exploration. The long-standing argument whether he was more of an explorer than a missionary—his latest biographer says he eventually became "less of a missionary as he became more of an explorer" [12] —or the reverse would have meant little to Livingstone himself. The mainspring of his life was his role as a missionary. With his usual determination, he decided upon his career at the age of twenty-one; thenceforth he never entertained thoughts of another way of life. "I am a missionary heart and soul," Livingstone later affirmed, continuing that "God had an only son, and he was a missionary and a physician. A poor imitation of Him I am or rather wish to be. In this service I hope to live, in it I wish to die." [13]

There are, and were, many ways of being a missionary, and Livingstone characteristically evolved his own approach. He was unfettered by any narrow approach in interpreting Christianity; that was why he joined the nondenominational London Missionary Society. He could honestly say: "I never, as a missionary, felt myself to be either Presbyterian, Episcopalian, or Independent, or called upon in any way to love one denomination less than another. My earnest desire is, that those who really have the best interests of the heathen at heart should go to them." [14] Livingstone decided soon upon his arrival in South Africa that the life of a permanently settled missionary was not for him. He had a painful belief that those heathen who were unaware of the message of Christianity would suffer eternal damnation. His duty, therefore, was to reach new African populations; those already hearing Christian doc-

12. Seaver, *Livingstone*, 63.
13. Schapera, *Family Letters*, II, 74.
14. Livingstone, *Travels*, 132.

trines had to make their own choice of accepting or rejecting the new religion, and they had to accept the consequences if the message were rejected. To Livingstone, "Those who never heard the gospel are greater objects of compassion than those who have heard it for seven years & rejected it." [15]

This conception, joined to a nature that wished to live free of any superior body's authority—"I did not come to Africa to be suspended on the tail of anyone," he said in 1842 [16]—led to travel and exploration for the young missionary. The very act of travel was immediately discovered to be pleasureful, and for the rest of his career Livingstone would brighten when he "felt the pleasure of looking on lands which had never been seen by a European before." [17] On his final expedition he exclaimed: "Now that I am on the point of starting on another trip into Africa I feel quite exhilarated! When one travels with the specific object in view of ameliorating the condition of the natives every act becomes ennobled." [18] It is the latter statement, however, which motivated Livingstone as he marched along in Africa. Travel and exploration were not aims in themselves; they were part of the mission he was sure he had from his god to spread his religion in Africa. When fellow missionaries questioned Livingstone's aims, he responded with a heated torrent of words. "A few I understand in Africa in writing home have styled my efforts as 'wanderings,'" he fumed. "The very word contains a lie coiled like a serpent in its bosom. It means travelling without an object, or uselessly. . . . So very sure am I that I am in the path which God's Providence has pointed out as that by which Christ's kingdom is to be promoted, if the Society should object I would consider it my duty to withdraw from it." [19]

Livingstone, even with this often expressed disclaimer, was all too human, wanting full credit for what he achieved. sometimes at the expense of earlier travelers. But he was aware of his attitude. "Some of the brethren do not hesitate to

15. Schapera, *Correspondence*, 150.
16. Seaver, *Livingstone*, 55.
17. Livingstone, *Travels*, 232.
18. Waller, *Last Journals*, I, 13.
19. Schapera, *Family Letters*, II, 228.

tell the natives that my object is to obtain the applause of men. This bothers me," he confessed, "for I sometimes suspect my own motives." [20] Even so, he could not at times resist the lure of being the first European to visit a location, and to do it without sharing the credit with European companions. For example, when he prepared to return to Sekeletu's country from Luanda, Livingstone did not allow the Portuguese-German naturalist Friedrich Welwitsch to accompany him because it "would have deprived me of all the credit due to my energy in opening up the path to Loanda." [21] But such reactions were minor peccadilloes that do not detract from the essential nature of the man. Livingstone might say, as he did of William Cotton Oswell and Lake Ngami, "I felt a little chagrined that he had, unintentionally, got the first glance," [22] but when first told of the presence of the nearby Victoria Falls in 1851, he passed up a visit because it did not agree with the scheme of missionary-oriented travels he had then mapped out for himself. Although Livingstone doubtless exaggerated when he said, "I am regardless of the fame of discovery," [23] his enjoyment of the spotlight of national attention was subordinated to his overall goals. If fame resulted, then the increased resources and opportunities available to the successful only made the remaining missionary tasks easier.

One reason for Livingstone's success in securing the support necessary for his missionary explorations was the fact that he, as befitted a Scot, was a well-educated man, much more so than most nineteenth-century missionaries. His early education, acquired through the competitive strivings of a youth rising from a working-class background, plus later medical and missionary studies, fed into a lively intellect which never neglected an opportunity for additional information. His broad range of interests, from the characteristics of plant life through the multifarious activities of the insect world and on

20. Schapera, *Correspondence*, 189.
21. I. Schapera (ed.), *Livingstone's African Journal, 1853–1856* (London, 1963), I, 151–152.
22. Livingstone, *Travels*, 72. See also Michael Gelfand, *Livingstone the Doctor* (Oxford, 1957), 101, for a similar episode.
23. Schapera, *Family Letters*, II, 85.

to his human brethren, were an integral part of that range of topics which interested the inquiring minds of nineteenth-century men reacting to a world which they were increasingly mastering. Problems of natural history, ethnology, geology, geography, history, and many others, including above all his own special field of medicine, were of lasting concern to Livingstone. One recent observer said, "I have never yet discovered any phenomenon in Africa which had not already been noted by Livingstone." [24] While traveling, he was continuously observing the new worlds opening around him, recording what he saw at length in his journals. After all, might it not serve his ultimate missionary designs? That the learned men of Europe found value in what he observed and reported would to Livingstone be only another indication of the divine favor he felt was shaping his life and work. As with his other interests, however, Livingstone kept his scholarly inclinations in hand, asserting of his favorite avocation, medicine, that he had to hold himself in check or "something like a sort of mania" would develop to interfere with the more important missionary work. [25]

With this sense of divine mission, and with his interest in all phases of African life, it is not surprising that Livingstone was a man of peace in his relations with Africans. To him, "the teacher should come unaccompanied by any power to cause either jealousy or fear," and "good manners . . . [were] as necessary among barbarians, as among the civilized." [26] When entering a new area, he was prepared to accept the local African power structure as a valid form of political authority, and consequently to pay, albeit often reluctantly, a reasonable amount for the right to pass through. Even the local medical practitioners were to be respected, "it being bad policy to appear to undervalue any of the profession." [27] Indeed, at least on the first and third major expeditions, the way in which he traveled, living largely off the good-will and generosity of Af-

24. Frank Debenham, *The Way to Ilala: David Livingstone's Pilgrimage* (London, 1955), 97.
25. Seaver, *Livingstone*, 62.
26. Livingstone, *Travels*, 224, 297.
27. *Ibid.*, 274.

ricans, left Livingstone little alternative. He and his few African followers were not powerful enough to benefit from continued hostilities, even if such a reaction had seemed necessary. Even on his second major expedition, when Livingstone did possess a greater military potential, he continued to avoid trouble, although his European companions killed two Africans, in what they described as self-defense, during the 1862 ascent of the Ruvuma.

Despite his efforts to avoid hostilities Livingstone was not a pacifist; he was ready, at least during his younger and vigorous days, to use stern discipline whenever he felt it essential. He reacted to the often disorderly conditions of Africa as was to be expected from a man stemming from the peaceful environment of the British Isles. Africa was a harsh reality since "Life is destroyed with a callousness which I cannot understand." [28] Thus, he concluded: "There is no law of nations here. The weakest goes to the wall. Though I am favourably disposed towards peace principles, I believe it extremely questionable whether any Peace Society man could travel ... unarmed." [29] Although often sorely tempted, Livingstone, except for his actions against African slavers in union with the men of the Universities' Mission, remained one of the most peaceful travelers to wander in nineteenth-century Africa. His impulses boiled at times, as at the Nyangwe massacre in 1871—"My first impulse was to pistol the murderers" [30]— but they were controlled except for the few times when his own men received corporal chastisement to control what he considered a difficult situation. And then, it was done reluctantly only because circumstances dictated that "subordination must be maintained at all risks," [31] even if it meant "a beating with a flat piece of wood about 2 inches broad and thin." [32]

Livingstone was able to live and travel in peace in Africa because of his basic attitude toward Africans. Unlike most explorers, and Europeans in general, he rejected "the stupid

28. Schapera, *African Journal*, II, 320.
29. *Ibid.*, 267.
30. Waller, *Last Journals*, II, 134.
31. Livingstone, *Travels*, 506.
32. Wallis, *Zambezi Expedition*, I, 125.

prejudice against color."[33] To Livingstone, Africans were fellow men. But they were a particular kind of men; they suffered, in varying degrees, because of their distance from Christian ways. His comments on the Ngwato, in 1842, expressed this feeling: "The population is sunk into the very lowest state of both mental and moral degradation, so much so indeed it must be difficult or rather impossible for Christians at home to realize anything like an accurate notion of the grossness of the darkness which shrouds their minds." Or, for the Kgatla, in 1844: "They seem to have fallen as low in the scale of humanity as human nature can."[34] This belief, after all, was what had brought Livingstone and other missionaries to Africa.

Most important in Livingstone's conception was that this "degradation" was not a hopeless condition fated to endure for all eternity, and was not confined to Africans. There were "degraded Irish,"[35] and some of the Boers were "as degraded as the blacks,"[36] and perhaps even "worse indeed than the heathen who have had no advantages."[37] Livingstone felt that, in all justice, this had to be said: "We can not fairly compare these poor people with ourselves, who have an atmosphere of Christianity and enlightened public opinion, the growth of centuries, around us, to influence our development."[38] Thus, "when rescued from the degradation and superstitions of heathenism . . . [the African] evinces improvement in an eminent degree."[39]

Still, improvable as Livingstone thought Africans might be, there was a strong element of nineteenth-century racism in his attitudes toward them. He knew which people had been chosen to lead. He told the European members of the Zambezi expedition in 1858: "We come among them as members of a superior race and servants of a Government that desires to

33. Livingstone, *Travels*, 36, 397.
34. Schapera, *Correspondence*, 18, 53.
35. I. Schapera (ed.), *Livingstone's Private Journals, 1851–1853* (London, 1960), 186.
36. Livingstone, *Travels*, 36.
37. Schapera, *Correspondence*, 287.
38. Livingstone, *Travels*, 122.
39. Monk, *Cambridge Lectures*, 26–27.

elevate the more degraded portions of the human family." [40]
Nor was he free of stereotypes in his descriptions of Africans
who bore "the low negro character and physiognomy," [41] and
to whom "the pleasures of animal life are ever present to his
mind as the supreme good." [42] Even racial mixing demonstrated
the inferiority of Africans. After his Angolan experience Livingstone concluded: "It is probable that there will be a fusion
or mixture of the black and white races in this continent, the
dark being always of the inferior or lower class of society." [43]

Perhaps this characterization is too harsh for a nineteenth-
century Christian unacquainted with the ideas of cultural
relativism. When Livingstone saw some "Christians" failing
to live up to his interpretation of Christianity, thus dashing his
early hopes for them, he lamented that "the education of the
world is a troubled one, and it has come down with relentless
rigour on Africa from the most remote times. What the African
will become after this awfully hard lesson is learned, is among
the future developments of Providence." [44] A consolation was
that, even if the converts he and his contemporaries made occasionally were failures, "such was also the case with the
Apostles." [45] The only course to follow was to preach and live
Christianity among the Africans: "Now is their opportunity,
and if they do not learn the guilt will rest on their own hands." [46]
This can be classified as racism perhaps, but it was far better
than the invectives against Africans poured forth by a Baker
or a Burton.

In spite of "degradation," the African was not in a hopeless
condition; it might take years of missionary effort, but in the
end Christianity could, and would, redeem all mankind. And
until this time, even among the non-Christian masses of Africa,
there were individuals and groups to whom Livingstone could
respond as he would have to a good man (his definition) any-

40. Reginald Coupland, *Kirk on the Zambesi* (Oxford, 1928), 107.
41. Livingstone, *Travels*, 479.
42. Schapera, *African Journal*, I, 226.
43. Gelfand, *Livingstone*, 96.
44. Waller, *Last Journals*, II, 81.
45. Monk, *Cambridge Lectures*, 27.
46. Schapera, *Correspondence*, 108.

where. Examples are seen in the missionary-explorer's relations with, and expressed feelings to, the Kololo leader Sekeletu and his people. "It is a pity," Livingstone said, "that such men must perish by the advance of civilization."[47] The Kololo, whose territory was a goal for Livingstone's early exploratory ventures, were always a favorite with him, perhaps because "they are a strange mixture of good and evil, as [men] everywhere else, the evil predominating."[48] Even the Arabs, proponents of the slave trade, were treated as individuals. This explains the good relations that have bewildered interpreters of Livingstone. He opposed their raiding, but individuals such as Muhammed bin Gharib, who aided and counseled him, were among his closest associates. Livingstone could observe that "the Zanzibar men whom I met between this [Ujiji] and Nyasa are gentlemen and they traded with honour"; they were not all like "the Kilwa traders, haters of the English."[49] It was well that Livingstone did make this distinction, because without Arab aid his 1866–1873 expedition would have ended before any of the significant discoveries concerning the Congo River system had been made.

One important facet of the concept of "degradation" did color Livingstone's value as an observer of things African. A principal lacuna in his writings is a lack of ethnographic information since, like many another less talented missionary observer, he lacked real interest in customs so foreign and repugnant to his Christian norms. "There is nothing interesting in a heathen town," he affirmed in 1867.[50] Nakedness, for example, was one custom he could never react to with equanimity: "I asked an old man if he did not feel a little ashamed to go in that state."[51] Livingstone's observations on African social life and customs could be of value, especially when they concerned medicine, or his special nemesis, the slave trade, but, too often based on

47. Schapera, *African Journal,* II, 324.
48. *Ibid.,* 320; see also his concern as expressed in Livingstone to Russell, Sept. 6, 1860, F.O. 63/894–1, and Feb. 22, 1862, F.O. 63/894–2, Public Record Office, London.
49. Livingstone to Kirk, May 30, 1869, E-57, Zanzibar Archives.
50. Waller, *Last Journals,* I, 214.
51. Schapera, *African Journal,* II, 348.

hearsay,[52] they were not equal to the observations of the best reporters—even the acerbic Burton.

This characteristic of Livingstone's writings grew in part from the essential purpose of his published works. He wrote to persuade others to come to redeem Africa, either through commerce or Christianity. In so doing he often emerged as a special pleader who argued his case on grounds far distant from reality. Reacting from his experiences with Livingstone, John Kirk not unfairly described him as "one of those sanguine enthusiasts wrapped up in their own schemes whose reason and better judgment is blinded by headstrong passion."[53] The Zambezi expedition provides an excellent example of this tendency, especially descriptions of the healthiness of the regions where activity was proposed, and of the possibilities of the growing and processing of cotton there on a significant scale. Such enthusiastic recountings helped to draw the Universities' Mission to Central Africa to venture into the regions described. Livingstone could not but be pleased at their coming, and he wrote to advise them that in this part of Africa, thanks to his remedies against fever, "there is no danger to life," since "with it the fever is not more dangerous than a common cold."[54] As for cotton, "the capabilities of the country for the production of cotton cannot be overestimated."[55] The missionaries learned—several at the cost of their lives—that conditions were not exactly as he portrayed, and that they could not be so without years, if not decades, of continuous striving.

Even then Livingstone remained convinced of the validity of his writings. Failure to him was a failure of human effort; suffering and even death were part of the sacrifice needed to Christianize Africa. Thus, when Bishop W. G. Tozer, successor to Bishop Charles F. Mackenzie as head of the Universities' Mission, decided to leave the Zambezi, Livingstone scornfully charged that he, "in fleeing ... to an island in the Indian Ocean, acted as St. Augustine would have done, had he located

52. *Ibid.*, I, xviii.
53. Seaver, *Livingstone*, 424.
54. Wallis, *Zambezi Expedition*, II, 354, 360.
55. *Ibid.*, 335.

himself on one of the Channel Islands, when sent to Christianize the natives of Central England." And further, "This is, we believe, the first case of a Protestant Mission having been abandoned without being driven away."[56] In Livingstone's view those missionaries not willing to pay the price—as he was—were better off not undertaking the effort.

As great a man as he was, Livingstone had other major flaws in his character. One was his inability to evolve satisfactory relationships with others, both intimate and casual associates, and Africans and Europeans. This man of determined and resolute mien could and did relate successfully with the great and small of the world while accepting their plaudits in Britain, but once in Africa, obsessed with the sense of his mission, all seemed to change. Even his family was sacrificed. During the years of marriage to Mary Moffat, 1845 to 1862, he spent only four out of the seventeen years with her in a normal family relationship. Traveling accompanied by his family in 1850 in southern Africa resulted in the death of a newborn daughter and the serious illness of his wife, and helped Livingstone decide to return his family to Britain for the duration of his 1853–1856 expedition. This separation was a great blow— "to orphanize my children will be like tearing out my bowels"[57] —and marked the end, except for two brief stays in Britain, of Livingstone's family life. Mary returned briefly to Africa to die on the Zambezi, and his children practically remained without contact with their father for the remaining years of his life.

Livingstone's trouble in working with others in Africa was almost the same. He had really only one successful traveling venture in which he was responsible for the direction of other men. This, his 1853–1856 crossing of Africa, came when his followers were men of one group, the Kololo, who were sent by their own leader, Sekeletu, and were working for a goal of as much interest to them as to Livingstone: the opening of a route to their territory from the Atlantic or Indian oceans. Individuals among the Kololo followers of Livingstone occa-

56. David and Charles Livingstone, *Narrative of an Expedition to the Zambesi and Its Tributaries* (London, 1865), 574.
57. Schapera, *Correspondence*, 178.

sionally balked at the difficulties which their European leader wished to overcome, but group loyalty, plus the weight of their orders from Sekeletu, kept all together and brought the expedition to a successful conclusion.

During his final African travels, from 1866 to 1873, Livingstone again had difficulties with the Africans working for him. In contrast to the integrated group of Kololo, he now worked with Africans who were joined to him in a purely business relationship, and who often were, as porters, experienced African travelers in their own right. They could not realistically be expected willingly to sacrifice their lives for the ends—which made little sense to them—Livingstone pursued. But the explorer took virtually no account of them, and, lacking the ability to win the loyalty of his followers, except for the notable few typified by Susi and Chuma, his last wanderings were a saga of continuous mismanagements leading to his own unnecessary death. In fact, the end would have come much sooner except for the aid supplied by certain Arabs and Africans whose inherent kindly nature and good breeding led them to assist a man they must often have thought close to insanity.

Livingstone's impact on the course of history in Africa was immense, perhaps greater than that of any other individual of the nineteenth century. It did not stem, however, from the personal contacts which he made with African groups and individuals while in their territories, but from the impact his character and way of life made in Europe. He became a popular hero, the missionary and explorer par excellence, who brought knowledge of hitherto unknown regions and peoples to an ever-increasing circle of individuals. The circumstances of Livingstone's death and his burial in Westminster Abbey confirmed the impact and brought even more people into contact with Africa. With this stimulation, missionary societies were able to raise the extra financial resources for new ventures into Africa, while those with secular and humanitarian ambitions were also able to take advantage of the new tide of interest. The final partition of Africa began about a decade after Livingstone's death, a decade of intense European effort in all parts of the continent. The speed of this process destroying the independent existence of most regions of Africa owed much to the publicity coming from his dramatic career.

Africans do remember Livingstone, as so many missionaries have pointed out in religiously edifying detail.[58] But how many would remember him if the consciousness of the importance of his career among the Europeans, who ruled and educated them, had not enshrined his reputation? Livingstone never remained to work for very long in one location, except during his initial years in southern Africa; admitting what he described as his "failure" among the Kwena, he soon was preparing to move on to regions beyond, where he would carry out "the introduction of the gospel wholly by my instrumentality."[59] On most Africans who met him as he passed on the way to a distant goal, Livingstone could have had little personal impact. He must have appeared as a gentle man, perhaps even a holy one, who met Africans with friendliness, and then puzzled and bored them with incessant talk of religion, rivers, and lakes. They would have been surprised, if not appalled, to learn that he was reporting to Europeans that, because of the supposed disorders of African political life, "a European colony would be considered by the natives as an inestimable boon to intertropical Africa."[60]

Among Europeans, however, Livingstone's reputation rests secure. His published volumes, plus the extensive editions of his letters and journals, remain one of the most complete records of the life and work of any African explorer of the nineteenth century. These accounts, and the interpretations stemming from them, stress his considerable geographical and scientific work, but it is not for this that he remains in the forefront of African explorers. We will continue to remember Livingstone because of the life he led, stemming from his inner vision of divine purpose, as an individual advancing to complete tasks he had set for himself, no matter what the

58. See, for example, the words of Chauncy Maples quoted in George Shepperson (ed.), *David Livingstone and the Rovuma* (Edinburgh, 1965), 52–53.

59. Schapera, *Family Letters*, I, 13–14, 17.

60. David and Charles Livingstone, *Narrative*, 199.

cost. If he could not work with individuals, they were discarded along the way, but Livingstone's work went on. It was this intense energy, with its concomitant focus on single goals, that led to Livingstone's great geographical and human feats. By stirring the European consciousness of Africa to increased action they left a lasting influence on both Europeans and Africans.

Richard Burton:
The African Years

by Caroline Oliver

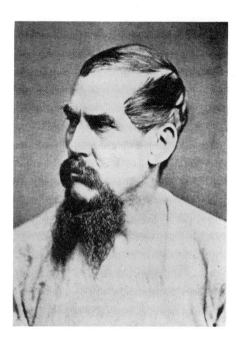

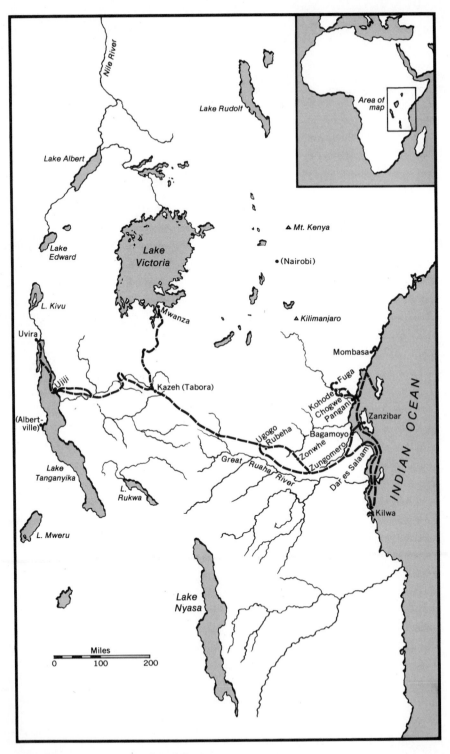

The explorations of Richard Burton

Richard Burton may have been the most brilliant personality of those who went exploring in Africa during the nineteenth century. But to the main achievements of his life, the continent was comparatively irrelevant, and even tragically irrelevant. He disliked and despised Africans, and Africans disliked, and, from his works, still dislike, him. Yet the fact that he was magnificently equipped to observe, understand, and interpret societies at a different state of development from his own is manifest in his detailed ethnographic studies, despite his arrogant, insulting, and at times almost naive derision.

Derision with Burton was by no means directed exclusively at Africans; it was a lifelong habit. In the beginning of the autobiography [1] which he dictated to his wife in later life, he painted a picture of the boyhood of two young scions of the Anglo-Irish upper classes, himself and his younger brother Edward. Instead of passing through the conventional channels of education of their kind, they spent a nomadic and undisciplined boyhood in the Europe of the 1820s and 1830s. Their playing fields were the small colonies of English people, either too unconventional or too disreputable to live in England, that existed at the time in France and Italy.

Their parents seem to have given up trying to control them at an early age. An English tutor traveled with them for many years, but does not seem to have interfered with their roistering way of life. The only subjects to which they gave serious attention were the study of languages, the use of firearms, and the art of swordsmanship. By the time the older boy was nineteen, their lack of discipline verged on the scandalous, and it was deemed expedient that they should be sent to England, Richard to Oxford, Edward to Cambridge. Their father, a disillusioned regular army officer, hoped that they were destined for academic careers.

1. Isabel Burton, *The Life of Captain Sir Richard F. Burton* (London, 1893), I, chapters 2 and 3.

In later life Burton realized the handicap of his upbringing.

The conditions of society in England are so complicated, and so artificial, that those who would make their way in the world, especially in public careers, must be broken to it from their earliest days. The future soldiers and statesmen must be prepared by Eton and Cambridge. The more English they are, even to the cut of their hair, the better. In consequence of being brought up abroad, we never thoroughly understood English society, nor did society understand us. And, lastly, it is a real advantage to belong to some parish. It is a great thing when you have won a battle, or explored Central Africa, to be welcomed home by some little corner of the Great World, which takes a pride in your exploits, because they reflect honour upon itself. In the contrary condition you are a waif and a stray; you are a blaze of light without a focus.[2]

But it was not only with English society that his unconventional childhood had left him unfitted to cope. He had formed the habit of being utterly contemptuous of anything and anybody that did not please him, and his rootlessness left him personally answerable to no one. His reactions to Oxford were typical; and though he recounted them nearly forty years later he did not trouble to temper them in any way. The dull, flat, rainy landscape was unendearing after Switzerland and Italy. The houses were mean. The place reeked of toadyism and flunkeyism. The dons were "queer things" who "walked the streets." The standard of tutoring was abysmal. The pronunciation of Latin and Greek was wrong. A fellow student guffawed at the splendid moustaches that had been the envy of the youth of the continental resorts, and when he seemed unable to comprehend a challenge to a duel, Burton was convinced he had fallen among *"epiciers."*[3] His brilliance and gaiety made him a popular undergraduate, though he professed, cynically, to have enjoyed nothing but the fencing and boxing.

2. *Ibid.*, 32
3. Grocers. Burton dearly liked to use occasional words from other languages.

The tragedy was that Burton's serious scholarly ability was not recognized at Oxford. He failed to get the professor of Arabic to accept him as a pupil; he then tried to study Arabic on his own—and suffered the indignity of being discovered writing it from left to right. In time Burton became a great Oriental linguist; the scholarly discipline of Oxford might have made him the greatest. His university career ended in his deliberately courting rustication and in his arguing so outrageously with the tutors who disciplined him that he was urged not to return. His parting shot was typically offensive. He told the college dignitaries that he hoped the "caution-money" deposited by his father would be honestly returned to him. He then drove himself away in a tandem, "artistically performing on a yard of tin trumpet, waving adieu to my friends, and kissing my hand to the pretty shop-girls."[4] Burton came to look at Oxford once again when he was nearly thirty, and after some hesitation decided not to stay and complete his terms. It was a decision which he often regretted.

From Oxford, Burton joined the Indian Army and spent seven years in India. Few who served there can have filled their time so productively. He studied eleven different languages, passed qualifying examinations in most of them, and published original grammars in two. His best Indian years were those in Sindh under Sir Charles Napier, one of the few people in high authority to recognize and harness Burton's exceptional talents. There he first practiced on a wide scale his gift for Oriental disguises, and it was as a half-Arab, half-Persian, that he went into the bazaars and out among the tribes in the hills. It was in Sindh, too, that he learned some geodesy.

In India, Burton's phenomenal literary energy, which lasted all his life, became apparent. The list of publications that resulted from the seven years is a long one, and the range of its subject matter is wide. Besides linguistic works it includes several volumes on the Sindh Valley and its peoples, a work on falconry, and monographs on swordsmanship and the use of the bayonet. But, for all the passion with which he studied

4. Burton, *Life*, 91.

India and for all his accomplishments, he wrote later: "My career in India had been in my eyes a failure, and through no fault of my own; the dwarfish demon called 'Interest' had fought against me, and as usual had won the fight."[5]

It is obvious that one demon responsible for the failure was his proclivity to jeer. All aspects of Anglo-Indian society came under the lash of his biting, snobbish, and sometimes witty tongue. He called it his "impolitic habit of speaking the truth," and doubtless there was some truth in his description. Of more serious consequence was a memorandum which he submitted to the Court of Directors of the Honorable East India company, in which he expressed himself forcibly on the subject of Anglo-Indian misrule. In an India moving rapidly toward the mutiny, there was doubtless truth in this too, but soldiers in their twenties did themselves no good by advising senior officers on how India ought to be governed.

Scholars maintain that a love affair with some part of the East is a necessary ingredient in the making of an Orientalist. Burton's was with Arabia and the Arabs. While still on the Indian List he tried unsuccessfully to obtain permission to explore central and eastern Arabia. In the autumn of 1852, he did succeed in getting a year's leave to study Arabic, and because of his frustration over the first project he decided to use it for a spectacular adventure. This took the form of a rapid journey to Medina and Mecca, the jealously guarded shrines of Islam. He went disguised as an Afghan doctor, and the part had to be sustained alone among Muslim pilgrims for many months, with never a moment of respite, sleeping or waking, from the danger of detection. Yet all of the time he was writing and sketching beneath his burnous, and the great journey was given to the world, in one of the most vivid and detailed of travel books.[6] The story is presented against an astonishingly wide background of reading, and a range of expertise. Even at the supreme moment when he was simulating the ecstasy of kissing the Black Stone in the Ka'abah, the Holy of Holies in Mecca, he opened one eye (or said that

5. *Ibid.,* 163.
6. Richard F. Burton, *Personal Narrative of a Pilgrimage to Mecca and El Medina* (London, 1855).

he did) and pronounced the stone to be an aerolite. It is significant that, although in the welter of detail the less pleasant jostles with the pleasant, Burton is patently in love with his subject in a way he never loved Africa. The jeering derision is all but absent. He found Arabs noble, manly, and demonstratively affectionate, and their language, especially in moments of passion and religious enthusiasm, imaginative and poetical.

Burton's ambitions as an explorer were whetted by the journey to Mecca. Further exploration in Arabia was impossible, owing to unsettled conditions, so he turned his attention to the vast areas of Africa awaiting European discovery. Characteristically he did so without delay. Ethiopia had already attracted European travelers, but the country of the reputedly inhospitable Somali was, except for the ports of Zeila and Berbera, comparatively little known. A journey[7] was planned in company with three other Indian Army officers, Lieutenants G. E. Herne, William Stroyan, and John Hanning Speke. Although the ostensible object was the exploration of Somalia, Burton's real intention was to continue south into the East African hinterland, possibly as far as the coast opposite Zanzibar. He, himself, made a brilliant and hazardous dash to the inland Muslim city-state of Harar, which he was the first white man to visit. Speke did some useful reconnaissance inland. But disaster overtook the expedition when it was ambushed by Somali tribesmen while still on the coast at Berbera. Stroyan was killed; and, though Herne, Burton, and Speke escaped with their lives, the latter two were seriously wounded.

Burton might have tried to enter Somalia again, but by the time that he had recuperated (in England) from his wounds, the Crimean War had begun and he was sent on war service. As soon as he returned from the Crimea, however, he began to make plans for another ambitious journey. This was to be the first modern exploration by a white man of the far interior of East Africa.

In the middle nineteenth century three German missionaries working for the British Church Missionary Society at Mombasa

7. Richard F. Burton (Gordon Waterfield, ed.), *First Footsteps in East Africa* (London, 1966).

had provoked considerable interest and speculation by the production of a tentative map of the interior of East Africa. They had traveled considerably in the interior and their map showed the snow peaks of both Mount Kenya and Kilimanjaro. They had also talked with Zanzibari merchants who had traveled much farther inland, and who had reported a great inland sea, which they called either the Sea of Ujiji, or the Sea of Tanganyika.[8] Burton proposed to determine the limits of this inland sea, to study the ethnography of the tribes in its vicinity, and to report on the trade and produce of the interior. The Indian Company was amenable to his request for a two-year leave of absence, and the enterprise was sponsored both by the Royal Geographical Society and by the Foreign Office, which contributed £1,000 to the expenses.

The possible discovery of so large a geographical feature as the Tanganyika lake was in itself attractive. But there was another more dramatic possibility. The upper courses of the river that had influenced so much of the history of mankind were still unknown. Somewhere in the East African interior, probably in this very Sea of Tanganyika, the Nile might originate. Ptolemy, the Egyptian geographer, showed the beginnings of the Nile as many streams coming from some "Mountains of the Moon" just north of the Equator. These streams converged into two lakes, from which two rivers flowed north to form the Nile. His map is detailed, not far from the truth, and was probably based on a firsthand account. The Scottish traveler James Bruce, in the eighteenth century, traced the source of the Blue Nile, which joins the main or White Nile at Khartoum. An Egyptian expedition sent by Muhammed 'Ali in 1839 reached Gondokoro on the White Nile. Other Egyptian expeditions followed, but there is no record of any successful penetration farther south than latitude 4° north, and little of value was contributed to the solution of the mystery of the Nile's origins, between the fifth century and Burton's expedition.

8. For details see Roy C. Bridges, "Introduction," Johann Ludwig Krapf, *Travels, Researches, and Missionary Labours During an Eighteen Years' Residence in Eastern Africa* (London, 1968), 39–42.

While making plans in London, Burton again met Lieutenant Speke. He had recovered rapidly from his many wounds and, like Burton, had served in the Crimea. Also like Burton, he was involved in plans for exploration, in his case in central Asia. But for a long time he had considered penetrating East Africa from the coast, returning, if possible, down the Nile; in fact, it was with some such object in view, that he had originally traveled to Aden, where he met Burton on the eve of the Somali expedition.

Speke was a complete contrast to Burton. In appearance he was tall, lithe, fair, and blue-eyed, with a tawny beard. Burton was shorter, very dark, almost gypsyish of countenance, with flashing dark eyes and the splendid drooping black moustaches that had astonished Oxford. Speke was in no sense an intellectual and had no great linguistic talent; but he was a much liked and tactful soldier, with solid qualitites of determination and dogged persistance. He was abstemious, trained rigorously, and had tremendous physical stamina. He was also a fine mountaineer. When not engaged in active service in India, his whole time had been spent on solitary wanderings in the Himalayas, with the ostensible object of shooting. In the course of five years a great collection of Himalayan fauna had found its way, via the taxidermist, to his father's country house in the west of England. He had been granted almost unlimited leave by his regiment to spend his time in this way, because, although he had begun without any of the necessary skills, he was in fact usefully charting unknown Himalayan tracks. Speke had acquired his skill as a surveyor in the hardest and best of schools, and in view of their subsequent serious disagreement about the geography of East Africa, Burton's own assessment of his qualifications is of interest.

Speke was the first to penetrate into some of the remotest corners of Little Tibet: and here, besides indulging his passion for shooting, collecting and preserving, he taught himself geodesy in a rude but highly efficient manner. . . . Some years of this work, tracing out the courses of streams, crossing passes and rounding heights, gave him an uncommonly acute eye for country,—by no means a usual accomplishment even with the professional surveyor.[9]

Burton invited Speke to join him, and helped him disengage himself from the central Asian venture and obtain further leave from the Indian Army.

There is no reason to think that the two men at the time were not reasonably good friends. Both wanted to solve the riddle of the Nile, but their motives for doing so differed. They must be seen against their period, when most young soldiers boasted frankly of their ambition to find hazardous fields in which to distinguish themselves. In spite of the support of the British Foreign Office, it was not yet the age of European imperialism in East Africa, and if either were imbued with fervor for imperialism it took second place to their ambition for geographical discovery. To Burton, whose background combined an unstable and nomadic childhood with exceptional talents which had as yet been scarcely rewarded officially, spectacular success seemed to provide the path to promotion and the unassailable social position which he craved. His facile pen would be well employed in presenting central Africa to the world. It is also clear that he was consciously building a pyramid to his own immortality. Speke, whose family were scattered among the manor houses of the west of England, had the security of background which Burton did not. He lacked Burton's brilliance, but in his own, less theatrical way, his determination to solve the Nile problem was probably as passionate. There was a great prize to win, the country he loved would be proud of him, and the collection of stuffed fauna in his father's house would grow even more magnificent. He seems to have been content to serve under Burton, his senior by six years. He became official surveyor to the expedition, while Burton's concern was with ethnography, and with the produce and commerce of the interior.

Near the end of 1856 they reached Zanzibar, where Sultan Majid had recently succeeded his father. The Omani Arabs

9. Richard F. Burton, *Zanzibar* (London, 1872), II, 376.

had first established their superiority over the East African coast at the end of the seventeenth century, when they defeated and expelled the Portuguese. But the colony was for a long time scattered and uncoordinated, until the reign of Seyyid Said, who had died a year previously. He had left Muscat, the Omani capital, to live for long periods at Zanzibar, and his development of the island's resources, chiefly cloves, had led to its becoming the chief slave market of the Indian Ocean. By 1856, the East African Arab empire that was ruled from Zanzibar had tentacles that reached over a thousand miles into the African mainland. Some of the traders who went inland were pure-bred Zanzibari Arabs. Their principal inland station was at the great caravan crossroads at Kazeh in Unyamwezi. The Swahili-speaking Arabized Africans of the mainland traded inland on their own account, and had their own inland capital at Mseni in Unyamwezi. There were also some Indian traders, who had long been established at Zanzibar and on the mainland.

Burton had no intention of breaking his own trail to the Tanganyika. Apart from potential African hostility, the traders with their vested interests could have made it impossible. The road to Ujiji was as much under the control of the Zanzibari sultanate as it was possible for such a road to be. With the help of the British Consul, Colonel Atkins Hamerton, and with his own ability to make friends with Arabs, he secured the Sultan's generous cooperation. He was provided with letters of introduction to the important merchants at the inland stations; he was lent a small detachment of Baluchi mercenaries as an armed escort; and the Sultan himself appointed Said bin Salim, a half-caste Arab, as Ras Kafileh, or caravan guide.

The expedition did not start for the interior until June. The intervening months were spent in making plans and in some preliminary travel. They sailed to the neighboring island of Pemba, thence to Mombasa, and on down the coast to Pangani. From there they took a brief inland trip through the Usambara Mountains. Being restricted as to time and money, it is puzzling that this preliminary canter was thought to be worthwhile. But some delay was necessary in order not to start for the interior during the rains, and possibly some experience in the management of East African caravans was useful. Also, there was good material for Burton's pen, which he published with his fine and detailed account of Zanzibar, presented against the usual background of reading—this time of Arab and Portuguese sources. But two good travel volumes scarcely seem to justify a diversion from the main objectives of the expedition.

There was a possibility of striking into the interior from the old Arab port of Kilwa, whence a caravan route led to a considerable lake or sea, known as the Malawi Lake.[10] But Burton was warned that this route was too remote from the Sultan's control for safety, and from inquiries in Zanzibar he was certain that Lake Malawi was divorced from Lake Tanganyika. So the immensely difficult task of assembling a caravan for the interior was undertaken at Kaole, opposite Zanzibar, the usual starting place for Kazeh and Ujiji. The recruitment was officially the task of Said bin Salim. Although commanded by the Sultan to do the job, he was less than willing and would have welcomed insuperable difficulties. Burton's linguistic ability gave him some advantage in the polyglot confusion of Kaole. Its range was unsuspected, and he could assess the local reactions to the European attempt to travel in the interior. It was generally reckoned that they would be unable to proceed more than a short distance from the coast, and the danger of traveling in a European's caravan made the recruitment of porters exceptionally difficult. Besides routine necessities and ammunition for a period of from eighteen months to two years, great quantities of cloth and beads had to be carried as currency, and to pay the *hongo,* or transit fees, of inland chiefs.

It proved impossible to find the force of about 175 porters which was needed. The best available porters came from Unyamwezi. These people had a rare bent for travel and had for a long time made the porterage on the Ujiji road their special preserve, even running their own caravans. Their number at the coast varied seasonally, and only 35 could be

10. Lake Malawi, known as Lake Nyasa during colonial times, has now reverted to its former name.

engaged. Under pressure from Burton a heterogeneous collection of coastal types was engaged, most of whom proved disorderly on the march. Many were the personal slaves of coastal merchants, and were bent on slave-hunting expeditions of their own or their masters. A number of asses were found to supplement the porters, but much of the baggage had to be left behind, to be forwarded when possible. Both Burton and Speke had Goanese personal servants and two freed slaves who acted as gun-carriers. One of them, Sidi Bombay, developed an interest in geography, and played a considerable part in the Nile quest.[11]

Much of the expedition's success was to depend on Burton's management of this multifarious collection of people. There were traditional caravan rules to be observed. For instance, the practice was for each group to have a leader with whom the Ras Kafileh dealt. But the orderliness which this suggests much belies the reality, and it was the white men who had to lead, encourage, humor, and coerce. Illness apart, the interminable nagging trials incurred in keeping the undisciplined throng on the move constituted the heaviest burden of East African travel. Quarrels, sickness, theft, disobedience, laziness, desertion, and fear were sometimes relieved by comedy, or by the euphoric elation of the good moments: the fanfared departures and arrivals, the occasional sudden improvement in the commissariat, the unexpected meetings with old friends. Burton's description of what was entailed in getting the first march under way shows that infinite patience had to be combined with pressure.

> At length by ejecting skulkers from their huts, by dint of promises and threats, of gentleness and violence, of soft words and hard words, occasionally combined with a smart application of the *bakur*—the local "cat"—, by sitting in the sun, in fact by incessant worry and fidget from 6 A.M. till 3 P.M., the sluggish unwieldly body acquired some momentum.[12]

11. He accompanied Speke on his successful descent of the Nile two years later.

12. Richard F. Burton, *The Lake Regions of Central Africa* (London, 1861), I, 51.

The only occasional use of the cat has a ring of truth, because Burton was capable of almost boasting of his competence in this respect. When later he generalized about the direction of caravans, he condemned the Nyamwezi caravans as being too strict and arduous, and the Arab as being too spoiled and pampered. He maintained that the Swahili,[13] whom he normally found inferior to the Arabs in everything, were the most successful. That he himself succeeded in assembling and commanding a caravan is some measure of Burton's own competence. But both Speke and Colonel Christopher Palmer Rigby, who succeeded Hamerton as consul at Zanzibar, were critical of his attitude toward his men, especially of the niggardliness of his ultimate financial settlements with them. It is likely that the more patient and diplomatic Speke played a bigger part in the direction of the caravan than Burton ever admitted.

The march to Kazeh took 134 days. They crossed swamps, marshes, deserts, and mountain passes on a trail littered with the bones of the casualties of the road. There was much sickness in the caravan, and the two Europeans suffered continuously from malaria, and what Burton called marsh fever. At times they were so ill that they had to be carried in hammocks. Sometimes, crossing the mountains, they were so weak that several assistants had to drag them up the steep cliffs. Weakness induced by fever made both deaf. And yet Burton was ceaseless in his quest for information of the peoples and of the country, and, as ever, scribbled incessantly.

There is no known African record of the passing of the first two Europeans ever seen in East Africa; no description of the first "anthropologist" who questioned. Prior to their arrival, reports had been spread of their monstrous physical features and habits, and of course of their suspected territorial ambitions. Nonetheless, the sightseers crowded to look, and sometimes followed the caravan with amused commentary. In one village Burton complained that the mob of starers made him feel like the denizen of a menagerie.

Burton's description of the Africans encountered is masterly,

13. The term Swahili is used for the arabized Africans of divers coastal tribes. Swahili was also the lingua franca of the interior.

though frequently marred by contemptuous criticism. In contrast, his portrait of the permanent settlement of Arab merchants at Kazeh is sympathetic and delightful. He probably overemphasizes the strictly Arab make-up of the society, which must have been very mixed, but it was an interesting oasis of comparative civilization buried deep in Africa. A trading station rather than a colony, it was sufficiently self-assured to be gracious in its welcome.

> Contrary to the predictions of others, nothing could be more encouraging than the reception experienced from the Omani Arabs; striking indeed was the contrast between this truly noble race, and the niggardness of the savage and selfish African—it was heart of flesh after heart of stone.[14]

In a detailed portrait of Snay bin Amir, who was his principal friend in the settlement, Burton gives evidence of a way of life that is something of a revelation.

> During two long halts at Kazeh he never failed, except through sickness, to pass the evening with me, and from his instructive and varied conversation was derived not a little of the information contained in the following pages. He had travelled three times between Unyamwezi and the coast, besides navigating the great Lake Tanganyika and visiting the northern kingdoms of Karagwe and Uganda. ... He had read much, and, like an oriental, for improvement, not only for amusement: He had a wonderful memory, fine perceptions and passing power of language. Finally he was the stuff of which friends are made; brave as all his race, prudent withal, ... and,—such is not often the case in the East, he was as honest as he was honourable.[15]

Snay bin Amir was the first to give Burton firsthand information about the rumored great lake to the north of Kazeh, which was known to the Arabs as the Sea of Ukerewe or as the Ny-

14. Burton, *The Lake Regions of Central Africa*, I, 323.
15. *Ibid.*, 325.

anza. He strongly recommended a visit there in preference to the Tanganyika, as he considered it a greater lake in every way. But Burton was determined to pursue his original course. Presumably he was prejudiced in favor of the Tanganyika as a possible fountainhead of the Nile. Contemporary maps, based on the speculations of armchair geographers, showed Ptolemy's Lunar Mountains as a chain running westward from Kilimanjaro to rumored peaks to the northeast of the Tanganyika. This chain, if it existed, would make the northward passage of a large river from a lake due north of Kazeh impossible; whereas a river flowing out of the northern end of Tanganyika could find a course round the western extremity of the chain, where the geographers had placed the great African depression. Speke at the time would have agreed with this, but had he rather than Burton been in command of the expedition, he would have turned north at Kazeh to look at the Nyanza.

It was only with Snay bin Amir's help that Burton succeeded in getting the caravan to go beyond Kazeh, which seemed to have been agreed upon by all parties as the ultimate limit of the journey. Finally, after many more trials and ills, he reached his goal on February 19 and looked down on the great narrow inland Sea of Tanganyika. Speke was suffering from inflammation of the eyes, the result of prolonged malaria, and was all but blind. Burton, who had to leave Kazeh in a *machilla*, had been stricken en route with a partial paralysis, also from prolonged malaria, and remained an invalid throughout the rest of the expedition. Many members of the caravan were sick, and all were lethargic in the humid lake climate. But the local information was exciting. Most of the Ujiji merchants were of the opinion that there was indeed a large river that flowed out of the northern end of the Tanganyika. None of them had seen it, but they knew that it was called the Ruzizi.

The subsequent difference of opinion between Burton and Speke about the geography of central Africa makes it necessary to follow their movements after their arrival at the Tanganyika in some detail. The first priority was to reach the northern end of the lake. Speke, whose illness was no longer as severe, crossed over to Kasenge, an island off the western shore, in order to negotiate the hire of a dhow from an Arab called Hamid bin Sulayman. The craft was not available, but the Arab claimed to have been to the north of the lake, and confirmed that the Ruzizi was an effluent and not an influent. "I went so near its outlet," he said, "that I could see and feel the outward drift of the water." This was splendid news for the sick and suffering Burton, but Speke, with his great experience and judgment of upland country, was puzzled. He made the altitude of the Tanganyika only 1,800 feet,[16] and he considered this to be too low for the ultimate source of the Nile. It was also but half the height of the general interior East African plateau. He guessed, correctly, that the deep narrow trough was of volcanic origin.

Having failed to obtain the dhow, they chartered two canoes, and embarked from Ujiji on 12 April, on a precarious voyage to the north. Burton, after nearly a month of rest, was still far from well, but doubtless the mounting hopes of a dramatic discovery proved stimulating. Speke had a distressingly painful poisoning, the result of a beetle's lodging in his ear. Besides the maddening discomfort, it had made him deaf, but the inflammation of the ear had drawn the inflammation from his eyes, which were greatly improved. The canoes were manned by Jiji boatmen, who, though noisily gay and brave on the water, stood in awe of the Tutsi of Burundi on the northeast of the Tanganyika. So, after hugging the Ujiji coast for a time, they crossed the lake to Uvira in the northwest, via the long northward-pointing peninsula of Ubwara that they thought was an island. Because of the reputation of the formidable Tutsi, this was the farthest north that the Arab or Swahili traders ever went, and it was impossible to persuade the Jiji crews to continue. Burton might have recruited local crews, but his great hopes that the Ruzizi might prove to be the earliest Nile stream were shattered. The sons of the chief of Uvira came to visit him; they were emphatic in declaring the river an influent, not an effluent, and a host of bystanders

16. John Hanning Speke, "Journal of a Cruise on the Tanganyika Lake," *Blackwood's Magazine*, 86 (September 1859), 352. The correct altitude is just over 2,000 feet.

confirmed the assertion.[17] When questioned, Bombay, who had accompanied Speke on his visit to Hamid bin Sulayman, said that he thought that Speke had misunderstood; and there was considerable doubt expressed as to the Arab having ever really been to the extreme north. It must have been a bitter moment for Burton. He had been very ill during the voyage; a horrible ulceration of the tongue made him almost inarticulate, and eating was a misery. He lacked the strength to make the probably hopeless effort of going to see for himself.

The information was not so surprising to Speke because the effluent theory had not made good geographical sense. He said, though significantly Burton does not, that the sons of the Uvira chief described high mountains encircling completely the northern end of the Tanganyika, which were drained to the south by the Ruzizi.[18] Before leaving Uvira he climbed some neighboring heights and looked across at the mountains on the eastern shore, at this point only seven miles away. He was convinced that they increased in height to the north, and that they rose to at least 6,000 feet. Burton, sick and bitter, jeered and later accused Speke of drawing in an imaginary "chancellor's wig" of mountains at the head of the lake. But the man to whom Burton himself imputed "an uncommonly acute eye for country" was correct.

They reached Ujiji again on 13 May, and Burton seems to have been more resigned. The spectacular prize of finding the early Nile sources had eluded him; but, though the non-arrival of the remainder of his baggage meant that he had not the means to explore southward, the many good informants at Ujiji made it possible to determine the limits of the lake and to describe accurately the people there and their commerce. He had therefore successfully carried out his brief from the Foreign Office and the Royal Geographical Society. While he was at Ujiji the rainy season ended, the climate became enjoyable and the lake very beautiful, though, typically, Burton could not resist comparing its lush beauty unfavorably with the austere beauty of the arid deserts of Arabia.

17. Burton, *The Lake Regions of Central Africa,* II, 117, 118.
18. John Hanning Speke, "The Supposed Source of the Nile," *Blackwood's Magazine,* 86 (October 1859), 392.

Anxieties over the return journey, with the hazards of feeding a caravan of seventy-five on the march to Kazeh, were at the last moment alleviated by the arrival of some of the lost baggage. It was battered and broken and depleted but, in Burton's poverty-stricken condition, blessedly welcome. With the usual frustrations, the expedition finally left Ujiji on 26 May, and reached Kazeh a month later.

On the journey back to Kazeh, Speke had already broached the question of his going to look at the northern lake. Apparently by then relations between the men were far from good, and Burton was content to remain in the comfort of the Arab settlement, and in the informative company of his friends. He later insisted that it was as much to be rid of Speke's company as to have the Arab reports on the great extent of the northern lake confirmed that he sent him. At all events, a small party was organized, including Bombay, who was developing into an enthusiastic geographer. A much recuperated Speke left Kazeh on July 10, and Burton settled down to amass a wealth of information about the countries and peoples of the interior, especially of the northern kingdoms of Karagwe, Bunyoro, and Buganda, to the west, northwest, and north of the Nyanza.

Suddenly, on the morning of August 25, shouts and gunshots announced Speke's return. He had made a successful and rapid trip to the northern water and back, and had found it to be a lake of even greater dimensions than they had expected. The two men had scarcely finished breakfast when Speke announced "the startling fact that he had discovered the sources of the White Nile." [19] Burton was dumbfounded.

Speke had reached his conclusion slowly, on the basis of a mounting sum of evidence. Before leaving Kazeh, informants, including Snay bin Amir, had described in detail the northward route up the western side of the Victoria Nyanza. All agreed that two large rivers and more than a hundred streams drained high mountains in the west and southwest and flowed into the Nyanza. The mountains were certainly those at the northern end of Lake Tanganyika. All were agreed that, as far

19. Burton, *The Lake Regions of Central Africa*, II, 204. See also below, 103.

as Buganda, on the equator, there was no west-east mountain chain, that the Nyanza stretched northward for at least 5° from its southernmost point, and that its northern extremity was unknown. It was said that somewhere to the north there was a great river, called the Kivira. One informant had seen it, and thought that it came from the generally acknowledged direction of the lake. Speke was not aware at the time that the Swahili word *nyanza* denoted any water, whether river, lake, or sea, but he must have begun to suspect something of the kind.

All of the reports about the southern shores of the Nyanza had proved accurate when Speke arrived there. He also had found good informants, who had traveled extensively by canoe along its coasts, and whose reports both confirmed and added to those of Kazeh. One African, known to have traveled widely, had demonstrated dramatically with his arm the endlessness of the waters to the north and had said that he considered that they extended "probably to the end of the world." [20]

Speke's own observations and calculations had further confirmed the general picture of his informants. He had found the Victoria Nyanza to be a high-level reservoir in a different category from the volcanic Tanganyika. He had reckoned that its southern tip was in latitude 2° 30' south, and that its altitude was about 4,000 feet.[21] The known altitude of the Nile, in latitude 4° north, was 2,000 feet. The comparative altitudes made it more than likely that the Nile River received water from the Nyanza. From a point of vantage by the lake he had been able to assure himself that the lost west-to-east mountain chain did not exist to the south of the equator. In the light of all this information, other facts had assumed significance. The rainy season in the mountains to the north of the Tanganyika was consistent with the times of White Nile flood. Rumors of sailors on waters in the far north, who used navigational instruments, and of trade beads that came not from Zanzibar but from the north, became plausible.

The greater part of this formidable build-up of evidence

20. Speke, "The Supposed Source of the Nile," 414.
21. The correct altitude is 3,700 feet.

must have been known to Burton; but he greeted Speke's announcement with utter derision, and a serious quarrel ensued. The bitterness of the next few days can be imagined. Finally any reference to what Burton called Speke's "trouvaille" had to be banned. It might have been reasonable for him to refuse to share Speke's conviction. To accuse a surveyor with great experience of unknown country, the official geographer of the expedition, of complete irresponsibility was intolerable. No doubt Burton's great talent for jeering had full play. The account of the incident in *The Lake Regions of Central Africa* gives some idea of its flavor.

> The fortunate discoverer's conviction was strong; his reasons were weak—were of the category alluded to by the damsel Lucetta, when justifying her penchant in favour of the lovely gentleman Sir Proteus:
>
> "I have no other but a woman's reason.
> I think him so because I think him so." [22]

This is followed by some pages of argument against Speke's "Pretended Discovery," based largely on his linguistic shortcomings and those of his interpreter, Bombay. Speke was bitterly angry too, but had the good taste, or possibly the good sense, not to publish his acrimony.

It is not evident when the relationship between Speke and Burton began to deteriorate. Perhaps both had too much personal ambition to work together. Their traveling priorities were different, and this, combined with his poor health, led Burton to prefer ethnographic research at Kazeh to a first glimpse of another lake. But it was his expedition that had led Speke to the Nyanza, and to the probability that they were on the track of the Nile at last; thus some of the credit was legitimately his. Perhaps "some" was not enough. The alternative was to sneer, with the result that Speke, probably already irked by his companion's ways, was estranged. And the pyramid of adventure that Burton was consciously building to his own

22. Burton, *The Lake Regions of Central Africa*, II, 204.

immortal fame was destined to be not the sublime cone of Cheops, but the bent and blunted pyramid of Snefru.[23]

The victim of his own temperament, Burton did not immediately realize that by the quarrel he had forfeited his stake in the Nile quest. His subsequent behavior was strangely inconsistent. The finances of the expedition precluded any further exploration of the northern lake, and yet a completely irrelevant expedition from Zanzibar to Kilwa was found possible. While still at Zanzibar he quarreled violently with Colonel Rigby, who was bitterly critical of him—and who became a firm supporter of Speke. At Aden he pleaded ill-health as an excuse for not accompanying Speke to England (though Aden in 1859 can scarcely have commended itself for convalescence). He always maintained that Speke, on leaving, gave him a friendly promise not to make any pronouncements on the results of the expedition in London, before his arrival. Yet in apparent contradiction (as well as to his reception of Speke's theories at Kazeh), Burton wrote to the secretary of the Royal Geographical Society, soliciting "serious attention" for Speke's map observations, and for his diary of his journey to the Nyanza, "as there are now reasons for thinking it to be the source or principal feeder of the White Nile."[24]

Speke, apparently against his own inclination, was persuaded by Sir Roderick Murchison, then president of the Royal Geographical Society, to speak briefly at a meeting already arranged for two days after his return home in May. It seems likely, perhaps understandable, that he presented his case to Murchison with a conscious eye to being sent again—without Burton. His single-minded preoccupation with the Nile and the reasonableness of his arguments were undoubtedly persuasive. So, when Burton arrived two weeks later to a triumphant reception at the Society, and to the award of the Gold

23. Isabel Burton in her biography of her husband (I, 304) quotes some verses of his, which she found scribbled on his Tanganyika Journal. They begin: "I have built me a monument, stronger than brass, / And higher than the pyramids' regal site."

24. Richard Burton to the secretary of the Royal Geographical Society, April 19, 1859, in Waterfield, "Introduction," *First Footsteps in East Africa*, 39.

Medal, its greatest prize, much attention already was focused on Speke. His behavior was correct. When receiving the medal, he gave Speke generous credit for the expedition's geographical findings. When they both spoke from the Society's platform in June, and Speke further developed his theories, he did not dissent. His official account of the journey, resulting from his journal and published in *The Proceedings of the Royal Geographical Society*, though arrogant at times about Africans, is reasonably disciplined and objective. It was only when Speke published his own journals in *Blackwood's Magazine*, in the autumn of 1859, that Burton realized that the future exploration of East Africa was in other hands than his. Then once more he let loose a barrage of derisive scorn against Speke and his Nile theory. It became an obsession which continued even after Speke's subsequent successful Nile exploration, and tragic death.

If his triumphant accomplishment of the aims of his East African journey was destined to appear in perspective as a personal failure, in Burton's great travel book *The Lake Regions of Central Africa*, he opened for the first time a brilliant window on to the eastern side of the Dark Continent. As well as the vivid picture of the Arabs of the interior, it teems with information, topographical and ethnographical. However, it is spoiled for many for two reasons. Speke, who was "Jack" in the original journal, more formally "Captain Speke" in the Royal Geographical Society's version, is never mentioned by name; but as "my companion" he is sneered at throughout. And the Africans, having failed to improve through the apparently civilizing influences of the slave trade, which, elsewhere in the book Burton maintained, "practically annihilates every better feeling of human nature," [25] are condemned to a limbo of eternal inferiority. Even in the official account, with its rapid condensed flood of information, Burton's opinions are strangely inconsistent.

> In intellect the East African is sterile and incult, apparently unprogressive and unfit for change. Like the uncivi-

25. Burton, *The Lake Regions of Central Africa*, I, 99.

lised generally, he observes well, but he can produce nothing profitable from his perceptions. His intelligence is surprising when compared with that of an uneducated English peasant; but it has a narrow bound beyond which apparently no man may pass.[26]

Despite the polished elegance of the book, the contempt at times seems ludicrous. The impulse to write and publish superficial opinions and Burton's indulgence in derision frequently seem to have mastered him and spoiled much that was excellent.

In 1860 Burton, who was still officially in the Indian Army, took a trip across North America by way of diversion and recuperation. On his return, he married Isabel Arundel, a member of the family of the Roman Catholic Dukes of Norfolk. She had hero-worshiped him for a long time, and her blind adulation was doubtless soothing. After his marriage Burton decided to look to the consular service for a job. He very much hoped that he might be sent to Damascus. But in spite of his achievements and the influential connections of his wife, he only received the offer of the comparatively lowly post of Consul to the Bights of Benin and Biafra, based on the island of Fernando Póo. The post, known as the "Foreign Office grave," provided a livelihood, but little more, and, as the West African climate was then proving lethal to Europeans, he refused to allow his wife to accompany him. The Indian Army, in which he had had official listing, if little conventional service, for nineteen years, saw in the new posting a chance to be rid of him. It would not have been inconsistent with the practice of the time for him to have remained on half-pay, but, to his great indignation and distress, he was removed from his regimental list and given no pension. It must have been infinitely galling to this brilliant man, now forty years old, to be starting at the bottom rung of the diplomatic ladder, going to a lonely post among the Africans whom he despised.

Consular functions in the West Africa of the 1860's were not very clearly defined. There was a considerable English trad-

26. Richard F. Burton, *Proceedings of the Royal Geographical Society,* XXIX (1859), 336.

ing community in the Niger delta and the Oil Rivers ports of what is now Nigeria. There the legitimate palm-oil trade, already valued at nearly a million pounds annually, had successfully replaced the centuries-old but by then illegitimate slave trade. This had brought about a great change in the trading pattern, and incidentally in the political pattern. To a certain extent the trade was passing from the hands of the rulers of small states into those of African trading families. In the course of the transition trading rules were loosely defined by precedent, and there were at the time no consular courts. The frequency of disputes had brought into being here and there voluntary tribunals known as Courts of Equity. During his term of office Burton made a useful contribution to the smooth running of commerce in the Bights by reforming the procedure of these courts. It was perhaps the most constructive contribution that he made to the consular office. For he was not temperamentally suited to the job. His snobbishness saved him from the overinvolvement with the trading community which had led to undesirable results for some of his predecessors. The naval officers engaged in the antislavery campaign were more congenial, and at times very useful to him. With some notable exceptions he despised the missionaries. He was capable of horsewhipping any African trader whom he considered bumptious out of his office. He prided himself on his ability to deal with African labor, though his methods do not commend themselves in the twentieth century. Yet, probably nobody more astute had served the Foreign Office in Fernando Póo and the Bights, and his acute powers of observation were conducive to valuable reporting home.

Burton devoted by far the greatest part of his consular time to traveling and to the acquisition of knowledge. Within two weeks of his arrival, he availed himself of an offer by the senior officer of the West African Naval Squadron of a passage to Lagos. He stayed with the Acting-Governor, since Lagos, long one of the most active ports of the slave trade, had been annexed as a British colony in 1861. He again enjoyed Muslim society, though even he found some imperfections in the Islam of the west coast of Africa. He also acquired a servant, Selim Aga, an ex-slave who had come to Lagos *via* Egypt and some education in Scotland. Apart from escaping from Fernando Póo, perhaps Burton's chief reason for going to Lagos was that he had the chance of accompanying what he called a "nautico-diplomatico-missionary visitation" to Abeokuta, the capital of the Egba group of the Yoruba peoples, about whom he had read a great deal. This was a treaty-making expedition by a naval officer, Commander Norman Bernard Bedingfield, to the King of Abeokuta. It was no concern of Burton's, who went purely "for the fun." Inevitably the fun and a great deal of information were put to paper for the wider world.[27]

Returning from Abeokuta to Lagos within a few weeks, he sailed in another of Her Majesty's ships to Victoria in the Cameroons. There a small party was organized for the purpose of climbing the peaks of the Cameroons Mountain. It consisted of Gustav Mann, a German botanist of some repute; the Reverend Alfred Saker of the Baptist Mission at Victoria; a Spanish judge, whom Burton had brought from Fernando Póo; Selim Aga; and a company of Krumen as servants and porters. In spite of incidental injuries and maladies, and an antagonistic rivalry that developed between Burton and Mann, it proved a delightful six weeks' Christmas holiday. A base camp was set up with many amenities, including a whipping post to strike terror into the hearts of the Krumen. From it the members of the party made arduous climbs of the volcanic peaks, gaily naming them after wives, relatives, and friends. Burton claimed to have been the first to reach the summit of the tallest peak. In this holiday spirit, however unsuitable his methods of controlling the Krumen seem a century later, he was able to laugh when he caught them out in an elaborate piece of trickery, as heartily as they did themselves. And he was so delighted with the countryside that he confidently reported home that the Cameroons was suitable for the sanatorium that could save the white man's life in West Africa. (Actually the area has the highest rainfall of the whole continent.)

After the Cameroons episode, Burton must have endured some weeks of Fernando Póo. But toward the end of March he

27. Richard F. Burton, *Abeokuta and the Cameroons Mountains* (London, 1863).

was again far out of his consular domain, and up the Gabon River looking for gorillas. While there he also studied the Fang peoples, whose probably exaggerated reputation for cannibalism and other practices interested him. After that he had an even longer spell in Fernando Póo, and began to pursue his anthropological researches among its island peoples. Then in the autumn, the tearful importunings of his wife at the Foreign Office resulted in his being granted home leave, and Christmas 1862 saw him in England.

He spent only one month in Britain, during which he gave his two West African travel books to the press, and played a large part in the launching of the Anthropological (later the Royal Anthropological) Society. The rest of his leave was spent belatedly honeymooning with Isabel in the Canary Isles. After his return to West Africa in 1863, he began to find Fernando Póo more congenial than before, but he still seized every opportunity to travel. He explored the Congo estuary, and he visited Luanda and penetrated some ways inland into Portuguese Angola. None of this activity was in any way connected with his consular business, which was carried on in his absence by an assistant; though on this, his second and last, short tour in West Africa, he did carry out one official diplomatic mission of some importance. This was to Gelele, King of Dahomey, the powerful, and in some ways notorious state, to the west of Lagos and Abeokuta.

In 1864, the slave trade, dead or dying along the greater part of the Guinea coast, was still thriving in Dahomey. The principal foreign merchants involved were half-caste Spaniards and Brazilians, based at the infamous slave port of Whydah. The principal source of supply were prisoners taken in the recurrent wars between Dahomey and its traditional enemy, Abeokuta. Several Englishmen visited the Dahomean court during the eighteenth century, and, toward the middle of the nineteenth century, the antislave trade campaign sent a number of humanitarian delegates, who were courteously received but who were quite unsuccessful in their efforts to persuade successive Dahomean kings to abandon the trade. In the 1860's, the annexation of Lagos, and the presence of English missionaries in Abeokuta, where they were in recurrent danger from Dahomean attack, added a political incentive to the humanitarians to bring pressure to bear on Dahomey. Invasion was discussed, and, indeed, confidently advocated by Burton, but the Admiralty was loath to add to its active commitments in West Africa. The only alternative was a diplomatic mission. In 1862 Commander William Eardley-Wilmot, the Officer in Command of Her Majesty's West African Naval Forces, went to Abomey, the capital, briefed to explore the possibilities of an antislave trade treaty. He was delighted by his reception by King Gelele, and reported, perhaps naively, that conditions were favorable for negotiation. He promised Gelele that he would return, but his naval duties prevented this, and the mission was deputed to Burton.

Burton was already interested in the Fon people of Dahomey. Rumors of sacrificial rites, performed annually and on a larger scale at the king's accession, had long since reached Europe. These rites were common to many West African courts, but those of Dahomey were especially notorious. There was also an unusual political structure, in which the whole range of officers of state was duplicated with women officers. There was also a female army, known to Europeans as the Amazons, whose military prowess had earned it the honored center position when the Dahomean army went to war. All this was intriguing to Burton. He had paid a brief visit previously, but as this was without Foreign Office sanction and possibly against his explicit instructions, he never wrote about it. Typically he had gone on preparing himself for another opportunity, both by reading and by studying the Adja dialect spoken by the Fon.

His brief from the Foreign Office was to endeavor to consolidate the renewal of friendly relations brought about by Eardley-Wilmot; to impress upon the King the importance which Her Majesty's government placed on the cessation of the slave trade; and, if possible, to sow some seeds that might result in time in the abolition of human sacrifice. As regards the slave trade, there was a chance of success, because by 1863 there were sound practical reasons for its replacement by other forms of commerce. The British naval squadron, which had done a great deal to end the trade on other parts of the coast, could, and very soon probably would, prevent the slave ships from leaving Whydah. A treaty with the United States already insured that no more American ships would participate in slave transport. On the other hand, the prospects of influencing Gelele on the subject of human sacrifice were negligible. The West African despots were themselves controlled by a despotic tradition. Burton commented: "It is evident that to abolish human sacrifice here is to abolish Dahomey. The practice originates from filial piety, it is sanctioned by long use and custom, and it is strenuously upheld by a powerful and interested priesthood." [28] He also came to the conclusion that the abolition of the slave trade would, in fact, result in more victims for the sacrificial rites.

On all three counts Burton's mission was a failure. He was so undiplomatic that the long tradition of friendly visits to the barbarous court was nearly broken. He was unsuccessful with regard to the abolition of the slave trade, and human sacrifice was not ended in Dahomey until the French conquered it in the 1890s. Probably no ambassador could have done any better. Others before him had received nothing but friendly hospitality and demands for extravagant presents. Burton more than any of them understood the nature of sacrifice; if he behaved badly by diplomatic standards, he was at least honest. His patience was outrageously taxed by Gelele's incessant postponement of a chance for serious discussion. Finally the great annual "customs," or sacrificial feast, intervened, and he had to sit in the hot sun through five days of bizarre spectacle, though by his own insistence he was spared the actual killing. When at last he tackled the king, his temper was frayed and—an unheard of thing at the Dahomean court—the interview took the form of a noisy quarrel. Burton admits this, and the episode is further commented on by Peter Bernasko, an African Wesleyan missionary based at Whydah, who accompanied him to Abomey. He reported to his missionary headquarters: "The manner and customs of the Dahomans, or Africans generally, are not as the civilised Europeans;

28. Richard F. Burton (C. W. Newbury, ed.), *Mission to King Gelele of Dahome* (London, 1966), 235.

therefore one who has an interest in their civilisation ought not to go among them with a hot passion and harsh temper. The C.[ommissioner] in fact Rev. Sirs, did not go to Dahomey with any patient heart." Bernasko described the actual leave-taking when Burton "put on a long face to the presence of the King which no European has ever done so." Subsequently, Gelele sent for Bernasko and told him "that if the Queen send such Commissioners to him [it] will spoil everything and break the friendship between England and Dahomey." [29] The party left for the coast immediately after and reached Whydah in late February 1864.

The most important result of Burton's visit was the book he wrote. It is the best description of Dahomey written while the monarchy was still a living force. It is also probably his best African book, because his interest in and understanding of much of his subject often surmounts the impulse to jeer. He describes Fon culture and religion, the Dahomean constitution, and the sacrificial rites with objective authority, and as usual the detail is astonishing. During the five-day ritual at Abomey, he recorded every dance movement, the pattern of every one of hundreds of decorated umbrellas, and every ceremonial wiping of the royal nose and face. As the record of a visit of little more than two months, it is a great achievement.

After the Dahomean mission Burton left Africa for home leave. In England, Speke had returned from his successful journey to Victoria Nyanza and down the Nile to Cairo. The two men never met again socially, but their lives were destined to interact in one final dramatic episode. A distinguished gathering was arranged by the British Association, to take place in Bath in September 1864. Among other scientific discussions, Burton and Speke were invited to debate their differences over the Nile sources. In retrospect, it seems an unfortunate bit of cock-fighting, got up for the sport of a learned company. Speke had never completely recovered from his deafness and would have been at a serious disadvantage in public debate. He had suffered greatly from Burton's derision, which had continued on the grounds that he had not actually

29. *Ibid.*, 23.

followed the Nile bank the whole way from the Nyanza to its known course. In doubting Speke, Burton had important supporters among the geographers present; yet he must have known that Speke had proved his contention. Speke tried to refuse the invitation, but was provoked into accepting by mischief-making intermediaries. The debate never took place. Both protagonists were present in the hall at Bath on the opening day, although their discussion was not due till the morrow. Speke found the presence of Burton intolerably disturbing, left before lunch, and drove to the house of a cousin who took him out shooting. Shaken by the event in which he was involved, and with his concentration impaired, he mishandled a gun when crossing a stone wall, and shot himself dead.[30] Burton heard the news the next day while waiting to begin the debate. His wife says that he went home and wept copiously. The two men had come to hate each other bitterly, but they had shared hardship and physical suffering on the long road they had traveled together, and doubtless this had bred some ineradicable affection. Also Burton in all likelihood was shocked by the tragedy into a recognition of what his own arrogance had done to his standing as an African explorer.

Since 1854 Africa had been the main focus of Burton's ambition. In 1864 he left it, never to return. He was posted to Brazil, and he continued, in a not very distinguished consular career, for the rest of his life. His greatest claim to fame was in the realm of scholarship, chiefly in the translation of Arabic literature, but he has undisputed claim to have been the pioneer of East African exploration.

30. The possibility that Speke committed suicide has frequently been raised. Sir John Milner Gray, Chief Justice of Zanzibar from 1942 to 1953, told me in 1958 that he had examined the evidence given at the Coroner's Inquest with great care, and that he fully concurred with the verdict of the Court: "accidental death."

John Hanning Speke:
Negotiating a Way to the Nile

by Roy C. Bridges

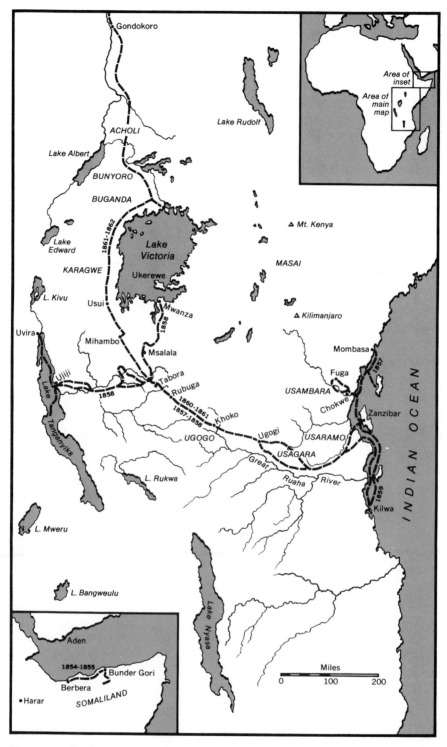

The trips of John Hanning Speke, 1857–1862

"Lord, let us kill this prodigy!" The call came from the chiefs, officials, and priests at the court in the royal palace of Buganda in February 1862. The "prodigy" was John Hanning Speke, who had recently arrived in the country to search for the source of the Nile. The lord was Mutesa I, *kabaka* of Buganda. Fortunately for the explorer, the *kabaka* refused to execute a man whom he had already welcomed as a friend.[1]

African accounts such as this are seldom available to record an explorer's arrival. In this instance, the recollections of a page at the court suggest that Speke may have been in much greater danger than his own published account would indicate. Big-game hunting exploits more often provide the excitement in the two books which Speke wrote to describe his African experiences. Nevertheless, there is enough evidence in them to show that his presence was always an important factor in local political situations, even if these did not necessarily involve a threat to his life. Few of the early journeys of East African exploration were adequately financed, and Speke's was no exception. Consequently, he was never in a powerful enough position to ignore local political realities, especially in a kingdom like Buganda. How quickly he was able to proceed to his next objective, how much *hongo*, or transit fee, he would have to pay, and how much food he could obtain for his porters all depended upon complicated factors which he might or might not comprehend.

By the time that he reached Buganda in 1862, Speke had accumulated a considerable amount of experience in the art of persuading African chiefs to allow him and a half-mutinous gang of porters to travel through a particular stretch of country. His own personality had something to do with the success. Although one verdict has it that "lack of education made him

1. From an account given in 1934 by a former page at Mutesa's court, Isaya Kasakya, as translated by Frederick B. Welbourn, "Speke and Stanley at the Court of Mutesa," *Uganda Journal*, XXV (1961), 220–223.

naive, over-confident and very susceptible to 'slights,'"[2] Speke was said by Harry Johnston to have "impressed the natives favourably wherever he went as being a man and a gentleman."[3] He may have been naive in many ways and he certainly had more than his fair share of pride, but Johnston's estimate reflects something of the skillful manner in which he managed his relations with local rulers. Even if he might allow it to be thought that he was a prince in his own country and refuse to prostrate himself before majesty, he never failed in some way to show sufficient deference to whichever potentate might control his destiny. Nor, and this was equally important, did he alienate the loyalty of the small group among his porters who were prepared to risk putting their trust in him to conduct them safely through the Nile region.

Speke's first African venture in Somaliland had taught him the futility of becoming involved in fighting when trying to explore. Born in 1827, he had entered the Indian army in 1844 and saw considerable service in the Punjab campaign.[4] Yet he was more of a sportsman than an all-round soldier: "I only liked my profession when I had the sport of fighting," he wrote. When there was no fighting, Speke spent his leaves shooting game in Tibet, where he also became a competent surveyor. When he qualified for leave in 1854, pursuit of the excitement of shooting big African animals made him arrange to join Richard Francis Burton's Somali expedition. At this time the human population was of little account to him; he arrived with a collection of cheap trinkets and baubles to tempt "the simple-minded negroes of Africa."

The expedition was not destined to meet many Negroes,

2. Richard Francis Burton (Gordon Waterfield, ed.), *First Footsteps in East Africa* (London, 1966), 28.

3. Harry Hamilton Johnston, *The Nile Quest* (London, 1903), 129.

4. A full-scale biography of Speke has never been written. Kenneth Ingham, "John Hanning Speke, A Victorian and his Inspiration," *Tanganyika Notes and Records*, 49 (1957), 301–311, is a useful short account of his life. The large literature concerned with the specific problem of Speke and the Nile sources is surveyed by Donald H. Simpson in the Royal Commonwealth Society's *Library Notes*, new series, nos. 93–94 (October–November 1964). A complete life of Speke is in preparation by Alexander Maitland.

simple-minded or otherwise. The plan was to penetrate from Berbera in Somaliland southwards into the parts of East Africa opposite Zanzibar. A series of delays and difficulties, culminating in the Somali attack on the explorers' camp at Berbera in April 1855, led to the abandoning of the scheme. Burton, it is true, had added fresh laurels to his personal reputation, which the Berbera disaster tarnished only a little, by penetrating to the "forbidden city" of Harar. Speke's achievements were hardly comparable. He was given the task of investigating the interior south of Bunder Gori, a town east of Berbera, and then moving westwards into the Berbera hinterland along the Wadi Nogal. Soon abandoning the Arab disguise he had assumed, Speke set off in late 1854 with an *abban* or "protector" called Summunter.

Speke had innocently supposed that present-giving to local chiefs was simply a matter of giving, receiving thanks, and then proceeding with the journey. As he was to learn on countless other occasions in Africa, it was not always easy for a traveler even to be given an audience with a chief. More than once he found that a chief would give help only on condition that Speke provide military support in one of his border wars. Protracted negotiations with rulers like Muhammed Ali of Bunder Gori or the ruler of the Dulbahantas tribe were made more exasperating by his growing conviction that his protector, who was supposed to be smoothing away the difficulties, was in fact dishonest and merely using Speke and Speke's goods to try to solve his own financial problems. There were also constant arguments with his camel men, on whom he relied to carry his supplies and equipment. In the end, because of these difficulties Speke had to return to Bunder Gori with very little accomplished. He had Summunter tried and imprisoned at Aden in February 1855. Burton recommended the abandonment of the use of *abbans* by British travelers, and Speke himself, after a minor trip along the coast near Berbera, made another journey from Bunder Gori without one.

The Somali disliked this departure from custom. It seemed particularly suspicious at a time when the various chiefs were warily watching the extension of British influence into the Horn of Africa from their base across the sea at Aden. Nevertheless, Speke reached Berbera without too much difficulty since he traveled only through the coastlands. But Burton's decision to wait for further equipment from Britain rather than join a caravan going south left the European party open to attack by the Habr Owel tribe. One of Speke's companions was killed, while he himself was wounded and then captured. He escaped and then almost died of his wounds.[5]

Some of Speke's subsequent adventures in East Africa were equally dramatic, but the physical danger usually resulted from animals rather than men. Relatively unimportant as they were, his early journeys had taught him some useful lessons, for his difficulties adumbrated those he was to encounter during his East African expeditions. Speke had rejected a Somali *abban*, but would he be able to do without a Zanzibari guide in East Africa? He had refused to be drawn into local wars in Somaliland. The Berbera disaster must have driven home the lesson that a small European exploring party could be in great danger if it encountered active hostility. It was a lesson Speke remembered in East Africa, although he was to find himself under great pressure to take sides in a dispute. The problems Speke had encountered in Somaliland over present-giving and managing his camel men were only brief foretastes of the endless troubles he was to have in negotiating *hongo* and leading his porters along the routes to the East African lakes. The experience was sufficient, however, to teach him to control his impatience and anger.

After he had served in the Crimean War, further opportunity for Speke to travel through Africa came in 1857, when a Royal Geographical Society expedition to East Africa under Burton was organized in order to test geographical speculation and follow up the limited practical exploration which had been carried out by Johann Ludwig Krapf and his fellow missionaries. Little information on traveling conditions in East Africa was available to the sponsors except for some rather optimistic suggestions by Jacob Erhardt, one of Krapf's companions. The cost of the venture was also seriously under-

5. John Hanning Speke, *What Led to the Discovery of the Source of the Nile* (Edinburgh, 1864), 2–4, 151, 19–23, 32–35, 45, 80, 109–115, 117–144. See also above, 69.

estimated, with the result that both Burton and Speke eventually had to pay considerable sums of money out of their own pockets. It was some months after the expedition's return in 1859 that wrangles over money matters completely snapped the already badly frayed thread of friendship between the two men.[6]

The disputes centered around how much should have been paid to the porters and guides who accompanied the explorers. To an even greater extent than with subsequent European ventures, in fact, the direction and pace of the expedition were determined by factors external to the strictly African scene. Burton, already Arab-oriented in his thinking and sympathies, could only imitate the organization of an Arab trading caravan in making his arrangements to penetrate toward Lake Tanganyika from the Zanzibar coast. When in the interior, he had to follow the normal Arab routes. It is notable that the explorers' attempt to reach the northern end of Lake Tanganyika was unsuccessful because there were no Arab facilities to help them. Speke himself tried to hire the only dhow then on the lake. He failed—perhaps because the owner was concerned only with crossing the lake to trade on its western side and had no interest in its northern end.

Conducting an Arab-type caravan, Burton and Speke were subject to all of the difficulties usually encountered by traders. Troubles with porters, often culminating in their desertion, were the normal order of the day. The porters were no doubt underpaid, but there were other reasons why the Nyamwezi carriers in particular absconded. Burton and Speke were entering East Africa at a period when competition between the coast-based Arab trading parties and the interior-based Nyamwezi caravans was growing acute. The Nyamwezi, beginning to lose their formerly predominant position to the much better-financed Arabs, reacted by charging more *hongo,* withholding food supplies, and refusing to enlist as porters. With the help of their own Arab caravan leader, Said bin Salim al-Lamki (d. 1879), and other Arabs in Tabora (the principal center for the Zanzibari traders in the interior), Burton and Speke man-

6. Roy Charles Bridges, "Speke and the Royal Geographical Society," *Uganda Journal,* XXVI (1962), 29–30.

aged to obtain more porters and more supplies, but they could not hope to reimburse themselves for the exorbitant costs by dealing in ivory or slaves. Europe would have been scandalized by the latter, and the Arabs would have withdrawn all support at the first sign of European economic competition.

The heavy dependence on Arab help and Arab methods, as well as the way all of Burton's information about East Africa was filtered through Arab informants, colored the whole expedition. Speke initially had little direct contact with African rulers, and his early reactions to the people whom he saw were superficial: "hideously black and ugly," was one of his first comments. Like Burton he was inclined to draw a sharp contrast between the Indians and Arabs of the coast and the apparently "savage" Africans. As the expedition progressed, Speke became more discriminating in his judgments; he met more Africans and came to know some of his porters better. The most important opportunity to learn more came in July 1858 when he seized the chance to organize his own minor expedition. This expedition was to be emancipated to a considerable extent from dependence on the Arabs.[7]

Having returned from Lake Tanganyika to Tabora, Burton was recovering from illness and attempting to recruit porters for the journey back to the coast when Speke sought approval for a "flying trip" to the southern end of the lake reported to lie to the north. The route to this lake, which Speke was to christen "Victoria Nyanza," was known but relatively little frequented by Arab traders. Most who ventured northward made for Karagwe, west of the lake, on their way toward Buganda; as yet, the water-borne trade from Mwanza to Buganda was not well developed.

Speke insisted at first on having Said bin Salim with him, but the Arab's refusal to accompany him, whatever the reason for it, left the European much more directly responsible than he had hitherto been for negotiating his passage with local rulers. Even so, Speke did engage a local Nyamwezi guide who obviously chose a route in accordance with his own knowledge and interests. For example, the guide arranged that the party

7. Speke, *What Led,* 240–245, 168–169, 190.

should make an elaborate detour in order to avoid passing through the territory controlled by one faction in a chiefdom split by a dynastic dispute. Such disputes were endemic to the region. Reigning *ntemi* clans provided candidates from among whom local elders from "commoner" clans would choose a chief. In this particular case, some brothers of the immigrant Bakamba clan seem to have been disputing the succession in Bumanda in the Msalala district. Frustrated by the delay caused by the detour, Speke contemplated employing some Baluchi soldiers of the Sultan of Zanzibar who were with the expedition to force a way through the dissident territory. Force would probably have been unnecessary; it was simply that the guide had a friendly arrangement with one of the rivals, a chief called Kurua. The chief wished to have Speke in his *boma* in order to demonstrate his superiority over his brothers. He also hoped that friendship with the explorer would bring him access to supplies of gunpowder, which could help his warriors triumph over his enemies.[8]

On attaining the lake and deciding (without much real evidence) that it was the source of the Nile, Speke was glad to meet Mansur bin Salim, the only Arab trader then resident in Mwanza. Mansur was in a curious position. Reports at Tabora said that the chief of Mwanza was holding him for ransom, but the situation was slightly more complicated. The chief, Muhaya, had recommended that Mansur should send all of his trade goods ahead to Ukerewe, a major trading center on the southeastern lake shore, but not risk going there himself for the time being. The goods had been detained by Chief Machunda of Ukerewe and Mansur was left destitute. Muhaya would not allow the Arab to take any steps to recover his goods nor permit him to leave Mwanza, but insisted that he himself would arrange matters with Machunda. Muhaya Rubambula

8. *Ibid.*, 251, 261, 266, 285–288, 353–354; Tanganyika District Book, Kahama and Nzega, George VI Museum, Dar es Salaam; Hans Cory, *The Ntemi* (London, 1951), 4; R. F. Burton, "The Lake Regions of Central Equatorial Africa, with notices of the Lunar Mountains and Sources of the White Nile; being the results of an Expedition undertaken under the patronage of Her Majesty's Government and the Royal Geographical Society of London in the years 1857–1859," *Journal of the Royal Geographical Society*, XXIX (1859), 265–268.

was the founder of the Mwanza chiefdom and a member of the Hindi clan fairly recently arrived from Buha to the westward. Perhaps, as he consolidated his chiefdom, he wished to counteract the growing economic importance of Ukerewe by giving it a bad reputation with coast traders and maintaining a stranglehold on its communications. Alternatively, Muhaya may have wanted to discourage any coast men from coming to this region and superseding the local traders.

Speke established a fairly amicable relationship with Muhaya, but soon realized that, as with Mansur, every obstacle would be placed in the way of his going on to Ukerewe to see more of Victoria Nyanza. On the other hand, Muhaya, indisposed to detain the explorer, soon facilitated his return southward.[9] Thus the extent to which Speke could investigate the lake was determined by the rather obscure political considerations of the Mwanza chief. The porters were also anxious to return for reasons which soon became apparent. Fifteen of them were local men who could use the trip to their own particular advantage. The cloth they received from Speke as wages was used to purchase iron hoes in the Sukuma region, hoes which would be sold in Tabora at a profit.

Consequently, Speke had a quick and easy passage. Although he objected to his carriers stopping to make a feast whenever they received meat, he had relatively little difficulty with them since their own traveling interests coincided with his. Perhaps the explorer was lucky not to encounter any trouble with the Ngoni warriors or "Watuta" then attacking Ujiji.[10]

The favorable conditions which had made the trip to Mwanza comparatively easy were not repeated when Speke was in the same general area three years later. It was undoubtedly the importance of the discovery that he had made and the apparent good management he had shown in organizing his independent venture that decided the Royal Geographical Society to send

9. Hans Cory, *The Indigenous Political System of the Sukuma* (Nairobi, 1954), 40. Speke, *What Led*, 261, 309, 313–316. Tabora traders believed Muhaya was trying to strangle the Ukerewe trade. Burton, "Lake Regions," 270.
10. Speke, *What Led*, 285–286, 300, 333–334; Richard Francis Burton, *The Lake Regions of Central Africa* (London, 1860), II, 76.

Speke back to East Africa in 1860 with a somewhat more generously financed expedition. His companion on this occasion was James Augustus Grant (1827–1892), an old Indian colleague. But Speke, for the first time, was in complete command of a major exploratory expedition.

Speke's 1860–1863 journey is the apex of his career and the basis of his fame. Not only did he substantiate his Nile claims (though these claims were to be disputed in some quarters for several years), but he also opened to European eyes the fascinating region of the interlacustrine states. The explorer himself was determined to profit from the mistakes made on the first expedition as far as organization was concerned. There would be proper agreements with the porters, and even deserters would be paid for the time that they served. Supply depots would be established ahead of the expedition in the interior, while arrangements would be made for it to be met in the Nile source area by a relief party coming up river. The latter task was entrusted to a Khartoum ivory trader called John Petherick. Speke seems to have been completely confident of his own physical fitness and his own competence; he expected to be able to leave Zanzibar and to join up with Petherick in about eighteen months. On his way to East Africa, Speke met Sir George Grey, the governor at Cape Town. Grey aided Speke by providing him with a guard of ten Hottentot soldiers. This added to the prestige which Speke was hoping to establish by arriving in a British warship with the clear blessing of the British authorities. Certainly the British consul in Zanzibar, Christopher Palmer Rigby, did everything in his power to facilitate the arrangements, including paying all of the remaining debts of the 1857 expedition so that there should be no local prejudice against British travelers. Because the British Government approved of Speke's expedition, the Sultan of Zanzibar, Seyyid Majid bin Said (d. 1870), had no choice but to do the same. He provided porters from among his own slaves and allowed Said bin Salim to be engaged once again as the caravan leader. Everything augured well for the expedition.[11]

In the event, Speke was not to have the easy passage that he

11. Bridges, "Speke," 30–34; Speke, *Journal of the Discovery of the Source of the Nile* (Edinburgh, 1863), 1–11.

had planned. Basically, he relied again on utilizing Arab resources and facilities. But the Arab position in East Africa had changed a good deal since the time of his last expedition. Even the preliminary arrangements Speke had made did not work smoothly. There was delay in obtaining the £2500 grant which had been promised to the expedition by the British Government and even longer delay in making financial support available for Petherick. In both cases the funds proved insufficient. The Hottentot soldiers were a burden rather than an aid. Rigby had been able to arrange for only one load of supplies to be sent ahead to Tabora, and in 1861, when he left Zanzibar, the expedition was deprived of its support at base. Support at destination was also to prove lacking for Petherick was unable to attain Gondokoro, much less the Victoria Nyanza region, in time to meet Speke. Speke's assumption that Petherick would be present, however, was to have an important bearing on the way in which he conducted his journey.

Despite these drawbacks, the local arrangements for the expedition went ahead with Speke still in a confident mood. The most important task was to recruit the members of the caravan. It was particularly important to include some men who could speak Hindustani. Although Speke claims to have learned some Swahili, it does not appear that he ever became really proficient. During the Somali expedition, the reason for recruiting the guide called Ahmed had been his knowledge of Hindustani. Now Speke was fortunate in being able to secure the services of some freed slaves, including Bombay, who had served with the former expedition, Baraka, Frij, and Rahan, all of whom knew Hindustani. Presumably even Speke's communications with Said bin Salim must have been made most easily through one of these interpreters. It is impossible to say how accurately the explorer's words were conveyed to the African chiefs with whom he negotiated during the journey; but double or triple translation could be a tedious process. Speke notes that Mutesa of Buganda could not be bothered to wait for the answers to his questions.[12] Speke's linguistic deficiency meant that there was a tendency for the actual work

12. Speke, *What Led*, 20–21, 199; Speke, *Journal*, 5, 294, 298–299, 327; James Augustus Grant, *A Walk Across Africa* (Edinburgh, 1864), 25.

of negotiation to be left to Bombay and Baraka. If only for this reason, the story of Speke's relationship with his African followers is an extremely important one.

Men like Bombay, Baraka, Mabruki, Uledi, and their fellows, who, usually because of the slave trade, had been drawn out of their tribal environments, are examples of the class of Africans who were closely associated with European or Arab activities to open up East Africa for commercial, exploratory, missionary, or imperial purposes. The Yao hunters, the Swahili *fundi* (itinerant trading agents), the freed slaves, the mission "boys," and their like were in fact the most fundamentally important group of Africans in East Africa in the nineteenth century. Certainly his porters were the Africans with whom Speke had the closest contact and certainly, too, the activities of the leaders amongst them had almost as much bearing on the way the expedition managed its transit as those of the two Europeans. The porters were also important as a group. As long as Speke could keep his caravan together as a viable unit, it was a factor to be reckoned with in any local situation, especially since it carried an armament of fifty carbines at a time when firearms were not as common in East Africa as they were later to become.

Bombay and Baraka are the outstanding figures among Speke's followers—part of the small nucleus of men who were said to have some "knowledge of English honour and honesty." During the "flying trip" to Victoria Nyanza in 1858, Speke had found it possible to leave much of the negotiating with African chiefs to Bombay.[13] A member of the Yao tribe, Bombay had been enslaved at the age of twelve and taken to India. The death of his master had resulted in his being freed and he returned to Zanzibar to take service with the Sultan's forces. While Bombay was stationed with a detachment at Chokwe in Usambara Speke met him, was impressed by his capabilities, and forthwith recruited him for the Lake Tanganyika expedition. On his return, Bombay seems to have joined Rigby's staff as a member of the consul's boat crew. Baraka, another member of this crew, had previously seen considerable service with

13. Speke, *Journal*, 11; Speke, *What Led*, 353.

the British Navy, presumably after being freed from slavery. Speke described Baraka as the "smartest and most intelligent negro" he ever saw.[14] These two men are early examples of the "Yao career servant," and Speke acknowledges his indebtedness to them and the other freed slaves for the success of the expedition: "a loose, roving, reckless set of beings, quick witted as the Yankee," they were the key men in the caravan.[15] Altogether, there were 33 men in the category of freed slaves. With the addition of 42 men who were either still servile or only recently released from slavery and 101 Nyamwezi carriers, the total original complement of the caravan included 176 men. Speke was to emerge in Egypt with only 18 of his employees still under his command.[16]

Not surprisingly, Speke and Grant tried to put their army experience to use in controlling the caravan. Grant claims that drill was beginning to develop some coherence and discipline among the freed slaves. Corporal punishment was sometimes resorted to, and rewards took the form of days of rest or feasts of meat when the Europeans happened to have a successful day's hunting. But on almost any issue the porters had the last word because they could desert or threaten to desert when a favorable opportunity occurred.[17] Almost 150 men did desert in the course of the journey. Ten of the carriers provided by Sultan Majid deserted on the first day and 8 more a few days later, taking all the goats. At various subsequent stages, further groups fled, although local replacements could sometimes be recruited. All but 3 of the original Nyamwezi porters had absconded by the time the caravan had traversed Ugogo.[18] War and famine in Unyamwezi made it impossible to recruit sufficient men for the march northwards to Karagwe despite

14. *Ibid.*, 176, 186, 210–212; Speke, *Journal*, 11, 20.

15. Robin C. H. Risley, "Burton, An Appreciation," *Tanganyika Notes and Records*, 49 (1957), 273; Speke, *Journal*, xxv, xxvii.

16. A guard of 26 Baluchi as well as the Hottentots accompanied the expedition through the coast regions. Thus, including Said bin Salim, 213 must have set out, but the figures given in Speke's text and in his appended lists of personnel are not in complete accord. Grant, *A Walk*, 22–23, has another slightly different version.

17. Grant, *A Walk*, 76; Speke, *Journal*, xxx.

18. Speke, *Journal*, 19, 27, 63, 72, 77.

the great amount of time and trouble Speke spent trying to do so through the good offices of Musa Mzuri (d. 1861), the principal Tabora financier. By a series of shifts and expedients, involving the engagement of local carriers for short stages or the practice of sending goods ahead and then bringing the freedmen back to take up further loads, Speke managed eventually to reach the interlacustrine area. The majority of the freed slaves were still with him. They, together with a handful of slaves and Nyamwezi recruits, gave him a complement of 45 men when he reached Buganda. However, the departure from Buganda in July 1862 saw the desertion of 15 of the freed men and 7 others; each carried off a carbine. Speke dubbed these deserters the "unfaithfuls." [19]

The defection of the "unfaithfuls" was a considerable blow to the expedition. It was the culmination of the struggle for power among the freedmen which had been going on almost throughout the journey. There were many divisions among the porters as a whole. For example, the Zanzibaris seem to have disliked the Nyamwezi carriers on whom Speke showered favors in an attempt to keep them with the party. The Sultan's slaves did not easily fit into the caravan. But the more fundamental disputes originated among the freedmen; those originally from the same Yao village or those who had previously worked for the same master might club together in groups of varying size. Doubtless these allegiances helped to determine which side a man would take in the principal disputes which arose during the journey.[20] The ostensible quarrel between the two main factions was about whether it was too risky to follow Speke into Buganda and beyond. Essentially, however, the division resulted from the struggle between Bombay and Baraka for personal ascendancy among the porters.

Rivalry between the two men had become a notable feature of the life of the caravan when it was still in the coast regions, but the quarrel did not attain the proportions of a crisis until

19. Speke, *Journal*, 357, 491–492; Grant, *A Walk*, 274.

20. Speke, *Journal*, 24–25, 28, 135. Of the "faithfuls" who were with Speke at the end, 5 were freedmen, 7 were Sultan Majid's slaves, and 5 were men recruited in the interior. Of those who deserted in Bunyoro, 16 were freedmen, 1 was Sultan Majid's slave (25 others had deserted at the beginning of the expedition), and 12 were interior recruits.

the departure from Tabora where Said bin Salim had been discharged as ill. Bombay and Baraka both thought themselves qualified to take over the position of caravan leader. Speke, drawn to Bombay by their association on the previous trip and his apparent devotion to the cause of the present one, chose him for the position. From that time on, Speke believed, Baraka deliberately tried to hinder the progress of the expedition. Most serious was his apparent attempt to sabotage a plan Speke developed in Uzinza to avoid the delays and exactions of the local chiefs. The plan involved sending messengers ahead to Suwarora, chief of Usui (Rusubi), asking him to send help to the expedition and save its goods from the depredations of the minor chiefs over whom he exercised a vague suzerainty. Baraka refused to go himself and persuaded Speke's local guide, Ungurue, not to cooperate either. In this crisis Speke was forced to return to Tabora to obtain guides who would also recruit porters. Actually, in spite of Baraka, one man, associated with a different trading party, had gone forward and acquainted Suwarora with Speke's situation. Suwarora sent help, and the caravan was soon on its way to Karagwe, but there is no doubt that Baraka's obstructive tactics made Speke's already very difficult situation a good deal worse.[21]

With only Speke's own evidence available, it is not easy to discover the real reasons for Baraka's attitude. A witch doctor is supposed to have warned him that disaster would overtake the party in the north,[22] but it seems likely that he was motivated more by jealousy of Bombay than by fear of Usui and Karagwe. His longer experience in serving Europeans and his seniority to Bombay in the consul's boat crew probably made him resent being introduced to Speke as a protégé of Bombay's and being given the demeaning job of valet to Grant. But Speke had soon remedied the latter situation, and began to give Baraka just as much responsibility as Bombay as an interpreter and ambassador. It was Baraka, for example, who acted as go-between when Speke tried to mediate in the war raging around Tabora. So useful was he that Speke made every effort to conciliate him and patch up his quarrel with Bombay, realiz-

21. Speke, *Journal*, 41–42, 94, 134–136, 151–152.
22. *Ibid.*, 176.

ing that his dismissal would lead to the complete disintegration of the expedition, with only a few "infatuated fools" like Bombay maintaining their loyalty.[23]

On his side, Bombay distrusted Baraka's eloquence, was jealous of the confidence Speke placed in the other's skill, and resented the European's weakness in allowing Baraka to buy and keep women, which was against the rules of the caravan.[24] The clue to what was really at issue may lie here. The ability to buy women depended on control of the expedition's stores of cloth, beads, and wire. Baraka obtained this control in July 1861 at Mihambo, when he was left in command while Speke, Grant, and Bombay were away trying to recruit porters. Defalcations were discovered when Bombay resumed his customary management of the stores. Baraka manufactured a story of its having been necessary to hand out presents to conciliate those among the porters who, unlike himself, opposed Sultan Majid, and were therefore trying to break up the expedition.[25] Possibly there was some division among the men on these lines, but by this stage on the journey it was probably more a case of Baraka's gaining supporters by exercising patronage through the distribution of stores—something it was normally much easier for Bombay to do. At Mihambo, Baraka's patronage had extended beyond the confines of camp and it may well be that he had begun to see the opportunities open in this region to a man of talent who had some trade goods and guns at his command; not only could he acquire women but also some measure of political influence. Other men were making themselves "warlords" in this region at the time. The later activities of some of Baraka's friends among the "unfaithful" porters, particularly Uledi, lend some color to this view.[26]

23. *Ibid.*, 20, 36–37, 108; "Nominal Roll of Baraka's Unfaithful Children," May 29, 1863, Zanzibar archives, Arc. 312.
24. Speke, *Journal*, 126, 189–190; Grant, *A Walk*, 22.
25. Speke, *Journal*, 141.
26. John Milner Gray, "Speke and Grant," *Uganda Journal*, XVII (1953), 148. There were three freedmen known as Uledi and it is not easy to distinguish them. The man in question accompanied Baraka on his Bunyoro mission (see below), did not return to Zanzibar but was found by Stanley in the area northeast of Stanley Falls, acting as a rapacious ivory trader. This was in 1887. Henry Morton Stanley, *In Darkest Africa* (New York, 1891), I, 206.

Yet to suggest that Baraka himself had warlord ambitions may be unfair. He remained with the expedition into Karagwe and continued to perform important ambassadorial tasks. And, after leaving the expedition, he did not remain in the interior to become a slave trader as did Uledi, but returned to Zanzibar.[27] Indeed, the whole idea of Baraka's being the leader of the "unfaithful children" who deserted on the border of Buganda and Bunyoro needs some modification.

There definitely were two factions among the men in Karagwe. According to Speke's journal, the basis of the division remained the dispute over whether it was safe to go on northwards. But this was actually Bombay's story. The dispute was probably still a personal one between the two rivals in which women and witchcraft allegations now figured. At any rate, it seems inconceivable that Speke would invite Baraka to conferences with Rumanika, the king of Karagwe, and then send him on a mission to open the route to the Nile, if he really believed that the man was continuing his attempt to sabotage the expedition. When he sent Baraka and Uledi to Bunyoro to establish contact with Petherick, Speke was asking them to accomplish a task upon which the safe and successful return of the expedition then seemed to depend.[28] Baraka's activities after he left on his mission are not well documented. He did, however, reach Bunyoro—where he could gain no precise news of Petherick. Kamurasi, the ruler of Bunyoro, did not allow him to rejoin Speke, who was by now in Buganda, but did eventually give him some ivory and send him back to Karagwe. It does not seem to have been Baraka's fault that he could not resume his place in the expedition.[29]

In a letter written at his journey's end in Egypt, Speke avers that it was the news of Baraka's return to Karagwe which made the "unfaithfuls" decide to desert. Yet, in the published version of his journal, Speke does not specifically link the two

27. Gray, "Speke and Grant," 148, shows that Baraka returned to Zanzibar and points out that not all the charges against him may have been justified.

28. Speke, *Journal*, 217, 232, 243. It was believed in England that the tribes on the Upper Nile were extremely fierce and that, unsupported, Speke's party would be unable to get through.

29. *Ibid.*, 413–414, 515. On the other hand, some of Rumanika's men who had been with Baraka were allowed to contact Speke.

events; nor does Grant. Both men explain the desertion as a consequence of the attempt of the *kabaka* of Buganda to persuade the expedition to return to his country. Mutesa kept the porters from advancing into Bunyoro by alleging that there was great danger there and in the countries beyond. This, coming at a time when the party was short of ammunition, may have proved effective propaganda. Besides, during their sojourn in Buganda, the porters must have learned how much safer it was to obey the ruler's every wish. And in this region, the *kabaka* possessed more sanctions than did the Europeans. The news of Baraka's return to Karagwe may have been only a contributory cause of the desertion.

Speke was angry about the desertion and tried to have Mutesa imprison the men, but he did not then attempt to make any similar arrangements for Baraka and Uledi.[30] On the contrary, another man, Msalima, was sent back to join them, carrying a draft on Zanzibar which authorized their pay. Speke also allowed Baraka to retain the ivory. His discharge does not therefore seem particularly dishonorable. It was only later, perhaps under Bombay's influence, that Speke decided that Baraka was a "devil incarnate." Probably as punishment for the trouble that he had caused on the middle leg of the journey, Speke included Baraka in his list of deserters who were to be imprisoned when they returned to Zanzibar.[31] Speke argued that an example must be made of deserters and 11 men were eventually imprisoned. What happened to the rest of the 42 men placed in the "unfaithful" category is not known. The 18 who stayed with Speke were given bonuses and medals; gardens and wives were procured for them in Zanzibar and many, including Bombay, served with subsequent European explorers. His teeth missing as a result of blows from Speke's fist—which he received on one of the few occasions when they disagreed—Bombay accompanied Stanley in 1871 and Cam-

30. "Nominal Roll of Baraka's Unfaithful Children"; Grant, *A Walk*, 229, 273–274; Speke, *Journal*, 447–448, 491–492. It is possible that some of the deserters took service with Mutesa.

31. Speke to Playfair, May 31, 1863: Zanzibar archives, Arc. 29. It is notable that a slave whom the expedition freed and who regarded Baraka as his particular benefactor did not desert, Grant, *A Walk*, 73.

eron in 1873, was given a pension by the Royal Geographical Society in 1876, and died in about 1884.[32] He is one of the most famous of a remarkable yet little celebrated group of men who helped to change the face of East Africa.

The behavior of Speke's porters and their interrelations and contacts with local Africans had considerable influence on the way in which the mission was conducted. By keeping the nucleus of able and intelligent freedmen together until they had reached Bunyoro, Speke ensured the success of his search for the Nile source. Undoubtedly the expedition would not have got as far had it not been for Bombay and Baraka. It was they as often as Speke himself who managed the extremely difficult business of negotiation with African rulers.

In 1860–1863, negotiating travel through East Africa had become particularly difficult. Rapid change throughout the region, especially in the central Tanzania area, often involved violence. Even since Speke's former trip there had been notable developments. Tabora, for example, had become more like a beleaguered fortress than an accepted settlement among friendly Africans. Many factors may be adduced to explain the changes and, particularly, the violence which was characteristic at the time of Speke's expedition. Famine was an immediate one which made it difficult for the increasing number of Arab and Swahili-led caravans going up country to be provided with food. High prices, amounting to extortion, were met by a propensity on the part of the Arabs to use force to obtain what they wanted. The incipient economic rivalry between the Arabs and the Nyamwezi now broke out into war. The receipt of firearms from Europe and America made the situation worse, and enabled several African chiefs to embark upon careers as warlords. An equally potent factor was the presence of groups of Ngoni. The raiding activities of the remnants of Zwangendaba's horde, who had fanned out from Ufipa after 1845, constituted both a threat and an example. Defense

32. Gray, "Speke and Grant," 148–149; Speke, *Journal*, 271–272; H. M. Stanley, *How I Found Livingstone* (London, 1872), 346–347, also reports Feraji, one of the "unfaithfuls," as serving him satisfactorily, *ibid.*, 350; Grant, *A Walk*, 355, shows that 19 men reached Egypt but that one deserted there.

was required by local Africans, yet the effectiveness of these *ruga-ruga* warriors encouraged some chiefs to copy Ngoni military tactics and to live by plunder. Masai incursions from the north were another unsettling factor.

Unsettled conditions extended into the areas nearer Victoria Nyanza, although the Arabs were not present there in any great strength. Even in the powerful kingdoms north and west of that lake, influences from the coast were strongly marked, although for the moment they were regulated by the local rulers with much more success than was the case further south. At the time of Speke's visit to Buganda, there were special local reasons for tension: the monarchy, in the person of Mutesa I, was emerging as a unique unhindered despotism,[33] and Bunyoro, harassed by an expanding Buganda, was, together with other peoples of the Upper Nile, beginning to feel the effects of the arrival of Khartoum-based slave traders.

Throughout the region traversed by Speke conditions were unstable—probably considerably more so than they had been fifty or a hundred years before.[34] The ultimate causes of most of the major changes can be found in the expansion of Western civilization. Yet that civilization's first direct representative in the region was powerless to control the forces at work. On the first leg of his journey the obvious and, indeed, only possible thing to do was to repeat the practice of Burton's venture by relying on Arab methods and Arab facilities to expedite the journey. Said bin Salim's presence is indicative. Speke's plans envisaged much help from Musa Mzuri in the handling of his goods and the recruitment of porters at Tabora. This heavy reliance upon the Arabs made it almost inevitable for Speke to become involved in the war that they were fighting.

The disorganization consequent upon the war meant that Arab help for Speke was restricted. Musa, caught up in the politics of the war and preferring to sit smoking opium rather than to travel with Speke, could afford little aid. With Said bin Salim remaining in Tabora, the expedition was thrown

33. Christopher C. Wrigley, "The Christian Revolution in Buganda," *Comparative Studies in Society and History*, II (1959), 39.

34. It is erroneous to assume a state of slow or practically nonexistent change before the nineteenth century.

much more on its own resources.[35] Nevertheless, on the second leg of the journey, Speke still looked back to the Arab settlement for help. The point at which he finally abandoned any reliance on the Arabs was very clearly marked in Karagwe. Upon Speke's arrival there, he flatly refused to be housed with the Arabs in their settlement at Kafurro.[36] He was now in an area of strong African government and could try to further his objects by courting the leading chiefs. On the last stage of his journey, Speke was once again dependent on invaders—in this case the rapacious agents of the Khartoum traders.

Each of the four stages of Speke's journey presented special problems. The record of his work shows how the explorer was forced to accept situations as he found them. But it also shows how he learned the technique of deploying the limited influence, prestige, and power at his command to the best advantage for the furtherance of his objectives.

It was fortunate that the first leg of his journey, during which Speke was still learning how to curb his anger, was a reasonably easy one. In the coastlands, among the Zaramo people, the headmen of the Sultan of Zanzibar made a rich living by taking their cut of the taxes that he imposed upon incoming caravans. Outward caravans like Speke's found them acting as though they were independent chiefs and charging *hongo*. Bargaining over *hongo* took a fairly normal course, with angry words and first offers being turned down. Speke may have meant his angry words but he might just as well have saved his breath. On one occasion, when he threatened to let a particularly avaricious chief "smell his powder," he discovered that Said bin Salim had already secretly struck a bargain. In Usagara, the detribalized and demoralized Khutu gave no trouble, and Speke claims that the British reputation as opponents of the slave trade made his passage even easier.[37]

More trying conditions still lay ahead; by January 1861 the caravan was entering the area disturbed by the break-

35. Speke, *Journal*, 10, 71, 94, 104, 120. Norman Robert Bennett, "The Arab Power of Tanganyika," unpublished Ph.D. thesis (Boston Univ., 1961), 11; Grant, *A Walk*, 49.

36. Speke, *Journal*, 201.

37. *Ibid.*, 17–18, 22–24, 35, 47–48.

down of relations between the Arabs and the peoples of the interior. In Ugogo, normal practice was for coastward caravans to sell slaves in return for ivory and food supplies. Up-country parties expected to get their food in return for cloth and beads. The area was a disturbed one at the best of times for food was not abundant and the Gogo were a people of disparate origins, often refugees from Masai raids, living under the rule of adventurers from Unyamwezi or Uhehe who set up as chiefs. With increasing difficulty, the caravan pushed on to the western side of Ugogo and reached Khoko.[38]

The chief of Khoko, Mguru Mfupi, had recently been slain by Muhinna bin Suleiman, a prominent Tabora trader who became leader of the Arabs there in 1861. In revenge for the murder, the people of Khoko had driven Muhinna out of their territory but were daily expecting him to return to try issue with them again as he attempted to make his way to the coast. All Arabs were now treated with great suspicion, but there was no hostility toward Speke's caravan since it was led by a European. Nevertheless, his situation became difficult because Manua Sera, the chief of Unyanyembe recently deposed by the Arabs, was making common cause with Gogo people, like those of Khoko, who had reason to dislike the Zanzibar traders. Specifically, he was trying to cut the caravan route between Ugogo and Tabora. A large number of Speke's Nyamwezi porters chose this moment to desert, alleging that they objected to traveling through the rains which had now begun. It seems much more likely that their compatriots among Manua Sera's marauders persuaded them to defect. Speke suspected that some of the coastmen were also involved. In his predicament, the explorer sent messengers ahead to Tabora appealing for help from the Arabs there. Help was not immediately forthcoming, and Speke had to bully his remaining men into making forced marches westwards across the wilderness until they were finally relieved by Baraka's success in negotiating food supplies and Bombay's in hiring seventy slave porters at exorbitant rates from Musa Mzuri.

Musa and his associate, Snay bin Amir, then the leader of

38. Tanganyika District Book, Dodoma, King George VI Memorial Museum, Dar es Salaam; Speke, *Journal,* 57–58, 61–62.

the Tabora Arab community, had decided to give Bombay help for not entirely disinterested reasons. Snay hoped that Speke's small force of riflemen, led by two Indian Army officers, would join the Arabs in a decisive encounter against Manua Sera. Musa, having originally supported the chief, was much less happy about the recent violent turn of events in Unyanyembe, where Tabora was situated, but hoped that Speke would in some way be able to use his prestige to bring about a settlement.

The incipient Arab-Nyamwezi rivalry had come to a head on the death of Chief Ifundikira of Unyanyembe in 1859. Manua Sera had secured the chieftainship after a struggle with his kinsman Mkasiwa. (Both claimed to be sons of the old chief.) He began to impose a tax on Arab caravans, but this the Arabs regarded as a breach of their 1839 agreement with Ifundikira so they promptly deposed Manua Sera, and installed Mkasiwa as a puppet chief in his place. Manua Sera took up arms; he was not finally defeated until 1865.

Speke, dependent on Arab aid and just as anxious as they were to open the routes into the interior, could hardly help becoming involved. But he was reluctant to commit himself deeply. This is apparent from the way in which he dealt with the situation in Rubuga, a small chiefdom on the caravan route just east of Unyanyembe. Its ruler, Maula, who had been a friend to the 1857–1859 expedition, now appealed to Speke because the Arabs had deposed him in favor of a mere slave for allegedly giving help to Manua Sera. Under the new dispensation, caravans were allowed to plunder at will in Rubuga. Speke was unable to prevent his own men from enjoying this right, and he would go no further with Maula than promising to insure the chief's personal safety. Given the depleted state of his caravan, he could not afford to appear before the Arabs as the champion of Maula. Far less could he take Manua Sera's part in the principal dispute. When he met the ex-chief, Speke offered to intercede with the Arabs, but only on condition that Manua Sera promise to restore free transit for caravans if he were given back his throne. To this the ex-chief agreed.

Both sides were now seeking Speke's support and both presumably regarded his little band of fifty riflemen as powerful enough to tip the scales. Speke probably would have liked to resolve the problem by setting up a council of conciliation as he did in minor disputes between his men and local Africans, but it is doubtful that either side would have accepted a compromise settlement. Plunder and violence were becoming normal; both parties really wanted to further their success as warlords by securing Speke's support in much the same way as they might (and did) obtain the help of the Ngoni.

Snay bin Amir was certainly not prepared for compromise; he refused to be deterred by Speke from setting out with an army of four hundred slaves to hunt down Manua Sera. Muhinna bin Suleiman and others professed themselves unsympathetic to the "hotheaded" Snay, yet plans were currently afoot to punish Chief Hori Hori, the successor to Mguru Mfupi in Khoko, for his support of Manua Sera. Snay failed to catch his quarry, and, together with five other Arabs, met his death in Ugogo by allowing the desire to plunder to overcome military prudence in an area where Masai warriors were at large. At Tabora, following the news of Snay's demise, Speke received new requests to mediate, but the Arabs' alliance with the Ngoni and their treacherous murder of Maula made him highly dubious of their good faith. Mediation was, he thought, merely a tactic to get Manua Sera into their hands. Nevertheless, because he remained dependent upon Musa for porters and had to stay in the region, Speke did initiate further peace moves. Through the unflagging diplomacy of Baraka, an armistice was arranged in March 1861. But Manua Sera was now quite inflexible, demanding nothing less than the throne and Mkasiwa's head as the price of peace. The Arabs offered only to give him alternative territory and would not allow him back in Unyanyembe, so, inevitably, the war broke out again.

Speke's force was far too small and too distant from its base for him to be able to impose an impartial settlement. His task, in any case, was to seek the Nile source, not act as governor of central Unyamwezi. Had he sided firmly with either side, the course of events in the war might have been very different. Victory for Manua Sera would have vastly strengthened the Nyamwezi position and perhaps have made Mirambo's rise of less consequence; but future explorers would have ceased to receive any assistance from the Arabs. On the other hand, immediate victory for the Arabs would have saved them from four more years of war but not, perhaps, from an eventual reckoning with the Nyamwezi. Speke's neutral attitude meant that he exercised only a passing influence on the course of events. Had he fought, he might have risked death for himself or many of his followers and not have been able to go on at all. As it was, the war affected him profoundly for it meant a dearth of porters and supplies. The next leg of his journey was thus incredibly difficult.

The expedition moved in small detachments, carrying supplies when opportunities of recruiting local porters resulted from the negotiations of Bombay or Speke. Even as late as July 1861, Speke was forced to return to Tabora to seek help. Grant was marooned in one spot for 109 days. The war, Musa's death, and the difficulties with Baraka contributed to the crisis.[39] The region through which the expedition was attempting to pass added its own hindrances. Petty Nyamwezi, Sukuma, and Zinza chieftaincies dotted the area, most of them with fairly recently arrived immigrant ruling clans. There were tensions between different members of these clans and, in certain cases, tensions between the new arrivals and the former class of *ntemi* rulers who headed the older established "commoner" clans. Many of the chiefs had come to rely on trade contacts, perhaps originally to obtain some of their insignia from the coast but increasingly to obtain the cloth, beads, and guns which made it possible to exercise patronage and impose sanctions.[40] To obtain what they wanted, some chiefs were prepared to detain caravans for long periods. Given the complex interrelations of the area, it was difficult for Speke to discover the relative powers of different chiefs and thus to learn which of them he could afford to defy. A complicating factor was the presence of Ngoni groups. It seems that chiefs often tried to detain the caravan as an insurance against attack by these

39. Grant, *A Walk*, 71; Speke, *Journal*, 9, 63–64, 69–70, 72, 90–91, 75–82, 81, 87–88, 93–98, 105, 107–109, 136–137.
40. Cory, *Indigenous Political System*, 17, 24, 31, 77–78; Cory, *The Ntemi*, 17; Speke, *Journal*, 183.

marauders.[41] In fact, although Speke's caravan never had any serious direct confrontation with the Ngoni, there was, on more than one occasion, news of an attack on a village that they had just left.[42]

Typical of the complications with which the explorer had to contend was the situation in Uzinza when he tried to avoid paying *hongo* by skirting the village of a sub-chief. The local guide, Ungurue (actually employed by an Arab trader called Masudi, who seems to have disliked Speke), insured that the caravan did stop at the village in question. Inevitably, the Hinda overlord of the area, Makaka, then demanded his quota of *hongo*. Speke says that he considered shooting Makaka, but Baraka persuaded him of the unwisdom of this act. Speke eventually agreed to "eat the dirt with good grace" over the *hongo*, but refused to put on a show of force against the Ngoni as he had been requested. Gradually Speke learned that he must play the politics of the area. At Bogwe, for example, he sowed dissension between Chief Lumeresi and one of his subordinates to some effect. His tactic of sending ahead for the help of Suwarora, banking on his cupidity and curiosity, has already been noted.

As Speke entered the territories of the more powerful chiefs of the interlacustrine area, some difficulties began to disappear. Just as Suwarora had helped him, Rumanika of Karagwe now rescued Speke from Suwarora's clutches. The friendly reception in Karagwe may have had something to do with the explorer's being able to claim an association with Musa Mzuri, for Musa had helped Rumanika to obtain his throne in about 1853. But the brother defeated at that time, Rogero, was still at large, and Rumanika hoped that Speke would now finish Musa's work by bringing about the final defeat of his rival. Rogero received his support from the Hima clans in the country, whereas Rumanika was backed by the commoner Banyambo, so, although he did not fully appreciate this com-

41. Suwarora of Usui seems to have tried to use Arab hostages for protection, having heard of the Arab-Ngoni alliance, *ibid.*, 112.
42. *Ibid.*, 105, 116, 125, 156, 161–162; Grant, *A Walk*, 119–120, 215.

plication, Speke was wise not to become involved.[43] There was relatively little Rumanika could do to force Speke to comply with his wishes since the real arbiter of events in this region was the *kabaka* of Buganda, to whom Rumanika was more or less tributary. Until the 1880's, Karagwe was a vital access route to Buganda,[44] and Mutesa kept a close watch on developments at least as far south as Usui. Suwarora, the chief of Usui, was at this time being prevailed upon to send his daughter as a wife for the *kabaka*. Speke was actually joined by a Nyamwezi witch doctor cum trader called Kiengo, who was carrying Suwarora's tribute to Mutesa. The man who had originally negotiated this affair now told the *kabaka* of Speke's proximity and Mutesa sent a party to fetch him.[45]

Meanwhile, life with Mutesa's "gatekeeper," Rumanika, was pleasant for Speke and Grant after the trials of the previous leg of the journey. The chief was intelligent and affable. In fact, Speke wrote, he was almost "civilized," for running in his veins was "the best blood of Abyssinia." So was born the "Hamitic myth." [46] Yet Speke's constant flattering allusions to the chief's racial superiority no doubt helped his cause —no matter the confusions to which they gave rise. Grant was particularly impressed by the "mild and gentlemanly" Kakoko, Rumanika's son, who was later to murder seventeen close relatives and put out the eyes of his youngest brother soon after Rumanika's suicide in 1878.[47] Days were spent in discussing

43. Speke, *Journal*, 127–132, 157, 165, 151–152, 196, 198, 207, 226; Hans Cory, *History of the Bukoba District* (Mwanza, n.d.), 25.

44. J. Ford and R. de Z. Hall, "History of Karagwe," *Tanganyika Notes and Records*, 24 (1947), 3–23. The development of waterborne trade from Buganda to Mwanza was one main reason for Karagwe's demise.

45. Speke, *Journal*, 184, 200, 244; Grant, *A Walk*, 187. Kiengo, one of the numerous Nyamwezi individuals who carved out an independent career for himself in the nineteenth century, was still in Karagwe in 1889. Stanley, *Through Darkest Africa*, II, 412.

46. This was the belief that the Hamites, in effect a mixture of Semitic and Bantu blood, were "the great civilizing force of Black Africa." See C. G. Seligman, *Races of Africa* (London, 1930), 10. A full discussion of the myth is given by Edith R. Sanders, "The Hamitic Hypothesis: Its Origins and Functions in Time Perspective," *Journal of African History*, X (1969), 521–532.

47. Speke, *Journal*, 203, 211; Grant, *A Walk*, 176; Cory, *Bukoba*, 29, 31–33.

geography, European wonders, and the Bible, while Speke developed plans for the "regeneration" of this region.[48]

Rumanika was not as helpful and disinterested as he at first seemed. Speke realized that some of the exactions in Usui had been on his behalf. More important, the explorer failed to appreciate how much his constantly reiterated plans for opening up the Nile route to these regions must have worried Rumanika, for the plan would have seriously diminished Karagwe's importance. As the chief was no doubt shrewd enough to realize, he gained by controlling the only existing route from the outside world. He seems, therefore, to have tried to keep Speke from going north by telling ridiculous stories about the need to dress the expedition's donkeys in trousers and for the Europeans to conceal their trousers before they entered Buganda. This did not deter Speke, but Rumanika was able to insist upon Grant remaining behind because he had an ulcerated leg. Eventually, Mutesa sent for him as he had sent for Speke. Even then, it seems that Rumanika was hoping to arrange for the explorers to return to Karagwe from Buganda rather than for them to go on down the Nile. He alleged that he would send Speke to the Nile from Karagwe via Bunyoro, but whether he would have done so may be open to question. The fact that, when Baraka did travel this route in search of the supposed Petherick, he was accompanied by some of Rumanika's men and was then forced to return southward may point to some subtle maneuvering by the ruler of Karagwe.[49]

Speke's belief that Petherick was reasonably close at hand colored his proceedings in Buganda; he constantly petitioned for permission to visit the Nile source and then travel northward to Bunyoro and Gani (Acholiland) as soon as possible so as not to miss him. Petherick's agreement with the Royal Geographical Society had envisaged his joining up with Speke

48. Gray, "Speke and Grant," 159–160; Speke, *Journal*, 208, 213, 226, 240–241.

49. *Ibid.*, 93, 215–216, 239, 242–245. Speke said there had been "cunning humbug," 268; Grant, *A Walk*, 153, says he was not well cared for after Speke's departure.

at any time between November 1861 and June 1862. It was already February 1862 when Speke entered Buganda.

The explorer's desire to travel northward presented Mutesa with a problem of foreign policy of more than temporary concern. Speke accompanied his request with constant discourses on how he proposed to open up the Nile route to facilitate direct intercourse between Europe and the lakes region; he even suggested that the Unyamwezi-Karagwe route would fall into disuse.[50] Although the *kabaka* could see the advantages of contact with Europe, it would hardly be welcome to have that contact come via Bunyoro, his kingdom's ancient rival. Acquisition of European firearms by the Nyoro would not only alter the balance of power in the region but also threaten one of the main bases of Ganda prosperity and power which, most authorities agree,[51] was the habit of raiding neighboring territories, especially Bunyoro, for women and cattle. These trophies helped to make possible the court patronage system.

There were good reasons, then, for not allowing Speke to go forward and establish a relationship with the Nyoro. Yet to send him back to Karagwe might mean that Speke would attain Bunyoro from there. The Karagwe-Bunyoro route was another which the *kabaka* preferred not to have opened to regular commerce, since the Nyoro might divert too much of the coastal trade from Buganda to their own country. Control of Buddu made it easier for him to prevent this from happening but, as Rumanika was obviously not averse to having the route to Bunyoro opened, there were dangers in the situation for Buganda. A way out of the dilemma might have been found by allowing Speke to leave Buganda by the third alternative path: the road through Busoga and Masailand toward the coast at Mombasa. The exploration of this route would have offered many attractions to someone trying to solve East Africa's geographical problems, but the supposed presence of Petherick forced Speke to insist upon the Nile route. For his part, Mutesa seems to have been genuinely in-

50. Speke, *Journal*, 422.
51. Christopher C. Wrigley, "The Changing Economic Structure of Buganda" in Lloyd A. Fallers (ed.), *The King's Men* (London, 1964), 19.

terested in the eastern route and had already sent some expeditions to probe it. The snag was that their reports suggested that great difficulties would be encountered along the way, particularly in the territory of the warrior Masai.[52]

One reason for Speke's enforced sojourn in Buganda must have been that Mutesa could not make up his mind what to do. He did allow various probings of the northern route by his own and Speke's men; perhaps he thought that it might be possible to find a way to the north which circumvented Bunyoro. At length, however, in July, he permitted Speke to leave his capital.[53]

There is more than a suspicion that the *kabaka* was banking on the refusal of Kamurasi of Bunyoro to welcome Speke into his kingdom. Certainly he allowed stories of the cannibalistic propensities of the Europeans to reach the Nyoro. Mutesa also attempted to recall Speke from the border and had something to do with the desertion of the "unfaithfuls."[54] But once the *kabaka* had allowed Speke to go north there was obviously a strong possibility that he would get through. Why, then, did Mutesa let him go? Perhaps it was worth taking the risk that when Speke returned, as he promised, he could be persuaded to make his home in Buganda rather than Bunyoro.[55] Or, very likely, Mutesa's decision may have been a personal favor to Speke, who had impressed him very favorably.

The way that the relationship between the *kabaka* and the European explorer developed makes a fascinating study. To a certain extent Speke relied on his uniqueness as a white-skinned, highly skilled stranger from a far-off country, and broke down a great deal of normal Ganda protocol in order to gain influence with the monarch. Yet he was really only using his unique qualities the better to be able to operate the right levers in the Ganda political machine. It has been said that

52. Grant, *A Walk*, 165–166; Speke, *Journal*, 374, 421, 428–434.
53. *Ibid.*, 302, 338, 384, 413, 321, 440, 445, 529. According to Speke, it was to avoid having to bow to Rumanika's wish to have them return to him.
54. *Ibid.*, 483, 489.
55. Mutesa's expectation of Speke's return is noted by one of his pages, Welbourn, "Speke and Stanley," 221.

Speke maintained "a rather good-natured detachment" about the situation in Buganda,[56] but the reverse is true; he was deeply involved in the system because, like others, he was jostling for favors from the ruler. In his case, the principal favor desired was an exit permit.

Although Speke successfully worked the Ganda political machine, it would be impossible to say that he completely understood it. Yet he learned a good deal. To take one example among many possible ones, his explanation of why the *kabaka's* subjects accepted even the severest punishments as if they were rewards accords almost exactly with the results of a modern sociological investigation of the phenomenon.[57]

The explorer was not prepared to give unquestioning obedience to the *kabaka* and would not grovel before him as did other courtiers while making their excessive thanks—"nyanzigging," as Speke called it. He would not always attend court when he was wanted, and he was inclined to walk off in real or simulated rage if he were kept waiting too long. He refused to accept the status of an Arab trader or to be given precedence behind the men bringing in Suwarora's tribute, especially as that tribute consisted of goods taken from him. On the contrary, he demanded to be treated like a prince and be given living quarters within easy reach of the palace. This was accorded him and he even had the audacity to flirt with the *kabaka's* wives and the Queen-Sister [58]—audacity which would have meant instant death for anyone else. For Speke, it was the right policy—his way of establishing and maintaining *kitiibwa,* the prestige necessary for a successful petitioner at court.

Speke was prudent enough not to overplay his hand. He would doff his cap for Mutesa; he agreed not to remain seated in the monarch's presence; and, as much as he and Grant were

56. Lloyd A. Fallers, "Despotism, Status, Culture, and Social Mobility in an African Kingdom," *Comparative Studies in Society and History,* II (1959), 20.

57. Speke, *Journal,* 256; Audrey Isabel Richards, "Authority Patterns in Traditional Buganda," in Fallers, *The King's Men,* 262–263.

58. "Nyanzig," properly "tweanze, tweanzege," means "we have received it, we thank you for it." Speke, *Journal,* 288–289, 301, 318, 322–323, 339, 376–379.

distressed by them, he only twice interfered to prevent the daily executions ordered by the *kabaka*. Speke was also wise enough to court the *namasole,* or Queen-Mother. Chiefs disliking Speke had earlier asked her to use her considerable power to get rid of him, but the Queen-Mother took a liking to the explorer and gave him another means of establishing his position in the kingdom, for he realized that it was possible to play off her court against that of the *kabaka*.[59]

It was, however, the guns which Speke carried and his skill in their use which provided the most effective key to influence with the ruler. Fascinated by the superior weapons at Speke's command, Mutesa eventually had the palace gates opened to him whenever he announced his presence by firing three rounds.

What did the *kabaka* hope to gain from Speke besides lessons in rifle shooting? It is said that he interpreted the first visit of a white man to Buganda as a sign that he was the rightful king; his coronation began soon after Speke had left. Put in another way, this may mean that Speke was used as some kind of pawn in a game that the *kabaka* was playing to establish his position as a complete despot. Was it, for example, merely a sight-seeing tour when Speke was taken on a visit to the shrine of the lake god Mukasa? Mukasa was one of the most important of the *balubaale,* yet the *kabaka* treated the god's medium with a good deal of contempt. In other words, this may have been less a show for Speke than a demonstration to the chiefs and priests that, in the European, Mutesa had at his command a more powerful influence than they did.[60] Possibly, too, the *kabaka* wished to have an alternative outside force to play off against the Muslim traders from the coast. Mutesa may even have been thinking of appointing Speke a *mkungu* (chief), as some Arabs, and a Baluchi whose qualities made him useful, had already been promoted. Speke, with

59. *Ibid.,* 254, 304, 306, 319, 329, 336, 343, 395; Welbourn, "Speke and Stanley," 221. One of the victims Speke saved, the son of Kunza, was executed on an alternative charge the following day, Grant, *A Walk,* 228.

60. Speke, *Journal,* 295–296, 352, 296, 543, 394; John Roscoe, *The Baganda* (London, 2nd ed., 1965), 290–293; Frederick B. Welbourn, "Some Aspects of Kiganda Religion," *Uganda Journal,* XXVI (1962), 173–174.

his skills and his following of armed porters, would have seemed a very great asset.[61]

Whether or not Mutesa had any such plans in mind, the great chiefs around the court may well have suspected something of the sort. They were jealous of Speke's favored position and of the easy way in which he gained access to the palace, as the recollections of Isaya Kasakya, quoted at the beginning of this chapter, bear witness. Yet concerted action against the explorer was unlikely since, mixed with hostility, was also the desire to secure influence with the *kabaka* through association with the favored one. For example, the *mutongoleh*, Maula, was apparently rewarded with women and promotion for his services in conducting Speke into Buganda from Karagwe. Typically under the system, however, he seems later to have intrigued against the explorer's interests.[62]

The *katikiro*, or chief officer in the Ganda state, to whom Speke refers as the *kamraviona*, did not appear to be helpful, although he was personally affable. Presumably he had not been in office long[63] and may have been suspicious of Speke's friendship with the Queen-Mother. After all, Kaira, his predecessor, had been deposed and his sons murdered by the *kabaka*, despite their ties of blood-brotherhood with the Queen-Mother. Moreover, Speke ignored the *katikiro's* normally most effective political perquisite—the control of access to the *kabaka*. Speke even earned the man a reproof from his sovereign by lodging a complaint about the *katikiro's* use of the expedition's porters for his own purposes. Probably trying to place Speke in the scheme of things, the *katikiro* asked him whether he wanted

61. Speke, *What Led*, 259; Grant, *A Walk*, 217; Speke, *Journal*, 276, 387, 431.

62. *Ibid.*, 309, 319–320, 364, 399; Ham Mukasa, "Speke at the Court of Mutesa I," *Uganda Journal*, XXVI (1962), 97.

63. Although *Kamraviona* (Kamala Byonna) was the personal title of Kaira, Kabaka Suna's last *katikiro*, it seems unlikely that, six years after Mutesa's accession, Kaira should still be in office. Moreover, Speke, *Journal*, 344, says the *kamraviona* he met was only twenty years old, although he is just possibly referring to the *namasole's katikiro*. After he left Buganda, Speke heard, *ibid.*, 463, that "two Kamravionas and two Sakibobos, as well as all the old Wakungu of Sunna's time, had been executed." But Sir Apolo Kagwa (Ernest B. Kalibala, trans.; May Mandelbaum, ed.), *The Customs of the Baganda* (New York, 1934), 83, says specifically that Kaira was not executed.

Ganda help to dethrone Queen Victoria and reign in her stead. The *katikiro* seems to have been particularly obstructive over the matter of food supplies for Speke's men; perhaps he hoped that the porters' behavior would lead to trouble for Speke.[64]

The *mugema*, chief of Busiro and one of the few remaining clan-nominated great chiefs in the country, may also have resented Speke. He put one of Speke's men in stocks and would not return the explorer's visit although, again, he was very polite when they eventually did meet.[65] On the other hand, the *kaggao*, chief of Kyadondo and a leading palace official, was helpful over the matter of food supplies. Also friendly was "General Congow," that is, the *kangawo*, chief of Bulemezi. Kunza, the executioner, sought Speke's aid in having his own son saved from the fate that he normally meted out. Both Usungu, another executioner, and the *kaggao* hoped that Speke would be able to cure them of venereal disease. The explorer thought that the chief of Gomba, the *kitunzi*, who was also the Queen-Mother's brother, was standoffish; he resented the unconventional way Speke was allowed to behave at court. In fact, Speke was obviously involved in a web of intrigues and rivalries, the precise nature of which it is impossible to delineate from his evidence alone. Information on this matter is poor, partly because he got to know few of the chiefs well; at one point they seem to have been ordered by the *kabaka* not to associate with the European.[66] No doubt Mutesa used Speke as some sort of counter in the policy of divide and rule which he constantly followed.

In one sense Speke played a normal role in Ganda politics, but in other respects he was a harbinger of change. His visit coincided with the full flowering of Mutesa's genius as a ruler. "Bana, I love you because you have come so far to see me and have taught me so many new things," Speke reports the king as saying to him. It was not just that the *kabaka* henceforward copied the idea of sitting in a chair and wearing trousers and a

64. Fallers, "Despotism," 20–21; Richards, "Authority," 275; Speke, *Journal*, 320–321, 326, 346, 355–356.

65. Roscoe, *Baganda*, 233; L. A. Fallers, "Social Stratification in Traditional Buganda," in Fallers, *The King's Men*, 96; Speke, *Journal*, 376, 378, 381.

66. *Ibid.*, 345, 354–356, 358, 359, 365, 386, 416; Roscoe, *Baganda*, 233.

hat like Speke's, although these things may be symbolic. Rather, he had now begun to see that Buganda was not the center of the universe and that he must adjust accordingly. Until more Europeans should arrive, he had to make do with Arabs as representatives of the outside world, but he later made it quite clear to Stanley that the Arabs were a second best. Relative superiority was doubtless gauged primarily in terms of who had the best guns. Mutesa, having told Speke that he would now never fight without guns, soon formed a standing army of musketeers; henceforward the percussion cap type of gun was known in Buganda as "Makoowa Speke." The desire to bolster the power of the kabakaship by monopolizing for it the available resources of Europe—of which guns were only the most obvious example—may reasonably be said to date from Speke's visit.[67]

Kamurasi, the *omukama* of Bunyoro, seemed less aware than Mutesa of the importance of Speke's visit, although he was equally determined to have rifles and any other less immediately useful European toys. Some of the difficulties of Speke's passage through Bunyoro have already been noted. Kamurasi was highly suspicious of a party which came from enemy Buganda, particularly as it approached in two separate detachments as if it were executing a military maneuver. Not until the Ganda escort had retired was the party allowed into Bunyoro. Speke's fumbling attempts to establish peace between the states were not appreciated by either. Bombay finally negotiated a meeting with Kamurasi, but he proved just as evasive about the road north as Mutesa had originally been.

Kamurasi had even more acute problems of foreign policy than Mutesa. To him Speke's airy talk of opening the Nile route probably seemed to threaten trouble from the "Turks." These agents of the Khartoum merchants were already spreading

67. Speke, *Journal,* 330–331, 356, 373, 388, 397, 427; Ham Mukasa, "The Rule of the Kings of Buganda," *Bulletin of the Uganda Society,* 3 (1944), 26; Kagwa, *Customs,* 97. See the significant comment on Arabs and Europeans by Mutesa as reported in H. M. Stanley, *Through the Dark Continent* (London, 1878), I, 321; Mukasa, "Speke at the Court of Mutesa I," 97. There is some dispute as to how successful Mutesa was in limiting the distribution of firearms, see Wrigley, "Economic Structure," and the comment by Martin Southwold, both in Fallers, *The King's Men,* 8, 25n, 61–62.

misery among the Acholi, news of which Kamurasi doubtless received from the Acholi messengers who were at his court when Speke and Grant arrived. The "Turks" were making nonsense of the *omukama*'s claim to sovereignty over Acholiland —a claim which arose from clan connections among the Bito. An even more immediate cause of concern for Kamurasi was the position of his dissident cousin, Ruyonga, then established at Magungo near the northern end of Lake Albert. Ruyonga not only intrigued with certain of the Acholi *rwots* and the "Turks" but also tried to arrange for the arrival of supplies from Zanzibar. Speke's refusal to make blood-brotherhood with a leading chief and his unwillingness to help the campaign against Ruyonga made it inevitable that he should not be allowed to visit Lake Albert. Kamurasi's fear that the explorer might aid Ruyonga was thus responsible for the continuing doubt in Europe about the precise geography of the upper Nile valley. Kamurasi did, after two months, allow the explorers to trek across Acholiland to join the Nile much further downstream. The delay allowed various diplomatic feelers to be put out to the north and was probably also designed to make Ruyonga believe that Kamurasi now had Speke's support. Certainly Kamurasi saw Speke's Nile plans only in terms of their being effected in such a way as to crush Ruyonga between forces from north and south.[68]

The somewhat unfriendly reception that Speke received in Bunyoro did not deter him from wanting to make it the initial target for his future efforts to regenerate this part of East Africa.[69] No doubt the logic of Bunyoro's position in relation to the Nile accounts for this desire, although Speke was wise enough to refrain from mentioning it in Buganda. Nothing came immediately of his ideas although they may have had a marginal effect on the Egyptian decision to occupy the lake regions. It was of course Speke who encouraged the man who

68. Speke, *Journal,* 483, 487, 490, 502–503, 509, 518, 521, 526, 535, 539, 544; F. K. Girling, *The Acholi of Uganda* (London, 1960), 85, 125–126, 130, 133–134. John Beattie, *Bunyoro, An African Kingdom* (New York, 1960), 17–18; Grant, *A Walk,* 298–299. Kiengo and his men were now in Bunyoro and had agreed to fight against Ruyonga.

69. For these plans, see Gray, "Speke and Grant," 150–151; Bridges, "Speke," 40.

was to lead the Egyptian initiative in 1872 to make his first visit to Bunyoro in 1864. Whether Bunyoro's history would have been a happier one if he had left no Nile problems for Samuel White Baker to solve is a moot point.

Speke was conducted through Acholiland by Nyoro forces. At Koich ("Koki") they met Cong Alwala ("Chongi"), who claimed to be governor of the region on behalf of Kamurasi. In fact, he was in league with Ruyonga and shortly afterward cooperated with the "Turks" in a raid on his rival, the *rwot* of Payera, who genuinely supported Kamurasi. But since Speke had Kidgwiga, Kamurasi's officer, and a Nyoro force with him, Cong Alwala gave no trouble. At Faloro, Speke came into the care of the "Turks," not Petherick as he had expected. The campaign of the "Turks" against Payera and their terrorist raids to recruit porters meant long delays which the explorer spent shooting. Much as he would have liked to protect the Acholi villagers, there was little he could do—in his depleted condition he was ten times more at the mercy of Mahammed, the Turkish leader, than he had ever been of the Arabs on the route to Tabora.[70] Mahammed was the agent of the Khartoum trader Amabile and his uncle, Andrea Debono. These men had every reason to dislike Petherick and they helped to poison Speke's mind against him. Speke was in a receptive mood because he was disappointed that, after all the efforts he had made in the lake regions to get in touch with Petherick, the man had not kept the rendezvous. Probably through Speke's influence, Petherick was later deprived of his position as British consul, and one small check on the slave trade was thus removed.

Speke's independent management of his caravan effectively came to an end at Faloro. Before he reached this point, his passage had had a considerable effect on East African developments. The presence of white men excited great curiosity of course, and there was the possibility of obtaining strange new medicines and fascinating new toys—like elastic bands, glass spectacles, and matches—as well as the conventional presents

70. Grant, *A Walk*, 331; Speke, *Journal*, 574–576, 578, 588, 590; Girling, *Acholi*, 129, 134.

of beads and cloth. Grant's sketching ability won him many admirers. It has often been assumed that the local impact of Speke's mission went no further, and that Africans were incapable of doing anything more than covet European goods. This is not the case; much more fundamental relations were involved. It is important to remember that Speke's party was not strong enough to ignore local realities. On the other hand, the party was not so weak and uninfluential as to be easily brushed aside by local potentates. For both reasons, Speke and his followers became deeply involved in local situations, whether it was a question of mediating in the Arab-Nyamwezi war or merely staving off a Ngoni raid on a small Sukuma chiefdom for a few days.

Some of the incidental effects of Speke's visits were severe, if temporary. It is said, for example, that Kamurasi's kingdom lost three hundred dead when Sudanese slave traders were allowed into Bunyoro because they claimed to be friends of Speke. Mutesa expressed his love for Speke in an extravagant way, executing five hundred slaves, two of whom he suspected of stealing the explorer's stores.[71] The introduction of a number of freed slaves into the interior and their subsequent activities, whether independently, like Uledi, or as members of subsequent European expeditions, was a further consequence of Speke's activities. But many of the more permanent effects were intangible. It is difficult to measure precisely, for instance, the extent to which Speke's association with the *kabaka* affected the development of that monarch's policy, but it seems undeniable that the visit played at least a significant part in the education of a mighty king.

The effects and importance of Speke's work with regard to European developments are easier to discuss. It is possible to review, for example, his motives as an explorer and the impact of his views in Europe. Indirectly such considerations may be of importance for East African history.

The explorer had been sent by the Royal Geographical Society to obtain accurate data about the interior of East Africa, particularly data that could be used to plot accurate maps. This

71. Beattie, *Bunyoro*, 18–19; Welbourn, "Speke and Stanley," 221.

scientific motive was sufficient in itself to justify the expedition; in arranging for the British government's financial support, the Foreign Secretary stated that £2500 was needed for the cause of "geographical science." The odd £500 was actually added in order to allow Speke to collect specimens of the fauna of the region.[72] These scientific motives were shared by Speke and Grant and they obviously did make fundamental additions to the map of East Africa as well as—in Grant's case especially—providing important zoological and botanical information.[73] But the geographical problem which assumed most importance was that of the source of the Nile and this quest involved more than just scholarly concern. The man who discovered the source would inevitably achieve fame and, through the medium of Sir Roderick Murchison, become the "lion" of the fashionable London season and noted in scientific circles. There is no doubt that Speke sought this fame. It might also be argued that, as far as the fauna were concerned, he was less interested in zoological science than in the adventure of big-game hunting.

Such motives would seem to have little to do with Africans and African societies. Indeed, the introduction to Speke's book dismisses "the negro" as merely one kind of fauna. He did not generally find "very marked or much difference in them," and was puzzled to account for their living "so many ages without advancing"; from the scientific point of view, Speke was not much of an ethnographer. Yet the explorer's attitude is in itself of some importance. Many other travelers provided similar impressions of "backward" societies in East Africa, with disorder and dishonesty considered the normal order of the day. Speke believed that Africans were kept backward mainly because of the operation of the slave trade and the turmoil which it produced—an explanation which continues to be offered by many modern scholars. The only solution he could see was the

72. F.O. 2/37: Russell to Treasury, 8 November 1859, Public Record Office, London; Committee Minutes, 21 June 1859, Royal Geographical Society Archives.

73. See, e.g., the appendixes to Speke's *Journal* or Grant's impressive flora published in the *Transactions of the Linnean Society*, XXIX (1873–1875). *passim.*

imposition of a "strong protecting government" similar to that in India. The image which Speke and others built up of Africans as backward people needing European rule undoubtedly influenced the assumptions which imperial rulers made when they took control some twenty years later; European overrule in East Africa was almost a duty. A corollary of this attitude was that East Africa's economic resources could not be tapped until order was established. When it was, Speke implied, European rule would pay dividends.[74]

The extent to which this sort of view actually influenced imperial adventures in the 1880's would be a matter of great controversy, but Speke's work was evidently read as some kind of textbook by men like Sir William Mackinnon and Lord Lugard. In another sense, too, the work may be seen as part of the imperial process for Speke's efforts were, in many respects, only the culmination of an increasing association between Africa and Europe. Although the Royal Geographical Society might eschew nonscientific motives, it had mentioned the advantages which might eventually accrue to "commerce and civilization" when applying to the government for funds for Speke's expedition in 1859.[75] It could be argued that the rise of a powerful society devoted to the exploration of little-known parts of the world and its backing by the government was a manifestation of the economic expansion of Europe. Speke could be considered one of the spearheads of that expansion even if he had no immediate economic objectives to fulfill.

A discussion of this kind is bound to deal in generalities for the most part, but there is one respect in which Speke's influence on European concern with Africa, and therefore, indirectly, his influence on East Africa itself, is clear and undeniable. The effect of Speke's discoveries was to direct European interest in East Africa to one particular region. Naturally, all eyes were drawn to the spot on his map which the explorer designated as the source of the Nile. The controversy which ensued kept attention focused on that spot, but Speke provided other reasons for maintaining interest in the region. For here, living near the

74. Speke, *Journal*, xvi, xx, xxii.
75. F.O. 2/37: Ripon to Palmerston, 16 August 1859, Public Record Office, London.

headwaters of the Nile, were "advanced" peoples, who constituted a ruling group—the Hima. The explorer wrote that he considered "the discovery of the Ancient Ethiopians detached from their country by the Galla and occupying all the country from the Kira [Nile] to Usui under the two kings Kamurasi and Rumanika the next matter of importance [after the Nile source] that the expedition has discovered." The Hima were specifically exempted from Speke's general remarks about the backwardness and inadequacy of East African peoples, and he was anxious to take some Hima princes back to England for education or to send teachers to them. His argument was that, in the lacustrine regions, the economic situation was favorable to the extent that there was a leisured class able to spare the time for education and other pursuits beyond mere subsistence.[76] Moreover, this racially superior class maintained enough order to make schemes for "regeneration" particularly apposite and European economic activity conceivable. Nearby, in addition, were large and navigable lakes which could solve some of the transport problems.

Subsequent European enterprise in this region and, particularly, the way in which Buganda was regarded as the prize at the time of the Scramble clearly indicate the effect of Speke's discovery on Europeans and Africans. The explorer's own plans for opening up the Nile route to the region had some limited importance in stimulating the Egyptian enterprise, which led to the foundation of the province of Equatoria. In a more general sense, Léopold II was obviously fascinated by the opportunities which seemed to exist in the lakes region when he founded the International African Association in 1876. Closely associated with Léopold was Mackinnon, who was to promote the chartered company which eventually took Britain irrevocably into Buganda.

In the long run Speke and Grant may be seen as explorers who were vital participants in the process which brought Africa and Europe closer. They influenced other participants whether these were Africans like Mutesa or Europeans like Mackinnon. In the shorter term, as this chapter has attempted

76. Speke to Murchison, 6 July 1862. Royal Geographical Society Archives; Speke, *Journal*, xvii, 558.

to show, Speke, whatever his prejudices about Africa and Africans, dealt with societies as he found them. His careful and often successful manipulation of the existing political situation was a vital element in his success. His arrival may also have been an important event in various local contexts—perhaps it served to defer a Ngoni attack or alter the course of the Arab-Nyamwezi war.

Finally, it is worth remembering that Speke's visits constituted the first chapter in the story of a hundred years of delicate race relations in the interior of East Africa. Speke was diplomatic and prudent when he had to be, and, by the standards of his time, kindly disposed toward the people he encountered. He was perhaps condescending rather than sympathetic, never for a moment doubting his own superiority as an individual and that of the civilization he represented. In dealing with Africans, Speke set a pattern of paternalism and amused, when not exasperated, tolerance for the vagaries of this seemingly backward and childlike people. Although seldom able to practice it himself, the explorer recommended the use of firm if benevolent control of Africans by Europeans. It is unlikely that many East Africans reciprocated Speke's attitude to the relationship that was developing, but the traveler was often regarded as the representative of a race which seemed to have material advantages worth sharing. In the next generation, Africans were to find that any such advantages were not to be obtained without European rule as a concomitant—a conclusion which Speke to a certain extent helped to bring about. Although these events are long past, his influence on East African affairs is by no means spent. His journals form a priceless source of information on a vital period in the history of the peoples of East Africa. Used with understanding, Speke's evidence now helps historians to assess this period without the distortions engendered by the intervening period of colonial rule.

Samuel White Baker:
Prospero in Purgatory

by Robert O. Collins

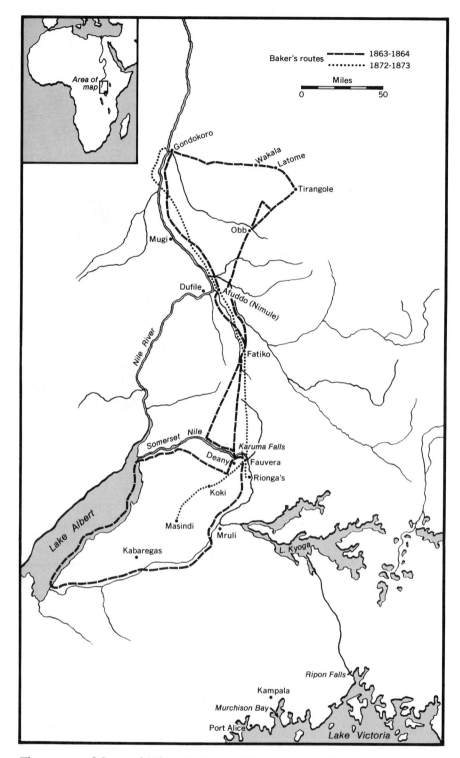

The routes of Samuel White Baker, 1863–1864 and 1872–1873

On February 2, 1863, Samuel White Baker landed at Gondokoro on the Upper Nile, accompanied by his beautiful wife, his guns, and his servants. He found only a few miserable grass huts, a hostile population, and the ruins of that former outpost of European civilization, the Austrian mission.

Baker had come to equatorial Africa to explore and hunt, to satisfy his own curiosity, and to provide his own amusement. He was sponsored by no society. He was dependent on neither private charity nor government philanthropy. He was required to obey no orders but his own. Moreover, he came prepared, not only with the finest and most expensive equipment, but with sufficient quantities to remain many months, if not years. Guns, supplies, and an independent spirit were not all that he brought to Africa. Baker also came with attitudes and preconceptions guaranteed to insulate him from the peoples through whom he passed. His family, his class, and his plantation life in Ceylon had shaped his assumptions about men and about life. His conservatism had transfixed these assumptions into rigid beliefs—an undeviating dogma by which Africa and its inhabitants were judged and condemned. During the eight years which he spent on the Upper Nile, he remained apart from and blindly insensitive to the Africans around him.

Samuel Baker was born in Enfield, England, on June 8, 1821, into an established, wealthy, and large pre-Victorian family. He never had to worry about status, money, or security. In fact he never really had to worry about anything—except what to do with himself—and his most pressing problem always remained the search for purpose as well as pleasure from his itinerant life. The pleasure he found in shooting was something he could understand. He thought that he had found a purpose by establishing a thriving plantation community from the wilderness of Ceylon, discovering Lake Albert—the western source of the Nile—and carrying the Egyptian flag into the Upper Nile. Certainly there was achievement enough in these adventures for any man, but purpose proved more illusory. What did the Ceylon plantation accomplish but add to his already sufficient wealth? What was Lake Albert but another Nile source? What had he accomplished in Equatoria but to intensify the violence in that unhappy land? The motivation which carried Baker to the heart of Africa can be measured in distances traversed, lakes discovered, and posts established, all the objectives of his deliberate perambulations. In the end his wealth had not diminished, his Nile quest remained unresolved, and his grand design for an Egyptian imperium in Equatoria was a failure. Yet Baker firmly believed that he had reached his goals and achieved his objectives. His self-delusion over the success of his undertakings perhaps explains the obscurity which still enshrouds their purpose.

Educated at home by a tutor and fitfully at Frankfurt, Germany, Baker did not receive the school experience usually reserved for members of his class. Perhaps his independent spirit would never have accepted the discipline and conformity of the English public school, but at least none was ever given the opportunity to institutionalize him. He remained forever outside the interlocking circles which dominated his class and England. He was never required to get along with others, and thus never had to accept them. He had few friends outside his family. Whether in equatorial Africa or on his Devon estate, Sandford Orleigh, Baker remained aloof, surrounding himself with friends and devoted servants, indifferent to and separate from all others.

At an early age he became interested in guns, to whose care and construction he applied all of his technical dexterity. His practical mind readily absorbed the transparent logic of firearms. His inventive skill found fulfillment in their operation. His curiosity was stimulated by their use. He hunted the game around Tottenham with the same intensity which he later displayed in Ceylon, the Balkans, and Africa. The rules of the chase were for Baker the discipline of school without its conformity. The hunt itself inculcated in him the ideas of fair play that his contemporaries were learning on the playing fields. Yet sport, guns, and a brief sojourn in Germany were hardly calculated to instill much breadth of vision, tolerance, or a speculative mind. In fact, Baker's education, or lack thereof, appears to have confirmed the conservatism of his class and the prejudices of his family.

In 1842 the Baker family moved to Gloucestershire in the west of England, the region with which the Bakers had traditionally been associated. Here, on August 3, 1842, Samuel Baker married Henrietta Martin, daughter of the Reverend Charles Martin of Maisemore, in a double ceremony in which Samuel's brother John married Henrietta's sister Eliza. Both young couples then went abroad. Although the west country was ideally suited to Samuel Baker's temperament, the family tradition of overseas enterprise could not be ignored, let alone broken. In 1843 he elected to go out to his father's sugar estates on the island of Mauritius in the Indian Ocean. He soon tired of the quiet sedentary life of the planter, however, and wandered to Ceylon in search of sport. He found sport and stayed to establish an agricultural colony in the highlands. After initial difficulties the plantations prospered, and the Bakers settled down to a rough but not uncomfortable English country-house life. Here in Ceylon his Victorian prejudices, unrelieved by the narrowness of his education, congealed, and the attitudes which he carried throughout the rest of his life were confirmed.

Although dissent in nineteenth-century Britain was accepted, even guaranteed, most Victorians regarded the greatness of their country with unquestioning faith. They came to assume that its civilization and race were preordained to occupy a superior position among peoples, and, although that assumption was in itself an article of faith, they arrived at this profound belief by experience and observation. To Baker the obvious fact that Great Britain dominated large regions of the globe established the superiority of British civilization and, of course, the British themselves. He was thus a confirmed racist before racism was seemingly later corroborated by nineteenth-century biology. Baker's racism predates the host of theories based on scientific evidence from cranial capacities, skin color variations, skull shapes, language distinctions, and climatic variations which concluded that the European, and particularly the Germanic, races, of which the English were the finest example, were superior to all others. These theories invariably equated race with culture. The best races would have the highest culture, and, since culture could be measured by experience and observation, the superiority of one race over another was self-evident. Samuel Baker did not have to wait for the Social Darwinists in order to arrive at such conclusions. The hunt had already established what more intelligent and thoughtful men later accepted, and, if there were any lingering doubts, his own physical strength made him conspicuously superior to other men. Thus, he dismissed the Sinhalese with the same intolerant contempt which he later reserved for Africans when they, without his strength, could not match his prowess or, without his knowledge of guns, display the same dauntless courage during the chase. Baker's physique clearly helped to shape his relations with those about him. In Ceylon and Africa he continually asserted his physical superiority, and for him the superiority of British civilization was not infrequently confirmed by his own ability to thrash the opposition with bare fists.

Within a few years the Ceylon plantation required less attention, and Baker devoted more time to hunting. This was a violent and restless period when neither contemplative nor philosophic speculation checked his pursuit of sport. He might easily have become a frontier roustabout had not the ever-growing Baker clan provided an anchor as well as responsibility. The American frontier would have challenged the young Baker; but, unfortunately, he never saw the Great West until he was too old to master it.

In 1855 Samuel Baker and his family returned to England. He had fulfilled his reasons for going to Ceylon—he had shot almost every kind of beast on the island and the plantation required no supervision other than a bailiff. He now had to seek another goal to provide an objective, if not a purpose, to his life. At first it was hard to find. In December 1855 Henrietta died of typhus, and thereafter he wandered aimlessly—to the Crimea, to Asia Minor, to the Balkans. Although assured of sympathy and support from his brothers, he seemed to slip increasingly into a life of wanton shooting and capricious wandering, until his marriage in 1860 to Florence von Sass, a Hungarian beauty, introduced a steadying influence and turned him once more to seek a purpose in his travels. On April 15, 1861, the Bakers started up the Nile. The formative years were over.

Baker brought to Africa very precise and very real conceptions of good and bad. If British culture was the culmination of a progressive assent up the ladder of civilization, then progress and British culture had to be good. It thus followed that lower cultures were bad. Their creators were inferior and, if not bad, certainly nowhere near as good. Those foolish enough not to acknowledge, if not accept, British superiority had to be inferior people against whom force was not only justified but desirable. Conversely, those who acknowledged British (which in Africa meant Baker's) superiority were children, to be led, disciplined, but, since they were inferior, never entirely trusted. With the paternalism of a West Country squire Baker would dutifully instruct in progress and civilization as he conceived it. His religious convictions must have placed these obligations upon him despite the fact that he despised missionaries. In Africa he always placed civilization before Christianity, perhaps because the missionaries represented, even if they did not act out, the ideals of Christian charity, tolerance, and humanitarianism which were inimical to Baker's belief in work, racial superiority, and the efficacy of force. Inferior peoples needed to be shown the way; it was the obligation of superior people, the British, to guide them. Equipped with these Olympian convictions, Samuel Baker marched through Africa without ever knowing the Africans, indeed convinced that they possessed little that was worth knowing or remembering.

Baker's racism was not the product of speculation or study. He was an empiricist. He went to Africa and looked at Africans. Unfortunately, he only saw what his preconceived ideas permitted him to observe. Within this structure he had a fixed idea of the black man first learned from his father. The elder Samuel Baker had gone out to the slave-worked plantations of his family in Jamaica where he formed deep racial prejudices, on the one hand, and developed complete contempt for abolitionists and humanitarians, on the other. Certain of the inferiority of blacks, the father passed on his convictions in no uncertain terms to his son. With his curious but uncritical mind young Samuel never bothered to question or even to reëxamine the stereotype. Moreover, abolition only seemed to confirm his father's opinions, for freed slaves were reluctant to work. Everyone knew that the Africans were inherently lazy, and, if the armchair philanthropists of Exeter Hall refused to believe the obvious, then let them follow Samuel Baker to Africa and see for themselves.

Although Baker's racism remained undeviating, it did not prevent genuine friendship with a few individuals whom he came to trust, despite their inferiority. A Sinhalese gunbearer, an Arab servant, an African child adopted by his wife were regarded as friends, but it was a friendship characterized by childlike devotion, on the one hand, and paternal concern on the other. Baker never considered that Saat or Richarn or Amara could be representative of his race. But how could they, since each had accepted the friendship on Baker's terms, not his own? The conduct and standards which Baker imposed on the recipients and which cemented these exceptional relationships were those of his own culture and not of Asia, Arabia, or Africa.

Although served by a few devoted friends, Baker remained alienated from the societies through which he passed. He understood the environment but never the people. His insularity was a product of his youth in England; his later travels only confirmed his isolation. His deep attachment to his family provided security and gave him pleasure, but it also discouraged wider associations. Wherever he went he always repeated the pattern of his nuclear family, surrounding himself with a closed circle of a devoted few. Throughout his travels Baker always remained at the center of this small intimate group, sallying forth to combat savagery, retreating to bask in the security of his own assumptions without fear of intrusion or challenge. Perhaps his search for security within an inner circle of close associates betrayed a deep psychological need to dominate without. Isolated himself, he could hardly expect to observe those whose precondition was to observe in return.

Baker's methods of exploration in Africa were as unsophisticated as his ideas. The objective was all-important, but everything else was assumed. Having decided upon the goal, the most suitable route was selected, the best equipment secured, and the appropriate number of servants employed. He then set out to attain the prescribed end. Failure was not considered, or, if so, quickly dismissed. For Baker all things were possible. He could overcome any challenge; in fact, he thrived on adversity. Baker was at his best when facing natural barriers, at his worst when dealing with human intransigence. The forces of nature could be overwhelmed by sheer physical strength. This same strength was of little use against the more subtle and complex ways of men. Given sufficient men, equipment, and time Baker always moved forward against natural obstacles. Perhaps that is why he never understood nor appreciated the desires and motivations of Africans.

Outwardly Baker was a simple, transparent man; inwardly he seems to have suffered from insecurity and, perhaps, even real inadequacy. He was motivated by fundamental but complicated drives which he attempted to satisfy by straightforward means. He sought to master affairs by ignoring their complexities and by applying direct solutions to what he regarded as simple problems. His two sojourns in Africa involved objectives. The personal relationships required to reach those objectives he abruptly reduced by direct action. Perhaps this was an attempt to impose order on a world inhabited by a people whom he regarded as incomprehensible. Perhaps this was a compulsive need to impose order, to resolve deeper anxieties. Wherever he went, he desperately sought to establish order in those societies whose regulation did not correspond to his ideas of how a society should behave. In Baker's words, "a savage who has led a wild and uncontrolled life must first learn to obey authority before any great improvement can be expected."[1] Only when he enforced his own conception of order, could he then seem to comprehend it.

Samuel Baker was typical of that group of Englishmen who sought hardship and adversity in the unknown reaches of Africa. Some have suggested that they were simply sensible

1. Sir Samuel W. Baker, *Ismailïa: A Narrative of the Expedition to Central Africa for the Suppression of the Slave Trade* (London, 1895), 146.

people escaping an intolerable climate; others have pointed to the exhilaration of African exploration and the cartographic sweep of its geographical riddles. In Africa Baker perhaps sought to escape the human problems in England which his class ignored and his prejudice obscured. He clearly regarded the Africans as natural rather than human obstacles. In Africa this was quite possible; in Great Britain quite illegal. The force which he could not employ in England, he could use without restraint in equatorial Africa. Even after he had officially settled at Sandford Orleigh, he continued to return perennially to wild lands to kill in regions where his guns and strength were law.

Unfortunately, Baker never served in the army although on numerous occasions he expressed his desire to become an officer. There was no profession for which he was better suited. He was a leader of men whose courage alone could command respect. Aloof and insulated, he demanded discipline and conformity at all times. He simplified objectives to understand them, then sought to attain them by discipline, order, and skill. Little power of reflection was required, and what his limited foresight did not perceive, he trusted to improvisation. Strong, dogmatic, insensitive, self-confident, and brave—this was Samuel Baker.

In 1860 the region of the Upper Nile had been opened to the world beyond for nearly twenty years. Ever since the expedition of Salim Qapudan had discovered a passage through the great swamps of the Nile in 1840, merchants and missionaries had followed to exploit the natural and human resources of the Southern Sudan. The merchants were first on the river. Led by the Savoyard Brun Rollet, a small group of tough-minded European traders organized regular commercial expeditions, despite official resentment by the Egyptian administration in the Sudan and the difficulty of navigation through the swamps. They traded cloth, beads, and wire for ivory, and their profits were considerable. In 1852 a dozen boats had sailed for Gondokoro; four years later the number had increased to over forty; by 1859 eighty boats set out from Khartoum for the southern

Sudan; and by 1863 the annual number had reached one hundred and twenty.[2]

Missionaries joined the merchants. As early as 1846 Pope Gregory XVI had created the Vicariate Apostolic of Central Africa, and the Congregation of Propaganda Fide sent out four priests to pioneer a route to the "pagans" living in the wild lands of the Upper Nile basin. Led by Ignaz Knoblecher, a Slovene, the first band of missionaries made a reconnaissance to the Upper Nile in 1849, and just over a year later Angelo Vinco settled near Gondokoro to proselytize among the Bari. Although the missionaries added to the river traffic, they were decimated by fever and the mission was abandoned in 1860, the year before Baker arrived in the Sudan. The missionaries had been devout and dedicated Catholic priests, but their ignorance of African cultures, combined with their own Christian zeal, prevented any meaningful communication with the Africans, and the cause would probably have foundered on the failure to communicate even if the missionaries had not succumbed to malaria.

The European merchants were a tougher lot. Hospitable and, above all, adventurous, they lived in Khartoum in relative comfort and sought their fortunes in speculative ventures on the new frontier to the south. They were not all, as many have supposed, the riffraff of Europe, but, without the restraints of European society, they frequently compromised their sense of morality for the sake of greater profits. The first contacts between the traders and the Africans had already been poisoned by the official Egyptian expeditions of the 1840s. These initial experiences in culture contact had seriously disillusioned the Bari who greeted the Egyptian expeditions when they emerged from the Nile swamps at Gondokoro. The Arab soldiers and sailors made no attempt to conceal their contempt for the Africans, their way of life, or their pagan practices, and heaped scorn on the naked "savages" whom they regarded as inferior beings.

Of all the African peoples living in the Southern Sudan, not

2. Richard Gray, *A History of the Southern Sudan, 1839–1889* (London, 1961), 50.

one was prepared to meet the forces of alien civilization which followed Salim up the Nile to trade, to proselytize, and, ultimately, to conquer. These forces arrived in equatorial Africa convinced of their own superiority and unwilling to compromise, let alone understand the African cultures which they encountered. Unprepared, on the one hand, unyielding, on the other, neither the Africans nor the intruders could find a suitable middle ground upon which to compose their differences and adjust their attitudes to the new situation. The result was a clash of cultures out of which rose a violent new world in which the artistic and social values of African civilization were overwhelmed by the superior technology of the invaders and made to appear as inferior as their primitive weaponry and rudimentary mercantile practices. In such a conflict the southern Sudanese could only delay their submission by isolating themselves behind the geographical defenses which had protected the region for so many centuries.

In 1850, when the European traders arrived on the Bahr al-Jabal, the gap between African and Mediterranean cultures was already too wide to bridge by simple good will. Nor were the activities of the traders and their demands upon the Africans calculated to inspire the peoples along the Bahr al-Jabal with confidence and friendship. The Africans met violence with violence, but their hostile reaction only hardened the determination of the merchants to continue the lucrative trade in ivory by war, if not by peace. Although equipped with technical superiority on the river, the traders were at first insecure on land, where they had to depend upon African cooperation for supplies as well as ivory. This equilibrium prevailed for only a few short years, however. By the 1860s the deadlock was broken by the traders who, unable to cooperate with the Africans, decided to penetrate directly into the interior, establish stations, and hunt and collect supplies and ivory. Such large operations could never have been carried out alone by the handful of European and Levantine merchants who had pioneered the Nilotic trade, and so large numbers of armed Arab servants were recruited in the north and employed to force a way into the land beyond the river.

The decision to plant the bitter seed of Arab intervention

quickly gave rise to the distrust and fear which dominates relations between the northern and the southern Sudanese to this very day. Under European direction the Arabs intruded by force not only inland from the Bahr al-Jabal but also up the Bahr al-Ghazal to Mashra' ar-Raqq and the plains beyond. Throughout the southern Sudan the Arabs established stations, seized wives and slaves from among the neighboring African tribes, and collected ivory. Once having settled in the country, the Arab retainers transformed themselves into a ruling caste through the power of their guns and by exploiting tribal rivalries and exacerbating sectional antagonisms. To divide and rule the disunited tribes of the southern Sudan required neither imagination nor skill and, by playing off one African group against another, the traders and their Arab employees soon established their political supremacy over the African peoples near their stations. This control was never used to produce stable conditions or constructive government; instead, the organizational and technical superiority of the newcomers was combined with robbery and pillage to achieve maximum profits. In alliance with local tribes or, frequently, on their own, the traders carried out systematic raids to collect ivory from supposedly hostile tribes. As one locality was denuded of ivory, the spiral of violence penetrated deeper and deeper into central Africa until the whole of the Bahr al-Ghazal and Equatoria were plundered by the marauders.

The ivory raids produced secondary commodities, principally cattle and slaves. Originally ivory had been purchased with beads, but soon the supply outstripped the demand, and the only medium of exchange which the proud Nilotes would consider was cattle. To import cattle was beyond the limited capital of the traders, who resolved the dilemma by helping friendly chiefs to rustle the cattle of neighboring rivals in return for ivory. These cattle raids produced not only animals but men, slaves swept up in the search for cattle and ivory.

As one area after another was hunted out, ivory grew increasingly scarce. At the same time the traders' policy of direct intervention resulted in the employment of large numbers of armed servants. To maintain these bands of retainers in the field required ever-increasing expenditures by the traders, precisely when the quantity and consequently their income from the sale of ivory rapidly diminished. Caught in a profit squeeze the traders could remain in business only by raising the price of ivory or diversifying their operations.[3] The gradual rise in prices, however, never offset the precipitous decline of profits, and so the merchants turned more and more to the trade in slaves in order to balance income against expenditure and still make a profit. At first the traders tried to cut their overheads by enrolling captured slaves into the ranks of their armed followings, but by 1860 this practice had been extended to include a regular export trade in slaves. Like the ivory trade in its early years, the export of slaves proved highly lucrative, and big profits attracted an ever greater number of speculators until the slave trade quickly eclipsed that in ivory. Along the Bahr al-Jabal and throughout the Bahr al-Ghazal a series of *zariba* or fenced enclosures were erected, manned by armed retainers who ranged far and wide in order to plunder cattle camps and villages and enslave their bewildered inhabitants.

Of all the peoples of the southern Sudan the Dinka and the Nuer were perhaps best able to protect themselves from the marauders, by retreating into the inaccessible swamps, sallying forth only to attack the *zariba* and recapture cattle. Further to the south the Azande were able to withstand the assaults of the slavers until the traders learned to exploit the dynastic squabbles of their Avungara leaders. Many Azande were captured as slaves, including some of the paramount princes, but their society never appears to have been totally disrupted. Between the Dinka and the Azande lay a belt of weaker tribes whose sedentary agriculture and decentralized society made them less resistant to the predatory bands of the slave traders. Stretching along the edge of the ironstone plateau from Daym az-Zubayr in the western Bahr al-Ghazal to Rumbek and beyond the Nile to Gondokoro and Tirangole in the east, over a hundred stations were concentrated from which armed raiders roamed the countryside, depopulating the Dembo, the Jur, and the Bongo west of the Nile, and the Bari, the Latuka, and the Acholi east of the river.

3. *Ibid.*, 50–58.

Of all the tribes on the eastern bank, the Bari were most exposed to the full impact of the commercial and technical superiority of the newcomers before which Bari institutions disintegrated and were very nearly totally destroyed. Before the coming of the traders the Bari were pastoralists in the best traditions of the Nilotic cattle cult; even today they regard themselves as cattlemen although they now derive their livelihood from the soil. The transition from pastoral pursuits to agriculture had probably been a steady process spanning many generations, but the depredations of the nineteenth century hastened it. Although inhabiting permanent villages, the Bari were as disunited as their Nilotic neighbors to the north. There was no single spiritual or temporal ruler, and they were splintered into mutually antagonistic clans with no concept of an administrative hierarchy. The men in position of authority—or rather influence, for their power to command was negligible—were the ritual experts and the village chiefs or clan heads. These spiritual leaders possessed no direct political control and their influence fluctuated with their success as ritual experts. The secular leaders appear to have had even less authority and that derived more from personal prestige than position. The same applied to the notable men, none of whom either through wisdom or wealth emerged to rally the Bari against the invaders. At no time were the leaders able to create institutions which could stand against the storm of invaders that poured into Bariland before and after Baker.

South of the Bari, Latuka, and Acholi, across the Victoria Nile, lay the interlacustrine Bantu kingdom of Bunyoro. Bunyoro was as centralized as the scattered clans and villages of the Bari were not. All political authority in the state emanated from the king, the *omukama*. The *omukama* appointed his territorial chiefs, and their authority, down to the lowest level, was confirmed by him. The *omukama* could depose a chief, but the office was usually conferred on an heir so that in practice chiefships soon became hereditary. The principal chiefs were expected to maintain themselves at court where they acted as advisers and where their presence checked potential rebellions. The chief, of course, was responsible for the administration of his area, from which came presents of grain, beer, and cattle for the *omukama* and fighting men in time of war. The great *saza* or provincial chiefs owed their position to the king and their relationship to him. Their wealth came from the control over land, which accompanied their political authority. Like their positions, this control was ultimately dependent upon the king. This elaborate political organization was infused with history, tradition, and ritual, all of which accompanied and helped it to operate effectively. Unlike the diffuse communities to the north, Bunyoro at the time of Baker's first visit was still a strong, self-contained kingdom. True, the *omukama* no longer had control over the former outlying provinces of Buganda, Karagwe, Busoga, and others, which had successfully asserted their autonomy, but the Nyoro had yet to experience the challenge to their society of the ivory and slave trade.

The disruption of African society among the Bari, Latuka, and Acholi might by itself have confirmed Baker's preconceptions of Africans. Politically disintegrated, in cultural disarray, implacably hostile to the traders and those who marched with them, Baker viewed them as "savages" with nothing of value to be observed, and he made little attempt to inquire into their past traditions or to examine the remains of their social and political life. Even in Bunyoro, which the violence further north had yet to reach, Baker pressed on toward his goals, impassive, insensitive, and undeviating.

When Samuel Baker and his wife arrived in Africa in March 1861, his objective was clear. Upon the return to England of John Hanning Speke and Richard Francis Burton in the spring of 1859, he had been deeply stirred by their exploration of Lake Tanganyika and Speke's discovery of Lake Victoria. Although Burton and Speke had hoped to determine the Nile sources, they actually raised more questions about the origins of that great river than they resolved. With the support of the Royal Geographical Society, Speke had returned to Zanzibar in August 1860 determined to march into the interior along his former route in order to confirm his assumption that Lake Victoria was the source of the Nile. Baker was not far behind. He appears to have decided privately to seek the Nile source, not by following Speke through East Africa, but by the direct, perhaps more obvious approach—straight up the Nile River itself.

Baker said little, but his preparations were thorough. By May 1861 he had reached Berber, only eight months after Speke and his companion, James Augustus Grant, had left the East African coast for the interior. At that time the two explorers were moving very slowly, and had yet to reach the Victoria Lake. Clearly, Baker did not regard his Nile quest as a race with Speke and Grant, but he was not far behind and, when he later met them at Gondokoro in 1863, he could not hide his disappointment that Speke had "settled the Nile" question before him. However, Baker was too experienced, too sensible, and too independent to plunge into an unknown land without proper preparation. Guns and supplies were no problem; courage and fortitude were taken for granted. Unhappily, language could not be bought or assumed, and by the time that the Bakers had reached Berber, he "felt convinced that success in my Nile expedition would be impossible without a knowledge of Arabic."[4] He decided to pause in his Nilotic march in order to learn Arabic while wandering up the Atbara River and along the Nile tributaries which flow down from the highlands of Ethiopia.

For twelve months the Bakers traveled spasmodically throughout the frontier marches between the Sudan and Ethiopia. They learned Arabic, and the customs and way of life of the Hamran Arabs with whom he hunted elephant and rhinoceros. Baker respected the Arabs of the Sudan frontier; like himself they were courageous, direct, and unsubtle. They were also foolhardy, fatalistic, and undisciplined. Like Burton, Baker regarded the Arabs of the Sudan as superior to the Africans of the Upper Nile; unlike Burton he was never blind to their participation in the slave trade. The Arabs of the northern Sudan might be brave, tough, and straightforward—preeminent qualities in Baker's pantheon—but they could scarcely be expected to bring civilization to central Africa as might Englishmen of Baker's class. In June 1862 the Bakers reached

4. Samuel White Baker, *The Albert N'yanza, Great Basin of the Nile, and Explorations of the Nile Sources* (London, 1866), I, 4–5.

Khartoum, by which the Nile flowed from the interior of unknown Africa.

In 1862 Khartoum was the capital of the Egyptian Sudan. It was governed by a Turk and inhabited by a motley collection of Turko-Egyptian officials, Sudanese, and a handful of Europeans. Despite his *firman* from Sa'id Pasha, the Viceroy of Egypt, ordering local officials in the Sudan to cooperate with him, Baker met only sullen antagonism. He was exasperated and contemptuous, but too intelligent not to perceive the reasons for the opposition to his proceeding up the Nile. Baker was the first European to seek the source of the Nile from the north. Burton and Speke had begun in East Africa, and James Bruce in Ethiopia. Moreover, the Upper Nile was the preserve of the slave traders, who carried on their activities with connivance of the Turko-Egyptian bureaucracy and did not wish to have their practices publicized by a meddlesome Englishman. The officials were as reluctant to aid Baker as the traders. Afraid to ignore the orders from Cairo, on the one hand, and, on the other, terrified of having their slave trade exposed, they generally resolved their dilemma by doing nothing and doing it very well. But Baker thrived on these obstacles, and bullied his way over the opposition. By December 1862 he was ready with a small flotilla of boats, an escort of forty-five men he had personally armed and placed in uniform, and supplies for several months. On December 18, 1862, the expedition sailed for Gondokoro (probably much to the relief of the officials and traders of Khartoum).

After a tedious journey up the White Nile and through the great swamps, Baker reached Gondokoro. His reception was unfriendly and inauspicious. His response was, characteristically, to take matters into his own hands, an action hardly calculated to allay the suspicions of the traders or the hostility of the local Bari. He refused to collaborate with the slave traders or be conciliatory to the Bari. The slavers had little trouble in subverting Baker's men against him, and, although he managed to preserve his own life, his men deserted. Nor were the Bari any more cooperative, and Baker's first encounter with Africans only seemed to confirm his well-defined assumptions of their inferiority. With the expedition on the verge of disintegration, the traders hostile, and the Bari ill-disposed to support him, Speke and Grant suddenly arrived at Gondokoro from the south on February 15, 1863. It was not entirely a happy meeting.

Speke had much to tell. He had skirted the western shore of Lake Victoria, visited the kingdoms of Karagwe, Buganda, and Bunyoro, and had seen Ripon Falls, the outlet of the Nile from Lake Victoria. He claimed that the Nile question was settled. Not even Baker's sense of sportsmanship could hide his dismay. It suddenly seemed that all he had to show for two years in Africa were trophies of the hunt. This might have satisfied a younger Baker, but at forty-two he had killed enough for any man. (Already he had become more selective in his targets, and the killer instinct was diminishing. In later life it became virtually satiated, and he hunted much but shot little.) Now at Gondokoro there seemed little more to do until Speke reported that he had heard of a second lake, the Luta N'zigé, west of Bunyoro, that might feed Speke's Victoria Nile. These reports provided the needed incentive for Baker to press on. He offered the weary explorers the use of his boat and saw them off to Khartoum on their final journey to London, fame, and controversy.

On March 26, 1863, the Bakers turned southeastward from Gondokoro with a handful of men and the remaining supplies. Their goal was the Luta N'zigé, and they hoped to travel alone through the interior in order to disassociate themselves from the traders whose caravans had sustained Speke and Grant on their march from Bunyoro. They failed and were soon overtaken by a large caravan under the command of Khurshid Agha. Khurshid Agha was the principal agent of Muhammad Ahmad al-'Aqqad, who, in partnership with his brother, Musa Bey al-'Aqqad, was one of the principal slave traders on the Upper Nile. Muhammad Ahmad al-'Aqqad came from a well-known commercial family in Aswan, but he had long lived in Khartoum where he had established the headquarters of 'Aqqad and Company. The Bakers had had no choice but to accompany the caravan (their own lacked sufficient porters) and become dependent on the generosity of 'Aqqad and Company or return to Gondokoro and abandon the expedition. They joined and continued to Tirangole, but thereafter their advance was compromised by their association with and dependence upon the local agents of 'Aqqad. They remained for nearly a year in the country of the Latuka and neighboring Madi, relying upon the slavers for supplies, servants, and even protection. By January 1864, the Bakers had not moved beyond Obbo. Eleven months had elapsed since they had met Speke and Grant at Gondokoro, and they had progressed little more than a hundred and fifty miles.

Although they were forced to depend on the goodwill of the slave traders at Tirangole and later Obbo, the Bakers attempted to disentangle themselves from them. They lived apart in their own camp, cultivated their own garden, and hunted. With one exception, Baker never went far from camp either to hunt or to explore. He was in fact very much a prisoner confined by circumstance to the environs of the station. Here he met the Africans, and his contacts and conversations confirmed the impressions formed at Gondokoro.

> The black man is a curious anomaly, the good and bad points of human nature bursting forth without any arrangement, like the flowers and thorns of his own wilderness. A creature of impulse, seldom actuated by reflection, the black man astounds by his complete obtuseness, and as suddenly confounds you by an unexpected exhibition of sympathy. From a long experience with African savages, I think it is absurd to condemn the negro *in toto,* as it is preposterous to compare his intellectual capacity with that of the white man. . . . In his savage home, what is the African? Certainly bad; but not so bad as white men would (I believe) be under similar circumstances. He is acted upon by the bad passions inherent in human nature. . . . He is callous and ungrateful. . . . He is cunning and a liar by nature. . . . In the great system of creation that divided races and subdivided them according to mysterious laws, apportioning special qualities to each, the varieties of the human race exhibit certain characters and qualifications which adapt them for specific localities. The natural character of those races will not alter with a change of locality, but the in-

stincts of each race will be developed in any country where they may be located. . . . Thus . . . the African will remain negro in all his natural instincts, although transplanted to other soils; and those natural instincts being a love of idleness and savagedom, he will assuredly relapse into an idle and savage state, unless specially governed and forced to industry.[5]

By January 1864 Baker had finally persuaded 'Aqqad's agents to take him and his wife south across the Victoria Nile into the kingdom of Bunyoro. The slaver did not require much encouragement, and his advance was not motivated solely by sympathy for the Bakers or their goal—the Luta N'zigé. For several years agents of the Maltese merchant Andrea Debono had operated in Bunyoro, trading principally in ivory. (One of Debono's caravans had brought Speke and Grant to Gondokoro.) Although there appears to have been a silent partnership between Debono and 'Aqqad in Khartoum, there was a good deal of rivalry between their agents on the Upper Nile. 'Aqqad's men hoped to break into the Bunyoro market and profit from the confusion created by Debono's traders.

On January 22, the Bakers and 'Aqqad's agent reached the Victoria Nile, marched east to the Karuma Falls, and crossed into Bunyoro. Here Baker was infuriated by the delay they encountered as the result of the procrastination of Kyebambe IV Kamurasi, *omukama* of Bunyoro. In Bunyoro he could not command. Baker's impotence in the face of this reversal of the master-servant, superior-inferior relation between the Christian Englishman and the pagan Kamurasi strongly affected his attitude toward the Nyoro in particular and Africans in general. Even under more congenial circumstances a man of his prejudices could not have examined Nyoro society dispassionately. Travel-worn in a strange land, frustrated by his dependence upon his slave-trading companions, and now finding himself being ordered to advance or halt at the whim of an African he considered more suited to be his servant than his master, were events hardly calculated to improve Baker's

5. Baker, *The Albert N'yanza*, I, 287–291.

mood or alter his preconceptions so that he might begin to understand and appreciate his role in Bunyoro.

Between Speke's departure from Bunyoro in November 1862 and Baker's arrival in January 1864, Debono's principal agent, Wad al-Mak, had crossed into Bunyoro, claiming to be a friend of Speke, and had intervened in the succession struggle taking place there between Ruyonga and his brother, the *omukama* Kamurasi. In support of Ruyonga, Wad al-Mak had conducted a *razzia* in Bunyoro, killing some three hundred of Kamurasi's subjects. Now Baker suddenly had appeared, professing to be a good friend of Speke and accompanied by a heavily armed band of traders. No wonder Kamurasi was suspicious, and delayed his advance to the capital, Mruli. Baker regarded the whole proceedings as "exceedingly unfair."[6] Nor were the *omukama's* apprehensions dispelled when Baker and his party reached Mruli on February 10, more than two weeks after arriving at the frontier. The explorer explained to the king that he had come to Bunyoro in search of the source of the Nile and the great lake, the Luta N'zigé. To Baker this was a perfectly sensible reason; to Kamurasi the explanation was absurd. Who would want to go to a lake simply to look at it? One might go to fish or to drink, but merely to see the lake and then go away made no sense. And, even if this were true, a man who wanted only to look at a lake had no use for so many guns.[7] Baker never understood Kamurasi's suspicions. Unable, if not unwilling, to believe that his motives might be misinterpreted, Baker was continually astonished and angered by the incomprehensible actions of the Nyoro and their king.

The depth of Baker's frustration, which blinded him to the motivations of those around him, was all the more surprising because previous conversations with Comorro, a Latuka headman, whom Baker regarded as "one of the most clever and commonsense savages that I had seen," should have enlightened him as to the attitudes and assumptions by which Africans made decisions. Instead of reexamining his own precon-

6. *Ibid.*, II, 37. See also above, 141–142.
7. Ruth H. Fisher, *Twilight Tales of the Black Baganda* (London, 1912), 157–158.

ceptions about Africans in the light of Comorro's arresting comments about life, death, good, and evil, Baker simply records them, oblivious to their implications. In discussing Baker's destination, Comorro inquired, "Suppose you get to the great lake, what will you do with it? What will be the good of it? If you find that the large river does flow from it, what then? What's the good of it?"[8] Just as Baker could not see the logic of Comorro's questions, challenging the very purpose of his African expedition, he never considered what Kamurasi's similar queries might imply. As a matter of fact, Nyoro traditions record that "Kamurasi knew that the stranger was speaking lies, for no man would leave his own country and people, and face danger and fatigue, merely to look at water."[9]

Baker could never understand why Kamurasi did not act like a European. If Kamurasi were king and master, he should behave as a ruler; if he were not, the *omukama* should have responded like a loyal servant to Baker's requests. Kamurasi did neither. His kingdom was based on conceptions far different from the foundations of the British monarchy. The Nyoro firmly, if mystically, believed that their prosperity and well-being derived directly from the *omukama*. If any weakness should appear in him, if any sickness or injury should befall him, there would be a corresponding weakness in the kingdom. Kamurasi could not be too careful. His life was the life of the kingdom. He could not permit harm to his person; therefore he sent his younger brother, Mgambi, to impersonate the *omukama* and to ascertain the intentions and objectives of the white traveler.

Little realizing that he had yet to meet the real Kamurasi, Baker pushed forward to the Luta N'zigé, which he reached on March 14 and promptly named Lake Albert. He then passed along the east bank by canoe to the Victoria Nile and Murchison Falls. His contribution to the history of African exploration secured, he started on the long journey home. Suddenly, on an island in the Victoria Nile, his porters deserted, leaving

8. Baker, *The Albert N'yanza*, I, 245–246, 251.
9. Fisher, *Twilight Tales*, 157.

the Bakers marooned without food or shelter. Although at first inclined to let Baker starve to death, Kamurasi finally decided that the explorer was of more use alive than dead, and an escort appeared to bring the Bakers to the real Kamurasi. Baker's indignation knew no bounds at the "deceit of this country," and he scornfully interpreted such conduct as "abject cowardice." [10] Yet the *omukama* remained convinced that Baker had come to seize his country. He had never accepted the validity of Baker's objective. Moreover, Baker had come with many guns and a wife to produce many sons to succeed him.[11] The cultural gulf between Baker and Kamurasi was too great for them to communicate, even if they had not had conflicting objectives.

If Kamurasi feared Baker and his guns, he also sought to enlist those powerful weapons in the struggle against Ruyonga. He first thought he could starve Baker into submission and so had arranged to have him abandoned on an island in the Victoria Nile. Kamurasi next tried to compromise, and in this he was not successful. Several weeks after Baker had been brought to the camp of the *omukama*, Ruyonga advanced against Kamurasi, supported by a well-armed party under the leadership of Wad al-Mak. Baker immediately raised the British flag, declared Kamurasi under British protection, and forced Ruyonga and the slavers to withdraw. His intrepid action was, of course, to be expected. All his life Baker had prepared for moments like these, and his heroism was marred only by his contemptuous laughter "at the miserable coward [Kamurasi] who represented a Kingdom." [12] Baker was too strong, determined, and dangerous, and like the officials of Khartoum, Kamurasi appeared only too happy to be rid of this terrible Englishman. Rejoining 'Aqqad's caravan, the Bakers left Bunyoro in November 1864. They reached Gondokoro in February 1865 and Khartoum in May, and thence left for Cairo and home.

Baker's discovery of Lake Albert was an important contribution to the geography of equatorial Africa. It did little, how-

10. Baker, *The Albert N'yanza*, II, 171.
11. Fisher, *Twilight Tales*, 157–158.
12. Baker, *The Albert N'yanza*, II, 193.

ever, to resolve the question of the Nile sources, and, in fact, added a new and confusing factor to the Nile quest. Baker also had traversed, with incredible deliberation, Bunyoro and the land to the north. He knew its mountains, lakes, and rivers. He knew its inhabitants less well. Despite the length of his sojourn, Baker's contact with the African peoples between Gondokoro and Bunyoro remained astonishingly superficial. His descriptions of the inhabitants and their surroundings are detailed and vivid. Unfortunately, while inanimate objects are precisely delineated, the people are not. Baker's Africans are stereotypes of what he had expected them to be, not what in reality they were.

Baker's narrative of his travels, *The Albert N'yanza,* published in 1866, was widely read. His opinions, judgments, and prejudices deeply influenced his contemporaries and have since misled historians. Not only was he read; he was believed. He was rewarded with a knighthood for "laborious research in Africa," and settled quietly in the country until the Viceroy of Egypt sought to employ his knowledge of the Upper Nile in the service of Egypt.

In 1869 Sir Samuel Baker and his wife accompanied the Prince of Wales on his official visit to Egypt to attend the opening of the Suez Canal. During the festivities the Viceroy of Egypt, Isma'il Pasha, inquired if Baker would undertake to lead an Egyptian expedition to the Upper Nile. Isma'il had been educated in Vienna and Paris, and when he gained the viceroyalty in 1863 he expanded the efforts of Sa'id, his predecessor, to modernize Egypt and the Sudan. Agriculture and commerce were encouraged, the postal service reformed, and the telegraph extended. Isma'il's feverish introduction of European institutions and technology was accompanied by a desire to expand the Egyptian imperium in any direction, but particularly up the Nile into the vast hinterland of the southern Sudan. Between 1863 and 1867 the European traders, who had played such a dominant role in developing the Nile trade, were taxed and discriminated against until they were driven from the Sudan. Debono sold out in 1865, and a few years later the last of the European traders, the Poncet brothers, Ambroise and Jules, left Khartoum. From that time on Europeans no longer played any part in the commercial life of the Nile, control of which fell to Egyptians and Arabs from the northern Sudan.

The disappearance of the Europeans did not mean an end to the Nilotic slave trade. The Arab traders continued the methods of the Europeans, so that, rather than diminishing, the slave trade flourished in the southern Sudan, thereby providing Isma'il with a second motive to establish Egyptian control in the equatorial regions. Not only was Isma'il sincerely opposed to the slave trade, but during a visit to Paris in 1867 he had vigorously repeated his intention to employ the resources of Egypt to end the Nilotic traffic. Isma'il required European capital for his schemes of modernization, and this capital was more likely to be forthcoming if he could win the sympathy of the powerful and influential abolitionists in Europe. By 1869 Isma'il not only had eliminated the European opposition, but had agreed to lead the fight against the slave trade in the Sudan. The decisive advance up the Nile could now begin. In April, Sir Samuel Baker agreed to lead that advance. He clearly understood the objectives of his mission.

> The principal objects of the expedition, *"after crushing the Slave Trade,"* were to secure for Egypt the Equatorial Nile Basin, to establish "a powerful government throughout all those tribes now warring with each other," and, having opened the Lakes to steam navigation, to found a chain of trading stations, "on the system adopted by the Hudson Bay Company" throughout the territory linking the north with the southern-most point. "The natural productions are ivory, native flax, beeswax, and cotton; but I take seeds of the finest quality of the latter from Egypt. Every tribe will be compelled to cultivate a certain amount of corn and cotton, in proportion to the population. No wars will be permitted. Each chief will be held responsible for the acts of his tribe. Tribute will be exacted in labour to be performed in opening-out roads, on the same principle as the road-tax in Ceylon." [13]

13. Gray, *History of the Southern Sudan*, 88, his italics.

After massive preparations for the most elaborate and best-equipped expedition ever to proceed to the Upper Nile, Baker arrived in Khartoum in January 1870. Here he met much the same delay and frustration that he had encountered at the time of his 1862 African expedition. It was, however, only the beginning of the sullen opposition which stalked this new mission until he left the Sudan. An insensitive man, he never appreciated his delicate position as a Christian Englishman with despotic authority over his Muslim subordinates. The very object of his mission—the elimination of the slave trade—meant disaster to the well-entrenched and powerful traders in the Sudan. Moreover, Baker despised the African people whom he had come to save, and later treated them to the only method of control which he seems to have understood—force. He was genuinely moved by the horrors of the slave trade, however, and one must distinguish between his belief that Africans were savages and his refusal to accept the idea that they should be transported away from their homeland. Obtuse, unsympathetic, and violent, he had no experience in governing and none in Oriental administration.

On February 8, 1870, Baker departed from Khartoum for the south only to find the way to Gondokoro blocked by masses of floating vegetation, called sudd, which closed the White Nile beyond Fashoda. After exasperating and futile attempts to clear the sudd and cut a passage through the Nile swamps, he was forced to admit defeat and retired to Tawfiqiyah near the Sobat junction in the Shilluk country. Here the expedition remained to refit and to await the rise of the river, while Baker observed the struggle between the Shilluk and Egyptian forces for control of Shillukland. He also intercepted a few slave ships making their way down the Nile to markets in the northern Sudan and liberated their cargoes. The experience aroused his moral indignation and confirmed in his own mind that the paramount objective of his mission must be to root out the slave trade. This preoccupation with the Nilotic traffic in slaves seems not only to corroborate Baker's extravagant assertions of its extent, but blinded him to the fact that much more ivory than slaves was passing by Tawfiqiyah from equatorial Africa. Ivory was still the dominant commodity of

White Nile commerce, to which the trade in slaves was an evil subsidiary. Simply to eliminate the trade in slaves would not result in the successful introduction of ordered administration and legitimate commerce on the Upper Nile. Although he might suppress the slave trade, it would not automatically result in establishing Egyptian control, and in the end Baker found himself employing "the violent expedients of his mercantile predecessors."[14]

With sixteen hundred men and fifty-eight vessels, Baker left Tawfiqiyah in December 1870, and, after five months of great exertions in the labyrinthine channels of the Bahr az-Zaraf, the expedition broke through the sudd. On April 15,1871, two years after Isma'il had signed Baker's contract, he had at last arrived in the land where he was supposed to establish Egyptian administration. He only had two years left to do it, for his contract expired in April 1873.

From the moment of his arrival at Gondokoro, Baker was confronted with the open hostility of the Bari. Rather than rush enthusiastically to place themselves under Egyptian protection from 'Aqqad's rapacious agents, the riverine Bari, under their headman, Alloron, had allied themselves with 'Aqqad. They wanted nothing to do with Baker, particularly when he demanded that they supply the expedition with building materials and foodstuffs. Baker's attitude toward the Bari did not smooth out the difficulties. He had loathed the Bari during his first expedition, and his opinion had not altered: "I always knew the Bari to be the worst tribe in the Nile basin." They were "naturally vicious and treacherous," "irrepressible vermin," who barred the way of progress and civilization.[15] Julian Baker summed up his uncle's attitude when he recorded that the Bari "have not the slightest feelings of gratitude, honour, fair dealing, but will always try to gain their point by the basest treachery."[16]

Unable to persuade the Bari to provide the expedition with supplies, Baker sought to purchase their cattle. Alloron re-

14. *Ibid.*, 94, 95.
15. Baker, *Ismailïa*, 108, 110.
16. The Journal of Julian Baker, quoted in Dorothy Middleton, *Baker of the Nile* (London, 1949), 192.

fused, and Baker regarded his refusal as a declaration of hostilities. This in part it was. Alloron even had the audacity to question Baker's right to occupy Gondokoro. But his reluctance to sell cattle was much more than a belligerent reaction to Egyptian encroachment. Cattle were the very foundation of Bari society, representing not only wealth but prestige. Their sale would mean not only an economic but a social deprivation. Nothing Baker could pay would compensate for their loss, except more cattle—which he did not have. Thus, Baker resorted to the expedients of the traders: he seized Bari cattle by force. His troops were thus fed, but he incurred the implacable enmity of the Africans of Gondokoro. The Bari might have been beaten into submission by Baker's superior firepower, but they were not beaten into cordial cooperation with Egyptian rule.

By December the dearth of supplies had become so acute that Baker's own men were scouring the country, stripping the Bari of corn or cattle with an intensity that surpassed that of the most ruthless trader. By January 1872 Baker had succeeded in alienating the very people whom he had come to protect. His expedition was a shambles; nearly a thousand troops who could not be fed had been sent north to Khartoum; and without local cooperation all hope of carrying the sections of the disassembled steamer around the rapids to the navigable Nile and Lake Albert had to be abandoned.

Baker had devoted nine months to the imposition of his authority in the Bari country. His contract had less than sixteen months to run, and he had to hasten southward to carry the Egyptian flag to the central African lakes. On January 22, 1872, with over two hundred men, he left Gondokoro for Fatiko, just north of the Victoria Nile and the Bunyoro frontier. Here Baker found Abu Su'ud, the principal agent of 'Aqqad and Company, surrounded by his Arab followers, the Danaqla, who had originally arrived on the Upper Nile to serve Debono, and now were in the service of 'Aqqad. They had settled in the country where they exploited the local inhabitants and intervened in the succession struggle in Bunyoro which followed the death of Kamurasi in 1869. As at Gondokoro, Baker faced at Fatiko a hostile Arab settler class, who were well-armed and bitterly resentful of his mission to check the slave trade and establish Egyptian control. Had it not been for the reaction of the local people, the Acholi, Fatiko might have become another Gondokoro.

Unlike the Bari, who had formed a strong alliance with the traders, the Acholi opposed them. They had struggled to maintain their independence and to check the raids of the slave traders on their cattle and persons. Baker was able to rally their opposition and thereby gain their cooperation, not only to oppose Abu Su'ud, but to press on into Bunyoro. To the Acholi he was a welcome force to counteract the traders, and they willingly placed themselves under his protection. Today Baker is as revered in Acholi traditions as he is vilified in those of the Bari.

Baker left Fatiko on March 18, less than a fortnight after his arrival. He was in a hurry. He had already abandoned plans to march to Buganda, and, so as not to lose Bunyoro, he moved more rapidly than at any time in his African experience. Sending gifts before him to Kabarega, the new *omukama* and Kamurasi's successor, Baker reached Masindi, his capital, on April 25, 1872. There is little doubt that Kabarega was a man of exceptional character and ability. Under his leadership the warlike traditions of the Nyoro were rekindled as he sought to restore the greatness of Bunyoro's past. Kabarega had come to the throne as the successful claimant in the succession struggles following his father's death. In two hard fought campaigns he had defeated his brother, Kabigumire, who was killed. He then prepared to attack Ruyonga, who had rebelled against his father and was, at the time of Baker's arrival, seeking to replace the son. Although Baker was impressed by the neat appearance of the *omukama*, he could not overcome his prejudices. Kabarega was the twenty-third ruler of his dynasty, an able king of a proud people. Yet Baker could only see "a *gauche*, awkward, undignified lout of twenty years of age, who thought himself a great monarch. He was cowardly, cruel, cunning, and treacherous to the last degree." [17] In fact Kabarega was none of these.

Upon arriving at Masindi, Baker had high hopes of quickly

17. Baker, *Ismailïa*, 309.

incorporating Bunyoro into the growing Egyptian empire on the Upper Nile, and his incredible inability to understand African aspirations deluded him into thinking that the Nyoro would willingly submit to Egyptian rule. At Masindi he talked trade and civilization; but Kabarega, like Kamurasi, spoke only of his need for support against Ruyonga, and Baker agreed to assist him. He was in a hurry. He had to have results and have them quickly, and, ironically, the most deliberate of African explorers jeopardized his future relations by hastily consenting to means inimical to the ends of his mission. At Masindi as at Gondokoro the humanitarian objectives of Baker's expedition were hopelessly compromised by his willingness to employ the violent methods of his commercial predecessors. Alliances, however, are not built on expediency; they are the result of common interests. There were none between Baker and Kabarega. To the *omukama*, Baker was a returned Cwezi who only sought to conquer Bunyoro.[18] To the explorer, Kabarega should have displayed cooperation, gratitude, and loyalty, not distrust, suspicion, and hostility.

Relations deteriorated. Kabarega tried to poison Baker's men. Baker retaliated by a demonstration which ended in a Nyoro attack, the burning of Masindi, and a fighting retreat to Fatiko. Baker could see no reason for the Nyoro assault except the treachery of Kabarega. He denied having done anything to warrant such a provocation, and lamented the ingratitude of African savages.

> The country had been relieved from the slave-hunters, and my people were actually on the road to Fatiko to liberate and restore to their families about 1,000 women and children of Unyoro. I was about to establish a school. No thefts had taken place on the part of the troops. The rights of every native had been respected. The chiefs had received valuable presents, and the people had already felt the advantage of legitimate trade.[19]

18. Fisher, *Twilight Tales*, 160–166. The Cwezi were the tall, red men from the north who, according to oral traditions, established the first states in the lakes region of equatorial Africa.

19. Baker, *Ismailïa*, 354.

Drawn from the prisons and the retinues of the slave traders, Baker's irregulars could hardly have been the virtuous men he made them out to be, and their behavior seems to have contributed to Nyoro hostility.[20] Even if Baker's troops had not alienated the Nyoro, Kabarega could not have been expected to remain idle while his country was reduced to an Egyptian province. Baker had castigated the Nyoro and their customs; he had enrolled slave hunters in his service; he had communicated with Mutesa, *kabaka* of Buganda and Kabarega's traditional enemy. In the end, it is not surprising that the *omukama* of Bunyoro seized the first opportunity to rid himself of Baker and his entourage.

Forced to retire from Bunyoro, Baker was next challenged by Abu Su'ud's irregulars at Fatiko. Although well-armed, the slavers were fighting for neither home nor country, and after a pitched battle they either fled to Khartoum with Abu Su'ud or capitulated and enrolled in Egyptian governmental service. With their labor Baker constructed a strong fort at Fatiko, and, despite plans to extend Egyptian rule into Buganda, this station became the southernmost Egyptian outpost of Baker's expedition and the symbol of Baker's futile attempts to occupy the interlacustrine kingdoms of the great lakes of equatorial Africa.

Baker himself was not only satisfied with his work but immodestly boastful about his accomplishments. With unjustifiable enthusiasm, if not culpable misrepresentation, he summed up his achievements on the Upper Nile: "All obstacles have been surmounted. All enemies have been subdued—and the slavers who had the audacity to attack the troops have been crushed. The slave trade of the White Nile has been suppressed—and the country annexed so that Egypt extends to the equator."[21] Isma'il received a similar and equally glowing account of the work which Baker had carried out on his behalf.

This exaggerated assessment does not coincide with the

20. K. W., "The Kings of Bunyoro-Kitara, Part III," *Uganda Journal*, V (1937), 64.
21. Samuel Baker to John Baker, May 20, 1873, quoted in Gray, *History of the Southern Sudan*, 102–103.

facts. Bunyoro and Buganda were not annexed nor was their independence disturbed. The Egyptian flag flew at Gondokoro and Fatiko, but in between the authorities could only claim nominal control. Rustling and the *razzia* still prevailed in the region ostensibly under Egyptian rule, and were carried out by the Arab settlers whom Baker had employed in government service. Moreover, in return for the greatest expense, Baker had managed to acquire very little territory for Isma'il. Gondokoro and Fatiko were not much more than a hundred fifty miles apart, and the interior to the east still remained unknown. All that Isma'il had to show for an expenditure of a million pounds and Baker's enormous salary of over £40,000 were a few isolated outposts. True, a considerable quantity of ivory had been confiscated, probably just enough to cover Baker's fee, and the equipment and steamers he had left behind proved useful for his successors in continuing Egyptian administration. Nevertheless, Isma'il had a right to expect more for his money.

Baker's failure contrasts sharply with the efforts of his successors, General Charles George Gordon and Emin Pasha. Baker remained isolated in Africa. He had troops which he displayed, fireworks, and a battery of guns which stunned the people. He was powerful, and he used his power to impress the Africans—more by fear than friendship. With his racist attitudes and his deep contempt for Africans, it is not surprising that he assumed that force was the only way to deal with savages. He entered Bunyoro ready to employ violence. It is no wonder that the Nyoro and their *omukama* felt uneasy. Just as Baker became concerned when Africans massed against him, so Africans were nervous when confronted by the power which he personified. Emin Pasha came alone. A small, deferential man, he brought no guns and made no threats. Kabarega was neither menaced personally nor was his kingdom in danger, and he talked more freely and confidentially to Emin than to any other European. Baker assumed that obstacles could only be overcome by force. He never perceived that often it was his force which created the obstacles.

Regrettably, Baker's use of violent methods set the pattern of future European relations with Bunyoro. Today in Alur traditions Baker repeatedly returns until he finally defeats Kabarega.[22] The traditions do not make any value judgment; they simply provide an Alur explanation for Kabarega's ultimate defeat by Europeans in 1899. They make no distinction between the methods of Baker and those who came after him. With the exception of Emin Pasha there are few distinctions to make.

The greatest impact of Baker's mission, however, was felt neither in Egypt nor on the Upper Nile, but in Britain itself. The very scale of the expedition aroused philanthropic, economic, and strategic interest in the southern Sudan. The tale of its hardships and difficulties stimulated the imagination of a romantic age, and in his letters and books Baker sustained the initial excitement long after his expedition had reached its melancholy conclusion. *The Times* seemed to speak for all of Britain when it compared Baker's work with the Spanish in Mexico and the English in India.[23] He had come to the Upper Nile to conquer and to colonize in a land reputed to be rich in natural products and blessed with an equitable climate. Here was fertile parkland suitable for civilization which seemed tragically to have slipped under Egyptian control. British humanitarians were deeply distrustful that a Muslim, slaveholding nation like Egypt could introduce Christianity and commerce to the Upper Nile, and Baker's expedition encouraged their proprietary interest in equatorial Africa. The apparent success of Baker in extending the Egyptian empire to the central African lakes did nothing to dissolve their fears that Islam and the slave trade would flourish there under the Egyptian imperium. English intervention was not only the obvious answer but the morally right solution, and Baker had demonstrated that it was not only possible, but probably profitable.

Baker retired to England to enjoy the prerogatives of fame and the privileges of authority. His opinions on African matters were constantly solicited, and, until his death on December 30, 1893, he remained Britain's foremost expert on the River Nile.

22. Aidan Southall, "The Alur Legend of Sir Samuel Baker and the Mukama Kabarega," *Uganda Journal*, XV (1951), 187–190.
23. *The Times*, August 15, 1873.

His pronouncements, usually couched in letters to *The Times*, were widely read and invariably believed. His influence upon the official minds which made policy in Britain was by no means negligible. But fame and fortune and influence and respect never seem to have resolved Baker's search for purpose nor satisfied his deeper anxieties. He continued to travel and shoot, and, although he no longer marched in the wilderness or killed with the abandon of youth, his prejudices remained to shield those inner conflicts which perhaps no man successfully subdues.

Gerhard Rohlfs:
The Lonely Explorer

by Wolfe W. Schmokel

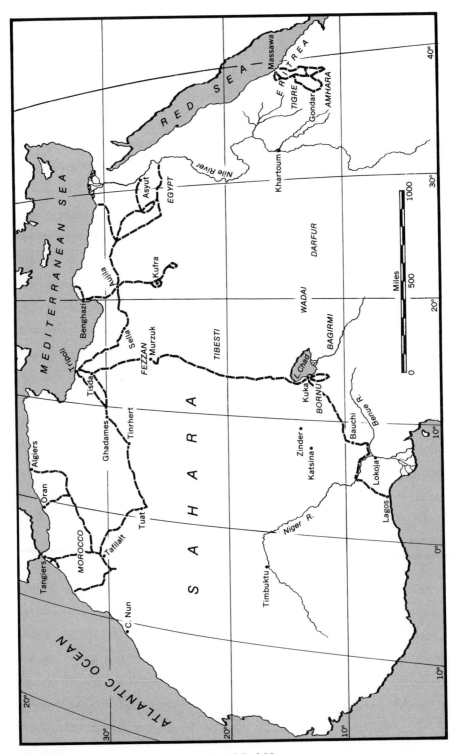

The many African travels of Gerhard Rohlfs

Friedrich Gerhard Rohlfs was the first European to cross Africa from the Mediterranean to the Gulf of Guinea, an accomplishment which made him widely celebrated in his time. Today few remember him, and he probably would not be included in a list of the leading African explorers, along with, say, Park, Livingstone, and Barth. This evaluation is not entirely unfair. Rohlfs came to northwest Africa too late to participate in the solution of such exciting geographical riddles as that of the Niger; many of his routes had already been mapped by other Europeans; his concept of a thorough exploration of north central Africa, to fill in the remaining blanks on the map, was eventually realized only by others.

It is also true that Rohlfs's scientific and linguistic accomplishments, gradually acquired in the course of his journeys, were too slight to enable him to see and describe his surroundings in the depth achieved, for example, by Barth; his strong prejudices and, in some respects, rigid personality vitiated any attempt on his part to understand and fairly to describe the Muslim peoples of North Africa and the Sahara among whom he sojourned for the better part of the nearly twenty years that he spent in Africa. This self-contained, self-conscious son of Hanseatic patriarchs, whose hunger for adventure was combined oddly with a distinct stiffness, would never have been capable of virtually adopting an African tribe, as did Livingstone, or of attempting to convert a powerful king and leading his war parties, like Stanley. In his case one is not even tempted to wonder—as one inevitably does about so many other Victorian explorers—whether his interest in exotic womanhood ever exceeded the requirements of ethnography.

But if Rohlfs as a geographer, an ethnographer, a figure in African history, and, in his later life, a rather unsuccessful diplomat is deserving of little more than the casual mention he usually receives in historical accounts, there is another aspect of him that looms larger: forced to make his living as a writer and lecturer, he became a tireless and highly successful publicist. His writings were so voluminous and his circle of acquaintances so large that there can be little doubt that Rohlfs was more influential in shaping the German public's view of Africa and Africans than anybody else in his time. He became Germany's Africa-expert par excellence, and as such was entrusted with several official missions, culminating in his brief Zanzibar consulship. To the extent that his writing and his personal persuasiveness helped to awaken and shape the Bismarckian empire's colonial attitudes, Rohlfs is indeed one of the shapers of modern African history. Beyond that he provides, because his personality was so monolithic and his prejudices so clear-cut and rooted in his age, a striking insight into the European mind at the time when Europe and Africa first came truly face to face, as well as an idea of the difficulties of that meeting. Finally, Rohlfs may best represent in this volume, among the savants, humanitarians, empire-builders, and missionaries, a type of motivation rationalized and submerged in those others, but basic to all of them—first and foremost he was an adventurer.

Gerhard Rohlfs, born in 1831, was the third son of a doctor in Vegesack, a little port near Bremen. His early education, at the hands of private tutors, was a rather slapdash affair, and he admitted in later life that he had been extraordinarily lazy and disinterested in all subjects except history, geography, and languages. He did not attend a formal school until he was fifteen. After a brief and miserable period in the Osnabrück *Gymnasium* he attempted to run away to sea, but his parents caught up with him in Amsterdam. A second bout with formal education was no happier. At eighteen Rohlfs left school and joined the Bremen Fusilier Regiment, hoping to see action against the Danes in Schleswig-Holstein, where both his older brothers were then serving as army surgeons. When the forces of the German Confederation withdrew from the war, Rohlfs transferred to the Schleswig-Holstein army, and, despite a rather casual attitude toward soldiering, distinguished himself in battle. Although he left the service as a lieutenant when the Schleswig-Holstein forces were dissolved in 1851, his interest in military matters was to last throughout his lifetime. Time and again, Rohlfs would intersperse his travel accounts with lengthy observations on the makeup and quality of the military forces of a country, the defensibility of its towns, etc. He generally foresaw the ease with which Europe's armaments would triumph over Africa's.

The Schleswig war had not satisfied Rohlfs's longing for activity and adventure. His attempt to study medicine thereafter proved a fiasco. He spent two impecunious years at various German universities, attending lectures at first sporadically, then not at all. (His medical notions were to remain exceedingly unorthodox.) Finally he joined the Austrian army, deserted after a short time, and made his way via Switzerland and Italy to France, where he enlisted in the Foreign Legion. In 1855 he arrived in Algeria, where he participated in the Kabylia campaigns of 1856–57, and was promoted to sergeant and acting surgeon. He seems to have been out of touch with his family, and later was extremely reticent about his experiences during this period. Clearly, however, his abiding antipathy toward things Muslim and Arab was formed then, as was his continuing sympathy with and interest in French colonial policy. He himself became French in outlook and manner, and seems to have entertained the idea of assuming French citizenship; it was not until after the founding of the German Empire that Rohlfs, like so many of his compatriots, became infected with national pride, and, in the process, something of a German super-patriot.

Upon his discharge from the Legion in 1861, Rohlfs set out to seek his fortune in Morocco, hoping to become a surgeon in the Sherifian forces, which, according to rumors current in Algeria, were to be reorganized along European lines following their utter defeat at the hands of Spain in 1859.[1] From Tangiers, where he had obtained letters of recommendation from the British Consul General, Sir Drummond Hay, Rohlfs set out into the interior dressed as a Muslim. His initial equipment on what was to become his first journey of exploration consisted

1. The only biography of Rohlfs, a good one, is by his nephew, Konrad Guenther, *Gerhard Rohlfs: Lebensbild eines Afrikaforschers* (Freiburg, 1912). For his early life, see 1–18.

of a notebook, a pencil, a few items of spare clothing, and the equivalent of about $25 in the money of the day—all of which was stolen within a week.

Penniless and regarded with suspicion by the Moroccans—who easily saw through his rather thin disguise, no matter how conscientiously he tried to follow their customs—Rohlfs made his way to Ouezzane.[2] There he was hospitably received by Sidi al-Hajj Abu as-Salaam, the Grand Sherif, who as the head of a Muslim brotherhood exercised an immense influence throughout the Maghrib, and whose patronage was greatly to facilitate his travels. Abu as-Salaam was a man after Rohlfs's own heart. His devotion to nineteenth-century progress and European ideas, and particularly to France, recommended him considerably less to his coreligionists; eventually he had to leave Morocco and seek French protection.[3] From him Rohlfs received further letters of recommendation—he seldom traveled without such documents and attached great value to them—before proceeding to Meknes, where he was accepted into the Sultan's service as a surgeon. After several months traveling with the Moroccan court, engaging in private practice in addition to performing his rather casual official duties, he discovered that he was unlikely to make his fortune in that manner. Moreover, he continued to be suspect, and was forced to curb his curiosity about the little-known country in which he was living:

> I made an excursion to Mulei Edris Serone, a town about three hours' distance from Mequinez, but I can say noth-

2. The spelling of non-European geographical names presents a thorny problem. In this case it is aggravated by Rohlfs's own theory that they should be written so as to accord with the orthographical rules of each writer's mother tongue ("Über die Schreibweise geographischer etc. Eigennamen," *Petermann's Mittheilungen aus Justus Perthes' Geographischer Anstalt*, XXV [1879], 347–349). I have generally followed the *Oxford Regional Economic Atlas of Africa* (Oxford, 1965). With regard to personal names I have followed Rohlfs's spelling, except in the case of some well known historical figures, and where his usage flagrantly conflicted with common modern rules for transliteration of Arabic (for example, I use "Muhammad," rather than "Mohammed").

3. "Marokko," *Westermann's Illustrierte Deutsche Monatshefte*, LXXIV (1893), 374.

ing further about this delightfully-situated place than I have already done in my description of Fez. Although I was physician-in-ordinary to the Sultan, lived in the first Minister's house, and followed most exactly all Mohammedan customs and usages, I was nevertheless always looked upon with distrust. To ask directly about any place would not do at all.[4]

Rohlfs's account of Morocco, partly at least because of such restrictions, is rather superficial.

Eventually released from what was becoming a condition of virtual bondage through the intervention of Sir Drummond Hay, and given freedom to travel wherever he pleased, Rohlfs resolved to penetrate the Saharan regions beyond the Atlas. His Arabic was still so poor, however, that he found it advisable to perfect it during a second stay in Ouezzane with his patron, the Grand Sherif, whom he accompanied on several visits to surrounding areas. Finally, in the spring of 1862, Rohlfs set off southward.[5]

He proceeded along the coast as far south as Agadir, making a side trip to Marrakech. On the way, having exhausted his supply of quinine, he suffered his first severe attack of malaria and was again robbed of all his possessions by a traveling companion. One of his most attractive characteristics was his readiness to accept such afflictions as matters that could not be helped. To that extent at least he did apparently share the philosophy of Islam.[6]

From Agadir, Rohlfs, traveling with merchant caravans, crossed the Atlas, and via Taroudant reached the Wadi Dra oases, of which he was the first European to give a detailed description (René Caillié and others had, however, visited them previously). Unlike earlier travelers, who had speculated about a Saharan lake as its terminal point, Rohlfs was the first to suggest that the Wadi seasonally carried its waters into the

4. *Adventures in Morocco and Journey through the Oases of Draa and Tafilet* (London, 1874), 199–200.
5. Rohlfs's early stay in Morocco is described in *ibid.*, 1–275.
6. *Ibid.*, 306.

Atlantic.[7] From Wadi Dra, Rohlfs traveled to Tafilalt, whose inhabitants doubted the genuineness of his pretended conversion to Islam. A phimosis operation which he had undergone years earlier in Wurzburg saved his life when they insisted on convincing themselves that he had been circumcised.[8] His next escape from death was closer yet. In Bouanane, a small oasis northeast of Tafilalt, the traveler unwisely let his host see his money. (It was little enough, about $70, which he had amassed by practicing medicine in the Moroccan manner, that is, with amulets and hot irons.) That night after leaving the oasis, alone, Rohlfs was robbed and left for dead, with his left arm and right hand partly severed, and a bullet wound through his thigh. A passing pair of marabouts found him nearly two days later and took him to the little oasis of Hadjui, whose inhabitants cared for him for nearly two months until he was able to drag himself on, via the tent village of the Uled Si Sheikh, to Géryville, the southernmost French outpost in western Algeria. Rohlfs retained a shortened left arm and stiff fingers on the right hand for the rest of his life. His major wounds opened sporadically until 1868, causing him considerable suffering during his journeys across the Sahara and in Ethiopia.[9] His continued energy and even more the virtual absence of any complaints about his personal health in his accounts is, under these circumstances, more than remarkable.

Just as striking was Rohlfs's ability to set aside his prejudices against whole peoples, and especially religions, in specific cases. He showed real warmth in expressing his gratitude to the inhabitants of Hadjui, among whom he convalesced, and in describing the life of the Uled Si Sheikh, where he made real friends—only to sum up, a few pages later: "After . . . two years of residence amongst these, by their religion, debased

7. "Gerhard Rohlfs' Tagebuch einer Reise durch die südlichen Provinzen von Marokko, 1862," *Petermann's*, IX (1863), 361–370. For Caillié's visit to the oases, see his *Journal d'un voyage à Temboctou et à Jenné dans l'Afrique Centrale* . . . (Paris, 1830), III, 45–91.

8. *Reise durch Marokko, Übersteigung des grossen Atlas, Exploration der Oasen von Tafilet, Tuat und Tidikelt; und Reise durch die grosse Wüste über Rhadames nach Tripolis* (Norden, 1884), 81–82.

9. Guenther, *Rohlfs*, 48.

people, I had the greatest desire to get once more to civilized life." [10]

This desire, if real, was not to be fulfilled immediately. Rohlfs, who pretended to be repelled by North Africa's religion, customs, and total unconcern with nineteenth-century ideas of progress and humanitarianism, was also fascinated by it. After a brief and imperfect recovery in Oran and Algiers, he set out again into the desert, revisiting his friends among the Uled Si Sheikh. He hoped to obtain their help in reaching the oases of Tuat, not previously visited by Europeans, and perhaps to travel on across the Sahara to Timbuktu. He still considered it essential to maintain his Muslim identity. When letters reached him from the Bremen Senate and the Royal Geographical Society, both of which offered financial assistance for his enterprise, this disguise was punctured so far as the Uled Si Sheikh were concerned. The traveler decided to turn back to Oran and to make a new start from Tangiers. [11]

Rohlfs had already been brought to the attention of the European public through his brother Hermann, who had come out to meet him in Algiers in the summer of 1863, and who had forwarded the explorer's brief diary to August Petermann, whose *Mittheilungen aus Justus Perthes' Geographischer Anstalt* had become Europe's foremost geographical journal and who was tireless in encouraging geographical discovery. In printing Rohlfs's diary, [12] Petermann pointed out that, despite its brevity and superficiality—to some extent unavoidable since Rohlfs had lacked all equipment for scientific observations—it was of first-rate importance as the fullest account of the trans-Atlas regions, aside from Caillié's. Through the efforts of Petermann and his own brother, Rohlfs was somewhat better equipped for his second journey. The Bremen Senate and the Royal Geographical Society each contributed $225, Hermann Rohlfs another $375. A further sum from the Berlin

10. *Adventures*, 360 ff.; "Si Sliman ben Hamsa und die Uled Sidi Schich," *Vom Fels zum Meer,* I (1881–82), 331–333. All translations from Rohlfs's German writings are my own.

11. "Algier und Oran," *Westermann's,* LXXIII (1892), 344–363.

12. "Tagebuch einer Reise durch die südlichen Provinzen von Marokko, 1862," *Petermann's,* IX (1863), 361–370.

Geographical Society failed to reach him in time. With this minimal financial backing Rohlfs carried out a journey that lasted nearly a year. His equipment was necessarily modest (he was unable, for example, to buy pack animals, and had to rent camels for the several stages of the journey) and his scientific apparatus consisted of little more than a few barometers and thermometers with which to make rough determinations of altitude. Even these instruments tended to create suspicion—Rohlfs still traveled as a Muslim—and had to be used with extreme circumspection. He generally traveled with merchant or pilgrim caravans, but sometimes marched alone with his one servant. The risk involved was decreased somewhat by his friendship with the Grand Sherif of Ouezzane, who provided him with letters to the local heads of his order. These introductions also enabled Rohlfs to obtain hospitality in most places, and thus stretch his meager funds.[13]

Leaving Tangiers in March 1864, the explorer traveled via Ouezzane and across the High Atlas to Tafilalt, and on through the Wadi Saoura to the Tuat oases. Once again, because of the delay occasioned by his change of plans, Rohlfs traveled into the Sahara in midsummer—something he warned others not to do. Despite his punctual observance of all religious prescriptions and prompt visits to the tombs of prominent holy men, Rohlfs was in continual danger from Muslims suspicious of the authenticity of his conversion. He also had reason to be apprehensive about the predatory habits of some of the tribes through whose territory he traveled. Nevertheless, he reached Tidikelt in Tuat without major incident, aside from being robbed of his provisions by members of the same tribe among whom he had nearly died during his previous journey.[14]

Already in Tafilalt, Rohlfs had begun to inquire about opportunities of reaching the Sudan, but he found that, despite the thriving appearance of the market of that oasis, most of the trans-Saharan trade was now in the hands of the inhabitants of Tuat. There, too, however, he found obstacles that could not be overcome. A long delay was expected before the next major

13. *Reise durch Marokko*, 116–117, 273–274, 42, 46, 65, 14–16, 55–56.
14. *Ibid.*, 115, 65, 74, 75, 81–82, 99–102.

caravan would leave for Timbuktu, and Rohlfs was running short of funds. There was, moreover, a growing suspicion in Tidikelt that Rohlfs was really a Christian, and possibly an agent of the French government. Rumors to that effect had reached the oases from Algeria and Morocco. Finally, conditions along the upper Niger River appeared unusually turbulent. The son and successor of al-hajj 'Umar, supported by Tuareg tribes, was besieging Timbuktu. All of these factors persuaded Rohlfs to postpone his journey to the Sudan, and thus the attempt to win the prize of 8,000 francs of the Société de Géographie de Paris for a cross-country journey from Algeria to Senegal, which apparently had been brought to his attention by Petermann. Instead, he decided to go to Tripoli, where he apparently hoped to obtain additional backing for his enterprise.[15]

In October 1864 Rohlfs left Tidikelt for Ghudamis (Ghadames), with a caravan led by Si 'Uthman b. Bekri, whose brother had been Major Alexander Laing's guide to Timbuktu and who had himself traveled with the French Saharan explorer Henri Duveyrier. The journey to Ghudamis, and from there, in the company of a Turkish military courier, to Tripoli, was uneventful if tedious. Rohlfs reached Tripoli on 29 December 1864.[16] Despite his earlier intention to start south again as soon as possible, he now decided to pay a visit to Germany in order to meet his principal backers and personally to organize support for his venture into the Sudan. This decision was to influence the objective of his next journey. Rohlfs never saw Timbuktu.

Nevertheless, Rohlfs's second journey, seen by itself, was

15. *Ibid.*, 75, 176–180, 183–184, 204; Guenther, *Rohlfs,* 50–51. Rohlfs implies that news of the death of al-hajj 'Umar al Tall had already reached the Saharan oases before his departure from In Salah in October 1864. This is barely possible—we do not know the exact date of the death of 'Umar. The reference to a siege of Timbuktu is either based on confusion with 'Umar's sack of that town in 1863, or refers to an attempt by 'Umar's son Ahmadu to regain control over Timbuktu, not reported by Eugène Mage, to whom we owe most of our information about events in the Western Sudan for that period. Cf. Abdon Eugène Mage, *Voyage dans le Soudan Occidental (1863–66)* (Paris, 1868).

16. *Reise durch Marokko,* 200–274.

perhaps his most important accomplishment. He had provided new information about southern Morocco, especially the Tafilalt oasis, had described the most practicable route to Tuat, had provided the first complete description of that group of oases, and had gathered the first information whatever on Tidikelt and In Salah, determining the location of these places as accurately as possible without making astronomical observations. He had obtained new information about Saharan and trans-Saharan trade and trade routes, and, perhaps most impressive, had managed to travel without major mishap in the midst of populations so suspicious and xenophobic as to prevent any other European from reaching Tuat until the French occupied the oases more than thirty years later.[17] All this had been done on a shoestring. Rohlfs's later travels, with far more elaborate preparation and equipment, were paradoxically to yield lesser results.

In early 1865, setting foot in Europe for the first time in ten years, Rohlfs paid a brief visit to his family, then proceeded to Gotha to discuss with Petermann plans for his next journey. The German winter seriously affected his health, his old wounds made traveling extremely painful, and the explorer was anxious for this reason to return to Africa as soon as possible. Petermann and he seem to have agreed on a general plan of striking out southwest from Ghudamis through the Ahaggar mountains to the upper Niger. Heinrich Barth, however, whom on Petermann's advice he saw in Berlin, had other ideas. He urged Rohlfs to follow his own old route, south from Fezzan to Bornu, then east to Wadai and the western tributaries of the Nile, solving if possible what Barth considered one of the greatest remaining geographical questions in Africa— the relationship between the rivers flowing into Lake Chad and the Niger-Benue system. Rohlfs, despite his great admiration for Barth, remained unconvinced. He felt that the dangers and difficulties of Barth's suggested route far outweighed any risk involved in the possibility that the inhabitants of Ghudamis might have learned that Rohlfs was a pseudo-Muslim, who had

17. *Ibid.*, VI–VII (foreword by Victor Adolphe Malte-Brun); "Tuat," *Globus*, LXIII (1893), 274–277.

changed into Christian garb upon reaching Tripoli. In the end, however, he was to follow Barth's plan.[18]

Concerned lest the European winter immobilize him indefinitely, Rohlfs left Germany for Africa in February 1865, stopping off in Paris to confer with French experts on the Sahara, including Duveyrier, and complete the purchase of his equipment. Rohlfs's third journey was a far more elaborately arranged expedition than his earlier ones, although still modest by the standards of most other African explorers. From various sources, including the Bremen Senate, the King of Prussia, and geographical societies, he had been provided with 9,195 thaler (about $6,900). This sum included funds that had been collected for the relief of two travelers, Eduard Vogel and Moritz von Beurmann, who, as had been learned in the meantime, had been killed in Wadai respectively in 1856 and 1863.[19] Petermann made this money available to Rohlfs on the understanding that he would, if possible, ascertain the circumstances of their deaths and recover their belongings, some of which had been left in Bornu. (This indicates the vagueness of Rohlfs's objective; he could hardly have expected to accomplish these assignments on the upper Niger!) In Paris, Rohlfs acquired his instruments—thermometers, barometers, hygrometers, hypsometers, and watches—some weapons, and medical supplies, notably quinine and extract of opium; rugs, blankets, some canned goods, general provisions, rifles, and other items were purchased in Malta; bulk supplies, water

18. *Quer durch Afrika. Reise vom Mittelmeer nach dem Tschadsee und zum Golf von Guinea* (Leipzig, 1874–75), I, 1–2. *Neue Beiträge zur Entdeckung und Erforschung Afrikas* (Cassel, 1881), 11–12.

19. On Vogel (1829–1856) and Beurmann (1835–1863) and their travels in the Sahara and Central Sudan, see the following: Victor Adolphe Malte-Brun, *Résumé historique de l'exploration faite dans l'Afrique Centrale de 1853 à 1856 par le docteur Edouard Vogel* (Paris, 1858); Adolf Pahde, *Der Afrikaforscher Eduard Vogel* (Hamburg, 1889); "Ermordung Moritz von Beurmann's an der Grenze von Wadai," *Globus*, V (1864), 120; "Beurmann's Tod nebst Übersicht seiner Reise (1861–63), sowie derjenigen von Overweg (1850–52), Vogel (1853–54) und Steudner (1861–63)," *Petermann's*, X (1864), 25–30; H. Lange, "Die deutsche Expedition nach Innerafrika und Moritz von Beurmann," *Globus*, I (1862), 68–85; John Petherick, "Noch einige Nachrichten über Eduard Vogel und Moritz von Beurmann," *Petermann's*, XIII (1867), 1; A. Merx, "Lebensbild eines zu früh Geschiedenen," *Jahresbericht des Vereins von Freunden der Erdkunde zu Leipzig*, VI (1866), 87–111.

bags, cooking utensils, packing cases, rope, tools, and presents were obtained in Tripoli. The last included a wide variety of items of clothing, perfumes, beads, needles, writing paper, and knives. Wherever possible, Rohlfs bought articles of German manufacture, a wide variety of which seem to have been available in the bazaars of Tripoli.

The expedition's personnel included Hamid al-Tandjaui, who had accompanied Rohlfs on his second journey, Muhammad Shtaui, a native of Tripoli and a pardoned murderer, and three others—a Kanuri, a Hausa, and a Teda. Muhammad Shtaui particularly commended himself to the explorer by his generally churlish behavior, which tended to discourage unwanted visitors to the camp and prevented the servants from agreeing on private arrangements to Rohlfs's disadvantage, as well as by his extreme stinginess, which also applied to the expedition's property. He was to accompany Rohlfs on future expeditions as well.

With only five servants and six camels, Rohlfs's was indeed a modest caravan. He felt that this was all to the good: "Large and luxuriously conceived expeditions are liable to be a hindrance in that country rather than of use." He saw Barth's "elegant" expedition as an exception to that rule, which had been borne out by Samuel Baker's journey—which he compared to Georg Schweinfurth's much more modestly conceived and more productive travels in the Sudan, and by the disaster that befell the Dutch heiress Alexandrine Tinné in the Sahara.[20] The validity of this opinion seems to have been borne out by

20. *Quer durch Afrika*, I, 3 ff. On Schweinfurth (1836–1925), see Konrad Guenther, *Georg Schweinfurth; Lebensbild eines Afrikaforschers: Briefe von 1857 bis 1925* (Stuttgart, 1954). He himself described his most important journey, through the area of the Niger-Congo watershed, in *The Heart of Africa: Three Years' Travels and Adventures in the Unexplored Regions of Central Africa, from 1868 to 1871* (London, 1873). Alexandrine Tinné (1835–1869) shares with most explorers from the minor European countries the fate of almost total historical oblivion. One of the few women explorers of the nineteenth century, she traveled widely in the Sudan, seeking to "find" Speke; she was killed by the Tuareg not far from Ghudamis while setting out across the Sahara to the Sudan. Clara Eggink, *De merkwurdige reisen van Henriette en Alexandrine Tinné* (Amsterdam, 1960); P. C. Mohuysen and P. J. Blok (eds.), *Nieuw Nederlandsch Biografisch Woordenboek*, I (Leyden, 1960), 1500; J. L. Walch, *Vrouwen van Format* (Amsterdam, 1941), 256–288.

the relative ease with which Rohlfs traveled through the Sahara and the Sudan, and particularly by the absence of any armed clashes on this journey. He was by no means a pacifist, but his belongings were too modest to excite cupidity or make robbery or extortion worthwhile.

Rohlfs left Tripoli in May 1865, traveling once again during a Saharan summer, and reached Ghudamis without major incident. Here things went wrong. Si 'Uthman b. Bekri, who was to accompany him to Ahaggar—his brother was an important Tuareg leader and Rohlfs considered this a guarantee of safety—had not arrived in the oasis. Eventually it transpired that he had gone to Algiers and might not return for months. The explorer suffered a severe attack of dysentery, and, attempting a cure with opiates, became addicted to narcotics. (The cure was inevitable when he ran out of his supply of drugs.) He spent a good deal of his time during his slow convalescence in various mosques (still pretending to be a Muslim), talking to the imams and making other friends. When he finally left Ghudamis at the end of August, having decided not to follow the invitation of one of his Tuat acquaintances to return to that oasis, he did so "not without regret," for during that hot, miserable summer he had "grown to like its inhabitants, despite their public display of bigotry." Once again we have an example of his ability to get along with individual Muslims, and even whole groups, while disliking Islam in general.[21]

Having decided to adopt the plan that Barth had suggested, Rohlfs returned to Mizdah, and from there marched south to Fezzan. He now shed his Muslim garb, seeing no further use for it in "tolerant Fezzan and in Bornu, where Europeans are received with kindness."[22] The desert journey to Murzuk was unremarkable. Rohlfs followed a track some forty miles east of Clapperton, Denham, and Barth's old route, arriving in Murzuk at the end of October. Here he spent nearly five months, awaiting further supplies and money from Tripoli. He also sought to attach himself to a suitable caravan for the trans-Saharan leg of his journey. During this time he became friendly

21. *Ibid.*, I, 85–96.
22. *Ibid.*, I, 108.

with Muhammad Besserki, the last descendant of the old rulers of Fezzan before the Turkish conquest of the 1820's. This somewhat seamy pretender offered to cede Rohlfs his "rights," arguing that he as a foreigner would stand a better chance of having them recognized in Constantinople, and suggested a marriage alliance. Rohlfs, who was also on the best of terms with the Turkish officials, declined with thanks.[23] He always considered himself a guest in Africa, and it was his policy not to become too involved. Thus, despite his abhorrence of the slave trade, which he found rampant in Fezzan, and whose horrors he described and abominated with a fervor equal to that of his contemporaries, he returned to his owner a runaway Bagirmi slave who had taken refuge with him. But first he pointed out to the owner that he had no legal rights since slavery had been officially abolished in the Ottoman Empire, and that he would therefore have to persuade the slave to return to him voluntarily. This the owner did with the promise of a wife and no work for a month.[24]

Rohlfs did, however, keep another slave, a Bagirmi boy who had been offered to him as a fee for medical services by a Kordofan slave trader. Named Noel, the boy accompanied Rohlfs to Lagos and on to Berlin, as well as on his first Ethiopian journey. He was educated in Berlin at the court of William I (although Rohlfs's suggestion that he be brought up as a companion of the later William II was not followed), later joined the German consular service in Egypt, eventually went insane, and died many years later in an asylum in Ancona, Italy.[25]

Another addition to Rohlfs's company, by way of replacement for a dismissed servant, was Muhammad al-Gatruni, a remarkable African traveler, who had been to Timbuktu with Barth and had journeyed with Henri Duveyrier, Eduard Vogel, and Moritz von Beurmann in the Sudan. He accompanied Rohlfs to Kuka, then the capital of Bornu, took back part of his baggage from there to Tripoli, and later accompanied Gustav Nachtigal to Lake Chad. His son, Ali, was with

23. "Gerhard Rohlfs Reise durch Nordafrika," *Ausland*, XLII (1869), 169.
24. *Quer durch Afrika*, I, 133.
25. *Ibid.*, I, 173; Guenther, *Rohlfs*, 90–91.

Rohlfs on the unhappy Kufra expedition of 1879.[26] Al-Gatruni, who had been recommended to Rohlfs by Barth, joined the expedition at about the time that the news of Barth's death reached Murzuk.

Since no caravans were then leaving for Wadai, Rohlfs had to abandon his hope to go there directly, exploring Tibesti on the way. Instead he joined the caravan of a Teda chief, who was returning to Bilma, on the route to Bornu. He left Murzuk on 25 March 1866[27] and, after a delay of some weeks in the Kauar oases, reached Kuka on 22 July. Aside from one occasion when the small caravan, traveling alone south of Bilma, got lost and ran out of water, the trip went smoothly.

There is, in fact, very little that is sensational about Rohlfs's travels or, at any rate, about the way in which he described them. His accounts lack any attempt to make his exploits seem dangerous or extraordinary by depicting Africa and Africans as wild, savage, or dangerous. The general tone is that of a matter-of-fact travelogue. The impression conveyed of a rather pleasant walking trip—sometimes one feels Rohlfs might as well be writing of a hike through the North German countryside—is produced partly by the vocabulary used: instead of tribes, Rohlfs speaks of peoples, instead of huts, houses, instead of chiefs, kings or mayors, instead of tribal elders, councillors. For military ranks and units he frequently uses European terms. Despite the simplification that this involves, it may be argued that Rohlfs's books conveyed to his readers a more realistic picture of African life than the more highly colored works of other explorers, many of which exaggerated the "exotic."

By the time of his third voyage Rohlfs had acquired considerable talent for observation. Although descriptions of places and the running account of his own activities still predominate in *Quer durch Afrika*, some passages show real insight into the meaning of African institutions, customs, and beliefs, as well as some rather finely drawn sketches of personalities,

---

26. *Neue Beiträge*, 1–3. Heinrich Barth, *Travels and Discoveries in North and Central Africa* (London, 1965), III, 21; Gustav Nachtigal, *Sahara und Sudan* (Berlin, 1879–1889), I, 19–20, 201, 242–244, 314, 357, 630; II, 746; III, 3.

27. *Quer durch Afrika*, I, 179–180.

for example, Sultan 'Umar of Bornu.[28] He had also become more skeptical about the facts and figures of other explorers, with whose works he was thoroughly familiar. Perhaps the most attractive feature of his writing—aside from the clear and straightforward, although grammatically sometimes rather tenuous, style and the absence of late-nineteenth-century cant —is his obvious delight in nature and his talent for describing landscapes. Thus, of southeastern Bornu:

> We were now in the province of Udjé and entered the splendid forest of Buddumáseli. It consists entirely of gigantic, perhaps 1,000 year-old trees: The majestic Anim tree, whose leaves are used for a green dye, competes in girth and height with the Tamarind and with the no less imposing Komána, whose fruits are of the size and have the taste of lemons. Overtopping them all there is the Kagui, reminiscent in the fullness of its light-green leaves of our beeches in their spring garb. These giant stems are often tied together by lianas into a high green wall, above which only the boles rise free into the sky; or the faintly green Kossásse bush, the Borúngo with its coral-red blooms, and other bushes form a thicket beneath them, impenetrable for man and beast. The mimosas, too, reach a height on the rich humus which I have not seen elsewhere.[29]

The route followed by Rohlfs from Fezzan to Bornu had been taken by several European travelers since the epic Denham-Clapperton-Oudney expedition. Nevertheless, Petermann found that Rohlfs's observations and sketch maps contributed considerably to geographical knowledge, and "that his results far exceed the accomplishments of his predecessors, Barth, Vogel, and Beurmann not excluded."[30]

In Kuka, Rohlfs was received in a friendly manner by Sultan 'Umar, who had welcomed earlier European travelers. The ruler was adamant, however, on the subject of allowing Rohlfs

28. *Ibid.,* II, 33.
29. *Ibid.,* II, 21.
30. "Neueste Nachrichten aus dem Inneren Afrikas," *Petermann's,* XIII (1867), 41.

to proceed to Wadai, where Vogel and Beurmann had met their deaths. Eventually, however, the explorer persuaded him to send messengers to the Sultan of Wadai, 'Ali b. Muhammad, asking permission to enter the country. While waiting for a reply, Rohlfs made himself at home in Kuka, living in the same guest house that had sheltered European visitors from the time of Denham and Clapperton. He was as impressed as they had been by Bornu's high degree of civilization, and particularly by the industriousness of the population. Compared with North African Arabs and Berbers, he considered the Sudanese in every respect superior. During September and October 1866 Rohlfs made a trip to Mandara, in what was to become the northern Cameroon. This area, then tributary to Bornu, had previously been visited by only two Europeans, Denham and Vogel.[31] He also made shorter excursions into the vicinity of Kuka. He was able to learn something in detail about the deaths of Vogel and Beurmann—but he was denied permission to enter Wadai. Rohlfs indeed had reason to doubt that the messengers whom 'Umar had promised to send to Wadai had ever left Kuka.

Judging it imprudent to go to Wadai without an invitation, he considered returning the same way he had come, suggesting to Petermann that on his return a new and larger expedition be organized, "consisting of six or seven specialists, escorted by a small armed force . . . in order to end once and for all our ignorance of the real interior of Africa."[32] Despite—or, rather, to some extent, because of—the hospitality he received in Kuka (it had to be repaid in presents to numerous court functionaries and hangers-on), funds were running low. Eventually Rohlfs decided to make for the Guinea coast. Borrowing money (to be repaid in Tripoli at 100 percent interest), dismissing all of his servants except for Hamid and Noel, and selling some of his possessions, he set out via Magumeri, Gujba, Duku, Bauchi, the Jos Plateau, and Keffi to Loko on the Benue. Al-Gatruni, after accompanying him as far as Magumeri, returned across the Sahara with the baggage that had been left in Kuka, including the botanical and geological collections. Rohlfs was

31. *Quer durch Afrika*, II, 7–63.
32. "Neueste Nachrichten," 46.

much impressed by the climate and the fertility of Bauchi. Together with his inveterate contempt for Islam, it inspired the following outburst, which nicely sums up many of the motives of nineteenth-century imperialism:

> May one of the Christian powers, using these advantages offered by nature, take possession of the Bauchi Plateau and colonize it with settlers from Europe under the protection of its arms! Here in the territory of the Haussa and Bolo Negroes, a great majority of whom are still pagans, and who despise the rule of the Muhammadan Fulanis, a strong barrier could be established against the continued spread of Islam. Islam fills its confessors with heartless contempt of the infidel heathen, with fanatical hatred of Christians. It is Islam which causes the outrageous manhunts among the Negroes; it is Islam which makes it difficult for European travelers to penetrate into the interior.[33]

It is interesting to note that Rohlfs, while already formulating colonial projects, had as yet no national egotism about them. On this journey he still carried the flag of the Free and Hanseatic City of Bremen, a power not likely to be interested in colonizing Bauchi, or any other part of Africa. Only with the creation of the German Empire was a nationalist flavor added to Rohlfs's imperialism.

In Keffi the traveler heard of the existence of a British settlement at Lokoja, near the confluence of the Niger and Benue rivers. Delighted at the prospect of meeting Europeans so soon, he hurried on, reaching the Benue at Loko, from where boats, rented with his last few cowries, took him to Lokoja, which he reached on 28 March 1867.[34] After a brief period of rest, during which Noel was baptized by a Sierra Leonean missionary, Rohlfs went up the Niger to Raba in order to deliver presents to the Etsu Nupe. He did so partly out of courtesy to the governor of the British post and partly because the direct route to the coast, down the Niger River, was considered too dangerous for his small party. His interpreter on this mission,

33. *Quer durch Afrika*, II, 163.
34. *Ibid.*, II, 230 ff.

interestingly enough, turned out to be a certain Durrugu, who had traveled with Barth and subsequently been educated in Britain. Finding that Etsu Massaban had been taken away from his capital by the needs of war, Rohlfs delivered the presents on the battlefield. His hurry to get to the coast, and back to Europe, nearly precipitated a diplomatic incident. Through a misunderstanding or a mistranslation Rohlfs departed without making his formal farewells. He was forced to repair that error when Massaban sent messengers after him and threatened to return the presents to avenge what he considered a slight. This was one of the few cases in which Rohlfs ever failed to observe local etiquette, but on this last leg of a long journey his patience ran short. When the ruler of Ilorin failed to grant him the farewell audience which Rohlfs had requested, he again left without permission. Rapidly marching through Yorubaland, Rohlfs reached the coast without incident, only to be nearly drowned during the crossing of the lagoon between Ikorodu and Lagos. He had been rumored dead during the last year of his journey, and was joyfully received by the Europeans in Lagos, especially by his compatriots at the factory of William O'Swald & Co.[35]

On his return to Europe, Rohlfs was heaped with honors, received by the Prussian King and Chancellor Otto von Bismarck, and given honorary memberships by all of the major geographical societies and medals from those of London and Paris. His servant Hamid Tandjaui was likewise honored with the silver Victoria Medal of the Royal Geographical Society. The journey had been short on real geographical discovery— little of Rohlfs's route had not been traversed by Europeans before—but he was the first to cross Africa from the Mediterranean to the Gulf of Guinea. In his native country he henceforth became something of an oracle on all things African, and was in this respect eventually superseded to some extent only by Nachtigal. Others planning explorations sought his advice, and Rohlfs acquired a huge circle of friends and acquaintances among travelers and explorers. Among his warm-

35. *Ibid.*, II, 246–247, 261–262, 270–276; *Land und Volk in Afrika* (Bremen, 1870), 16–26; "Übersicht von Gerhard Rohlfs' Reise durch Afrika, 1866–67," *Petermann's*, XIII (1867), 372–381.

est admirers was Georg Schweinfurth, with whom, by sheer chance, Rohlfs was to establish a family connection through marriage.

As one of the immediate results of his new prominence Rohlfs was sent by the Prussian government to accompany the British expedition of Sir Robert Napier to Magdala as an observer. This journey was unremarkable and routine, and Rohlfs's account of it even more so. Attached to General Charles Staveley's advance column, he was plainly bored:

> One will find little new on this my route. Abyssinia has been crisscrossed by travelers in all directions, the land and the customs have been so thoroughly described that no one will expect much from the little time [I spent there]. Also, I don't have such interesting adventures to report as those related by Bruce, and I believe that these are the exception.[36]

Rohlfs met some of the giants of African exploration in the British camp—James A. Grant, Johann Ludwig Krapf, Henry M. Stanley, and Werner Munzinger—but seems to have established close relations with none of them.[37] On the return march from Magdala to the coast he left the British column to visit Lalibela, with its wondrous monolithic stone churches, and Axum. Of both he provided no more than a routine descrip-

---

36. *Land und Volk,* 125.

37. Werner Munzinger (1832–1875) is another explorer who has received far less attention from historians and biographers than his adventurous life and his active and important role in the history of Africa warrants. He traveled widely in northern Ethiopia and in the Sudan, became a first-rate naturalist and linguist, as British consul in Massawa was responsible for the preparations of the Napier expedition to Magdala, and was finally appointed Egyptian Governor of the eastern Sudan and the Red Sea. He was killed, along with his Ethiopian wife, in a Galla ambush. J. V. Keller-Zschokke, *Werner Munzinger-Pascha, Sein Leben und Wirken* (Aarau, 1891); Lee van Dovski (Herbert Lewandowski), *Ein Leben für Afrika; Das abenteuerliche Schicksal van Werner Munzinger-Pascha* (Zürich, 1954); Hugo Dietschi, "Werner Munzinger-Pascha," *Grosse Schweizer* (Zürich, 1938), 619–623; J. V. Keller-Zschokke, *Betätigung Werner Munzingers bei der Aufsuchung Dr. Ed. Vogels von Krefeld* (Solothurn, 1912).

tion, despite the fact that Lalibela had been previously visited only by Arnaud d'Abbadie, who had failed to publish an account, and by Francisco Álvares in the sixteenth century. On the whole, Rohlfs was unimpressed by all things Ethiopian. He considered its people "the dirtiest... in all Africa," and compared the country in its degree of civilization, the quality of buildings, and most other matters highly unfavorably to the Western Sudan. Rohlfs's anticlericalism no doubt played a role in forming these opinions; he used the lamentable state of Ethiopia as a stick with which to belabor Christianity.[38]

Soon after his return from Ethiopia in the summer of 1868, Rohlfs was again in Tripoli. He had been requested to organize the transport of some presents which William I was sending to 'Umar of Bornu. ('Umar had solicited them through Rohlfs.) Originally Rohlfs planned to entrust the mission to al-Gatruni, but, when that old traveler could not be found, he accepted the offer of a fellow German, Gustav Nachtigal, lately physician to the Bey of Tunis, to undertake the journey. (Al-Gatruni eventually showed up and accompanied Nachtigal.)

While overseeing the preparations for this expedition, Rohlfs visited the classical sites of Sabratha and Leptis Magna. These tours, as well as his subsequent journey through Cyrenaica, and, via the oases of Aujila, Gialo, and Siwa, to Alexandria, yielded little in the way of new discovery, but they provided material for a two-volume book, a rash of articles, and a project for the colonization of Cyrenaica. Rohlfs's observations are among the earliest European reports on the rise of the Sanusi movement. His (inexact) measurements, showing the oases to the south of Cyrenaica to lie below sea level, led him to some bold speculations on the extent of that depression, and thus furnished one of the reasons for the Libyan Desert expedition of 1873–74. Already in 1868–69 his real objectives were the oases of Kufra, but it proved impossible to engage a

38. *Im Auftrage Sr. Majestät des Königs von Preussen mit dem englischen Expeditionscorps in Abessinien* (Bremen, 1869), *passim; Land und Volk,* 1–196; "Die Christlichen Wunderbauten zu Lalibala in Abyssinien," *Globus,* XIV (1868), 364–370.

guide to take him to that area, hitherto never visited by Europeans. He was to reach there only ten years later.[39]

Back in Europe, while maintaining an astonishing literary productivity, Rohlfs was constantly engaged on the lecture circuit. In Riga, in the course of a Russian lecture tour, he met and married Lony Behrens, the eighteen-year-old niece of Georg Schweinfurth. In the fall of 1870 the couple established a home in Weimar, still a center of artistic and scientific life. Rohlfs's activities as a lecturer and publicist allowed him to live well and to extend hospitality to a circle of acquaintances which included celebrities as diverse as the Weimar Grand Duke, the Austrian polar explorer Julius von Payer, and the composer Franz Liszt. His contribution to the Franco-Prussian War was a rather farcical attempt, devised by the Prussian Foreign Office, to raise the tribes of southern Algeria against the French. Rohlfs and his companion, a leading academic Arabist, got as far as Tunis, where as a result of French prodding they were arrested and deported. Rohlfs received the title of Prussian Court Councillor anyway. The war and its splendid outcome turned him, like so many other Germans, into a jingo. He would, for example, scrupulously avoid "foreign" words, going so far as to coin his own German equivalents for such terms as *Äquator*.[40]

Germany's new might and importance were brought into play to assist Rohlfs in realizing his plans, formed as a result of his previous journey, for a thorough exploration of the Libyan Desert. The German Consul General in Egypt intervened on his behalf with the Khedive, who appropriated £4000 for the enterprise, and also provided transport and local personnel. That he did so willingly may be doubted, since he complained bitterly to Rohlfs of the cost of Sir Samuel Baker's expedition

39. *Von Tripolis nach Alexandrien* (Norden, 1885), *passim;* "Leptis Magna," *Ausland,* XLII (1869), 473–477; "Sabratha," *ibid.,* 222–226; "Die Jupiter Ammons Oase," *ibid.,* 985–989, 1018–1022, 1065–1070; "Bengasi," *ibid.,* 947–952; "Audjila und Djalo," *ibid.,* 1153–1158; *Land und Volk,* 230–240; "Gerhard Rohlfs über die grosse Depression in der Libyschen Wüste," *Ausland,* XLIII (1870), 427–428.

40. Guenther, *Rohlfs,* 118–136.

on the Upper Nile, which he saw as a failure,[41] and since Rohlfs himself stressed the role played by the German Foreign Office in obtaining the funds.[42] The Libyan Desert Expedition was, with respect to staff and equipment, the most elaborate of Rohlfs's journeys. Its personnel included a paleontologist, Karl Zittel; a surveyor, Wilhelm Jordan; a photographer, Philipp Remelé; and a botanist, Paul Ascherson, who was a personal acquaintance of Rohlfs and had also been recommended by Schweinfurth. There were five German servants and ten African ones, aside from the camel drivers and guards furnished by the Egyptian government. As the caravan left Asyût it consisted of 95 persons and 102 camels. None of the Europeans, aside from the leader of the expedition, had traveled in Africa before, none spoke Arabic, and one of them, Ascherson, proved capable of such gross tactlessness and stupidity as feeding pork to an Egyptian child. While Rohlfs, unlike so many explorers, managed to maintain tolerable relations with and among the other Europeans—the German servants, incidentally, seem to have been treated pretty much like the Egyptian ones—he became highly irritated with the local personnel.[43] On his previous journeys he had gotten on well enough with his few subordinates; one must conclude that his temperament was simply not well suited to the organization of such a large enterprise. There were other difficulties as well. Rohlfs, whose experience had been gained in the western Sahara, was surprised and appalled by the utter barrenness of the Libyan Desert, which made it necessary to carry camel feed, which in turn meant that other baggage had to be left behind and the scientific program of the expedition curtailed.

Basing himself at the Dakhla oasis, Rohlfs attempted to march due west to Kufra. He discovered the Great Sand Sea, which proved impassable for his camels, and was forced to turn north, eventually reaching Siwa on 19 February 1874,[44]

41. "Beginn der deutschen Expedition in die Libysche Wüste unter Führung von Dr. G. Rohlfs," *Petermann's*, XX (1874), 81.
42. *Drei Monate in der Libyschen Wüste* (Cassel, 1875), 2–3.
43. *Ibid.*, 282, 33.
44. *Ibid.*, 161 ff.

after his caravan had spent thirty-six days in the desert without finding a single waterhole. Thanks to the metal water containers carried by the expedition, there had been no losses, or even undue suffering. To that extent at least the expedition could boast of a record accomplishment. The return journey via the western oases to the Nile Valley proved uneventful.

This expedition seems to have been considered largely a failure by everyone but Rohlfs himself.[45] He claimed to have accomplished his main purposes by establishing the nonexistence of a rumored old Nile bed in the Western Desert and the limited extent of the depression area around Siwa. An interesting historical result was the corroboration of reports of direct trading connections between Wadai and Egypt via Dakhla, during the reign of the Wadai Sultan Salure (about 1810).[46] Kufra, on the other hand, had once again proved unattainable.

During the next several years Rohlfs was kept occupied writing and lecturing. A tour through the United States in the winter of 1875–76 provided new topics for popular articles. In September 1876 he attended, along with Nachtigal and Schweinfurth, King Léopold's Brussels conference, which led to the founding of the African International Association. Like everyone else, Rohlfs was taken in by the wily monarch: "The fact that in the midst of such turbulent times a conference could gather under the presidium of the generous King of the Belgians which determined to seek exclusively humanitarian purposes surely is one of the outstanding signs of our century." [47]

In a sense Rohlfs's last major journey resulted from this conference. The German section of the International Association offered him the leadership of an ambitiously conceived expedition, whose objectives were as grandiose as they were vague.[48] It was to explore "the whole eastern interior of North

45. See especially "Gerhard Rohlfs' Expedition in die Libysche Wüste," *Petermann's*, XX (1874), 178–185; *Ausland*, LI (1878), 81–85.

46. *Drei Monate*, 249–255, 337.

47. *Neue Beiträge*, 3; see also "Die Brüsseler Conferenz zur Erforschung und Regeneration Afrika's im Palais des Königs der Belgier Leopold II, 12–14 September 1876," *Petermann's*, XXII (1876), 388–393.

48. "Rohlfs' Projekt zur Erforschung der Östlichen Sahara," *Ausland*, LI (1878), 81–85; "Gerhard Rohlfs' neues Afrikanisches Forschungsunterneh-

Africa," filling out the map between the Mediterranean, Lake Chad, and the Nile. There were even hopes that it might penetrate to the sources of the Benue, the Shari, and the Ogooué! It was estimated that such a journey would take five years and that the required funds would run to 15,000 marks a year—a rather modest budget. Petermann, who considered Stanley a model explorer, urged a military escort of a hundred men, an idea which, fortunately for all concerned, was abandoned.

Despite the fact that the main objectives of the expedition lay in tropical Africa, Rohlfs insisted on following a desert route. He argued that connections with Europe could be more easily maintained across the Sahara than over any other route and that Tripoli was the traditional "German" base in Africa, since Hornemann, Barth, Overweg, Vogel, Beurmann, Nachtigal, and he himself had used it as a starting point. There was also the matter of transport. Pack animals could be used in the desert, and Rohlfs appreciated their advantages over human bearers. He was so unfamiliar with conditions in Equatorial Africa, however, that he proposed to use mules and donkeys in that area as well, considering "the fear of the bogeyman Tsetse" to be based on exaggeration. Further advantages of the northern route were the opportunity it offered for gradual acclimatization, and the degree of law and order prevailing in the Turkish sphere of influence.[49]

Preparations for the journey consumed most of the summer and autumn of 1878. From among the hundreds who volunteered to accompany him, Rohlfs chose Dr. Anton Stecker, a zoologist who was also able to handle astronomical instruments, and two assistants, Franz Eckart and Karl Hubmer. An Austrian aristocrat, Leopold von Czillagh, accompanied the expedition at his own expense as far as Socna. (He later died on the road from Ghudamis to Tripoli.) As he was about to leave Europe in October 1878 Rohlfs received news of the suicide of his long-time friend and patron, August Petermann, and delayed his departure to attend his funeral. In Paris he was

men," *Petermann's*, XXIV (1878), 20–22; *Kufra; Reise von Tripolis nach der Oase Kufra* (Leipzig, 1881), 5–7.
49. *Ibid.*, 8–10, 12–15.

greeted with suspicion. The press speculated about a "Prussian Trans-Saharan railroad project" from Tripoli to Lake Chad. The days when African exploration had been a nonpolitical, cosmopolitan concern were passing.[50]

Having brought camels and completed the last preparations, Rohlfs set out from Tripoli on 22 December 1878. The first few marches established the uselessness of the camel carts, which Rohlfs had designed for the expedition; they were so slow and cumbersome that they had to be abandoned. Other delays were caused by (unfounded) rumors of a threatened ambush, which caused the column to retrace its steps for a considerable distance and Rohlfs to request a Turkish military escort, and by delay in the arrival of the presents which the German Emperor was sending to the Sultan of Wadai. Traveling via Socna and Zella, the caravan eventually reached Aujila. Its reception was far more inhospitable than the one Rohlfs remembered from his visit ten years earlier. Religious intolerance had intensified—by now the oasis was entirely dominated by the Sanusi order—and there was a further reason for tension in commercial jealousy: the local caravan traders feared for their monopoly of trade with Wadai. Rohlfs's pet dog was poisoned, he himself had to draw his revolver on one occasion to protect himself from a mob intent on stoning him, and there was no question of finding a guide to Kufra. Eventually Stecker with most of the caravan was sent to Benghazi to obtain the assistance of Turkish authority, while Rohlfs, motivated largely by considerations of prestige, stayed in Aujila. (He managed with considerable cool-headedness and forbearance eventually to establish fairly tolerable relations with the inhabitants.) Even the Turkish governor, however, found it difficult to procure guides, and delays mounted. When it appeared that the expedition might not be able to get started for Kufra and Wadai before the autumn of the year (1879) Rohlfs resigned his leadership, stating that he had not planned to stay away from

50. *Ibid.*, 17–18, 37 ff. One application was received from a French musicologist, who endeavored to investigate "whether 'les extremes se touchaient,' i.e., to what extent there were similarities between Wagner's compositions and those of Negro masters." Rohlfs, an ardent Wagnerian, frowned on the suggestion.

Europe for more than two or three years and that the journey would now probably be more prolonged. He reconsidered when a contract was unexpectedly concluded with the shaykhs of the Suya tribe, by which they assumed the obligation to get the expedition safely to Kufra. On 5 July he was thus able to leave Benghazi, where he had gone to support Stecker's efforts.[51]

The methods used (in agreement with Rohlfs) by the Turkish authorities to compel the Suya to guide the expedition—the shaykhs were imprisoned until they agreed to go and hostages were held in Benghazi, under degrading conditions—were among the main reasons for the disastrous end of this enterprise. Another was the fact that Rohlfs apparently made no secret of the large amount of ready cash (in Maria Theresa thalers) which he carried.

After a record march from Gialo to Kufra (the waterless distance of about 275 miles was covered in five days) Rohlfs found, on reaching the oases, that he was kept prisoner in his camp, subject to threats, insults, and extortion, and prevented from communicating with Benghazi. Warned by a sympathetic local elder of a plan to kill him, he and the other Europeans fled to the latter's protection. The camp, however, was raided and looted that night, most of the equipment scattered or destroyed, and the money stolen. Caught between two factions in the oases, one of which wanted to kill him, while the other counseled caution—especially in view of the possibility of Turkish reprisals—Rohlfs was finally saved by the arrival of a messenger from Jughbub, the Sanusi headquarters in eastern Libya, who urged that the Europeans not be harmed. Accordingly, he and his companions were escorted safely back to Benghazi, but the expedition was ruined, with the partial description of Kufra as its only result.[52] (The Turkish government, under pressure from the German Foreign Office, and in accord with the usages of that punctilious era, eventually paid part of a 20,000 frs. damage claim to the German African Society, even though its responsibility for the fiasco was at best tenuous.)

51. *Ibid.*, 98, 101–115, 122–144, 206–240.
52. *Ibid.*, 260 ff.; *Quid Novi ex Africa?* (Cassel, 1886), 119–131; "Das Ende der Rohlfs'schen Expedition," *Globus*, XXXVI (1878), 346–347.

After the Kufra expedition Rohlfs, now forty-seven, had had enough. To his wife he wrote: "Now I crave rest and hope to find it. I have aged a great deal; this one year with its many emotions and cares has turned me grey. . . . I wouldn't again go through such days . . . for a fortune, and yet I am glad that I experienced them."[53]

If Rohlfs's career as an explorer was over, his connection with Africa was by no means at an end. He was hardly back from Kufra when Bismarck personally requested him to go to Ethiopia in a quasi-diplomatic capacity, to deliver the reply to a letter from the Emperor Yohannes IV, who had written William I, as well as other European monarchs, requesting mediation in Ethiopia's conflict with Egypt. Rohlfs was accompanied on this mission by two of his Kufra companions, Stecker and Hubmer. He liked Ethiopia somewhat better on this second visit, praising in particular the honesty of his servants and pointing out that the whole people could not be considered savage because of the deeds of Theodore and those who followed his commands.[54] In Yohannes he found a man after his own heart:

> I found in him quite a reasonable man. He doesn't want to suffer missionaries in Ethiopia? We, too, have expelled the Jesuits; he is master in his country, his will is law, one must obey the law. He prohibited smoking? With us, too, it was once prohibited, who could accuse him of anything there? He imposes cruel punishments on many occasions? In this he bases himself on the Old Testament![55]

Yohannes urged Rohlfs to enter his service and negotiate peace with Egypt; the traveler promised to do what he could. He did later urge the Egyptian government to conclude a peace, and corresponded on the matter with Colonel Charles George

53. Guenther, *Rohlfs*, 172.
54. *Meine Mission nach Abessinien* (Leipzig, 1883), 51; *Land und Volk*, 125.
55. *Mission*, 223–224. (The expulsion of the Jesuits to which Rohlfs refers was one of the anticlerical measures of Bismarck's *Kulturkampf*, of which Rohlfs, incidentally, approved enthusiastically.)

Gordon, who also felt that the Egyptians were in the wrong—but all to no avail. (In 1884, while Gordon was besieged in Khartoum, Rohlfs in a letter to *The Times* advocated a relief expedition from Ethiopia. A British committee approached him about assuming the leadership of such a force, but, on Bismarck's advice, he refused.)[56]

On the return trip from Debra Tabor, Rohlfs was much annoyed by the behavior of his Ethiopian military escort: "How I internally cursed this escort, which marched plundering through the land, causing misery and lamentations everywhere, trampling down the fields, ransacking the houses, and generally conducting itself with great arrogance."[57] The explorer made some scientific observations on this journey, established that the maps of Ethiopia produced by Wilhelm Schimper, a long-time German resident of the country, whose son acted as Rohlfs's interpreter, were based on "sheer fantasy," and cleared up some minor geographical misunderstandings. Nevertheless, this trip must be considered essentially a diplomatic mission, rather than an exploring journey.[58]

Through his connections, and driven by his now ardent interest in German colonization,[59] in 1884 Rohlfs became directly involved in the diplomacy of the Scramble for Africa. In May of that year Bismarck, who was still mystified as to the intentions of Léopold, urged the explorer to submit proposals to that monarch under which Germany would either buy out his enterprise, or at least receive most-favored-nation rights in the territories he had acquired. Some time later Rohlfs was offered the German consulate in Zanzibar. His brief career as a diplomat, which brought him into conflict with Sir John Kirk, his British counterpart, and the reasons for his sudden dismissal after less than half a year are no part of the concern of this essay, which

56. *Ibid.;* Guenther, *Rohlfs,* 260–262, 327–328. Rohlfs's letter, actually addressed to Charles H. Allen, Secretary to the British and Foreign Anti-Slavery Society, was printed in *The Times* (30 April 1884), 6e.

57. *Mission,* 248.

58. Aside from the full account in *Mission,* the journey is described in "Ergebnisse meiner Reise nach Abessinien," *Petermann's,* XXVIII (1882), 401–405; *Quid Novi,* 40–59; *Land und Volk,* 120 ff.

59. See, e.g., *Angra Pequena; die erste deutsche Kolonie in Afrika* (Bielefeld, 1884).

deals with Rohlfs as an explorer. Basically it was his brashness in pressing Germany's claims that got him into trouble; moreover, the career officials in the Foreign Office had mistrusted this outsider from the beginning. In Zanzibar, Rohlfs involved himself in the attempt by the brothers Gustav and Clemens Denhardt to establish a German colony in Witu. He acquired land claims there, but did not press them when Witu became British as a result of the Anglo-German treaty of 1890.[60]

Rohlfs was aggrieved by his sudden dismissal, and refused proffered consulships in Jerusalem, Messina, and Tangiers. Since the Foreign Office refused to establish a consulate in Tripoli, a post he would have been willing to take, Rohlfs never returned to government service, but spent the last eleven years of his life in comfortable semi-retirement, writing about and maintaining an active interest in African affairs. He was in contact with all of the major German African figures, including Count Joachim Pfeil, Carl Peters, Karl Jühlke, Adolf Lüderitz, and Wilhelm Junker. During the 1890's he established a friendship with Rudolf Said-Ruete, son of a Hamburg merchant and a Zanzibari princess, and made various unsuccessful efforts to assist him in obtaining a financial settlement from Sultan Barghash's successors. Failing gradually after 1894, Rohlfs died of a heart ailment in June 1896.[61]

In appraising Rohlfs's work and stature, and in attempting to analyze the reasons for his successes and failures as an explorer, we must look first to his more striking character traits for explanations. He was, for all his occasional surface gregariousness and his undoubted ability to get on with others, essentially a lonely man. A biographer remarks on this quality, and points to the absence of anyone who might be called a disciple of Rohlfs.[62] It is tempting to speculate that for him, as for other seekers of the desert, the fascination of the Sahara lay in its very quality of loneliness. Rohlfs's wanderlust, the quintessential urge to cut loose from familiar settings and

60. Guenther, *Rohlfs*, 327–328, 217–239.
61. *Ibid.*, 262–286, 344–352.
62. Viktor Hantzsch, "Gerhard Rohlfs," *Allgemeine Deutsche Biographie*, LIII (Leipzig, 1907).

seek the unknown, is very much part of this basic trait of his personality. Travel was an object in itself—the destination was secondary.

On his earlier journeys—his most "successful" ones—Rohlfs had only the most nebulous of objectives. He was extremely flexible about changing course in the face of obstacles: he was never to see Timbuktu, but he saw much else and brought it to the attention of Europe. In comparing him with other explorers we must contrast him with Stanley, or Rohlfs's compatriot Nachtigal, men who set themselves objectives and then single-mindedly pushed on to achieve them in the face of all difficulties and dangers. Rohlfs was more in the mold of Livingstone (whom he greatly admired), a wanderer, ranging almost aimlessly over the unknown, making discoveries rather than seeking them. Paradoxically, the one journey during which he stuck to a clear objective, and achieved it (the Kufra expedition), became his most signal failure. Another factor was involved here: on later journeys Rohlfs was no longer traveling alone, responsible only to and for himself, for his sponsors insisted upon clear objectives. He thus lost the advantages of complete flexibility, and on the whole was not particularly successful in carrying out these later expeditions.

A quality which served Rohlfs well, particularly on his earlier travels, was his ability to adjust to conditions—to do as the Romans, or the Africans, did. He was certainly not free of cultural arrogance, as his remarks about Islam especially attest, but he was able to curb his prejudices in practice. Thus, to support himself on his first and second journeys in Morocco and Algeria, he practiced indigenous medicine, relying heavily on amulets and such heroic treatments as hot irons, leeches, and Spanish fly (cantharides) compresses.[63] Even when not wearing indigenous dress he was generally punctilious in observing local customs, such as kissing the door posts of Ethiopian churches:

> Many people will consider this hypocritical, but I did it because of the experience I had gained on my travels that

63. *Reise durch Marokko*, 148.

one travels best when one assimilates as much as possible to the customs and usages of the peoples among whom one is sojourning. And if it is expected in a European church that everyone, even nonbelievers, uncover their heads on entering the house of God, no one can find anything remarkable in participating in a custom in Ethiopia which we consider unnecessary.[64]

It is fairly obvious from his works that Rohlfs was not particularly gifted as a linguist; nevertheless, he tried manfully to master local languages, and used them wherever possible.[65] He was courteous to local dignitaries and in his works acknowledges favors in much the same terms that would have been used of highly placed Europeans. In a material sense, too, Rohlfs assimilated, living off the country wherever possible. He carried only minimal food supplies, depending for the most part on local hospitality or purchase.

Yet, despite this ability to blend into the local background, Rohlfs, unlike some other African explorers, refused to become too deeply involved. In Tafilalt, for example, the Sultan's governor asked him whether he knew how to serve some old cannon, which no one there knew how to use. Old soldier Rohlfs denied any such ability: "I was careful not to get mixed up in their disputes."[66] This was a general policy.

By no means was he a pacifist. After his first two journeys he always traveled armed and did not hesitate to give practical demonstrations of the efficiency of modern weapons when he felt it called for. Thus, when the inhabitants of a Bornu village "showed an inclination to oppose forcefully our camping there . . . a few blind shots made them see reason." When the leader of a gang of outlaws in Mizdah offered to convey him safely to Ghudamis—for a consideration—Rohlfs demonstrated his Lefaucheux rifle and automatic carbine to him instead. For all that, he never found it necessary actually to fire at a human being. In the account of the trans-Saharan journey he pointed out that there was only one occasion when his life was

64. *Mission*, 303; cf. 304.
65. E.g., *Quer durch Afrika*, II, 84.
66. *Reise durch Marokko*, 78.

seriously threatened by Africans, and that resulted from a misunderstanding; a group of drunken villagers in northern Nigeria mistook Rohlfs and his companions for a Fulani raiding
party.[67]

The explorer was also well endowed with simple common
sense. Thus, while some of his medical opinions can only be
described as peculiar, he took an eminently reasonable view
on tropical clothing, attacking the insane custom of wearing
woollen underwear in equatorial climates, and denying roundly
that the tropics were unhealthy because of the climate per se;[68]
he also recognized that exposure of one's head to the sun need
not necessarily lead to fatal consequences. About food, he felt,
"one shouldn't be overly afraid . . . and should especially try
to become familiar with native food as soon as possible."[69]
The fact that Rohlfs survived twenty years of travel in Africa
in reasonably good health and that he lost not a single traveling
companion to disease on any of his journeys adds a good deal
of weight to these views, and must be considered a genuine
accomplishment in an age when so many travel accounts read
like collections of medical case histories and obituaries.

Rohlfs, unlike so many African explorers, managed to maintain harmony with and among the personnel of his expeditions.
He was careful in his choice, preferring, if possible, to travel
with servants he knew. Thus Hamid al-Tandjaui accompanied
him on three journeys, Muhammad Shtaui on two. On the
Kufra expedition he was joined by a son of Muhammad al-
Gatruni. Occasionally he used force to maintain discipline.
When one of the European assistants refused to carry out an
order during the Kufra expedition, "Rohlfs simply drew his
revolver and yelled at him that he would shoot him on the spot
if he didn't do as he was told." Apparently this was effective,
for Hubmer not only became one of the most dependable hands
on that expedition, but subsequently accompanied Rohlfs to
Ethiopia.[70] In the same manner he unhesitatingly beat Tandjaui over a missing franc piece, which he himself had mis-

67. *Quer durch Afrika,* II, 21; I, 45; II, 183–184.
68. "Soll man unter Tropen Wolle tragen," *Quid Novi,* 262–266, 248–250.
69. *Kufra,* 30, 33–34.
70. Guenther, *Rohlfs,* 142.

laid, but apologized later and praised Hamid for not carrying a grudge.

Rohlfs felt that the bickering and strained relations that had marred such expeditions as that of Denham-Clapperton-Oudney and Richardson-Barth-Overweg had largely been the result of a lack of a clear division of tasks. He felt that his experiences in the Libyan Desert, where he had led a large expedition, supported his approach:

> The leader of the expedition must possess an unquestioned authority over his companions, must be older than they, and it must be assured that all participants of the expedition are well educated. Precisely in this lies the great secret. Not every scholar is educated, and even less can it be said that every scholar is well brought up.

Overfamiliarity should be discouraged. Rohlfs agreed with Schweinfurth that the best method of avoiding bickering and petty disagreements was to talk as little as possible on the march. Servants were treated as such. During the Libyan Desert expedition they addressed Rohlfs and the scientific personnel by their titles and camped "with their African friends," while the leaders had their own tents.[71]

Rohlfs himself, in summing up what he considered the most important qualities of an African explorer, put self-knowledge at the head of the list, followed by an understanding of others, and patience. An explorer "must be able to bear all kinds of hardship, hunger and thirst, and even insult and abuse."[72] On the whole, he possessed these characteristics.

In the introduction to this chapter it was argued that the main importance of Gerhard Rohlfs lay in the influence he exercised as a prolific author and lecturer in shaping the views of Europeans, and of Germans in particular, toward Africa and its inhabitants. He himself, on the other hand, was also most thoroughly rooted in the *weltanschauung*, not to say prejudices, of the educated German middle class of the

71. *Kufra*, 21–22, 23.
72. *Quer durch Afrika*, I, 5–6.

late nineteenth century. It can safely be assumed that his success as a publicist was in considerable part attributable to this fact. He was an anticlerical positivist, convinced that history was progress, that progress was inevitably good, and that the Darwinian thesis applied to social as well as to biological categories. To a remarkable degree Rohlfs clung to these views throughout his life and refused to abandon prejudices inherent in them even in the face of contrary evidence—which occasionally makes him appear inconsistent.

Most striking among these prejudices was his thorough theoretical dislike (he got on well enough with them as individuals) of the people among whom he spent most of his years in Africa—the Arabs and Berbers of the north and the Sahara. He took every opportunity to denounce them in violent terms:

> How often have I shaken my head at the standard descriptions of the character of the Arabs, when there is talk about their generosity, their virtue of keeping their word, even with enemies, their liberality, their courage, and even their historical accomplishments. If only people would begin to judge a nation by its material and, even more importantly, by its intellectual productivity. The Arabs have always been parasites and will always remain so.
>
> Spain can be happy that she expelled the Semites in the past. True, she is not in the most splendid condition, but had she kept this appalling gang, she would be on a level with Morocco.[73]

The historical greatness of medieval Islamic civilization, in Rohlfs's view, was the product of non-Muslim populations living under Arab rule.

It was religion which had depraved the North Africans, not some inherent racial characteristic:

> Morocco has one of those despotic and tyrannical governments which are only to be found where the spiritual and secular power is united in the person of one man, and the

73. *Kufra*, 244–245.

cause of this absolute despotism is not in any way to be attributed to the character of the Arab and Berber peoples, but solely to the Muhammadan religion.[74]

Clinging to an outmoded religion, such peoples as the Arabs opposed progress and invited their own doom:

One cannot repeat often enough that some nations aren't capable of being civilized—simply because their own spiritual makeup doesn't permit civilization. Wouldn't we Europeans perhaps be in the same condition if by chance we hadn't liberated ourselves from a religion which was fitting for entirely different peoples, with different needs, in times long past. . . . But fortunately for us our Christianity today is no longer the Christianity of the first centuries; whoever desires that, let him go to Abyssinia, or visit the Copts or other people who have strictly clung to the laws of the Church, and let him see what has become of them.

Or again:

I don't mean . . . that they wouldn't be capable of civilization. They have the same talents, abilities, and feelings as we. But they don't want civilization, their religion doesn't permit it. And just for that reason they will disappear, for civilization cannot be halted, and the peoples that don't wish to march along will be absorbed or annihilated.[75]

To help along this process, Rohlfs felt that France should push the Muslim populations of Algeria back into the Sahara or forcefully amalgamate them, for example, by compelling them to wear European clothing and give up nomadism.[76] European control was inevitable and necessary to bring civili-

74. *Adventures*, 208.
75. "Leptis Magna," *Ausland*, XLII (1869), 476; *Von Tripolis nach Alexandrien*, 2–3.
76. *Land und Volk*, 4; "Largeau's zweite Expedition nach Rhadames und einige Worte über Algerien," *Petermann's*, XXII (1876), 250–253; "Si Sliman b. Hamsa und die Uled Sidi Schich," *Vom Fels zum Meer*, I (1881–82), 331–333.

zation to such countries as Morocco, unless they had the good fortune to find indigenous leaders "not afraid of blood and iron, men like Mahmud, or Mehmed Ali." [77] Rohlfs greatly admired the latter and his successors, especially Isma'il, for what they had done for the modernization of Egypt.[78] (In 1879, incidentally, Isma'il appealed to him to intercede on his behalf with Bismarck in an attempt to regain the throne of Egypt. Rohlfs agreed, but nothing came of the matter since Francesco Crispi, the Italian Foreign Minister, who had also been approached, failed to send an agreed-upon telegram.)[79] But on the whole, Rohlfs was skeptical about the ability of Muslim states to develop in the modern world without European intervention. Quite perceptively, he saw the main obstacles in the absence of a true nationalism, which was stifled by the universality of Islam, and of truly national dynasties identifying with the people. Eventually, he thus accepted the British occupation of Egypt as necessary.[80]

In Rohlfs's harangues against Islam, an anti-Christian, and especially anti-Catholic, bias is implicit as well: "The Muhammadan bonzes differ from the Christian zealots merely in that the latter send us to hell personally, while the former curse our elders and forefathers."[81] He considered it scandalous that "in the age of electricity and steam people could seriously discuss the infallibility of a man, the miracles of dead men, and the heresy of people who taught differently."[82]

Still, Christianity, even Catholicism, might be useful for some peoples at a certain stage of their development, for the educational work done by their missions, and even for their message:

> It is quite conceivable that [Catholicism] is more convincing for the Negro, at this time still at a lower stage of cul-

77. *Quid Novi*, 175.
78. *Mission*, 22, 30; "Ein Blick auf Ägypten," *Deutsche Rundschau*, VI (1876), 381–392; *Quid Novi*, 72–81.
79. Guenther, *Rohlfs*, 148–149.
80. *Quid Novi*, 157–158; "Die Lage in Ägypten," *Deutsche Rundschau*, XXXII (1882), 460–465.
81. *Quer durch Afrika*, I, 118.
82. *Quid Novi*, 24.

ture, than the evangelical devotion, which believes in abstracts. . . . The Catholic worship of pictures, after all, is basically so closely related to the fetishism of the Negroes that it would exercise a greater attraction, precisely for that reason.[83]

But missionaries should not go where they weren't wanted, Ethiopia, for instance, for

> the laws of a country, and not religious commands, must constitute the ultimate guideline for those who live in it. And if we in Europe consider the observance of the laws of our countries obligatory . . . we should fairly take account of this demand in other countries as well.[84]

Rohlfs's opinion of the North Africans, those "most abominable of all peoples,"[85] was largely determined by his religious or, rather, antireligious views. He was much fairer in his appraisal of black Africans. The advanced civilizations of the Western and Central Sudan impressed him as much as they had impressed his predecessors. Oddly, he managed to overlook the fact that they too were Islamic, or at any rate Islamized. Perhaps it was a matter of degree, just as Berbers were, to Rohlfs, better than Arabs because their Islam was more casual:

> Because Islam . . . has not been accepted by the Berbers to the same extent as by the Arabs, the former have maintained a far greater freedom and love of freedom, and because they have more sense for freedom they are . . . better than the Arabs. Enslaved peoples, no matter whether oppressed by alien force . . . or by an indigenous one, e.g., by their own government or priesthood, have always proved the worst and morally the lowest.[86]

83. *Land und Volk*, 57 (cf. 107; *Mission*, 124).
84. *Mission*, 114–115.
85. "Neueste Nachrichten aus dem Inneren Afrika's," *Petermann's*, XIII (1867), 46.
86. *Beiträge zur Entdeckung und Erforschung Afrikas* (Leipzig, 1876), 95.

The development of Rohlfs's views on the worth and future of Africa and Africans demonstrates strikingly how the imperialist fever, which was in his case at any rate in large part a direct product of his worship of progress and acceptance of Social Darwinism, could insidiously corrupt good judgment and even the evidence of a fair observer's own eyes. Rohlfs started as a remarkably open-minded observer, greatly impressed by Africa's civilization and its inhabitants' abilities, and as an explicit opponent of racism. His positivist belief in progress at any price made him an apologist and then an active advocate of imperialism, and eventually came close to making him a racist as well.

His journey through the Sudan and Nigeria had convinced Rohlfs of the Africans' capacity to build civilizations and share in the world's progress. He admired their accomplishments in statecraft, domestic architecture, and handicrafts, and their personal qualities of cleanliness and honesty. In all of these respects he considered the Western and Central Sudanese more advanced than North African populations.[87] If there were a gap between African and European cultures, its causes were the fault not of the Africans, but of geographical isolation and the slave trade, which he abominated. The Europeans, "by their manhunts through the years," were themselves largely responsible for the Africans' tendency to look with mistrust upon strangers and to isolate themselves.[88] The gap which existed must be closed gradually, and it was being closed: In Lagos, for example,

> Morality and civilization are increasing among the natives to a satisfying extent. If missionaries would act on the assumption that a people which has always been isolated from the culture of civilized nations can only with great difficulty be brought from a primitive level to the same standard of culture which it took us almost 2,000 years to reach, then they would proceed more slowly and apply more

87. See, e.g., *Quer durch Afrika*, II, 100, 131, 133, 212–213, 261; *Beiträge*, 42; "Gerhard Rohlfs' Reise durch Nordafrika," *Ausland*, XLII (1869), 173–174; *Land und Volk*, 47.
88. *Quer durch Afrika*, II, 249; *Neue Beiträge*, 82.

patience in their civilizing endeavor. If one looks at today's Negroes, especially the inhabitants of the great empires of Central Africa, and compares their condition with that of Europe 2,000 years ago (excepting, of course, Greeks and Romans), then any unprejudiced man will agree that the advantage is on the side of the blacks. The great realms of Bornu, Sokoto, Gwando, etc., give splendid testimony of the extent to which Negroes have been capable of civilizing themselves, and Gen. Faidherbe is certainly not wrong when he considers the blacks more receptive to civilization than Berbers or Arabs.[89]

Again, he pointed out that

the generalized view that the black population is not at all capable of civilization is very insufficiently based. To be sure, those who hold that view apparently base it mainly on the black population of America; but to draw conclusions about a whole race from a population oppressed by slavery for centuries is just as nonsensical and ridiculous as it would be to accuse the whole European family of political immaturity because the Greeks can neither bear nor use their freedom which they have only just regained.

As an example of "the Negroes' ability to educate themselves" he cited acquaintances in Lagos, an African businessman and his wife, who had once been a slave at the court of Dahomey and who was, when Rohlfs met her, "one of the most charming salon ladies of Lagos," who particularly delighted him by her ability as a pianist.[90]

Liberia, which to be sure he saw only from his ship, he considered "the most striking proof of the level of culture and civilization which the Negro can reach as soon as he is left alone administratively and supported by able missions." At

89. "Lagos an der Westküste von Afrika," *Ausland*, XLIII (1870), 487–488. Rohlfs refers to a conversation he had with Louis Léon César Faidherbe. The General expressed similar views in his *Le Sénégal* (Paris, 1889), esp. 36–45.
90. *Land und Volk*, 35–36.

Monrovia his vessel took on several passengers, including a number of young ladies going to England to "be finished."

> Needless to say (the English are much too bright to grasp in any way whatever the swindle of our armchair intellectuals who write endless and meaningless monographs about racial differences) there was perfect equality on board between black and white, and Herr Bull, which was the name of our black traveling companion, proved one of the most interesting and most genial fellow travelers.[91]

Rohlfs continued to reject the idea of basic biological differences between races. "The hypothesis that . . . we and the blacks are of the same descent will hardly be gainsaid by anyone in this day and age."[92] But his simplistic view of progress, which implied the total acceptance of all facets of European civilization by everyone—he was capable of seriously suggesting that Egypt should "abolish" the Arabic language and adopt Italian instead[93]—coupled with his Social Darwinism made him increasingly dubious about the future in store for Africa's people. He felt that they might not be able to make the jump from the early Iron Age into the nineteenth century that circumstances required of them. Therefore, they might eventually be absorbed by the Europeans, just as, in Rohlfs's view (the analogy is obviously not only shaky, but utterly fantastic, even if the facts had been right), the Fulani populations had been largely absorbed by the tribes among whom they lived. On the other hand, they might be "wiped out earlier by overly rapid methods of civilization," by which apparently he meant the massive imports of cheap gin. Rohlfs, in fact, believed that such a process was already underway and that the population of Africa had declined by 50 percent in the course of his century. As a Social Darwinist, he was no more concerned about this imaginary development than he was over the prospect of the total annihilation of Africa's elephants: "Since

---

91. *Land und Volk,* 51–53. The author is unable to identify Bull. Rohlfs may have used a pseudonym.

92. *Quid Novi,* 220–221.

93. "Ein Blick auf Ägypten," *Deutsche Rundschau,* VI (1876), 390.

the White Man, physically and intellectually, is the stronger, he will be the survivor in the Black Continent as well."[94]

To Rohlfs's honor it must be said that he did not translate such speculations into a recipe for a colonial policy. His basic good sense and humanity asserted itself in his writings on colonial policy, and in practice his colonialism was of the "white man's burden" variety. Especially in East Africa, whose populations were less advanced, Germany, he said, must "lead them to a better state, must ennoble them." To be sure, that might entail obligatory labor (Rohlfs's scheme called for a daily maximum of six hours of paid, government-supervised labor for natives between the ages of eighteen and thirty). On the other hand, he felt that white men going to Africa should do physical work themselves rather than expect to exploit African labor (his domestic political views were a curious mixture of Bismarck-worship and strong liberalism, even socialism), and that, above all, indigenous land rights should be respected in the German colonies:

> The East Africa Company, which by its treaties has acquired the sovereign rights and ownership of the country, would fall into a severe error if it believed itself to be the personal owner of the whole country. That would be as if, e.g., Germany when it reacquired Alsace-Lorraine thereby had also become the owner of the land in private hands. Everyone will admit that it is simply ridiculous to express such an idea.[95]

It is clear that Rohlfs had little knowledge of African systems of land tenure; he seems to have assumed that land in East Africa was in fact held as "private property," so that the colonial power simply had to fix and guarantee local titles.

In discussing the colonial policies of other European powers,

94. "Pfahlbauten der Neger in Centralafrika," *Globus*, XVIII (1870), 358–359; *Beiträge*, 63; "Über Reiz- und Nahrungsmittel afrikanischer Völker," *Ausland*, XLVI (1873), 297–299; "Die Verwendbarkeit des Elefanten zur Erforschung unbekannter Gegenden," *Petermann's*, XXXIV (1888), 140; *Quid Novi*, 222.

95. *Quid Novi*, 223–242, esp. 242.

Rohlfs emphasized his opposition to what he considered French Arabophilia and, similarly, to British policies in Nigeria which, he felt, unduly favored Islam.[96] On the whole, we find little of the spirit of colonial rivalry in his work, even though he was a tireless advocate of German colonization projects. (A favorite was a plan for the German colonization of the Cyrenaica, a plan which he several times attempted to submit to his government. It met a cool reception. Later he encouraged the notion of a Zionist colony there.)[97]

In general, Rohlfs favored any project for the colonization of any part of Africa by any European power[98]—not for the sake of permanent political domination, for he held that all colonies would sooner or later break with their mother countries and foresaw the day "when Great Britain will be confined to its two islands,"[99] but for the sake of progress. European influence would speed up the evolution of the other races, "and finally peoples of the most different characters [will] cooperate in the common tasks of civilization."[100]

Of the economic resources of Africa he had the sanguine expectations common among colonial enthusiasts of his age: he expected it soon to outstrip India as a source of wealth.[101] Perhaps that expectation, too, can be considered an expression of his all-embracing nineteenth-century optimism and belief in progress, which was so pronounced that it is at times almost a parody of itself. Even the climate was getting better: "Just as everything on earth improves, so does the climate and all conditions that affect the health of men." He believed that the Sahara was shrinking "and that in some centuries or millennia, if necessary [!], there won't be any more Sahara. Thus all is being prepared for man, and while fearful people are thinking about overpopulation of the world, nature itself prepares the soil where man . . . may later build his home."[102]

96. E.g., *Land und Volk*, 2, 4, 7; *Quer durch Afrika*, II, 234.
97. Guenther, *Rohlfs*, 256–259.
98. See, e.g., *Quid Novi*, V; "Übersicht von Gerhard Rohlfs' Reise durch Afrika 1866–1867," *Petermann's*, XIII (1867), 379.
99. *Land und Volk*, 4.
100. *Mission*, 180.
101. *Neue Beiträge*, 28.
102. "Die madagassische Gesandtschaft," *Deutsche Rundschau*, XXXVI

Of his fellow explorers, Rohlfs generally spoke well and evinced no jealousy. An exception in this regard was Stanley, whom he took to task for "achieving his successes and making his way with powder and lead," while making constant references to God and Christ in his travel account.[103] He particularly and warmly admired Livingstone, Barth, and Cameron.[104] Making a distinction between broad exploration, which required a generalist and something of an adventurer, and detailed investigation of territory, which was the province of specialist scientists, he realized by 1886 that the time of African exploration was over.[105]

Speaking of the continent as a whole, he was right of course. It was Rohlfs's misfortune, however, that in that part of Africa to which the vagaries of his early life had drawn him, and in which his main activity remained centered, the great age of exploration had actually ended earlier. Rohlfs there followed in the footsteps of such giants as Barth, Denham, Clapperton, and Caillié. The greatest geographical questions had been answered by others. On the other hand, Rohlfs came to Africa too early, and his means and capacities were too limited to qualify him as a scientific investigator.

The importance of Rohlfs to African history is not comparable to that of the bearers of the "fatal impact"—whether missionaries, traders, or mere explorers—who first made Africa aware of the world beyond and opened up the great avenues for further penetration. Nor did he come, like later travelers, as the agent of empire, representing the power that was to change the physical and political face of the continent. He was no Hermann von Wissmann, Louis Binger, or Harry Johnston. Rohlfs, to emphasize this point once more, was a loner, a wanderer through Africa, not, in any major way, an actor in the historical scene. His historical importance therefore must be sought almost wholly in his "discovery" of the Dark Continent for a vast reading public. In spite of occasional absurdities

(1883), 131; "Neueste Nachrichten aus dem Inneren Afrika's," *Petermann's*, XIII (1867), 43.

103. "Cameron's Afrika-Reise," *Ausland*, L (1877), 918–919.
104. *Ibid.; Kufra*, 1–2; *Quer durch Afrika*, I, 179.
105. *Neue Beiträge*, 12.

and inconsistencies, forgivable and perhaps unavoidable in a literary output of such dimensions, he enriched Europe's understanding of Africa, not least by his constant endeavor to demolish the clichés about the savagery of that continent. In some measure he thus facilitated the complex interaction between the civilizations of Africa and Europe, which, after all, was the main historical result of the age of African inland exploration. In addition, Rohlfs's contributions to Europe's geographical knowledge, especially when measured against the very modest means with which they were achieved, were far from negligible. For these reasons, and to that extent, the high regard in which Gerhard Rohlfs was held by his contemporaries was justified.[106] For these reasons also, this attractive figure today deserves to be rescued from oblivion.

106. See, e.g., the obituary by Georg Schweinfurth, *Westermann's*, LXXXII (1897), 565–568.

Henry Morton Stanley:
The Opening Up of the Congo Basin

by Eric Halladay

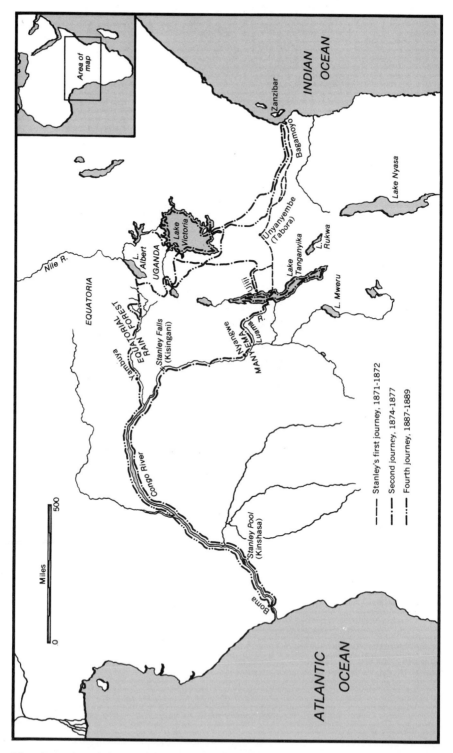

The three journeys of Henry Morton Stanley

H. M. Stanley was and still remains a figure of controversy. Doubts have been cast[1] on his own vivid account of his childhood and youth.[2] His death was the occasion for a disagreeable squabble when the Dean of Westminster exercised his right to refuse the expected burial in the Abbey. The arguments have continued ever since.

Stanley's early life as an abandoned orphan, the fearful regime in the St. Asaph (Wales) workhouse, and, ultimately, a new independence and the beginnings of self-respect under his foster-father in the United States left a marked impression on his personality and character. After managing to fight on both sides during the American Civil War—perhaps the only time in his life when he was as a result completely impartial —he became a journalist. In 1871 the *New York Herald* sent him on the mission to find Livingstone. His initial reaction to tropical Africa was unfavorable. "I do not think I was made for an African explorer," he wrote, "for I detest the land most heartily."[3] Yet Stanley was to make three more important journeys. In 1874 he set off on an expedition that took him across the continent from east to west and ended in 1877; between 1879 and 1885 he worked in the Congo for Léopold II's International African Association; and between 1887 and 1889 he commanded the Emin Pasha Relief Expedition.

A recent essay ranks Stanley with Livingstone as one "of the two greatest of African explorers."[4] And yet, if he were, it was almost in spite of himself. He was unable completely to lose that initial hostile attitude to the continent. Stanley never really savored the essence of Africa in the sense that Livingstone did. He was as much proving himself as he was exploring

1. Jack Simmons, *Livingstone and Africa* (London, 1955), 140.
2. Dorothy, Lady Stanley (ed.), *The Autobiography of Sir Henry Morton Stanley* (London, 1909), part I, 3–215.
3. Frank Hird, *H. M. Stanley: The Authorized Life* (London, 1935), 94.
4. J. H. Plumb, *Men and Places* (London, 1966), 219.

Africa. Restless, energetic, dissatisfied, he wrote after one of his expeditions: "When a man returns home and finds for the moment nothing to struggle against, the vast resolve, which has sustained him through a long and difficult enterprise, dies away, burning as it sinks in the heart; and then the greatest successes are often accompanied by a peculiar melancholy." [5]

The reservations that many people expressed about Stanley during his lifetime contributed further to this attitude. Criticism and distrust of his motives mingled with strictures on his methods. Savorgnan de Brazza, his rival in the Congo between 1881 and 1882, spoke disparagingly if perhaps a little complacently of the way Stanley conducted his expeditions. "I never was in the habit of travelling on African soil in martial array like Mr. Stanley, always accompanied by a legion of armed men, and I never needed to resort to barter, because, travelling as a friend and not as a conqueror, I everywhere found hospitable people. Mr. Stanley had adopted the practice of making himself respected by dint of gunfire; I myself travelled as a friend and not as a belligerent." [6]

Brazza had his own special axe to grind, but he reflected accurately the kind of criticism that was leveled at Stanley. Reports of his cruelty and unsympathetic attitude toward Africans were grist to the mills of those who had distrusted him ever since the Livingstone expedition. They objected to the "parvenu" American journalist-turned-adventurer who seemed to have "appropriated Livingstone and the credit of befriending him." [7] There was as a result a degree of prejudice against Stanley that he himself never fully understood. [8] The young Frederick D. (later Lord) Lugard, for example, refused the invitation of George S. Mackenzie, a director of the Imperial British East Africa Company, to meet Stanley after the Emin Pasha expedition. "Between ourselves," he wrote to his half-sister, "I did not care greatly about meeting Stanley. Letters of his that I had seen had made me disinclined to fall

5. Stanley, *Autobiography*, 536.
6. Albert Maurice (ed.), *H. M. Stanley: Unpublished Letters* (London, 1957), 152.
7. Reginald Coupland, *Livingstone's Last Journey* (London, 1945), 182.
8. Hird, *Stanley*, 177.

down and worship him, so I went up country again . . . and did not wait for him."[9] A few years earlier, Richard Burton, after reading Stanley's account of his punishment of the natives of Bumbire Island on Lake Victoria, wrote indignantly to Sir John Kirk: "Of course you have seen Stanley who still shoots negroes as if they were monkeys. That young man will be getting into a row—and serve him right."[10]

There was some justification for the way Burton wrote. There were times when Stanley had only himself to blame for the rough treatment that he received. Léopold once asked despairingly (and possibly anxiously in case too many secrets were revealed), "What can be done to make Stanley keep quiet?"[11] The answer was nothing at all. In his speeches and writings Stanley could be blunt and honest to the point of insensitivity. But what was good for the *New York Herald* was not necessarily good for Stanley.

This outspoken approach was doubly unfortunate in that it came at a time when many in Britain, in the United States, and on the European continent were more interested in and better informed about Africa than at any time during the nineteenth century. To some extent Stanley himself had contributed to this awareness. The dramatic meeting with Livingstone at Ujiji, followed in 1877 by Livingstone's death, quickened interest in central Africa. "The work of England for Africa," wrote Livingstone's obituarist in the *Daily Telegraph*, "must henceforward begin in earnest where Livingstone left it off."[12] It was this attitude, the obverse of the strident jingoism associated with the period, that gave meaning to the idea

9. Margery Perham, *Lugard, The Years of Adventure, 1858–1898* (London, 1956), 177.

10. Reginald Coupland, *The Exploitation of East Africa, 1856–1890* (London, 1939), 327. During his journey by boat down the western shores of Lake Victoria in late 1875, Stanley's attempt to obtain supplies from the inhabitants of Bumbire Island involved him in a fierce and almost disastrous fight. On his return to Uganda the following June, Stanley attacked the islanders, inflicting heavy casualties. The incident is the most noteworthy example of the ruthlessness toward African tribes that hindered Stanley's progress. (H. M. Stanley, *Through the Dark Continent* [London, 1899], I, 179–186, 212–230).

11. Maurice, *Unpublished Letters*, 151.

12. H. M. Stanley, *How I Found Livingstone* (London, 1913), lxxviii.

of "the white man's burden." It demanded not just new avenues of approach into Africa but also a sense of responsibility and justice in those entrusted with the task. Those associated with Exeter Hall and the Aborigines' Protection Society were the self-appointed guardians in this matter, and too often Stanley's methods failed to satisfy their standards. He could hardly expect a sympathetic hearing when he jocularly threatened to give Exeter Hall "seven tons of Bibles, four tons of Prayer Books, any number of surplices, and a church organ into the bargain" if they could reach longitude 23°, "without chucking some of those Bibles at some of the negroes' heads." [13] It was typical of Stanley to misread the point of view of his critics in this way and to fail to understand the climate of opinion at home. But, however heavy-handed and misplaced the humor, it indicated his fierce distrust of those in Europe who failed to appreciate what he took to be the realities of the African scene.

Stanley was quite uncompromising in his belief that in Africa his methods were best. Before setting out on the Livingstone expedition, he had carefully read as many relevant books as he could find, especially those of Burton, Speke, and Grant. His admiration for them was tempered by some criticism.[14] The same was true of his attitude toward Livingstone in spite of the devotion and reverence he felt toward him. They had had their disagreements, especially on Lake Tanganyika, where Livingstone had on more than one occasion to prevent Stanley from firing at some threatening Africans. Stanley was prepared, however, to defend his own point of view. "I wish to harm no one," he wrote, "quite as little as the Doctor; the wish to do them good is just as spontaneous in me as it is in him; but where we differ is, that whereas every instinct is prompt in me to resent evil, or a deadly menace, he appears indifferent almost to carelessness." [15] He further criticized Livingstone because "the natives took advantage of his weaknesses, and tyrannised over him at every point." [16] Stanley drew his own

13. H. R. Fox Bourne, *The Other Side of the Emin Pasha Relief Expedition* (London, 1891), 19.

14. Stanley, *Livingstone*, 20–21.

15. Hird, *Stanley*, 97.

16. Stanley, *Autobiography*, 268.

conclusions. "My methods, however, will not be Livingstone's. Each man has his own way. His, I think, had its defects, though the old man, personally, has been almost Christ-like for goodness, patience, and self-sacrifice. The selfish and wooden-headed world requires mastering, as well as loving charity." [17]

This remained Stanley's basic philosophy. It did not however imply unbridled ruthlessness, and he continued on more than one occasion to refer wistfully to "the gentle-souled Livingstone." [18] Even while he had been in his company, he had noted with some envy the contrast between himself and the older man. He wrote that, "to men differently constituted, a long residence amongst the savages of Africa would be contemplated with horror, yet Livingstone's mind can find pleasure and food for philosophic studies." [19]

Their differences, however, were more than those of personality. Stanley was subject to a number of embarrassments that no previous explorer in Africa had experienced. Basic to these was the extent of his financial backing, greater than that enjoyed by any of his predecessors. For the Livingstone expedition, James Gordon Bennett, the editor of the *New York Herald*, told Stanley to "draw a thousand pounds now; and when you have gone through that, draw another thousand, and when that is spent, draw another thousand, and so on." [20] The tycoonery of the *Herald* was tempered on the second journey by the respectability of the *Daily Telegraph*, but the outcome financially was much the same. When Stanley returned to the Congo in 1879, £20,000 was put at his disposal for immediate use and beyond this he could draw upon the private fortune of Léopold II. The total receipts of the Emin Pasha Relief Fund were over £33,000, of which Stanley spent nearly £28,000. [21]

The extent of Stanley's financial thralldom placed him under

17. *Ibid.*, 295.

18. Richard Stanley and Alan Neame (eds.), *The Exploration Diaries of H. M. Stanley* (London, 1961), 125; Stanley, *The Dark Continent*, II, 167–168.

19. Stanley, *Livingstone*, 357.

20. *Ibid.*, 2–3.

21. H. M. Stanley, *The Congo and the Founding of Its Free State* (London, 1885), I, 26–27; H. M. Stanley, *In Darkest Africa* (London, 1890), II, 461–462.

a special obligation to his employers to complete his various missions with the utmost dispatch. "Livingstone trudged across Africa," wrote Coupland, "Stanley strode." [22] Even as a newcomer to African exploration in 1871, there was a sense of urgency about his conduct. During a period of peculiarly bad rains, he was able to reach Unyanyembe in four months, a journey that had occupied Burton and Speke a month longer under far better conditions. This same drive characterized the march across Africa and the Emin Pasha expedition. The many hazards and frustrations that he encountered merely served to increase his impatience. Only during the years that he spent in the Congo basin on behalf of Léopold II did he refuse to be pressed. Significantly, in that case Stanley's obstinacy was largely due to his belief that speed would not serve the best interest of the venture. "If my mission simply consisted of marching for Stanley Pool," he wrote to Maximilian Strauch, "I might reach it in fifteen days, but what would be the benefit of it for the expedition and the mission that I have undertaken." [23]

Another result of the funds at his disposal was the sheer size of Stanley's expeditions, far larger than any previously seen in Africa. Livingstone in 1852 had set out with 27 men, and in 1866 with 60. Stanley's parties were far less modest: 804 men embarked from Zanzibar on the Emin Pasha Relief Expedition, a figure that dwarfed the 356 who had set out with Stanley in 1874. The size of the other expeditions was smaller but still significantly larger than those of other African explorers. [24]

The massive scale of his ventures and the need for urgency, both directly attributable to the financial backing he received, are fundamental to an understanding of Stanley's role in Africa. These were objective facts that he could not shirk, but by themselves they do not go quite far enough as an explanation of his conduct. To them must be added the virtues and

22. Coupland, *Livingstone*, 159.
23. Stanley to Colonel Maximilian Strauch, 6 February 1880, in Maurice, *Unpublished Letters*, 34.
24. Stanley left Bagamoyo to search for Livingstone in March 1871 with a party of 187.

blemishes of his own character. "I have a most anxious temperament," he wrote with more truth than grammar, "it is to my interests that things should go on right and proper." [25] When they frequently did not, Stanley was capable of a ruthlessness the sole redeeming feature of which was the honesty with which he wrote about it.

The preparation and conduct of expeditions of this kind demanded an organizing ability of the highest order. Stanley would have subscribed to the view that good leadership is in part close attention to detail. He devoted a whole chapter in *How I Found Livingstone in Central Africa* to the question of preparing for a journey to Africa, annoyed that he had found no such similar guidance in the writings of other explorers or from the white residents of Zanzibar. [26] He found the whole problem "a most sobering employment. . . . You are constantly engaged, mind and body; now in casting up accounts, and now travelling to and fro hurriedly to receive messengers, inspecting purchases, bargaining with keen-eyed relentless Hindi merchants, writing memoranda, haggling over extortionate prices, packing up a multitude of small utilities, pondering upon your list of articles, wanted, purchased, and unpurchased." [27] He found the Arab merchants invariably helpful in providing him with information. It was from them that he learned of the preferences of the various tribes of East Africa for different kinds of cloth, beads, and wire that were used as currency—the legacy of years of Arab trading. Stanley's account of the rough turmoil of Zanzibar during the preparation of an expedition suggests not so much frustration as the eager anticipation of a man doing something that he enjoyed. The apprenticeship that he had served in the office of the New Orleans shipping merchant and of his foster-father stood him in good stead.

Collecting material together in quantities great enough to cover every eventuality posed its own problems. "I confess I was rather abashed at my own temerity," he wrote before leav-

25. Stanley to Strauch, 7 April 1882, in Maurice, *Unpublished Letters*, 119.
26. Stanley, *Livingstone*, 20–21.
27. Stanley, *The Dark Continent*, I, 43.

ing Zanzibar to look for Livingstone, "there was at least six tons of material. 'How will it be possible,' I thought, 'to move all this inert mass across the wilderness stretching between the sea and the great lakes of Africa?' Bah, cast all doubts away, man, and have at them! Sufficient for the day is the evil thereof, without borrowing from the morrow!" [28] Stanley was quickly to find the truth of these pompous if brave platitudes.

Although he took a few horses and donkeys with him, Stanley, like all other African explorers of his day, relied in the main on porters recruited from Zanzibar and the east coast. He was fortunate when organizing the Livingstone journey to find some volunteers who had already served under Europeans.[29] In 1874, a number of Zanzibaris from that expedition volunteered to accompany him again. It was from among these men that he chose his leaders or chiefs as well as his own armed escort. Stanley took great pains in the selection of these men since the success or failure of a journey largely depended upon them. They were as a result contracted at higher rates of pay and Stanley took special precautions to win their confidence. He was also careful to explain the exact purpose of his mission and the likely tribal areas through which they might pass.[30]

As far as he could, Stanley arranged for all members of his party to agree to a special contract. In 1874 this was done before the American Consul at Zanzibar. The terms of the 1874 contract were quite specific. In the presence of their relatives, the porters were given an advance of four months' wages and ration money from the day that they had enlisted. In return, they promised "to serve for two years, or until such time as their services should be no longer required in Africa, and were to perform their duties cheerfully and promptly." Stanley for his part agreed to treat them kindly, to administer medicines, to arrange proper care with local tribes for any unable to proceed through illness, to judge impartially between them in

28. Stanley, *Livingstone*, 31.

29. *Ibid.*, 26–30. Among these volunteers were Uledi, who had served as personal servant to Grant, and five who had been porters under both Burton and Speke. Of the latter, the most colorful and determined was Seedy Mbarak Mombay, known by Stanley as Bombay.

30. *Ibid.*, 26–29; *The Dark Continent*, I, 44–46.

disputes, and to protect them against attack.[31] He did not regard these contracts lightly. On his return to Zanzibar from the 1874–1877 expedition, he paid in full to their relatives the wages of those porters who had died or been killed.[32] He was indignant in 1882 when one of his German assistants tried to stretch the contract of some of the Zanzibaris to make them stay longer in the Congo. "When their time is up," Stanley told him, "they must be allowed to depart with all kindness and courtesy. Whatever is good for their comfort must be done, but no attempt civilly or otherwise must be made to impede their departure."[33]

Stanley himself was often forced to break his side of the bargain but only because he felt that the porters were incapable of keeping theirs. Writing of some of the disasters of the Emin Pasha venture, he observed "that almost every fatal accident hitherto in this Expedition has been the consequence of a breach of promise. How to adhere to a promise seems to me to be the most difficult of all tasks for every 999,999 men out of every million whom I meet. I confess that these black people who broke their promises so wantonly were the bane of my life, and the cause of much mental disquietude, and that I condemned them in their own hearing as supremest idiots."[34]

The organization of any expedition into the African interior normally meant a flood of applicants from the Zanzibaris. In Stanley's case the situation was aggravated both by the large size of his expeditions and by the experience of those who had served on his first journey, since they had "returned to their homes to enjoy the liberal pay awarded them, feeling rather the better for the trip than otherwise." He claimed that in 1874, "almost all the cripples, the palsied, the consumptive, and the superannuated that Zanzibar could furnish applied to be enrolled on the muster list." More serious, "hard upon their heels came all the rogues, rowdies and ruffians of the island, and these, schooled by their fellows, were not so easy to detect."[35]

31. Stanley, *The Dark Continent,* I, 51–52.
32. Stanley, *Autobiography,* 331.
32. Stanley to O. Lindner, 13 February 1882, in Maurice, *Unpublished Letters,* 100.
34. Stanley, *Darkest Africa,* II, 21.
35. Stanley, *The Dark Continent,* I, 43–44.

Recruitment then was a far from easy task and it laid Stanley open to the damaging charge that he deliberately recruited slaves whose Arab owners received the wages.[36] In the 1874 expedition, he admitted that, in spite of close scrutiny, "many were engaged of whose character I had not the least conception until, months afterwards, I learned from their quarrels in the camp how I had been misled by clever rogues."[37] Henry Richard Fox Bourne, who first laid the complaint against Stanley that he had enrolled slaves, was nearer the truth over the Emin Pasha expedition. The porters in Zanzibar were recruited by an agent, George S. Mackenzie, but not only did he have to find them in far larger numbers than ever before but he had to do so quickly. Stanley was far from happy about the result and admitted after he had been some time in the Congo that "I was of the opinion that only about 150 were free men, and that all the remainder were either slaves or convicts."[38] It was probably inevitable in such a large organization that a proportion of the porters should be men whose credentials were suspect.

Stanley defended himself against the charge that the recruitment of slaves was deliberate. He pointed out that each of his porters had to declare in front of two witnesses that he was a free man, but in spite of this precaution, he agreed that a few slaves did slip in. He managed, however, to convince himself that, "since they had been able to earn their own living, their slavery had been merely nominal, and all their earnings were their own to do what they liked with, and their owners never saw them except when, at the end of Ramadan, they called to pay their respects."[39]

The presence of so many unreliable men necessarily affected

36. Fox Bourne, *Emin Pasha,* 49.
37. Stanley, *The Dark Continent,* I, 44.
38. Stanley, *Darkest Africa,* I, 65, 93.
39. Stanley, *Autobiography,* 421. About this particular matter Stanley may well have been guilty of special pleading or of an exaggerated generalization. The evidence of at least one slave, Rashid bin Hassani, would suggest that slaveowners were not always as generous or as disinterested as he suggests. According to Rashid, an owner would normally demand at least half of the payments made to a slave who had acted as porter to a European (Margery Perham [ed.], *Ten Africans* [London, 1963], 103).

Stanley's conduct of operations. As a consequence, much of his time was spent teaching "the novel lesson of obedience." He recognized that others had faced this same problem, but he felt, for example, that, "to the faithlessness of his people may be attributed principally the long wanderings of poor Livingstone." Stanley wished to avoid this kind of experience. The answer, he thought, lay in having a systematic routine, "the true prophylactic against failure." [40] Whenever possible, each march en route was to be made during the early hours between 6 and 11 A.M. This meant that it could be completed before the hottest part of the day, allowing time in hostile areas for a defensive stockade or "boma" to be built where there were no abandoned native villages. Each porter knew his place in the column and exactly what he had to carry, the weights varying between sixty and seventy pounds. Stanley contrasted "the feeling one possesses after a good journey briefly accomplished" with the weariness and irritability after a disorganized march.[41] In particular, he emphasized the advantages of such a routine for a large-scale expedition if the recalcitrant members could be controlled and disciplined. "The day ends happily for all," he wrote, "and the morrow's journey has no horrors for us." [42]

Inevitably, plans of this kind could easily be ruined. The early part of any journey was always the most difficult as far as discipline was concerned. "For the first few months," Stanley suggested, "forbearance is absolutely necessary. The dark brother, wild as a colt, chafing, restless, ferociously impulsive, superstitiously timid, liable to furious demonstrations, suspicious and unreasonable, must be forgiven seventy times seven, until the period of probation is passed." [43] Desertion at this stage was a frequent occurrence and remained so as long as an expedition was near Zanzibar and the coast or was in the proximity of Arab trading depots and caravans. It was partly to avoid this problem that Stanley decided against the

40. Stanley, *The Dark Continent*, I, 51–56.
41. Stanley, *Livingstone*, 32; *The Congo and Its Free State*, I, 46, II, 314; *Darkest Africa*, I, 148.
42. *Ibid.*, 84–85.
43. Stanley, *The Dark Continent*, I, 56.

east coast route in 1887, although he could not prevent a serious fight between his porters on the ship taking them to the Congo. Stanley wasted valuable time searching for deserters, and lost a considerable amount of costly equipment that they stole.[44] Almost as serious were the false rumors that such men circulated about Stanley's plight. These were intended to justify their abandonment of the expedition but, in the case of the Emin Pasha expedition, they increased the anxiety of the already depressed rear-column at Yambuya.[45] The disintegrating effects that deserters could have on an expedition had been emphasized for Stanley by what he took to be Livingstone's mildness in dealing with this problem. He claimed that "Livingstone lost at least six years of time, and finally his life, by permitting his people to desert." He agreed, however, that "over-severity is as bad as over-gentleness in dealing with these men. What is required is pure, simple justice between man and man."[46]

Discipline was made more difficult to maintain by loss of life through fighting and disease and by the shortage of supplies. The death of some members of an expedition did not mean automatic compensation in the form of increased rations for those who were left. On the contrary, during the voyage down the Lualaba and Congo rivers and the treks through the rain forest, lack of food was a major source of unrest. "Rigid discipline, daily burdens, and endless marching into regions of which they were perfectly ignorant, never seemed to gall our men when their stomachs were pampered, and abundant provender for their digestive organs were provided; but even hanging unto death was only a temporary damper to their inclination to excessive mischief when pinched with hunger."[47] It is difficult to believe, as Lugard reported, that in

44. Stanley, *Darkest Africa*, I, 45, 72–73; *The Dark Continent*, I, 86–87, II, 52. The problem of deserters was not the only reason why Stanley decided not to use the east coast route in 1887. He was at that time still an agent of Léopold II, who was very anxious that the relief expedition should proceed via the Congo (Roger T. Anstey, *Britain and the Congo in the Nineteenth Century* [Oxford, 1962], 219–224).
45. Stanley, *Darkest Africa*, I, 154.
46. Stanley, *The Dark Continent*, II, 52.
47. Stanley, *Darkest Africa*, I, 256.

such circumstances Stanley would issue some of his men with a few rounds and tell them to loot. On one occasion on the lower Congo he did threaten an obstinate chief with the possibility that his men might turn cannibal and consume the chief's tribe! This is just the kind of incident which the more ignorant of his porters might have misunderstood and embellished in years to come.[48] Nor was Stanley unwilling to occupy villages from which the inhabitants had fled and to encourage his men to collect what they could from the fields round about. "It seemed to me an excellent arrangement," he commented somewhat complacently, "it saved trouble of speech, exerted possibly in useless efforts for peace and tedious chatter. They had only one night's inconvenience."[49] But a policy of indiscriminate looting conflicts absolutely with Stanley's concept of the conduct of an expedition. He realized that it was not only prejudicial to the discipline which he was attempting to maintain, but, much worse, would irritate the local tribes unnecessarily. There were times when compulsory requisition of supplies was unavoidable. But the evidence of Emin Pasha's lieutenant, Gaetano Casati, a witness normally hostile to Stanley, indicates that in such circumstances attempts were made to keep the situation under control. "In these raids," Casati wrote, "Stanley strictly forbade the use of violence, maltreatment of the natives, and the stealing of bullocks and goats; corn, ban[an]as, beans, tobacco, and poultry were the only kind of food they were permitted to take."[50]

Stanley's view of punishment for offenses was far from straightforward. The size of his expeditions meant that he had to coax and coerce in a manner that at times invited criticism. He never, however, made any attempt to hide the truth on this matter, and he was indignant at his critics. "An unreflecting spectator," he wrote, "hovering near our line of march might think we were unnecessarily cruel, but the application of a few cuts to the confirmed stragglers secures eighteen hours' rest to about 800 men and their officers."[51] Thomas

48. Perham, *Lugard*, 282; Stanley, *The Dark Continent*, II, 349.
49. Stanley, *Darkest Africa*, I, 148.
50. Gaetano Casati, *Ten Years in Equatoria* (London, 1891), II, 255.
51. Stanley, *Darkest Africa*, I, 85.

H. Parke, the surgeon on the Emin Pasha expedition, defended Stanley's conduct, with a similar argument. "To say that he was needlessly cruel or tyrannical is absolutely untrue: the beatings inflicted on the carriers which have furnished so much material for comment to the Aborigines' Protection Society . . . were only such as were absolutely necessary to maintain the discipline on which the very existence of the Expedition, and its officers, depended." [52] Stanley later confessed that he disliked the whip and preferred irons, a method of punishment he had devised during the Livingstone expedition. The whip, he felt, "wounds, disfigures and renders disgusting the very person in whom you wish to plant self-respect, and invest with a certain dignity, and for whom you desire to entertain a certain degree of liking—if anything is disgusting—you cannot like it." He added, practically, that overuse of the whip also added to the sick list. He preferred therefore to put persistent offenders in chains, a punishment normally only applied while the column was at rest. [53]

In desperate circumstances Stanley was prepared to go further and to threaten and use hanging. As with other punishments, he always set up some form of court-martial in which the chiefs and defendant's companions acted as jury. [54] It is possible to detect some uneasiness in Stanley's mind about this question of execution. He had no qualms about turning hangings as well as floggings into public spectacles. Their intention was as much to impress as to punish. But the fact remains that, of the five men whom he sentenced to be hanged during his African journeys, three—one a murderer, and two deserters—were subsequently released. [55]

Necessary as discipline and punishment were, Stanley found "it terrible trouble to take charge of so many people totally innocent of anything approaching to manliness. . . . It is one protracted torture, chest aches with violent shouting and up-

52. Thomas Heazle Parke, *My Personal Experiences in Equatorial Africa* (London, 1891), 513.
53. Stanley to Strauch, 12 June 1881, in Maurice, *Unpublished Letters,* 49–50.
54. Stanley, *Livingstone,* 95.
55. Stanley, *Darkest Africa,* I, 201–206, 209, II, 197–198.

braiding them for their foolish cowardice, voice becomes hoarse with giving orders which in a few seconds are entirely forgotten." He went on, "They are terribly dull people to lead across Africa. . . . It took me nearly two years to teach my boatman how to row a boat and to take charge of her. After two years' practice, one fellow, Muscati, loaded his gun with paper and a bullet and was surprised that his gun did not fire." [56]

As hard a taskmaster as Stanley was, these strictures hide a note of tenderness and admiration that he genuinely felt for a large number of his followers. "However stupid they were," he wrote, "I could not help forgiving and forgetting." [57] By the second half of a journey, Stanley's coaxing and the dangers that they all had to face had produced the necessary changes. [58] When he came to leave those remaining after the 1874–1877 expedition, the tribute he paid them was heartfelt: "For me, too, they are heroes, these poor ignorant children of Africa for, from the first deadly struggle in savage Ituru to the last staggering rush into Embomma, they had rallied to my voice like veterans, and in the hour of need they had never failed me." [59]

A revealing parallel can be drawn between Stanley's treatment of his African followers and his attitude to the Europeans who accompanied him. Herbert Ward, one of the survivors of the rear-column, wrote: "The explorer, I knew, was a practical man, who leant more towards action than words. With him there could be no more powerful or persuasive argument than proof of energy and ready adaptability." [60]

There were times when Stanley's assistants could regard this attitude with an ironic detachment. A Belgian officer in the Congo wrote to his parents in 1881 to say that he was ill, but continued, "Mr. Stanley had taken great care of me during these bad days. He brought to bear the sort of care a blacksmith applies to repair an implement that is most essential

56. Stanley and Neame, *Exploration Diaries,* 146.
57. Stanley, *Autobiography,* 348.
58. Stanley, *Livingstone,* 529.
59. Stanley, *The Dark Continent,* II, 373–374.
60. Herbert Ward, *My Life with Stanley's Rear Guard* (London, 1890), 3–4.

and that has broken down through too rough usage, and he is in dread of losing."[61] Others found service under Stanley a good deal more difficult. This was especially the case in the Emin Pasha expedition when a number of his assistants found his behavior extraordinary as they moved up the Congo, felt they had been abandoned with the rear-column at Yambuya, and objected to his apparent refusal to treat them like the officers and gentlemen they in fact were.[62]

Stanley's distrust of his European companions was occasioned largely by the failure of some of those sent out to help in the Congo between 1879 and 1885. In particular he disliked those who "were continually at the military pose,"[63] and "whose dignity is so measureless that it chills the native onlooker on coming within its presence."[64]

The fact remains that, as long as these assistants played their part fully and efficiently, they could be assured of Stanley's respect. "It is solely a question of capacity and industry,"[65] he wrote, but his methods of gaining their cooperation were not always effective. He recognized that the tension of an African journey could lead to difficult personal relations, and, as far as he could, he messed separately from his European companions. He refused to shower them with compliments because he thought that "they were superior natures, and required none of that encouragement, which the more childish blacks almost daily received."[66] This rather conventional attitude to the question of command had some serious drawbacks. The high standards he expected of his assistants could lead to harsh judgments. "He believes all the Zanzibaris sooner than us," wrote Barttelot, "and they bring him no end of tales."[67] This is a familiar situation for anyone in authority, but, although he may have given offense, it was probably

61. Maurice, *Unpublished Letters*, 44.
62. Walter George Barttelot (ed.), *The Life of Edmund Musgrave Barttelot* (London, 1890), 81–113; Fox Bourne, *Emin Pasha*, 103–140.
63. Stanley to Strauch, 7 April 1882, in Maurice, *Unpublished Letters*, 118.
64. Stanley, *The Congo and Its Free State*, I, 248, II, 238–255.
65. Stanley to Strauch, 8 September 1881, in Maurice, *Unpublished Letters*, 77.
66. Stanley, *Autobiography*, 385.
67. Barttelot, *Barttelot*, 118.

unintentional and resulted mostly from Stanley's efforts to allow justice to be seen to be done as far as his African porters were concerned.[68]

A more serious consequence of Stanley's aloofness was his inability to delegate authority. On the march up the Congo River in 1887, he occasionally fell back to lead the rear-guard, presumably to set an example to the Europeans in charge. This was a mixed blessing for all concerned. "Stanley, as rear-guard," wrote Barttelot, "got on A1. He flogged loafers and they all kicked amazingly"; but a little later, irritated at Stanley's behavior, he could describe him "as usual, jumping, shouting, and finding fault with everybody."[69] But it is possible to go further and see in this attitude a grave fault in Stanley's method of command, a fault that was magnified by the size of his expeditions. The written instructions for the rear-column were quite specific, but as one of the officers at Yambuya pointed out, "Mr. Stanley is not one who allows any latitude with written orders—he demands strict obedience . . . but one contingency he did not provide for in the written instructions and we had no authority shown to us for acting in the way now outlined at the end of Mr. Stanley's first volume."[70] Stanley's attitude stifled initiative among his subordinates, a point he himself made to Barttelot: "I would only trust a white man to a certain point, and no further, as my letter of instructions showed."[71]

Like Livingstone, Stanley was often uneasy in the company

68. Parke, *Equatorial Africa*, 513.

69. Barttelot, *Barttelot*, 80, 99.

70. J. Rose Troup, *With Stanley's Rear Column* (London, 1890), 5, n.2; Stanley, *Darkest Africa*, I, 478–498.

71. Barttelot, *Barttelot*, 113. The instructions (Stanley, *Darkest Africa*, I, 114–117) were detailed and didactic. They covered a number of contingencies, all based on the assumption that the rear-column would move from Yambuya and follow Stanley's route through the Equatorial Rain Forest. The controversy over these orders arose largely from Stanley's bitterness when he discovered that Barttelot, the commander of the rear-column, had not advanced after him. The situation was complicated by Tippu Tib's inability to provide extra porters between the Congo and Equatoria, although in his instructions Stanley had foreseen this possibility and suggested an alternative course of action. Rose Troup considered that the instructions placed too heavy a burden on the officers of the rear-column; "It would have taxed a man even of Stanley's resources" (Rose Troup, *Stanley's Rear Column*, 209).

of white men. It can be argued that his strict paternalism toward his African porters owed something to his years in New Orleans and the American South, and that his strained relations with his European assistants were complicated by his own deficiencies when it came to personal relationships. He had had more than one unfortunate experience with upper-class Englishmen, and the treatment that he received from the Royal Geographical Society and other public bodies after the Livingstone expedition did little to improve his confidence. "I have had no friend on any expedition," he wrote, "no one who could possibly be my companion, on an equal footing, except while with Livingstone." This was a simple statement of fact, not a confession of loneliness. He continued: "Though altogether solitary, I was never less conscious of solitude. . . . My only comfort was my work. To it I ever turned as a friend. It occupied my days, and I dwelt fondly on it at night." [72]

The single-minded desire to complete successfully the main objects of his expeditions determined his relations with the indigenous peoples he met. To some observers, however, the methods that he used appeared unlikely to win the confidence of Africans. Sir John Kirk, in particular, was highly critical. After the 1874–1877 expedition, and especially following Stanley's account of the incident at Bumbire Island, Kirk was asked to make a confidential investigation for the Foreign Office. He wrote that "if the story of this expedition were known, it would stand unequalled in the annals of African discovery for the reckless use of the power that modern weapons placed in his hands over natives who never before had heard a gun fired." [73] The Reverend Alexander M. Mackay, admittedly a believer in the need for firmness in dealing with Africans, was less peremptory in his judgment of Stanley's methods. "Whenever I find myself in Stanley's track," he wrote, "I find his treatment of the natives had invariably been such as to win from them the highest respect for the face of a white man." [74]

72. Stanley, *Autobiography*, 351.
73. Coupland, *Exploitation of East Africa*, 329.
74. Fox Bourne, *Emin Pasha*, 13–14.

Stanley was not blind to the consequences of his actions as he traveled through Africa, but he believed that a major cause of the difficulties Livingstone had faced was his refusal to take a harsh and uncompromising line with recalcitrant African tribes. Stanley was careful not to make a similar error, but the size of his columns and the need to push on as fast as he could reinforced his determination to take a firm line with the Africans encountered. This did not mean that he was always prepared to use force or similar harsh methods. Those who assisted his expeditions received praise, condescending though some of it may have been. "The conduct of the first natives to whom we were introduced pleased us all," he wrote as he approached Nyangwe in 1876, "they showed themselves in a very amiable light, sold their corn cheaply and without fuss, behaved themselves decently and with propriety." [75] He was less generous to those who would not assist him or resisted his passage. "My blood is up," he recorded in his diary as he sailed down the Congo. "It is a murderous world, and I have begun to hate the filthy, vulturous shoals who inhabit it." [76]

The result was that Stanley's behavior toward the Africans swung like a pendulum according to the reception given to him by the local tribes. Too often, however, time was against him; this was at the root of his frequent inability to foster friendly relations with the Africans. He admitted that "one must not run through a country but give the people time to become acquainted with you and let their worst fears subside," but, he continued, "on the expedition across Africa I had no time to give, either to myself or to them. The river bore my heavy canoes downward; my goods would never have endured the dawdling required by this system of teaching every tribe I met who I was. To save myself and my men from certain starvation, I had to rush on and on right through." [77]

This rushing on and on inevitably produced hostilities that did little to improve Stanley's reputation as an explorer. There were occasions when Stanley tried to soften the blow by using

75. Stanley, *The Dark Continent*, II, 53.
76. Stanley, *Autobiography*, 327.
77. *Ibid.*

hostages and captives as levers with which to open negotia-tions.[78] When African intransigence made such maneuvers impossible, his behavior could be rough, precipitate, and often irresponsible. Once his "blood was up," he would pursue Africans "up to their villages; I skirmish in their streets, drive them pell-mell into the woods beyond, and level their ivory temples; with frantic haste I fire the huts, and end the scene by towing the canoes into mid-stream and setting them adrift." [79]

There were moments, especially as the expedition moved down the Lualaba and into the Upper Congo in 1876 and 1877, when fighting proved unavoidable. African suspicion of stran-gers, and what Stanley called their "contempt of people of whom they knew nothing," [80] made negotiations difficult, especially as they moved away from the area where Swahili was generally understood. "Natives are so wild here," Stanley wrote in his diary, "they will not stay to be questioned, they are only to be captured by stratagem and made friends by force." [81] African hostility also increased, especially in the dis-tricts beyond Nyangwe, when Stanley's expedition was con-fused with Arab slave and ivory traders.[82]

It would be easier to accept the necessity for Stanley's use of force if he had not himself been so insensitive when writing about it. He could say of the burning of a native village that "fire had a remarkable sedative influence on their nerves." [83] He argued that when he attacked the natives of Bumbire

78. Stanley, *The Dark Continent*, II, 205–206.
79. Stanley, *Autobiography*, 327.
80. Stanley, *The Dark Continent*, II, 253.
81. Stanley and Neame, *Exploration Diaries*, 141. In his books Stanley has little to say about how he communicated with Africans. In his account of the Livingstone journey, his reports of conversations with tribal chiefs are normally written in the third person as if an intermediary were being used. By the time of his subsequent journeys, however, it is clear that he had a work-ing knowledge of Swahili. Beyond the great lakes, Stanley was at a disadvan-tage in this respect but he tried to obtain a rudimentary vocabulary from hos-tages. He was conscientious enough about the language problem to compile a simple comparative word table of the different tongues spoken along the Lualaba and the Congo (Stanley, *The Dark Continent*, II, 375–391).
82. Stanley and Neame, *Exploration Diaries*, 160; Stanley, *The Dark Con-tinent*, II, 118–126.
83. Stanley, *Darkest Africa*, I, 300–301.

Island it was because force was the only method they would respect, and, startlingly, he invoked Livingstone's authority in support.[84] But there is a disturbing contrast between the use of elephant guns and explosive bullets and Grant's conduct in 1862 in the same area when he ordered his men to load their guns with "shot-sized pebbles."[85]

In spite of the Bumbire Island incident, Stanley realized that "blood-letting breeds resentment, feeds rumour, and rumour exaggerates and breeds general distrust."[86] Expediency demanded that where possible he should avoid hostilities and engage in patient and often protracted negotiations. As his penetration of the Congo between 1879 and 1885 proved, he was quite capable of doing so, but then the comparatively slow pace of his expedition worked in his favor; it gave him the time that he needed to win the confidence of the chiefs through whose terrain he passed. Stanley's letters to Strauch, irritated as he was by some of the suggestions from Brussels, indicate how successful he thought that he had been. He talked about "chattering and bargaining with the cute natives of the Congo regions," and told Strauch not to be concerned about native risings since "the stations are mine, the people guarding them are my people—therefore any party making hostile demonstrations against them would be making them against me." He concluded by saying that they are "by no means warlike, or inclined to hostility, and they have all become so intimate with us that there is not the slightest fear of rupture."[87] These were confident claims in the light of his fierce reception from these same Africans in 1877 and in view of Kirk's pessimistic conclusion in his report that Stanley's "proceedings will prove one of the principal obstacles that future explorers and missionaries will have to meet when following his track."[88]

But for once in his African life, time was on Stanley's side and he could deal with Africans in terms reminiscent of

84. Stanley, *The Dark Continent*, I, 216–217n.
85. Coupland, *Exploitation of East Africa*, 325–327.
86. Stanley, *The Congo and Its Free State*, I, 523.
87. Stanley to Strauch, 23 June 1881, in Maurice, *Unpublished Letters*, 60, 62.
88. Coupland, *Exploitation of East Africa*, 329.

Livingstone. He counseled one of his European assistants to be patient, good-tempered, and prepared to mix freely. "They will be sad triflers with your time," he told him "and will dawdle over trifling matters, but they will sharply note any exhibition of bad temper and their confidence in you will at once shrink. . . . The natives are suspicious, slow to give their confidence to persons of other colours, so strange in their customs, dress, colour, speech, and gesture as European, but if you are engaging, frank in manner, offering your confidence fresh, unrestrained in habit, you will soon gain their goodwill and confidence." [89]

Stanley's impact on the African peoples whom he encountered is not easy to gauge. Although his writings often include full accounts of indigenous customs and manners and as much historical background as he could discover, he had a tendency simply to label tribes as fierce or docile according to the reception that he had received. When Ward asked him what impression he thought the arrival of his Congo expedition in 1879 had made on the local Africans, Stanley replied brusquely, "In this world we can't stop to think about the impressions we create—no time for that sort of thing." [90] Clearly, however, African reaction varied from area to area according to the treatment that Stanley had meted out. Where there was fighting, as in the Upper Congo in 1877 and the equatorial rain forest ten years later, a whole region could be roused against him. But, as his pioneering work for Léopold II in the Congo indicated, the legacy of bitterness was dispelled with surprising speed. The reaction of the African chiefs when they realized that Stanley was not just a bird of passage was in complete contrast to their previously unfriendly behavior as he sailed down the Congo for the first time. He became a respected figure among them and was irritated whenever his European assistants upset the friendly relations that he had established.

When they were not in his way, Stanley's sympathy for

89. Stanley to Lieutenant Braconnier, 8 April 1882, in Maurice, *Unpublished Letters*, 127.

90. Herbert Ward, *A Voice from the Congo* (London, 1910), 166.

Africans could be aroused quickly. His remained largely an objective, European view of African society, usually patriarchal and patronizing, occasionally naive. When he met African leaders of real authority, he could behave in a manner normally reserved for court functions at Osborne or Balmoral. He treated Mutesa of Buganda and the imperious Gankabi, queen of a tribe on a tributary of the Kasai River, with exaggerated respect.[91] When he at last met Mirambo, the "condottiere" chief who had hindered his progress during the Livingstone journey, he was greatly impressed and described him as "a thorough African *gentleman*," his italics being presumably suggestive enough to his readers to require no further explanation.[92] In all these cases, Stanley's treatment indicated an impressive degree of sympathy and understanding of the African personality. Mutesa, in particular, normally critical and suspicious of strangers, responded to Stanley with enthusiasm.

The aspect of life in central Africa that caused Stanley most concern was the treatment of the Africans by the Arab slave and ivory traders. Like Livingstone and Cameron, he was indignant in spite of the often close relations that he had established with the Arabs, relations which in the case of Tippu Tib appalled his critics. The fact remained that the Arab presence, especially in the area of the great lakes, made some form of mutual dependence between them and the Europeans inevitable.[93]

Stanley's first evidence of the slave trade had not disturbed him. He saw the slave caravans as an inevitable part of the landscape and compared the slaves themselves to Martin

91. Stanley, *Autobiography*, 312; Stanley, *The Congo and Its Free State*, I, 425–428.

92. Stanley, *Dark Continent*, I, 306.

93. Roland Oliver, *The Missionary Factor in East Africa* (London, 1952), 100–101; Fox Bourne, *Emin Pasha*, 37–41. In 1871 Stanley had aided the Arabs at Tabora in an unsuccessful war against Mirambo. For five years Tippu Tib (who had earlier assisted Cameron) was employed by Stanley on his journey north from Nyangwe. During the Emin Pasha expedition, Stanley made the arrangements leading to Tippu Tib's becoming Governor of the Stanley Falls region for the Independent State, but was subsequently let down by him when he failed to provide his promised assistance to the rear-column at Yambuya.

Chuzzlewit's jolly servant.[94] His long conversations with Livingstone, however, and above all the latter's account of the Manyema Massacre—whose grim story Stanley first revealed to the public[95]—turned him into a firm opponent of the slave trade.

By the time that Stanley entered Africa, the main centers of the slave trade had already shifted westward. The export of slaves from the east coast had dwindled to practically nothing and in its place traders had begun to exploit the ivory resources of the region, particularly the supplies from the Lualaba and the Upper Congo. During the 1870s and 1880s, the Arabs and their auxiliaries spilled into the area in great number. The incidence of slave-hunting, however, remained high in the interior since slaves were still needed for carrying and in some districts were an acceptable form of currency to be traded for ivory. Also, as Stanley noted in his diary, those tribes which had little to offer in the way of ivory sold slaves in return for firearms.[96]

At first the European consulates in Zanzibar only dimly understood what was happening. Kirk, for example, aware of the small number of slaves reaching the coast, was puzzled by Livingstone's reports of large-scale slave-trading in the far interior.[97] One of the important results, therefore, of Stanley's journeys was the information that he was able to provide about the nature of this continued trading. In particular his exploration of the region between the great lakes and the Lualaba and the Upper Congo rivers revealed the full effects of the trade on the local peoples. He was acute enough to realize that the sad state of the area, more especially among the Manyema, could not entirely be blamed on the slave-traders themselves. The peoples of this area were often disunited and constantly at war with each other, Stanley himself being asked on three occasions to assist in these intertribal disputes. It was these

94. Stanley, *Livingstone*, 91–92. The reference is to Mark Tapley in Charles Dickens' novel *Martin Chuzzlewit*.

95. *Ibid.*, 381–384.

96. Roland Oliver and Gervase Mathew (eds.), *History of East Africa* (Oxford, 1963), I, 274; Stanley and Neame, *Exploration Diaries*, 124; and Ruth Slade, *King Leopold's Congo* (Oxford, 1962), 85.

97. Oliver, *Missionary Factor*, 100.

weaknesses that gave the men of the coast their opportunity.[98] "Slaves cost nothing," Tippu Tib told Stanley, "they only require to be gathered."[99] It can perhaps be argued that Stanley's awareness of the state of affairs among the Manyema and his subsequent agreements with the Arabs in the Upper Congo in 1877 indicate his recognition of Tippu Tib as a political figure able to bring some benefit to the region.

Tippu Tib was unusual among Swahili-speaking traders in realizing that if the ivory trade were to flourish it involved the establishment of some form of political power. By 1876, when Stanley first visited the area, the process had not gone very far. In any event, such authority rarely extended far beyond Manyema, and as the Arabs pushed north into the Upper Congo in Stanley's wake, it was very tenuous indeed.[100] It was Arab activity in this area that most angered Stanley. "It is simply incredible," he wrote, "that, because ivory is required for ornaments or billiard games, the rich heart of Africa should be laid waste."[101] The evidence was not difficult to find. As he was moving up the Congo basin in late 1883, he arrived at a group of villages that only hours before had been raided by Arabs and their Manyema warriors. A little later he overtook the Arab caravan and was able to view the captured slaves, noting that there was an almost total absence of adult males.[102] To Stanley, the scene was only slightly less horrifying than the Manyema Massacre had seemed to Livingstone in 1871. It left just as deep an impression.

Stanley's experience of the worst aspects of the Arab trade reinforced his conclusion that the only solution for Africa lay in an active European interest in the continent. "Every man I saw, giant or dwarf," he wrote, "only deepened the belief that Africa had other claims on man, and every feature of the glorious land only impressed me the more that there was a crying

98. Stanley, *Dark Continent*, II, 66–68.
99. Stanley and Neame, *Exploration Diaries*, 134.
100. Slade, *Congo*, 89.
101. Stanley, *Darkest Africa*, II, 230. For the price of ivory in the Zanzibar market at this period, see Norman R. Bennett, *Studies in East African History* (Boston, 1963), 89.
102. Stanley, *The Congo and Its Free State*, II, 138–151.

need for immediate relief and assistance from civilization." [103] Among the specific remedies he suggested for halting the slave trade was a total prohibition on the import of firearms into Africa and the building of railways. He also urged Léopold II and the Independent State to attack the Arabs as soon as seemed prudent.[104]

Stanley's preoccupation with the need for greater European interest in Africa dates from his second journey that took him across the continent from east to west. This particular expedition has been seen as leading "directly to the Partition of Africa," [105] a view which the supporters of the Robinson-Gallagher thesis might want to question.[106] The claim emphasizes that Stanley saw beyond the mere solution of vexing geographical problems and was acutely conscious of the wider significance of his work. For Stanley, Africa represented a rich field for humanitarian activity and commerce. In this context he sounded a note of realistic optimism, not least about the Africans themselves. "Africa is inhabited," he wrote in a letter to *The Times,* "by millions of robust, courageous men. It is no cant or sentimentalism, it is an obvious dictate of ordinary prudence, to say that, if we are to hold these men in such control as shall make Africa equal to any continent in serviceableness to mankind at large, it is by moral superiority, first of all, that control must be won." [107]

Stanley accepted that a necessary part of this process was the introduction of Christianity, but he sounded a note of caution. His own experience with Mutesa of Buganda had made him realize that the *kabaka*'s sympathy with the Christian story rested largely upon his admiration for what Europeans appeared to represent.[108] In this he was near the truth, although

103. Stanley, *Darkest Africa,* II, 246.
104. Stanley, *Darkest Africa,* I, 229–230, II, 246; Stanley, *The Congo and Its Free State,* I, ix–x; Hird, *Stanley,* 274–275.
105. Margery Perham and Jack Simmons (eds.), *African Discovery, An Anthology of Exploration* (London, 1942), 32.
106. Ronald E. Robinson and John Gallagher, *Africa and the Victorians* (London, 1961); Ronald E. Robinson and John Gallagher, "The Partition of Africa," in F. H. Hinsley (ed.), *The New Cambridge Modern History,* XI (Cambridge, 1962), 593–640.
107. Stanley, *Autobiography,* 377.
108. Stanley, *Dark Continent,* I, 318.

Mutesa's motives were even more complicated than he had guessed.[109] Stanley maintained that the introduction of missions on too small a scale would do more harm than good and that it needed to be linked with a wider and more effective European presence. The essential condition that the missions had to recognize was that the Africans had "material wants which crave to be understood and supplied. . . . My experience and study of the pagan prove to me . . . that if the missionary can show the poor materialist that religion is allied with substantial benefits and improvement of his degraded condition, the task to which he is about to devote himself will be rendered comparatively easy." [110]

Stanley was disappointed when his attempts in 1878 to interest both governmental and business circles in Britain in a more forward policy in Africa proved unsuccessful. Only Léopold II was sufficiently impressed to emphasize consistently, though privately, the commercial aspects of his Congo enterprise.[111] But Stanley had no doubts that Europeans in Africa would find that the continent had its own rewards from both the commercial and humanitarian points of view. Africa had resources and riches as yet untapped, and he claimed that the Almighty had "surely intended that it should be reserved until the fulness of time for something higher than a nursery for birds and a store-place for reptiles." [112] Further, and as important, Stanley's own experience of the vigorous intertribal commerce of the Congolese and their sharpness and shrewdness in trading matters suggested that European enterprise would not be wasted on the Africans themselves.[113]

For Stanley the ultimate answer was European occupation of the continent. During the period of the Scramble for Africa, he played a significant if at times marginal role in events. It was his careful work in the Congo basin between 1879 and

109. John Milner Gray, "Mutesa of Buganda," *The Uganda Journal*, I (1934), 2–49.

110. Stanley, *Dark Continent*, I, 63–64.

111. Jean Stengers, "Quelques observations sur la correspondance de Stanley," *Zaïre*, IX (1955), 922–924.

112. Stanley, *Darkest Africa*, II, 246–247.

113. Stanley, *The Congo and Its Free State*, I, 137; Maurice, *Unpublished Letters*, 107–108.

1885 that enabled Léopold II to establish his Congo claims at the Berlin Conference of 1884–85. The relief of Emin Pasha involved Stanley as a political agent for both Léopold II and William Mackinnon, the Chairman of the Relief Committee and, subsequently, Chairman of the Imperial British East Africa Company.[114] To Fox Bourne this serving of two masters inevitably implied "jiggery-pokery" and formed a useful preliminary to the other criticisms that he had made against Stanley's conduct of the expedition.[115] When, in 1890, Stanley took the lead with Lugard in the agitation that ended in the assumption of a British protectorate over Uganda in 1894, he met the same negative response from the British Government that he had received twelve years earlier when he had tried to persuade Britain to take an active interest in the Congo. Lord Harcourt wrote to William Gladstone in October 1892: "The Uganda smoke is only scotched. The whole force of jingoism is at the bellows. I see Mr. Stanley leads the way—a worse guide no one could have." [116]

Harcourt misjudged Stanley. The label of jingo was neither useful nor accurate. He was, however, voicing the general distrust of the explorer that was felt in and near government circles—the legacy of which has never disappeared. The importance and value of Stanley's work in solving the outstanding geographical problems of the African watershed was not in question; the efficacy of his methods, however, has always been questioned. Such matters have been further complicated by the natural tendency to compare him with Livingstone, in spite of Stanley's own disclaimer that, however much he admired that missionary-explorer, he was unable to accept his methods.

Stanley made no attempt to hide his view that firm, even harsh, methods were necessary. His behavior toward his followers and African tribesmen indicates his unwillingness to yield to pressures that might prevent him from fulfilling his aims. There were occasions, such as the Bumbire Island incident, when it is difficult to excuse or explain his actions. But,

114. Anstey, *Britain and the Congo*, 215–225.
115. Fox Bourne, *Emin Pasha*, 30–46.
116. Perham, *Lugard*, 410.

in the main, the methods that he adopted can be defended since they were the direct outcome of the special factors that distinguished his journeys from those of his predecessors.

Among these the most important was the generosity of his patrons and the consequent lavish scale of his expeditions. Far from making Stanley's task an easy one, the wealth of his resources merely complicated his work and presented him with a number of novel problems. In particular, the relatively large size of his columns frequently intimidated local tribesmen, and Africa at that time could not easily support or absorb expeditions of the kind he led. Unlike Livingstone, Stanley could not afford to be on sufferance in his relations with the Africans. His sense of urgency, except when he was pioneering for Léopold II, was the unavoidable result of the size of his columns. In such circumstances, especially in those areas where a European had never been seen before, it was difficult to avoid intimidating the Africans that he encountered.

Stanley's character was equally important. He was neither so hard nor so cold as his conventional Victorian photographs suggest. Behind the stern image was a complicated, far from simple character, never wholly at ease and unable completely to overcome the sense of inferiority that was the legacy of his early years. But, though the circumstances of his upbringing meant that he drove himself harshly and with an uncompromising zeal which he expected from others, they also generated in him a degree of sympathy for the Africans. He was never committed to Africa in the sense that Livingstone had been, and as a result had fewer inhibitions about treating harshly those who annoyed him or who impeded his progress. But when he had the time to cultivate their friendship, Stanley's judgments of Africans were not ungenerous. This side of his conduct is not often enough stressed, mainly because he seldom had occasion to reveal it. But it is important in any attempt to assess his role in the exploration of tropical Africa.

Stanley's complex character, the massive size of his expeditions, and the need for him so frequently to complete his missions as quickly as possible explain, if perhaps they do not always excuse, the controversial methods that he used. He was a prisoner of attitudes and circumstances not always under his control. There were, however, moments when he was able to free himself. On such occasions, he could behave toward the people of Africa with a generosity of spirit that Livingstone himself might have admired. But too frequently the strains and pressures under which he worked meant that his conduct was harsh and uncompromising. His understanding of African life was all the more real and genuine in that at first he had found the continent unattractive. Stanley was too honest a man to conceal his blemishes and his immediate reactions to Africa, but this characteristic in its turn lent authority to his actions and his judgments as one of the great African explorers.

Verney Lovett Cameron:
A Sailor in Central Africa

by James R. Hooker

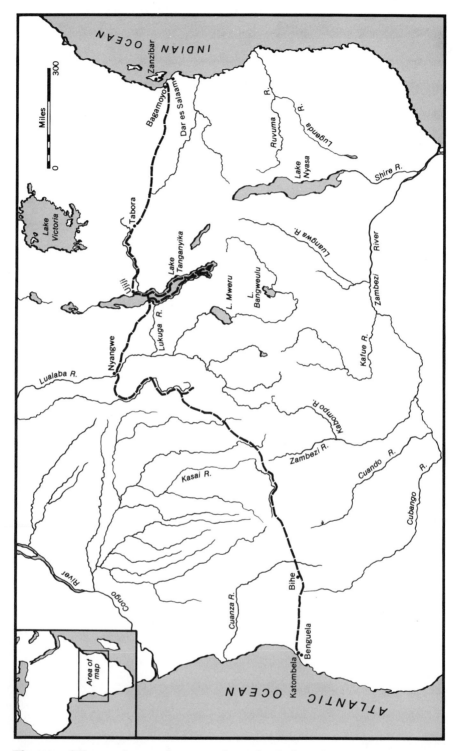

The trip of Verney Lovett Cameron from the Indian Ocean to the Atlantic

Verney Lovett Cameron was the first European to traverse Africa from east to west, in the process adding much geographical, political, and anthropological information about central Africa and further documenting the fragility of Portuguese pretensions in the interior of the continent. His observations had a great influence upon the course of European expansion into this area, especially into the Congo. He was the first to suggest the probable course of the Congo River and among the earliest to recognize the potential of Katanga—although in the popular mind his successor Henry Morton Stanley is associated with these developments. Cameron's naval career was solid, if uninspiring; his business ventures were substantial, though not glamorous; he wrote numerous books, technical, descriptive, and fictional, for both adults and boys; he was accorded great honors by his own and other governments. But he does not spring to mind when the great explorers of the middle nineteenth century are named. In large measure this obscurity was a result of his modesty and lack of ruthlessness. He achieved one great exploit as a young man, and then became an English gentleman.

Cameron was born in Weymouth, on 1 July 1844, to Frances, wife of Jonathan H. L. Cameron, Rector of Shoreham, Kent. Although the explorer's biographer suggests a substantial family connection, this seems to enlarge the case.[1] The boy was sent to school in Somerset and, soon after his thirteenth birthday, during the Indian Mutiny, joined the Royal Navy. After training he was posted to the eastern Mediterranean, where he spent four years, in the process becoming a midshipman. Late in 1861 he was sent to the West Indian Squadron. While on this tour, he observed the capture of New Orleans by the United States forces. (Henry Stanley was in the Con-

1. W. Robert Foran, *African Odyssey: The Life of Verney Lovett-Cameron* (London, 1937), 20–25. The idea of hyphenating the surname would appear to be Foran's, as Cameron called himself "Cameron."

federate Army at that time.) For the next two years Cameron served in the Channel Squadron, attaining the rank of lieutenant in the autumn of 1865. The twenty-one-year-old officer was then transferred to Indian Ocean patrol duty. He was decorated for his services in the Abyssinian Campaign of 1868. The routine duties of this period, however, seem to have been more important in forming Cameron's views of Africa. He had considerable experience of antislavery patrols in East African waters, and the misery and extent of the illicit trade profoundly impressed him. In 1870, having received no further promotion, Cameron was placed on the steam reserve at Sheerness, a most uninspiring assignment for a twenty-six-year-old man with a taste for travel and an increasing interest in the African hinterland. Within a few months he offered to lead the Royal Geographical Society's proposed expedition to ascertain the whereabouts of Livingstone.

According to the by then well-known journalist-traveler Stanley, who was Livingstone's last European contact, the Scots clergyman intended to explore the last unknown parts of the region of the Great Lakes. Some months had gone by without word from the missionary, and concerned followers of his exploits began to urge that two relief columns should be dispatched, one from each coast. Cameron was among those who applied for work. He was unknown, without money or connections (though shortly he came to the notice of Clements Markham of the Society's Council), and possessed no appropriate experience. However, after Livingstone was "found" by Stanley in November 1871, the Royal Geographical Society decided to place another expedition under Livingstone's command, and, after some further disappointments, Cameron was given charge of this party. The "Livingstone East Coast Expedition," as Cameron called it, first had to find Livingstone, who was thought to have headed south toward Lake Bangweulu after parting from Stanley, and then accept his instructions.

Cameron and his chosen companion, Assistant-Surgeon W. E. Dillon, a former messmate, left England at the end of November 1872 for Zanzibar, which they reached in January

1873. There they encountered every difficulty spoken of by previous travelers: the high cost of goods, the scarcity of carriers, the absence of trustworthy guides, and the intense suspicion accorded to their proposals to visit the interior. No one was prepared to accept the unofficial character of the expedition, especially as they had arrived in Zanzibar in the company of Sir Bartle Frere, who was to be so instrumental in the further extension of British influence over the Swahili coast. Not until March were Cameron and Dillon able to set out from Bagamoyo, the mainland town to the north of Dar es Salaam which was the traditional starting place of Arab traders. Stanley had preceded them here. Meanwhile, they had been joined by Lieutenant Cecil Murphy of the Royal Artillery, who was stationed at Aden, and Robert Moffat, a Natal sugar planter and nephew of Livingstone.

Desertion of carriers and guards began immediately, for Cameron, most unwisely but in desperation, had honored the custom of advance payment. He also encountered what became his principal problem, the demand for tribute in every petty chiefdom which he traversed. Very quickly, he perceived that the real, as opposed to the claimed, power of the Zanzibari sultanate was of little concern to people but a few miles removed from the coast. Cameron was skeptical that the slave trade could be ended by decrees published in Zanzibar, even if the coastal Arabs in fact had wanted to comply with British policy.

At his first stop he learned how precious food was in this seemingly rich land. What little surplus was offered came exorbitantly high, and Cameron soon realized that his supply of currency—bolts of cloth and East Coast shells—looked inadequate for any lengthy trip. Moreover, he constantly entered regions where large slaving parties had gone before, taking what foodstuffs he might have bought and creating an attitude of fear and hostility toward all subsequent caravans.

Despite these worries, Cameron faithfully recorded his impressions of the people he visited. As his biographer has remarked, he was almost alone in being interested in people rather than animals. He showed no great taste for hunting, except for the pot; indeed, he seemed "only mildly interested in the fauna of the country."[2] In this regard he was markedly different from many of his contemporaries, as well as most subsequent travelers.

The route followed was generally westward for about 150 miles and then west-northwest for the next 300 miles to the vicinity of Unyanyembe, which he reached in August. This important trading center (the modern Tabora) was garrisoned by nearly a thousand Arab and Sudanese troops under the governance of Said ibn Salim, who placed at Cameron's disposal the house previously occupied by Livingstone and Stanley.[3] The Governor had an extensive acquaintance with Britons, having accompanied Burton, Speke, and Grant on their journeys to the lakes.

The district was at this time, and had been for many months, in turmoil, owing to a guerrilla war waged by Mirambo, a chief of the area, against the Arabs. Cameron noted that "on both sides the war was prosecuted with the utmost revolting barbarity and cruelty," being aimed chiefly at small parties and innocent villagers.[4] Although he received extremely civil treatment from his host, the lieutenant was inclined to blame the Arabs for starting trouble and expressed some sneaking admiration for Mirambo's resistance.

At this point all of the Europeans came down with fever again. Many porters had contracted to go only this far and so were paid off; the remainder struck for higher wages. Once more Cameron was forced to dip into his declining stock of cloth.

Meanwhile, a caravan from Mutesa, ruler of the Ganda, arrived with a letter for Livingstone from Samuel Baker, then at the royal seat of Mengo. Under the circumstances, Cameron felt authorized to read it, but learned nothing about the missionary's whereabouts. As Mutesa's men were anxious to re-

2. *Ibid.,* 67.
3. For a photo and sketch plan of the dwelling, see *ibid.,* 74.
4. Verney Lovett Cameron, *Across Africa* (New York, 1877), 115. The American spellings in subsequent quotes are accounted for by my use of this edition, a one-volume version of the two-volume London original of the same year.

turn to the lake, and thinking that he might be sent to that region by Livingstone eventually, Cameron dispatched them with a note for Baker and a gift of cloth for the King. He was anxious to get away himself, but could not find carriers, and his days dragged by with numerous petty disappointments. His hosts were exceedingly helpful, on one occasion breaking up a revolt of his gun bearers, but Cameron could not get them to extend their influence to the labor question. His cloth was running out and he had to pay a 400 percent premium to replenish it. Meanwhile, fever came and went, each time weakening the Europeans more. When not delirious, they were too listless to work. Cameron managed to attend the great slave auction at Tabora, but this was his only venture away from his house for more than two months. Moffat had already died of fever, and Dillon was very sick.

On 20 October came the most depressing news of all: a letter telling him (the writer, Livingstone's servant, hearing of Europeans, had presumed that Cameron was the missionary's son Oswell) that the doctor was dead. His body and journal were being carried to Tabora.[5] Dillon, ill as he was, preserved his clinical interest, and upon reading it pronounced that Livingstone's ruthless disregard of his person was responsible for his death by dysentery.

The object of the expedition was at an end, and Murphy and Dillon decided to return to their duties. Cameron, however, said he would go inland at least as far as Ujiji on the lake, where Livingstone's books had been left. They parted on 9 November. Within a few days, Cameron learned that Dillon, while delirious, had killed himself. Much dejected by the loss

---

5. *Ibid.*, 123–124. The letter from Livingstone's servant is reproduced between pages 122 and 123 of Cameron's account, as follows: "Ukhonongo October 1873 Sir We have heared in the month of August that you have started from Zanzibar for Unyanyembe, and again and again lately we have heared your arrived. Your father died by disease beyond the country of Bisa, but we have carried the corpse with us. 10 of our soldier are lost and some have died. Our hunger presses us to ask you some clothes to buy provision for our soldiers. And we should have an answer that when we shall enter there shall be firing guns or not, and if you permit us to fire guns, then send some powder. We have wrote these few words in the place of Sultan or King Mbowra. The writer Jacob Wainwright Dr Livingstone Exped."

of his old friend, Cameron still set out for the interior, this time with a skeleton crew and short rations. The rains had started and no one was willing to leave his village during the crucial planting season.

His route now lay generally westward through Ugunda, toward Uvinza and Ujiji on Lake Tanganyika south of Kigoma. This path was south of Burton's and north of Stanley's, and it was extremely difficult to recruit bearers to traverse an unknown region. Before reaching Ugara he was frustrated once more, for the road was blocked because of a dispute between the inhabitants and the Arabs at Unyanyembe. Cameron could not prevail and was doubtful whether he could afford the three weeks or so necessary to circumvent it, so he was obliged to return to the next village east. Christmas came and went, and still he heard nothing of the negotiations in Unyanyembe. Then, toward the end of December 1873, he was allowed to proceed, and, with the usual delays over food and transport, slowly made his way toward the lake, passing scenes of great devastation. "Africa," he wrote, "is bleeding out her life blood at every pore. A rich country, requiring labor only to render it one of the greatest producers in the world, is having its population—already far too scanty for its needs—daily depleted by the slave trade and internecine war." [6]

Finally, in February 1874, he arrived at Ujiji, fifteen years after Richard Burton first saw it. Livingstone's papers were intact in the hands of an Arab trader, Mohammed ibn Salib, who had not ventured eastward in thirty-two years. He assured Cameron that travel west of the lake would be impossible for at least another three months, because of transport difficulties and unrest, and added that Livingstone's papers would never get through Unyanyembe in the current state of warfare, unless they were carried in some large convoy. None was in the making.

Cameron therefore decided to explore those southern portions of the lake as yet unseen by Europeans. This decision led to one of his most important discoveries: the lake's outlet and its connection (as he supposed) with the Congo riverine system.

6. Cameron, *Across Africa*, 152.

He had already made an important contribution by examining the principal streams flowing into the Malagarasi River from the south, thus completing the mapping of that large river's basin. Now he hoped to conclude the researches begun by Burton and Speke in 1858 and continued by Livingstone and Stanley in 1871. After some haggling, he procured two boats and set out down the eastern shore of the lake. Cameron's impatience with inefficiency manifested itself at this stage, for he was afloat again. The propensity of his crew, even the sailors among them, to hug the rocky shoreline and their evident fear of slight seas provoked the naval officer, though he had remained philosophical in the face of much greater provocation ashore. "What would I not have given for a man-of-war's whaler and crew for six weeks!"[7]

All told, Cameron was away 88 days, during much of which he could not get his men moving, partly through their stubborn fear of water, partly because he was too ill to overawe them. However, he made frequent observations, often being irritated at the confusing interchangeability of place names. As he rounded the bottom of the lake for the first time people began to speak of the Portuguese, those men in the far west who had two rulers, one called Mwene Puto, the other Maria, a woman whose image was preserved in various large houses. They were said to be rather like the Wazungu, or white men, although accounts varied.

Nearly opposite his starting point, Cameron encountered the Lukuga River (near Albertville), which people told him flowed into the Lualaba River. However, Arab traders who should have known the facts disputed this statement, claiming instead that the Lukuga was a swampy stream which flowed *into* the lake. One is tempted to presume that the Arabs did not wish the Englishman to learn too much, although at Ujiji they had assured him that the Lualaba flowed into the Congo, so it may be that they themselves had been deluded by local inhabitants. In any case, Cameron was much taken with this information and tried to navigate the stream. But his way was blocked by an enormous mass of drifting vegetation a short

7. *Ibid.*, 186.

distance inside the putative outlet. Travelers insisted that one could walk down its banks for many months, but no one volunteered to guide him and it looked like an expensive project, so Cameron abandoned it. He sailed back across the lake to Ujiji, which he entered again on 9 May 1874, and found a packet of mail from England waiting for him, some of which was nearly a year old. All told, he had plotted ninety-six rivers flowing into the lake, and one flowing out of it. His observations, though challenged by some, were ultimately substantiated.[8]

Although he might have been satisfied with his already considerable achievements, Cameron was bemused by the question of the source of the Congo River, which seemed more complex every time he investigated it with his Arab informants. Some insisted that fifty-five marches to the north there was salt water where white men traded in palm oil. Guessing that they alluded to the mouth of the Congo, though very much aware of their indifference to the niceties of compass points and distance, he decided to return to the western shores of Lake Tanganyika and go overland until he struck the Congo River, down which he hoped to canoe to the Atlantic Ocean, perhaps in two or three months' time. Once more he had to pay off his staff, most of whom refused to go beyond the lake. One of them was entrusted with Livingstone's and Cameron's papers, which reached England some months later. Markham, the Secretary of the Royal Geographical Society, put Cameron's diary into narrative form and revealed the lieutenant's discovery of Lake Tanganyika's outlet in a paper delivered the following March, while Cameron still was in the Congo.[9]

8. Those who held that Tanganyika fed the Nile system resisted, but the researches of Joseph Thomson and Captain Edward Coode Hore tended to support him. Thomson was rather acid about Cameron's way of defining a stream and Hore theorized that the Lukuga must be a new river, perhaps coming into existence only in the middle 1870's. See Joseph Thomson, *To the Central African Lakes and Back* (London, 1881), II, 6–8; Edward Coode Hore, *Tanganyika: Eleven Years in Central Africa* (London, 1892), 147. See also below, 298.

9. Clements Markham, "Examination of the Southern Half of Lake Tanganyika, by Lieutenant V. L. Cameron, R.N., compiled chiefly from Lieu-

On the last day of May 1874, Cameron headed for Ruanda, apparently the capital of the district north of the present Albertville (and unconnected to the northern kingdom of that name). Thence he hoped to proceed to Nyangwe, where he was promised canoes for the Lualaba River. One of his Arab merchant friends at Ujiji said there would be no trouble, as he was quite friendly with chiefs there. Cameron at this point noted that currencies suddenly shifted, cloth and beads being replaced by copper crosses from Katanga—or Urua, as his guides called it.

Somewhat to his dissatisfaction, at the village of Pakwanywa, twelve marches to the northwest, he learned that an Arab caravan was waiting for him in the next village of Pakhundi. The Arabs welcomed the protection afforded by his repeating firearms, but felt that he would spoil their slaving chances, while Cameron feared to associate his reputation with theirs, for he knew that they intended plundering as they went. Nevertheless, to avoid trouble he joined them on the march through the tall hot grass of Uhiya, where he recorded Fahrenheit 142° at noon. It was the dry season and fires roared across their path both night and day. The Arabs feared the men of Manyema, as this large district was called, though Cameron noted that those inhabitants who had seen Livingstone showed no reluctance to let another Briton pass. His men, perhaps with the Arab example before them, grew unruly and dishonest in their dealings with local people. "I gave my men extra rations to prevent their thieving, and in two or three cases paid natives who complained of them, and I treated the offenders to a sound flogging to show that I, as an Englishman, had no intention of making my way through the country by means of looting and force. Yet I fear when my back was turned they were fully as bad as the others." [10]

His fears were realized before the columns reached Nyangwe. The scene no doubt was common enough, but now Cameron was a witness and near participant. Local rulers banded

tenant Cameron's diary," *Journal of the Royal Geographical Society*, XLV (1875), 184–228.

10. Cameron, *Across Africa*, 253.

together to create an incident which would force the Arabs to assume responsibility for the prior depredations of their fellows. A petty theft from the Arab encampment led to Arab demands for restoration, which were in turn countered by African insistence upon compensation for past plunder. The Arabs refused to assume responsibility, insisted upon the return of their goods, and fighting began, evidently by plan. The Africans, although superior in number, were unable to withstand their opponents' musketry, and the Arabs went on to burn villages, seize women, children, and goats, and carry off grain and whatever other few possessions remained.

Cameron attempted to intercede, although the best that he could do was to confine his own men to quarters during the affair, meanwhile leading the Arabs to believe that he would protest to the British Consul in Zanzibar. They seemed to have misgivings about the effect of this policy; at least Cameron concluded that they recognized that their Sultan was already under heavy British pressure. In any case, the Arabs entered into negotiations on the following day. After a peace was patched up and prisoners returned, the Anglo-Arab forces departed, the Arabs still feeling themselves in the right. Cameron was in no position to report the African viewpoint. At the very next encampment he discovered that some of the captives had not been released. However, he had lost his influence. Once out of danger, the Arab leader, Muinyi Hassani, was not so ready to be overawed by threats of ultimate British displeasure. Nevertheless, for the first time Cameron insisted on having his way. "I told him plainly that I did not and could not interfere with the buying and selling of slaves by him and his friends, or with their seizing them by the strong arm when alone; but I was determined that the English colors, which had brought freedom to so many on both coasts of Africa, should not be disgraced in the center of the continent." [11] He prevailed, and the prisoners were freed—a sufficiently rare event to be recorded in some detail.

On 3 August 1874, he reached the Lualaba, "a strong and sweeping current of turbid yellow water fully a mile wide."

11. *Ibid.*, 256–257.

The population was densely settled along its banks and Cameron contracted with some fishermen to be taken downstream to Nyangwe, which he reached the following day, much to the astonishment of the Arabs there, who had heard nothing of his approach. The first part of his western travels was concluded. It remained to be seen how he would fare on the Congo.

Nyangwe itself consisted of two towns, the Arab traders occupying the high and healthy right bank, which was a permanent center of commerce, while the insubstantial huts of the Africans littered the mud flats on the far side. Cameron was not favorably impressed with many of these Arabs, who seemed far more interested in the delights of alcohol, Indian hemp, and their concubines than in conducting business with the east coast. They refused to accept his insistence on an early departure; indeed, a visit of less than a month's duration appeared too brief to consider, for what after all was hospitality for? Each day the Englishman's efforts to find canoes and paddlers were frustrated politely. In fact, Cameron would have had trouble even without Arab interference, for the trade now seemed to be conducted in west coast (Angolan) cowries, and he had none. The four-day market cycle prevailed in Nyangwe, and as each came around Cameron sought transport without success. Some elders opined that no good ever came to people who helped strangers, while others, unimpressed with this dictum, let it be known that they perhaps would part with their canoes for slaves. Cameron had to reply that Britons could not engage in this traffic, which must have seemed the utmost foolishness. The economic basis of domestic slavery was revealed fully by one potential seller, who explained to Cameron that if he accepted cowries rather than slaves for his canoe, he would have to waste time trying to exchange the Englishman's coin for the slaves he needed, whereas, if Cameron sold slaves initially, then they could be put to work at fishing, pottery-making, or farming right away. "In fact, he did not want his capital to lie idle," Cameron wrote with irritated knowledgeableness.[12]

Of course, the overland route provided another possibility,

12. *Ibid.*, 267.

but the smallness of his party and the evident reluctance of the Nyangwe people to venture down the Lualaba ruled out the idea. To while away his hours, Cameron did what he could to clear up various points of geographical interest. His observations of its flow led him to conclude that the Lualaba River must be one of the principal sources, if not the primary source, of the Congo, while its elevation seemed to defeat the theory that it flowed into the Nile, which at its lowest point was higher above sea level than Nyangwe. This disposed of Livingstone's speculation, which Cameron had hitherto accepted.

By mid-August 1874, with every hope gone, Cameron was ready to give up. Then came the advance party of the greatest Arab captain of the region, Hamed ibn Hamed, whom the Belgians and British later styled Tippu Tib. "He was a good-looking man, and the greatest dandy I had seen among the traders; and, notwithstanding his being perfectly black, he was a thorough Arab, for curiously enough, the admixture of Negro blood had not rendered him less of an Arab in his ideas and manners." [13] The great sultan-trader, who claimed to represent the power of remote Zanzibar, was just back from two years in Katanga. He urged Cameron to proceed to the Atlantic coast by the southerly route, agreeing with the Nyangwe Arabs that the Lualaba/Congo approach was out of the question. Cameron was enthusiastic about this man,[14] and the lieutenant's biographer readily accepted that Tippu Tib had the white man's interests at heart. This may be; at a later date he entered King Léopold's employment, after a fashion, and ended his days as a celebrated member of the Zanzibari community. Still, the skeptic might be allowed to wonder whether Cameron's intrusion was all that pleasing to the despot of the interior. What the Arab did after Europeans were

13. *Ibid.*, 270.

14. His estimate of Tippu Tib is interesting, considering Cameron's aversion to slavery and the trade. He found that slavery was a by-product of the Arab's activities, and that if alternative transport were available, he would have used it. Though substantial numbers of prisoners sat about camp in chains, they seemed well-fed, and very few were destined for the coast and overseas. Nevertheless, somewhat contradictorily, Cameron also believed that slavery was on the increase in the interior because of the entry of more and more Arabs who wanted slaves for purposes of prestige. *Ibid.*, 281.

established, however tentatively, in the Congo is one thing; what he proposed before any other Europeans had been there is quite another. What is certain is that Tippu Tib suggested a way to the coast which involved, as he saw it, passage through Portuguese-, not Arab-controlled territory.

Whatever Tippu Tib's reasons for proposing this alternative, Cameron accepted the offer and went with him to his base camp near the Lomami River (northeast of present-day Kamina). By month's end he was well away from the Lualaba. Thus ended his projected Congo voyage. In retrospect one can deplore his mistake, but he was ill and discouraged and Tippu Tib's apparently sound advice must have been easy to accept. The fact remains that Cameron might have done in 1874 what Stanley did three years later. That Stanley built upon Cameron's foundation frequently escapes notice. *Force majeure* was not Cameron's specialty, although reasons for saying so mostly derive from his own modest account.

While stalled at Nyangwe, Cameron had been regaled with stories of a great lake to the west, apparently downstream on the Lualaba, which was frequented by Europeans. Sankorra was its name, and Cameron tentatively (and quite erroneously) put it on his map somewhat near what later was called Lake Léopold II, into which the Lokoro River flows. He wanted very much to see this body of water, but was assured that the local people were irrevocably opposed to foreigners. He considered asking Tippu Tib for military aid, but his scruples overcame him: "the merit of any geographical discovery would be irretrievably marred by shedding a drop of native blood except in self-defense." He was, of course, badly misled, although perhaps unintentionally, by his informants, for the Lualaba certainly did not flow westwards. The only "lake" which fits at all is the string of lesser bodies west and north of Lake Mweru on the river. The problem is resolved quite easily with air photos; on the ground it must have been maddening, and Cameron's account reflects it. These are the most confusing pages of his narrative.

Accepting Tippu Tib's advice, Cameron struck southward toward Urua/Katanga, hoping that when he turned west again he might reach the lake from the southeast. From the time that he parted with the Arab sultan, Cameron was in trouble with his men, who lacked guides and persistently tried to turn the party eastward. They were now in the vicinity of the Lomami River, well on their way toward the principal town of Urua. Cameron constantly nagged his carriers and produced new courses, but only somewhat successfully.

Now came his first armed conflict with local Africans. It was occasioned by the theft of his mascot goat. Until then, the lieutenant had avoided ultimatums; this time he felt it necessary to be firm in recovering his property. His demand was rejected truculently, and great crowds of angry men began to press about his column, all over-reacting to what looked like a minor matter. Cameron was puzzled, angry, and not a little nervous. Nevertheless, having started boldly, he dared not slink away. Suddenly great showers of arrows were shot at his party, although to Cameron's astonishment no one was hit. Finally, reluctant to do so because of his superiority in fire power, Cameron ordered his guards to volley. One of the local notables was hit at long range and a truce was arranged. Unfortunately, at this point reserves appeared and the conflict was renewed. Cameron managed to withdraw to the next village, which he seized and fortified, naming it Fort Dinah, after his purloined goat. Several tense days went by and another peace was patched together. Cameron got away, and only then learned the nature of the dispute. It appeared that a "Portuguese" slaving party had been nearby; naturally his own group was mistaken for a part of the raiding force. It was precisely to avoid this sort of mistake that Cameron had been reluctant to march with Arabs; now his troubles with the Portuguese began.

Soon after this contretemps, the Englishman came upon another of the great traders to the interior, an Arab called Jumah Merikani (presumably after the New England textile, American cloth, which at this time dominated the east coast trade). Cameron thought him "the kindest and most hospitable of the many friends I found among the Arab traders in Africa." From questioning him, Cameron was able to piece together a very fair picture of the riverine system draining into the Lomami and, ultimately, the Lualaba.

While with Jumah, Cameron was visited by a messenger from a Portuguese caravan, evidently another set of slavers, who announced that his master, one José António Alvez, whom Africans styled Kendele, proposed to visit a fellow European. Cameron was excited at the prospect of a white visitor. Alvez, it seems, thought he was going to call upon Livingstone. Both were disappointed, for, if Cameron were not the missionary, neither was Alvez white. "Great was my disappointment, however, when an old and ugly negro turned out of the hammock. Certainly he was dressed in European fashion and spoke Portuguese; but no further civilization could he boast of." [15]

Alvez, who was from Dondo in western Angola but who had been trading inland for nearly twenty years, dissuaded Cameron from a further attempt to reach Lake Sankorra and a visit to the court of Mwata Yamvo of the Lunda, stressing the remoteness and the danger in both instances. Instead, he proposed to guide the Englishman either to Luanda or Benguela. Cameron accepted the offer, although he knew that Alvez had no intention of starting for at least another month. In the meantime, Cameron pursued his local researches. "Notwithstanding my occupations, the Christmas of 1874 . . . passed drearily indeed." [16] Here, Cameron is less than frank, nor does his biographer mention the matter, but we now know that Cameron spent at least part of his time in the fashionable enterprise of treaty-making. It appears that he went so far as to declare a British protectorate over the Congo basin on 28 December 1874. He forwarded the instruments to the Foreign Office, which in February 1876, upon the advice of the Colonial Office, declined to approve them. [17]

The local ruler, Kasongo of the Urua, was away. He laid claim, Cameron learned, to all of the territory between the Lomami River and Lake Tanganyika, although much of it likewise was subject to Mwata Yamvo of the Lunda state. At last the chief returned. He was a very young and self-assured man who was willing to grant equal status to the ruler

15. *Ibid.*, 299.
16. *Ibid.*, 321.
17. Roger Anstey, *Britain and the Congo in the Nineteenth Century* (Oxford, 1962), 54.

of the Lunda, but was dubious of British pretensions. Cameron was not amused. "I then informed this self-important chief . . . that my chief was far greater than he, and, indeed, that he could have no idea of the magnitude of her power." [18] There is something risible about this boasting match, but to his credit Cameron reproduces it. The lieutenant's certainty depressed Kasongo, who allowed that Cameron might be right, though he privately expressed the belief that his visitor was supernatural.

In Kasongo's train came various undesirable attendants, among them the son of a Portuguese officer, a young man named Lourenço da Souza Coimbra, whom Cameron "awarded the palm for having reached the highest grade of ruffianism among them all." This man's importunate requests, his apparent connection with the sluggish Alvez, coupled with Kasongo's bombast and casual cruelty (many of the ruler's hangers-on were mutilated in various ways), led Cameron to renew his attempts to leave Jumah Merikani's home. It was quite clear that no one would help him to visit Lake Sankorra, all alike contending that they lacked the force to effect passage. But they were reluctant to let the English officer out of their hands so long as he had money. Not until mid-February 1875 could Cameron contrive to negotiate his passage to the coast.

Cameron's rather impatient but precise description of the formalities prevailing at a "sudanic" court is noteworthy. One must respect his ear for transcription of praise names: "Kalunga Kasongo, Kalunga, Moene Munza, Moene Banza, Moene Tanda." (This has been translated rather delightfully by Irvine Richardson of Michigan State University as "O, Lord Kasongo, Owner of all within the world, Owner of all inhabitants of the earth, Owner of the Portuguese." A separate essay could be based on this ultimate claim.) His serious depiction of the abasement ceremony performed by sub-chiefs is also interesting. Cameron was no anthropologist; he would have been staggered by the anthropological assertion that cultures cannot be rank-ordered, but he could report without

18. Cameron, *Across Africa*, 326.

scorn the affectations of another elite. "After all the chiefs had saluted, Kasongo delivered a long speech about himself, his divine rights, greatness and powers, declaring that the only person who could be compared to him was his relative Mata Yafa." [19] One is reminded of the Venetian ambassadors' reports concerning the early Tudor court.

Finally, in late March 1875, Cameron persuaded Alvez to move toward the coast. From the beginning he was outraged by his guide's conduct. "On this march with Alvez, I was disgusted beyond measure with what I saw of the manner in which the unfortunate slaves were treated, and have no hesitation in asserting that the worst of the Arabs are in this respect angels of light in comparison with the Portuguese and those who travel with them. Had it not come under my personal notice, I should scarcely have believed that any men could be so wantonly and brutally cruel." [20]

In short, Cameron was party to a slaving expedition, and his best intentions had come to very little precisely in the territories where he most hoped to show the British flag. He pleaded with the restless Kasongo, who moved about like a medieval English king, to give him some canoes, so he might return to the river by way of the Lomami, but without success.

Early in May he sent a scouting party forward. Its report was discouraging: all the land that they had traversed was in ruins, apparently from the efforts of Kasongo and his Portuguese associate. "Under the combined influence of immoderate drinking and smoking bhang, Kasongo acts like a demon, ordering death and mutilation indiscriminately, and behaving in the most barbarous manner to any who may be near him." [21] In this fearful situation, Cameron was reluctant to leave his camp, for he knew his pathetic stock of supplies would be stolen in his absence. Not until early June was he free to move toward the Angolan coast.

All along the road Cameron's associates disgraced them-

---

19. *Ibid.*, 329–330.
20. *Ibid.*, 331. These remarks occasioned considerable indignation in Lisbon. See James Duffy, *Portuguese Africa* (Cambridge, Mass., 1959), 357; also James Duffy, *A Question of Slavery* (Cambridge, Mass., 1967), 75–78.
21. Cameron, *Across Africa*, 334.

selves, ruining unharvested crops, seizing food stores, and cutting down banana trees in the name of Kasongo, whose writ still ran for many marches to the west. And the enforced halt had spoiled many of Cameron's carriers, who, out of practice, no longer could or would handle their allotted loads.

With much urging, the caravan finally dropped from the wooded highlands into swampy country which Cameron reckoned was impassable during the rains. It was bad enough at present, an exercise in struggling from grass tuft to grass tuft, always fearful of quicksands which underlay even apparently swift, clear streams. Cameron was ill and hungry, but traveling light; for his men the exertion must have been appalling. At last they struggled through the Njivi marsh and entered lands known to European traders. Here the terrain changed markedly, and on the dry plain he noticed gigantic white ant hills, some nearly fifty feet high. When he encountered the local chief, an old man named Lunga Mandi, who seemed to be a dependent of Kasongo, the ruler fled his village. Cameron thought that word of his own good conduct would suffice, but rather unfortunately he gave the chief a demonstration of his firepower (none of these people had seen repeating, rifled weapons), which proved unnerving.

Coimbra, the slaver, still had not come up with them, though he was intending to travel with Cameron's party, and once more Alvez announced his intention of waiting for his friend. Cameron urged some bearers to go along with him, and told Alvez that he might do as he wished. Unwilling to lose his fee, Alvez reluctantly followed, and early in July they began their final march to the coast. The hungriest days and hardest marches, although Cameron did not know it, lay before them.

Some of Alvez's slaves immediately ran away, to Cameron's delight. He reconsidered when he witnessed the punishment of those who were recaptured. On the following day Coimbra caught up with them, dragging 52 women slaves behind him. Cameron was horrified, though still prepared to distinguish between the policy of Portugal and the acts of her citizens. "Indeed, the cruelties perpetuated in the heart of Africa by men calling themselves Christians, and carrying the Portuguese flag, can scarcely be credited by those living in a civilized land; and the Government of Portugal can not be cognizant of the atrocities committed by men claiming to be her subjects."[22] He worked out a formula which indicated that at least ten villages had been destroyed to procure these unfortunate women, that is, about 1500 persons must have been killed, injured, or driven into the bush without resources, merely to produce these wretched captives. This calculation was much copied in later years, when it became authoritative in antislavery circles. Working with those figures, and those he garnered from Stanley's writings, Cardinal Lavigerie was able to say in 1888 that the annual loss of life in the African interior was about 400,000 persons.[23]

Cameron now entered the domain of another despot, Msiri, the overlord of Katanga, who roamed freely throughout that copper-laden region by virtue of firearms and audacity. Cameron gathered that Msiri traded from the Atlantic to Unyanyembe, mostly in copper and slaves, as ivory-bearing elephants long since had been shot out. His trade with the west coast had gone on for more than twenty years and had recently expanded. His slaves for the most part never reached Benguela, being exchanged along the way, but Cameron was persuaded that of those who reached the ocean many were shipped abroad, despite "the lives and treasure that England has expended in the suppression of this inhuman traffic."[24] It was all most discouraging. Besides, food again proved difficult to obtain, as most of the villages they passed had but a little of last year's grain.

At this point they reached the source of the Lomami River, a large swamp near the spot where the Belgians later erected Kamina. Much copper, in the usual form of St. Andrew's crosses, was traded thereabouts. Cameron understood that the mines were located some fifty miles to the south. He was the first European of modern times to come this close to the min-

22. *Ibid.*, 351. This earned Cameron some approval in Portugal years later.
23. Ruth Slade, *King Leopold's Congo* (London, 1962), 102.
24. *Ibid.*, 354. Msiri originally had supplanted the rightful overlord of the greater Katanga, Kazembe of the eastern Lunda, by using his firepower to support various factions. Kasongo and the Luba state experienced the same fate somewhat later in the nineteenth century. See August Verbeken, *Msiri, roi du Garenganze* (Brussels, 1956).

eral zone, and, although he never saw it, he retained the conviction that Katanga offered great hope to European entrepreneurs. He became, on the strength of this near-visit, the reputed expert on the resources of central Africa.

Several more days of struggle through canebrakes and swamps brought them at last to the borders of Lunda country. Here Alvez again turned southeast, although Bihé lay to the southwest. Cameron tried to maintain the proper road, but was forced to retrace his steps and follow Alvez, for his men refused to traverse this unknown region without the dubious benefit of Portuguese protection. Finally, the sullen travelers came to the village of sub-chief Mwene Kula, which Cameron identified as that visited by the two *pombeiros* in the first quarter of the century.[25] The land was densely populated, although the poverty and absence of trade goods suggested that no recent caravans had preceded the Englishman and his Portuguese guide. Mwene Kula's realm lay between the headwaters of the northbound Lulua River and the southerly flowing Zambezi River, or Liambai, as it was known locally. The nights now were intensely cold (Fahrenheit 38° at dawn) and ice stood on the low ground, which much delighted the European, although he was sensible that his servants, lacking clothes and shoes, took another view of the weather.

They had reached what later became the Congo-Angola frontier, too far south for Cameron's liking, though some of his associates wished to walk even farther in that direction before turning toward the coast. (Letters which he sent to the British Consul in Luanda at this point were never received, and Cameron later believed that Portuguese officials would have been embarrassed by English communications from the remote Portuguese-claimed interior.)

For the first time since leaving the region of the lakes, Cameron began to see cattle again. But, though the countryside was rich, he was unable to buy much food, for slaves, cloth, and gunpowder were the only acceptable currencies. His march across this vast flood plain led Cameron to conclude that with certain improvements, such as a twenty-mile canal,

25. See Richard Burton, *The Lands of Cazembe* (London, 1873), for an English edition of their journals and reports.

the Congo-Zambezi systems could be linked, providing a trans-continental water route. Though he qualified his estimate, his enthusiasm remains difficult to explain, for he was not given to rash engineering projects.

Fish were available in great profusion. In fact, dried fish was the principal trade item, and Cameron turned to this imperfectly prepared food with relieved repugnance. To this point Coimbra had been in the background; now it was his turn to wrong the Lieutenant. The Portuguese bribed one of Cameron's best men to steal his employer's few remaining trade goods. When the attempt failed, Coimbra not only demanded that Cameron repay the bribe, but also compensate him for the dried fish which the purloined goods might have bought. The alternative, the astounded Englishman gathered, was the forcible seizure of the unreliable thief. The man was too good to lose, and upon Alvez's urging Cameron reluctantly gave in to this fantastic proposition. "Perhaps some who do not weigh the whole circumstances and surroundings of this affair may possibly think I erred in yielding; but I could not fail to see, much as it annoyed me, that this course was absolutely necessary to prevent the wreck of the expedition," Cameron explained with extraordinary patience.[26]

The bested traveler reckoned that he had roughly four days' supplies left, consisting only of rice and cassava flour, and he knew he was in for a slim time until he reached Bihé district, where Europeans had been trading for many decades. However, he could attain Bihé if valuables were jettisoned and enough determination shown. As usual, at this point Cameron was frustrated again, for news reached camp that the road from Bihé to the coast was closed. But the story proved false and, after additional delay, in late September he set out from the village of regional chief Mona Peho, who supported the difficulties of office by remaining drunk on mead concocted in his honey-laden realm. The chief had mentioned that another European was on the road before them, and Cameron eagerly sought to meet this unknown white.

Shortly thereafter they came upon a caravan of a merchant

26. Cameron, *Across Africa*, 379.

from Benguela. The column was led by a slave, who was utterly perplexed by Cameron's presence; nor was he satisfied with the Englishman's extraordinary assertion that his object was the collection of information. By this time the Lieutenant was reduced to selling his shirts and pieces of his coat in order to feed his men. Although he at last was in the basin of the Cuanza River and hence, he knew, reasonably near the coast, the strain began to tell. Alvez was if anything even more unbearable. One of the Ovimbundu chiefs, taking pity on Cameron's condition, freely gave him a calf, the first meat which he had seen for many days. Alvez tried to claim it, but there was a limit to the Briton's patience, and he refused to part with the animal.

On the last day of September, the quarreling men camped on the banks of the Cuanza. Sight of the river aroused Cameron's nautical and commercial instincts. He knew that a steamship company operated a vessel between the coast and Dondo, and he saw no reason why shallow-draft vessels could not be placed in the stream beyond the Dondo falls, thereby intercepting the overland trade to Benguela. In this, he was anticipating arguments later used by many, especially Léopold II.

Portuguese material culture was much in evidence. Pigs were everywhere, cattle abounded, and a substantial mulatto population lived amongst the local people. There was even a white man, an anonymous Portuguese known to Cameron only as Chico, who had escaped from a coastal penal colony and become an assistant to Alvez. For the first time in a year, Cameron at last bathed properly and drank coffee. Though Alvez had lived in Bihé for thirty years, he had not bothered to build anything permanent. He managed to overcharge Cameron considerably for the ivory and beeswax which was needed to buy cloth.

Early in October 1875 Cameron set off for the coast, first calling on the overlord Cagnombe (Portuguese: Camanongue), whose town, some three miles in circumference, was the largest encountered on the crosscontinental trip. Even in this far western place, Msiri's mark was visible, for many of the locals had adopted the cicatrices of the Nyamwezi, which markings Msiri had decreed for all his people, regardless of origin. Cameron was convinced that east-west communication would be an easy matter if Msiri's men could be enlisted. Upon his dismissal by the sovereign, whom he thought a braggart, Cameron moved to the compound of a resident European, one Senhor Gonçalves, who had been in Bihé thirty-three years, owned six villages, and traded mostly in ivory and beeswax. Cameron was delighted with the man, whose display of a breakfast tablecloth seemed a good omen. If only, he wrote, more such Portuguese gentlemen settled in the Angolan highlands, "much might be done toward opening up and civilizing Africa." [27]

The delights of rosé wine and bed sheets were not sufficient to keep Cameron in this place for more than a day, however, and he pressed on across country which promised to produce wheat. On the morrow he stayed with another trader, João Baptista Fereira, who, though he lived much like Alvez, seemed to be a different sort, one easier for an Englishman to accept. He was kind to animals, a mark in his favor—so much so, that Cameron was inclined to overlook certain other aspects of his host's manner of life, such as slaving. "I must acknowledge that to me and mine he showed great kindness, and I wish I were not compelled, in the interests of Africa, to make any allusions to the dark side of his character." [28] At that time the trader was enlarging his stock of muskets, preparatory to a visit to Kasongo's realm for slaves.

Cameron now was but a little more than two hundred air miles from the coast, at the place called Silva Porto on today's maps, though by that Portuguese settler named Belmonte. When Cameron called, António Francisco da Silva Porto had retired to Benguela and his citrus orchards and formal gardens were in ruins. Soon, however, Cameron entered a pleasant wooded region, where the villages had stone walls, quite like "farms on the Wiltshire downs." Their villages may have been pleasant, but the inhabitants were not. Cameron did not extend his comparison. The local people disliked strangers, for, as they remarked, one tends to bring another, and then

27. *Ibid.*, 401.
28. *Ibid.*, 403.

where is one's trade monopoly? Food was plentiful, but Cameron had trouble buying any, for there was a surplus of cloth so near to the coast, and farmers wanted only gunpowder or alcohol.

At the next village, Komanante, the expedition once more halted, since the foreman of the carriers refused to move his sick wife. Cameron applauded this unexpected display of marital affection but regretted its expression in his vicinity. While waiting impatiently, he was visited by a young Portuguese trader. Cameron's visitor was in pawn to the local chief and could not leave without satisfying his creditors, some indication that the Portuguese state did not extend its influence this far inland. On the other hand, the debtor did not seem to mind, for to Cameron's way of thinking he was well looked after by his captors.

After another protracted beer-drink amid scenes "of licentiousness almost beyond belief," Cameron moved into wooded, hilly country saturated with water courses and clothed in flowering shrubs. He was enchanted. "Neither poet with all the wealth of word-imagery, nor painter, with almost supernatural genius, could by pen or pencil do full justice to the country of Bailunda." [29] Nevertheless, he was bereft of cloth, rain made each night a misery, and some of his men were quite ill. Numerous streams had to be crossed, several of them actual rivers now that the floods were in progress, and the hazards of travel were magnified. Cameron took to guiding from the rear, so as to close up the stragglers, on one day spending over four of nine and a half hours trying to keep his men in line.

The only food now available was a swarm of locusts, which, stunned with cold, clustered on branches of trees in their path. Of the six hours which they spent on the road one bad day, only a third counted as marching time. More travelers met them now, but the only news of the coast which they felt worth mentioning was that slaves no longer could be brought to Benguela, a situation which did not please Cameron's companions.

29. *Ibid.*, 411.

After this day's exhibition, I saw that the marching powers of my men had gone from bad to worse, and that some decisive steps must be taken, or the caravan would never reach the coast, now only one hundred and twenty-six geographical miles distant. . . . I sat down for half an hour's reflection, and then resolved on the action to be taken. It came to this: throw away tent, boat, bed, and everything but instruments, journals, and books: and then, taking a few picked men, make a forced march to the coast, sending thence assistance to the main body.[30]

Picking five men, all east coast Muslims, Cameron set out over extremely high and rugged ground, camping at an altitude of 5,800 feet on the first afternoon. Caravans heading inland were frequent, most of their members carrying umbrellas and empty kerosene tins. (He was too distracted to inquire the purpose of the latter.) Some of these travelers expressed astonishment at the furious pace the strange white man was setting.

Shortly, they began their descent to the sea, in one march of eleven hours dropping nearly 2,000 feet. All the while they continued to meet upward-bound trading parties, evidence of a permanent commercial connection between the coast and Bailundu. No one would sell Cameron food, despite the region's fertility. His temper became dangerous. Passing one caravan, whose people tried shoving his scarecrow party off the narrow path, he lost it. "One fellow knocked up against me purposely, upon which I tripped him just as purposely, though seemingly by accident, and sent him sprawling with his load, by way of a hint that he could not expect to have his own way in everything."[31]

The going now was exceedingly rough, and the road was littered with evidences of exhausted slaves: clogs, forks, and shallow graves were everywhere; even skeletons were visible. One more day of stiff climbing, again without food, and Cameron at last saw, beyond the summit of the next

30. *Ibid.*, 421.
31. *Ibid.*, 425.

range, the distant sea. He was barely in time, for something clearly was wrong with him. Purple blotches disfigured his skin, and his mouth bled when he smoked his pipe.

He camped that night just short of the coast, amid the fires of numerous caravans on their way inland. Here one of the men he had sent ahead met them with a basket of wine, sardines, sausages, and bread, gifts of a trader at Katombela. Though exhausted, Cameron could not sleep, nor was he able to eat much because of the condition of his mouth, so he spent the night packing for the last march. At false dawn they started and within minutes were on the shore. The Union Jack was unfurled and the party staggered into town, where a retired officer of the French Navy, named Cauchoix, broke out a bottle to celebrate the first European passage from the Indian Ocean to the Atlantic by way of land. The date was 7 November 1875.

Cameron's savior had a large and civilized establishment. This was fortunate, for the Englishman now became seriously ill from scurvy. His tongue swelled till his mouth was filled, blood poured out copiously, and doses of carbolic acid were not enough to halt it. He had to be carried down the coast to Benguela, where he was saved by the resident surgeon.

When Cameron had recovered, his first concern was to dispatch his men back to Zanzibar. This arranged, he sailed up the coast beyond the Portuguese frontier to a free trade port, Kinsembo, halfway between Luanda and the mouth of the Congo. The actual border seemed to be at Ambriz, some twelve miles south. The information, of no great consequence then, came to seem very important when in the next decade the Portuguese argued an effective control to 5° north of the Congo River.

By February 1876 his men had sailed for St. Helena, where they hoped to transship for the Cape of Good Hope and eastward, and Cameron himself boarded the coaster S.S. *Congo*, destined for Liverpool after an interminable series of ports of call. Along the way, he met many of his old friends and superiors, some of whom had not connected the name of the African explorer with that of the young midshipman they had known. At last, on 2 April 1876, Cameron reached Liverpool, three years and four months after his departure to contact Livingstone.

The British scientific world acclaimed him. Nine days after his arrival in England, before an admiring audience in St. James's Hall, Cameron described his journey at a meeting of the Royal Geographical Society. Other explorers, such as James A. Grant, and geographers of the stature of Sir Clements Markham, paid tribute to Cameron's enterprise.[32] The British Treasury, not easily persuaded to spend public monies on such matters, provided £3,000 to help defray the costs of his expedition, which had exceeded £12,000. Some private donations also were accepted, but the Royal Geographical Society paid for substantially all of Cameron's trip. It was from start to finish a British undertaking. King Léopold, for example, when he learned that Cameron was short of funds for his return to England from Angola, offered to pay for the hero's passage, but his gesture was declined.[33] Cameron was awarded the Society's coveted gold Founder's Medal; the University of Oxford made him an honorary Doctor of Civil Law; the Queen announced his induction as a Companion of the Bath; finally, the Navy promoted him to Commander.

Friends had persuaded him to write up his narrative and he acceded, thus revealing a literary talent. In clear, sympathetic prose he noted that much still remained tentative. He believed that he had grasped the outline of the lakes region and the watersheds of the principal rivers; given an account of the soils, rains, and products of the central zone; and described political conditions in the interior, especially concerning Arab and Portuguese slave-raiding. Originally, he had believed, along with Livingstone, that the stream called Lualaba probably flowed into Albert Nyanza, and thus formed a part of the true Nile.[34] But his investigations west of the lakes persuaded him that the Lualaba was, as his Arab informants

32. Markham, "Cameron's Diary"; James Augustus Grant, "On Mr H. M. Stanley's Exploration of Victoria Nyanza," *Journal of the Royal Geographical Society*, XLVI (1876), 10–33; "The Founder's (Gold) Medal Presentation Ceremony," *ibid.*, cxxii.

33. Slade, *King Leopold's Congo*, 36, n. 4.

34. *New York Times*, 20 August 1874.

insisted, in reality a tributary of the Congo.[35] His examination of the Lukuga River tended to confirm this view. Moreover, he was convinced that the ultimate affluents of both the Congo and Zambezi rivers were intermingled in the upper Lozi flood plain and that some manner of linking them could be devised.

There were, he wrote, four principal ways to reach central Africa: from the Arab-controlled ports of eastern Africa; up the Nile Valley; inland from Angola (though the Congo River might supersede this path); and northward from Natal through the Transvaal. The latter, he supposed, would prove of great importance in the future. But all of these paths required men to carry burdens. With the extinction of the slave trade and the disappearance of elephants, alternative transport and commodities would have to be found. He was ready with suggestions. Sugar, cotton, coffee, palm oil, and tobacco sprang to mind, but many other equally useful items could be instanced. Besides, he believed that Africa contained great and as yet only imperfectly understood mineral deposits, particularly of copper, gold, coal, and silver. Enterprise and manpower would be needed to exploit them, and there were signs that both might be found. Missionary bodies were pressing into Africa, taking with them small steamships, and constantly struggling to suppress slavery and slave wars. "Missionary efforts, however, will not avail to stop the slave trade, and open the country to civilization, unless supplemented by commerce. Commercial enterprise and missionary effort, instead of acting in opposition, as is too often the case, should do their best to assist each other. Wherever commerce finds its way, there missionaries will follow; and wherever missionaries prove that white men can live and travel, there trade is certain to be established."[36] For the remainder of his life, Cameron sought to encourage these twin approaches, though, it should be added, with ever greater emphasis on the commercial side of the equation.

This emphasis upon the benefits of commerce might appear unusual in one so early trained in naval matters, especially one

35. *Ibid.*, 5 January 1875.
36. Cameron, *Across Africa*, 476.

from a clerical background. But Cameron was no stranger to his times; he subscribed to the ideas of his age with ever-increasing enthusiasm, until finally he came to devote most of his attention to the promotion of companies interested in Africa. He thoroughly approved of Stanley's efforts to induce British participation in African ventures, and he likewise grieved at their sluggish response. When Léopold II convened an international group of Africanist geographers in September 1876, Cameron was enthusiastic.

It appears that the King of the Belgians, either to spur his countrymen or to lay the basis for some sort of future action in Africa, visited London in the spring of Cameron's triumph. There he conferred with the explorer and Sir Henry Rawlinson of the Royal Geographical Society. Plans for an international geographical convention were outlined. In August, Léopold asked the Prince of Wales, his cousin, to advise him on the composition of the British delegation. The Prince recommended Cameron, Grant, Baker, and a few armchair notables from the Royal Geographical Society. Ten men finally were sent invitations and a position paper in which Léopold stressed the disinterested nature of his commitment to the cause of African civilization. He suggested that delegates might wish to consider establishing bases at the mouth of the Congo and on Zanzibar, from which interior routes of communication and supply could be projected. A string of interior stations was designed to further the twin goals of pacification and scientific advance.

The conference opened in Brussels on 12 September 1876. The British delegates appear to have been enthusiastic, in some ways even going beyond Léopold's introductory proposals. Sir Rutherford Alcock, the president of the Royal Geographical Society, suggested that the King might establish a consulate at Ujiji to encourage a beneficial commercial presence. All the British delegates approved Cameron's suggestion that steam vessels be placed on the upper Congo and the Great Lakes, while Sir Bartle Frere proposed what Léopold clearly wanted, that the King be president of the organization they decided upon—the Association Internationale Africaine. Nevertheless, for reasons which have already been explored at length,[37] the Council of the Royal Geographical Society decided in January 1877 to support the aims of the new association, but independently through British means.

Cameron remained impressed with the King's vision. "The philanthropic efforts of His Majesty the King of the Belgians, if they meet with the support they deserve, although not either of a missionary or commercial character, must also materially assist in opening up the country."[38] He went beyond Léopold in suggesting that some port, such as Mombasa, be acquired and a light line of rail projected from it to lakes Victoria and Tanganyika. The Congo especially intrigued him. Its mouth was owned by no European state, and above the rapids some 110 miles upstream, which Captain James Kingston Tuckey had reached in 1816,[39] the river was broad and tranquil. "We may well ask ourselves why we allow such a noble highway into regions of untold richness to lie neglected and useless. Why are not steamers flying the British colours carrying the overglut of our manufactured goods to the naked African, and receiving from him in exchange those choicest gifts of nature by which he is surrounded, and of the value of which he is at present ignorant?"[40] We may suspect an enthusiast, for this picture consorted oddly with the harrowing chapters of Cameron's book.

The commander was impatient with those who argued that indigenous rights would be trampled. Those chiefs who were

37. For the fullest account of the motives entertained by the directors of the Royal Geographical Society, see Roy C. Bridges, "The Royal Geographical Society and the African Exploration Fund," *The Geographical Journal*, CXXIX (1963), 25–35. Bridges concluded from an examination of the Society's papers that, although Sir Rutherford Alcock wished to support Léopold, and certainly did not wish to irritate Queen Victoria, he feared that the Charter of the Royal Geographical Society made formal association impossible. The Royal Geographical Society existed for the "advancement of science," and Léopold certainly envisioned far more than this. Moreover, it was the opinion of the Crown's Law Officers that the proposed international body might embark upon programs inimical to British interests. The Society therefore established an African Exploration Fund early in 1877. The Fund lasted nearly three years. Its most important (and final) work was carried out by Joseph Thomson.

38. Cameron, *Across Africa*, 477.

39. James Kingston Tuckey, *Narrative of an Expedition to Explore the River Zaire . . . in 1816* (London, 1818).

40. Cameron, *Across Africa*, 479.

not incompetent were barbarous, and their unwilling subjects gladly would trade them for the security of European rule. Naturally, the line of communications posts would assume the responsibilities of government: "in any scheme for forming stations in Central Africa—be they for missionary, scientific or trading purposes—the fact that those in charge would soon have to exercise magisterial powers must not be lost sight of." [41] Here he seems to have been as clear-headed as the King of the Belgians. Cameron was not sanguine about the early extirpation of domestic slavery. Certainly, there was much in Africa which was repugnant to Europeans, but it did not follow that European dislike would carry the day. Nor was it altogether advisable to rush matters. "Our own civilization, it must be remembered, is the growth of many centuries, and to expect that of Africa to become equal to it in a decade or two is an absurdity." [42]

When the hero's welcome was over, Cameron returned to regular naval duty, but the routine of gunnery courses and peacetime discipline bored him; in 1878 he again went on leave, this time travel across Turkey to India. With the recent acquisition of Cyprus and a new set of Near Eastern strategic interests, he believed that the notion of a railway linking British India with Asia Minor would be feasible. While in India he learned of the British disaster at Isandhlwana and volunteered for service in the last Zulu war. Through some mix-up he was not permitted to go to Natal, so he went home from Karachi and wrote his second book, *Our Future Highway*, an account of his trip.

His desire to see more of Africa remained unsatisfied. The Navy bored him. So, in the autumn of 1881, he joined Sir Richard Burton, who had been asked to examine some Gold Coast mining concessions for James Irvine, a Liverpool merchant with extensive west coast investments. Burton, the older and more eminent man, had first traversed these regions two decades earlier, when he had reported favorably on their gold-mining potential.[43] It was Cameron's first contact, except for ports of call, but, though inexperienced, he was stronger and

41. *Ibid.*, 480.
42. *Ibid.*, 482.
43. See his *Wanderings in West Africa* (London, 1863).

consequently did much of the actual mapping of the lands embracing the Ankobrah River, the center of the gold fields. Both men displayed considerable expertise in the problems of mining, and their resulting joint publication, *To the Gold Coast for Gold,* gave much solid information to prospective British investors. They made a joint presentation to the members of the Royal Geographical Society in June 1882.

This was Cameron's last year on active duty with the Royal Navy. He retired a quarter-century after entering upon that service, and thereafter devoted his full time to African affairs and to directing companies with African interests. The most important of these were the African International Flotilla and Transport Company, the Central African and Zoutpansberg Exploration Company, the Companhia da Zambezia, and the Katanga Company. The latter was the link between British capitalists and the Belgian ruler's domain. Cameron was very anxious to interest the British business community in Congo adventures but, disappointed in his inability to excite his compatriots, turned increasingly to King Léopold's Independent State, and in so doing helped deny Katanga to another British exponent of the forward policy, Cecil Rhodes. When Captain William Grant Stairs secured Katanga for Léopold, Rhodes effectively lost his chance for a Cape to Cairo railway under British control.[44] Not that this could have grieved Cameron very much, for he was in conflict with Rhodes in other areas as well.[45] Besides, Cameron later contended publicly that he first had put forth the Cape to Cairo notion.[46]

In the 1880's Cameron amused himself by writing adventure tales for various boys' magazines, mostly with an African or nautical setting, somewhat in the manner of that other ex-Naval officer, the popular and prolific Captain Frederick Marryat. On 27 March 1894, while returning from a hunt near Leighton Buzzard, he was thrown by his mount and died

44. See Joseph A. Moloney, *With Captain Stairs to Katanga* (London, 1893), and his "The Stairs Expedition to Katanga," *The Geographical Journal,* II (1893), 238–248.

45. For this see R. J. Hammond, *Portugal and Africa, 1815–1910* (Stanford, 1966), 169–173.

46. *Dictionary of National Biography,* Cameron entry, 381.

of head injuries. In his fifty years he did much to link Livingstone's Africa with the world of modern commercial development. He brought Europe's attention to the Congo, although it was Stanley who demonstrated what Cameron suggested. He had an unremitting faith in the beneficence of British institutions, especially capitalism, but his vision was not distorted by the racism so fashionable in his time. He was, to use a very old-fashioned word, a gentleman.

It is relatively easy to estimate Cameron's significance for and relation to his own, the European, world. It is more difficult to place him in an African context. He clearly was no cultural relativist, nor was he a romantic where indigenous customs were involved. His writings abound with strictures regarding the cruelty of rulers, who he was persuaded had no popular support, and there is a sufficiency of references to barbaric rites. But he was no racist in the generally accepted nineteenth-century meaning of the term, that is, he did not presume some congenital inferiority in Africans, nor was he disposed to believe in some connection between race and culture.

Given time (he thought at least in terms of a generation), Africans would become Europeans: Christian, monogamous, capitalist—in short, civilized. The process would be arduous as well as lengthy, but the material benefits of commercial expansion, coupled with the spiritual consolations of missionary enterprise, would combine to provide a framework for the regeneration of the native peoples. The word regeneration is operative here. Cameron did not suppose that Africans, any of them, had declined from some former glory, that their age of gold was past, but he did seem to understand that the conditions which he witnessed were at base the product of outside forces at work. His despots and savages tended to be Arabs, Portuguese, or Swahili interlopers, armed with European weapons and catering to demands which originated either in Europe or Asia. He distinguished between domestic or household slavery, which does not seem to have overly offended him, and the slave trade, which he detested thoroughly. The trade was not, however, so extensive as some critics held; the great majority of captured persons probably never left Africa's shores. Still, if most of them were spared the horrors of the middle passage or a cramped trip by dhow across the Arabian Gulf, substantial numbers did die as atoms in the commercial universe.

Being British, Cameron naturally felt a special necessity for crushing the trade in humans, quite apart from any obligation laid upon him by virtue of his naval commission. Moreover, he appears to have been an extremely compassionate man, very reluctant to inflict harm upon others. An unusual air of gentleness pervades his account; even in the passages which relate great provocation, his tone suggests that the loss of one's temper requires apology. On the one occasion when he fought to defend himself, he made it clear that his African enemies had very good reasons of their own to be hostile.

Time and again one is struck by Cameron's cool acceptance of the unknown. It is easy to forget that the regions which he entered were in fact dangerous. Warfare and despoilment of the stranger were typical patterns of behavior on the part of the strong; distrust and evasiveness characterized the weak. To people who knew only of Arabs and Portuguese Africans, the Lieutenant must have seemed ominous. His motives were unknown, his story was suspect, even implausible (who could take seriously the assertion that a man would undergo a hazardous journey because he wanted to know which way a river flowed?), and his relation to various Arabs seemed altogether too close. Moreover, as his trip went on he became progressively shabbier and, apart from his weapons, hardly could command respect. The Nyamwezi, with many years of commercial experience, no doubt could fit him into their universe, but for the Lunda and to a lesser extent the Ovimbundu, his posture seemed unlikely.

From an African viewpoint Cameron represented nearly the last of the inadequately equipped Europeans who had to rely upon good will and common sense in their dealings with native peoples. Within a few years the pattern set by Stanley would prevail, and Europeans would presume their right to shoot their way through whatever piece of the world they chose to visit. To this extent Cameron might be taxed with providing a poor model for Africans to examine, in the same way that successive generations of missionaries taught Africans to presume improbably correct behavior from all white men, especially those in the distant metropoles. The question arises: would he have sacrificed the chance to acquire scientific information, had he possessed the means to force his way? One is inclined to think so, but it is a guess. Cameron did not live long enough to become aware of reality in Léopold's private estate, or in Rhodes's counterpart, but his descriptions of African resistance to Arab and Portuguese depredations suggest that he would have distinguished between popular struggle and the warfare conducted by local despots whose unjust ways were in jeopardy. He worked from the premise that Europeans were just and that, as conditions were, African rulers could not be accorded the same presumption. This said nothing about the abilities of Africans, but it said a good deal about their polities, which he knew to be in ruins. In all likelihood, such polities never had been very satisfactory, but to him they then seemed scandalous.

It is important to remember that when Cameron castigated Africans, or Arabs, or the Portuguese he did so for other than racist reasons. What he objected to was not a man's color, but rather his pretension to an appellation which implied a higher set of standards. When he met an Arab or a Portuguese, he expected to meet someone who conversed in Swahili or the European tongue, dressed appropriately, conformed to certain standards of behavior toward others, especially those weaker or female others, was kind to animals, did not indulge his passions unrestrainedly, and had an eye for business (which would be exemplified by punctuality, truthfulness, and self-respect). The few who came up to this mark were treated by Cameron with great sympathy in his book. The many who fell short were treated less well. It was not that the Portuguese had given great responsibilities to half-castes in the interior of Angola which bothered Cameron; it was simply that these agents had not done their duty. It was in his eyes all right that Arabs on the shores of Lake Tanganyika claimed to represent the Sultan of Zanzibar; but they seemed to him to have failed to perform their functions. Similarly with African rulers: Cameron was prepared to acknowledge the claims of a Kazembe, but when that prince ruined his subjects to satisfy some perverse whim, he undercut the basis of his own position. African kings might be acceptable, but bad African kings were an abomination, especially in a region given over to bad Arabs and bad Portuguese.

Though not so detailed and erudite an observer as Burton, and certainly not so good a writer, Cameron included in his narrative much sound ethnographic material and displayed a lively sense of curiosity about daily existence as well as about the more bizarre customs which he encountered. He had a very good ear for language and accurately transcribed many key words in the Bantu languages he heard. His descriptions of "sudanic" courts are especially good and his understanding of political conditions in the interior was informed. Apart from the geographical value of his book, which was considerable, its main importance might appear to be its emphasis upon the human side of things. Although he was a careful student of his environment, Cameron showed no exclusive interest in its nonhuman aspects. Those lengthy accounts of big-game hunting which burden the pages of so many African travelers are not found in his volume. Nor was he much interested in glamorizing himself. This tendency to be matter-of-fact in unusual circumstances was useful in Cameron's relations with Africans. "I knew very well when I was in Africa that I was not there to play" was the way he put it when he accepted the Royal Geographical Society's Founder's Medal.[47] There was work to do, and as an officer he undertook to do it. The primary task, after learning of Livingstone's death, was to plot elevations and record the position and flow of rivers in the continent's heartland. The fellows of the Royal Geographical Society were not primarily interested in the peoples of Africa, and Cameron was not expected to provide them with ethnographies, except as they were pertinent to an understanding of the environment of the interior. This he did admirably.

Were it not for the worrisome business of the treaties that he made in the Congo, we might be justified in crediting

47. *Journal of the Royal Geographical Society*, XLVI (1876), cxxii.

Cameron with completely disinterested motives for his exploit. As it is, these forays into diplomacy need not bother us too much. There is no need to see the Lieutenant as a front-runner of rampant imperialism, as a Stanley, Brazza, or Peters prototype. He was distressed at the misdeeds of Portuguese and Arab slavers (though he found individuals congenial enough), convinced that most chiefs were barbarous incompetents who ruled without popular mandate, and certain that European supervision would be acceptable or even welcome to the harried peoples of central Africa. It was natural for a man with the Queen's commission to suppose that the best European protection would be afforded by Britain.

He showed no inclination to acquire lands indisputably in the possession of effective governments. The Swahili coast and the Atlantic provinces of Angola did not entice Cameron; in the case of the latter, he hoped that more Portuguese of the right type would appear on the scene. It was only in those areas where benevolent external influence was unknown or at best indirect that he contemplated a British sphere of influence. But this sphere was not to be confused with sovereign acquisition. Without doubt, a European enclave would become a power center and take on the trappings of local government, but this would not signify colonization. When Cameron spoke of opening a region, he meant to merchants and missionaries, not settlers. At least a part of the appeal which Léopold's African Association had for him was its international character, representing the concerted benevolence of European civilization brought to bear on a huge field of darkness.

Cameron found many Arabs acceptable, and was not a strenuous opponent of Islam. In this, too, he was at one with many of his contemporaries, both lay and clerical. After all, Islam was a world religion with historic connections to the other great Semitic faiths. It was, in his eyes, a white man's religion, and one remarkably resistant to external pressures and evidently able to proselytize with ease in Africa. Cameron was aware that many of the Muslims whom he encountered were only nominally so by the standards of Mecca, yet even such beliefs were preferable to pagan superstition which bound a man to ancestors and an unprogressive life. While Cameron stressed the advantages of Christian proselytism, he was no enemy to other "civilized" beliefs. Still, there is no doubt that Christianity and capitalism were part and parcel of his world view.

Africans were redeemable, but it would require great European effort to create the appropriate conditions for Africans to shake off the apathy to which custom, climate, and warfare had brought them. It was inconceivable that they could do so without European aid on a very large scale. Cameron believed very strongly in the educational value of work, as did most men of his class, and he saw the chartered companies and the African International Association as the proper means for effecting social change. These great employers of labor, with their schemes for bridging rivers, laying tracks, and placing steamers on the inland waterways, offered limitless scope for African advancement. If this advance went step by step with a moral advance resulting from missionary effort, Africans might be expected to show astonishing results within a generation.

To us, accustomed to dream of change in the very short run, this may seem impossibly dilatory, but in Cameron's age the discrepancy between Africans and Europeans was painfully obvious, far more so than in later times when so much of European material culture had been transmitted to non-European peoples. Moreover, Cameron's generation was quite aware of the price paid for industrialization, and it was not clear that just anybody could do it. Africa's wealth most likely would be extracted, not manufactured; consequently, Cameron thought Africans probably would remain primary producers of crops and minerals for the urban world to consume. Not very much has occurred in the intervening ninety years to alter this conclusion.

Cameron was an enlightened observer of the central African scene, and a conscientious and pacific traveler in one of the last zones to receive the mixed benefits of European attention. He was a practical humanitarian and a realistic assessor of African potentialities. It is in some ways to his credit that he has not achieved more fame; at least his memory lacks notoriety.

Joseph Thomson:
Energy, Humanism, and Imperialism

by Robert I. Rotberg

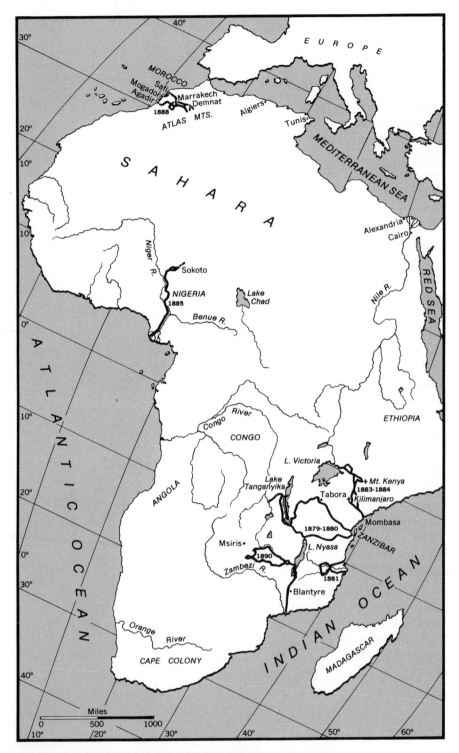

The six explorations of Joseph Thomson

Joseph Thomson made his name during the period of transition that marked the close of the great age of European exploration in Africa and the beginning of the phase of scramble and partition. His activities exemplified the era: He undertook journeys of heroic proportions into the unknown, and also ran the mundane errands of imperialist expansion; he contributed to both the ordered accumulation of scientific data and the intensification of alien political hegemony; and he caviled against, but nevertheless furthered the aims and dictates of commerce. His reputation, however, has always depended more upon his methods than upon his accomplishments. He was and is known as an energetic, intrepid, and courageous traveler who never failed to pursue his chosen tasks with the utmost dispatch and, unusually, a heightened respect for Africans as individuals and groups. Unlike his contemporaries and competitors, Henry Morton Stanley and Carl Peters, rough swashbucklers both, Thomson prided himself on a gentle, humane disposition. His explorations occasioned no unnatural loss of life; Thomson consciously cut a peaceful swath across Africa, nowhere fostering resentment or enmity.

Between 1879 and 1891 Thomson was almost always in Africa. His career, in accord with the dictates of the period of transition, naturally encompassed a series of journeys to geographical goals that were interspersed with sorties for largely diplomatic or commercial ends. The death in early 1879 of Keith Johnston, Jr., the leader of the Royal Geographical Society's expedition from Dar es Salaam to lakes Nyasa and Tanganyika, gave Thomson his first taste of responsibility in Africa. Then barely twenty-one years old, Thomson had joined the expedition as a geologist after spending three sessions at the University of Edinburgh and a few years in and out of his father's quarry in Dumfriesshire. "I felt," he wrote after Johnston's death deep in the interior of East Africa, "I must go forward, whatever might be my destiny.

Was I not the countryman of Bruce, Park, Clapperton, Grant, Livingstone, and Cameron?"[1] Guided and counseled by James Chuma and Makatubu, headmen attached to the expedition, he successfully led it through the troubled country of the Mahenge and the Hehe to the northernmost extremity of Lake Nyasa. Then he and his companions made the first European-directed traverse of the high plateau between that lake and Lake Tanganyika, proceeded around the western shores of Lake Tanganyika to the Lukuga River—where Thomson verified the existence of an outlet that governed the varying water levels of the lake—and continued up the Lukuga virtually to its confluence with the Lualaba (Upper Congo) River. At that point Thomson was compelled by African hostility to retrace his steps along the Lukuga River to Lake Tanganyika. He sailed south along the eastern shores of the lake, disembarked, became the first European in recorded history to descry the shores of Lake Rukwa, and then marched with his entourage *via* Tabora to the Indian Ocean.

His trek of more than 3,000 miles had consumed a mere fourteen months and had answered a number of important questions about the geographical and geological configuration of eastern Africa. Thomson was everywhere praised for his courage and skill and, considered simply as a complicated exercise of daunting proportions, it was the most successful journey of exploration that had ever been undertaken by whites in eastern Africa. Thomson generously gave most of the credit to Chuma and Makatubu, but was himself proud that the expedition had returned to the coast intact. There had—most uncommonly—been no defections and relatively few contretemps between the men and their leader; moreover, Thomson said proudly, they had fired no shots in anger.

In 1882 Thomson and Chuma took a small caravan up the Ruvuma and Lugenda rivers in a vain attempt to find coal and other minerals for the Sultan of Zanzibar. The exploit for which he is best known, however, the traverse of Masai-

1. Joseph Thomson, *To the Central African Lakes and Back* (London, 1881), I, 150. The present article draws upon and synthesizes Robert I. Rotberg, *Joseph Thomson and the Exploration of Africa* (London, 1970), where fuller references will be found.

land to the Victoria Nyanza, occupied most of 1883 and 1884. For the Royal Geographical Society, which sponsored the resultant expedition, and for geographers everywhere, the terrain between Kilimanjaro and Victoria Nyanza comprised the last significant unopened region in tropical Africa. Masailand was the heart of this area, and its occupants blocked the direct route to the supposedly great untapped markets of the flourishing interior kingdom of Buganda. The Masai, reputed, if undeservedly, to be bloodthirsty, had, by virtue of their uncompromisingly militant expressions of xenophobia, hitherto managed to discourage the penetration of Europeans beyond Kilimanjaro. But Thomson, confident that his methods would prove their equal, once again welcomed the opportunity to unveil a beshrouded portion of Africa. His first attempt to breach the Masai barricades failed, however, and he was forced for the first time to retreat, reorganize his caravan, and join forces with a large party of traders. Together they all passed with deceptive ease through Masailand. Thomson and a few of his followers also managed to charm their way across hostile country to the foot of Mount Kenya, confirming the much earlier sighting by Johann Ludwig Krapf. They delineated the previously exaggerated configuration of Lake Baringo, traversed the Uasin Gishu plateau, passed through Kavirondo to Victoria Nyanza, visited the lower reaches of Mount Elgon, and then, after Thomson had succumbed to a very debilitating attack of dysentery, returned slowly to the coast. To have traveled as far as he had (nearly 3,000 miles) and to have both surmounted so many obstacles and survived to retail the excitement of their conquest proved deeds sufficient to dramatize the magnificent quality of Thomson's achievement. As a dogged personal triumph over adversity and infirmity, it is unsurpassed in the annals of African exploration. And so it and Thomson were acclaimed in Europe.

After the passage through Masailand, the remainder of Thomson's life, although not devoid of excitement, was to a large extent anticlimactic. The heyday of exploration for its own sake had passed and been succeeded by the Scramble for Africa. By late 1884 France had added parts of the Western Sudan to its traditional holdings on the coasts and rivers of

Senegal and Guinée, occupied ports on the western Slave Coast, acquired stations on the Ogooué and Congo rivers, and declared protectorates in the Niari Valley. Stanley, on behalf of King Léopold II of the Belgians, had claimed Kinshasa on the south bank of the Congo. The Germans had annexed Southwest Africa and proclaimed protectorates over the Togo and Kamerunian coasts. Germany was about to claim sovereignty in eastern Tanganyika, and Britain to extend her holdings in Nigeria and on the Gold Coast. Although at first Thomson refused to acknowledge that he had already contributed to the expansion of imperialism, he soon played an active part in the drama of colonial rivalry. In 1885 he ascended the Niger River on behalf of the National African (later the Royal Niger) Company and obtained two important and surprisingly full treaties from the Sarkin Musulmi, the Fulani ruler of Hausaland, and his near equal, the Emir of Gwandu. Thus excluding the Germans from the rich and vast area that was later called Northern Nigeria, Thomson had, in his own words, "at the expense of a few pounds and a demoralised stomach . . . bloomed forth in all the glories of a diplomatist."[2] By the end of the decade he had briefly explored sections of the Haut Atlas mountains of southern Morocco and, on two abortive occasions, been suggested as a rescuer of Emin Pasha.

His next foray into the interior of Africa was made at the behest of Cecil Rhodes and the British South Africa Company. Thomson traveled from and to Lake Nyasa and the vicinity of the Kafue River, concluded fourteen valuable if spurious treaties of cession from chiefs, headmen, and pretenders of the future Zambia, but was unable even to visit Msiri, the Yeke chief who controlled the copper deposits of Katanga. Rhodes subsequently wanted him to try a second time to attain Msiri's capital, but by then the explorer's health had failed. In 1895, after vainly seeking to recover his strength in South Africa and the Mediterranean, Thomson died of pneumonia after suffering acutely from a probable combination of tuberculosis, schistosomiasis, and cystitis.

2. Thomson to Noake, n.d., quoted in James B. Thomson, *Joseph Thomson, African Explorer* (London, 1896), 162.

What drew men like Thomson again and again to Africa? "I died," Thomson summed up his life two years before his death, "with the Spirit of Africa at my lips." He wanted his epitaph to read: "The Last Tramp, or How Thomson found the true Spirit of Africa, and pegged out his last claims on the Dark Continent."[3] But such a poignant evocation provides only a partial and somewhat mystical explanation of the motives of exploration. Certainly Thomson had always been curious about the unknown; even before he attended the University of Edinburgh, he had demonstrated a keen interest in the geological configuration of his native Nithsdale. He read two reasonably mature papers about his investigations before the county scientific society and was lavishly praised by Professor (later Sir) Archibald Geikie, of Edinburgh for his enthusiasm, insight, and skill as an embryo geologist.[4] The testimonies of other instructors and his academic and professional contemporaries provided further evidence of Thomson's quick and inquiring mind. He doubtless was in part attracted to African exploration by the intellectual challenge involved. And his subsequent botanical and conchological collections, together with his various geological, zoological, and ethnological appraisals, indicate a real rather than a perfunctory desire to add to the store of Europe's knowledge of the "dark continent."

This was a quality that Thomson shared to a greater or lesser degree with nearly all of the well-known explorers of Africa. In his case, as in that of many others, there were additional considerations of importance. Livingstone's dramatic crossing of central Africa, his subsequent speeches and writings, and the tumultuous way in which his exploits were received in Victorian England had made exploration fashionable. With a bit of luck, a modicum of endurance, and some literary talent, men could make their names and reap the glories of fame by discerning and describing the physical features of inner Africa. Burton, Speke, Stanley, and Baker had done so successfully. Thomson clearly was driven by an urge to emulate the achievements of his predecessors and to claim a psychic reward equal

3. Thomson to Gilmour, 26 June 1893, in *ibid.*, 293.
4. Quoted in Thomson, *Thomson*, 42; Archibald Gᴇikie, *A Long Life's Work: An Autobiography* (London, 1924), 165–166.

to theirs. When the Royal Geographical Society sought a leader of its potentially hazardous expedition to Masailand, Thomson joyfully embraced what appeared to be the unexpectedly perfect opportunity to secure a suitable place among the ranks of Africa's great explorers. As a result of his first *safari* his name had indeed become known; but the achievement of greatness depended upon the exploits that would excite the popular imagination. Thus he wrote earnestly to his close friend J. M. (later Sir James) Barrie: "It is very wrong of you to wish me so ill as to incapacitate me from going again to Africa. Why, if I were to stop now I would simply be forgotten and drop out of sight." It was an honest assessment. And Thomson lacked no faith in his own abilities. "If you mean," he told Barrie, "that I shall be to some extent famous, you may be right."[5] He persuaded the Society to provide funds sufficient for a large, strongly defended caravan, and refused to be daunted by a series of initial reverses on the borders of Masailand itself. In the end, he "conquered" Masailand, opened a road to Victoria Nyanza, and returned home to the well-deserved plaudits of fellow geographers and the press. He also became a public figure of some note, particularly in Scotland. By ordinary standards he had in fact achieved fame. And he was only twenty-eight. But the time was past when explorers, no matter how mightily they strained, could excite the public as had Livingstone and Stanley. This limitation Thomson to some extent accepted; for the remainder of his short life he nonetheless continued to try, alas unsuccessfully, to add luster to his Masai glory.

Thomson explored because of a combination of inner drives. The quest for fame drove him. But no matter how much ambition may have dominated his approach to Africa, there were other constitutional and practical factors that seem to have sent him back to Africa again and again. He was primarily a doer, for whom creative activity held an immense attraction. He hated enforced idleness, and drove himself and his followers unceasingly. Even more, once he had successfully proved his mettle in Africa and had savored the adventuresome

5. Quoted in *ibid.*, 96.

essence of the continent, not even the delights of his beloved Scotland or the salons of bustling London could content him for long. He also always felt a need to maintain and enhance his reputation as a *wünderkind;* fame had been thrust upon his shoulders too early in life. It is also true that Thomson, being of the Scottish middle class and possessing few skills for which there was a demand at home, could earn a modest living more enjoyably by traveling in Africa and writing up his exploits than he thought he could by resting on his reputation or taking up a profession in Britain. Materially, however, he never asked for or commanded from the Royal Geographical Society and his other sponsors the lavish rewards that were obtained by Stanley and Cameron. Unlike Baker, Bruce, and Speke, he had no independent income, nor could he depend— as could Stanley—upon the munificent support of patrons and employers. At the end of each of his pioneering expeditions he claimed no more than bare expenses—£360. The National African Company remunerated him only a little more handsomely, and Thomson had himself to find the funds for the Moroccan tour. Thus, in strictly financial terms, Thomson profited little from his explorations (his books sold reasonably well, but never produced much revenue) and never amassed capital resources sufficient to have enabled him to live quietly in some Scottish retreat.

But Thomson never dreamed of a Scottish retreat. He was an incurable romantic for whom the mystery and drama of Africa held a compelling attraction. Livingstone was for him, as for so many other Victorian adolescents, a childhood hero. The youthful Thomson had also avidly read tales of adventure, some of which concerned Africa. He had wanted to volunteer for a Livingstone relief expedition, and, in the summer of 1878, impulsively applied to join the Royal Geographical Society's expedition to Lake Nyasa after reading a short item in his local newspaper.[6] Fortunately, his initial experiences in Africa satisfied many of his instinctive yearnings. The potential danger, the challenge of the unknown, the vast and seemingly pristine nature of his surroundings, a sense of following in the

6. "New Exploring Expedition for Africa," *The Dumfries and Galloway Standard & Advertiser* (19 June 1878), 3.

footsteps of Livingstone, a delight in commanding, and a feeling of "freedom" all enhanced his appreciation of Africa. Thomson pictured himself as a friend to and patron of "gentle savages"; he saw himself as one who brought light to the dark continent—as a latter-day Livingstone as well as a fearsome adventurer and a discoverer of geographical and scientific secrets. Only in the course of his autobiographical novel did he fully express the extent to which the arid plains, lofty mountains, miasma-drenched swamps, and lazy rivers of eastern Africa, her warm days and chilled nights, and the qualities of her varied peoples satisfied a deep streak of romance.[7] His published narratives seek to obscure such feelings and present their author as a more down-to-earth, conscientious traveler than he was. In the last analysis, Thomson returned repeatedly to Africa because it was there.

Stanley was a realist, and consequently viewed Africa as a field of endeavor. If Africans (or whites) stood in the way, they were pushed aside. Baker and Burton shared this point of view substantially. But Thomson was of a gentle disposition, his methods of exploration thus differing considerably from those adopted by many of his predecessors and contemporaries. No bully, he made his own the motto *Chi va piano va sano, chi va sano va lontano* (He who goes softly, goes safely, he who goes safely, goes far). Its lesson conveyed him with comparative ease to and from Dar es Salaam and Lake Tanganyika, Mikindani and the Lugenda River, and Mombasa and Victoria Nyanza. In situations where others might have aroused the wrath of Africans and thus forfeited their lives, Thomson held his tongue and acted judiciously. He, almost alone of the whites who crisscrossed Africa in the decades after Livingstone's first journey, was content to go in peace. He was prepared for the most part to persuade rather than to order, and to suffer indignities if they served to enhance the ultimate accomplishment of his objectives. When the chiefs of southern Tanganyika demanded that he tarry awhile in their villages, Thomson reluctantly acquiesced. Stanley or Burton in similar circumstances might have unlimbered his guns. When chiefs

7. Joseph Thomson and E. Harris-Smith, *Ulu: An African Romance* (London, 1888), 2v.

in the eastern Congo refused to let him pass up the Lukuga to the Lualaba River, Thomson decided that their right to prevent his travels ought to be respected. Sometimes, however, his contentions were misunderstood and warfare seemed imminent. In such circumstances he refused to take fright. He stood his ground—but peacefully and without a display of arms—when threatened by the Mahenge and the Nyiha in Tanganyika, the Holoholo in the Congo, the Samia in Kenya, a mob in Sokoto, and the peoples of the Haut Atlas. Only from the Masai and the Ngoni did he flee, and then prudently.

Thomson was usually prepared to seek the goodwill of—and come to terms with—the indigenous inhabitants of Africa. Any means short of war would do. He bribed; he gave presents in the usual way and not infrequently yielded to the most outrageous extortion. Two barrels of gunpowder persuaded Chief Kokomero of the Kilombero Valley to permit Thomson's caravan to proceed toward Uhehe. Wire and beads in vast amounts managed on several occasions to calm the passions of the worrisome Masai. Mangi Rindi (Mandara), the powerful chief of the Chagga of Moshi, mulcted Thomson of a complete suit of thick tweed, a pair of shoes, a steel box, the explorer's own double-barreled smoothbore rifle, and numerous other incidental accouterments. Even Thomson appreciated that his generosity had been unusually warm: "I beg to state," he told Dr. (later Sir) John Kirk, "that I have been to Mandara and there received in a very royal and pleasant fashion, but left with feelings of mingled character, leaving several desirable objects behind. Mandara desires it to be known that he is anxious to receive a shoal of European visitors in the same manner. . . . Let no one go with empty hands."[8] Similarly, to ensure a safe passage through the lands of the Masai and their equally fierce Iloikop cousins, Thomson posed as a man of magic. He pretended to exorcise their ills and, for some weeks, daily beguiled his antagonists with the fizzy frothing of Eno's Fruit Salts and the manipulation of his false front tooth. No trick was too juvenile—mirrors had their uses—if it would gain him an "open road" into the interior. Everywhere he flattered. He

8. Thomson to Kirk, 7 July 1883, enclosed in Kirk to R.G.S., 11 February 1884, R.G.S archives.

compromised. When the occasion demanded it, he humbled himself—even before his own porters. But these tactics were all means to an end which conceivably could not have been attained in another, unmartial, manner.

Thomson, more so than many other explorers, was pre-eminently flexible and pragmatic. He preferred and usually managed to be gentle, but virtually any means would do. On occasion he even altered his objectives (his experiences along the Lukuga River, in Masailand, and in the Haut Atlas provide examples) to suit the constraints of a particularly difficult situation. Whenever the wind of opposition blew too briskly, he tacked. By so doing, of course, he accomplished more than might have proved possible for others in the same or similar circumstances. Moreover, despite his reputation, when gentle methods failed he employed threats of force. He thus pushed his way through parts of Kavirondo, refused to countenance opposition in Nigeria, bullied the local people and his own porters in Morocco, and displayed his guns in trans-Zambezia. If the strength of his caravan were greater than that of the peoples through which his route passed, and if the occasion demanded it, he had little compunction (although he experienced feelings of guilt) about displaying the banners of war.

These martial moments dimmed, but were sufficiently rare not to demolish Thomson's reputation as a man of peace. "My fondest boast is," he told his townsmen after returning the first time from Africa, "not that I have travelled over hundreds of miles hitherto untrodden by the foot of white man, but that I have been able to do so as a Christian and a Scotchman, carrying everywhere goodwill and friendship, finding that a gentle word was more potent than gunpowder, and that it was not necessary, even in Central Africa, to sacrifice the lives of men in order to throw light upon its dark corners."[9] Overall, he merited the sobriquet "gentle," and no African or white lives were lost as a result of his tactics or initiative. He trekked about 15,000 miles in Africa without causing more than occasional hard feelings among his own men or the peoples through whom they passed. Barrie argued that Thomson was "tolerant and

9. Quoted in *The Dumfries and Galloway Standard & Advertiser* (15 September 1880).

conciliatory beyond almost all who have headed caravans, and
...left a sweet name behind him among all the tribes with
whom he had sojourned. It is responsible for much of his popu-
larity with the natives." [10] Explorers and administrators who
followed his footsteps into the interior nearly always discovered that Thomson's example made their own tasks easier
to accomplish. Henry Hamilton (later Sir Harry) Johnston, who
climbed Kilimanjaro in 1884, testified that he had found it "a
very great advantage to follow in the footsteps of Mr. Thomson.
There had been some travelers in Africa whom it was no advantage to follow, but in the case of Mr. Thomson it was a positive help, because of the excellent impression that he had left
behind among the natives. [I] never heard a single complaint
with regard to the conduct of Mr. Thomson's expedition;
though very few expeditions would traverse so difficult a country without leaving some friction behind." [11] Despite occasional
lapses, particularly his uncharacteristic truculence in the
streets of Marrakech, Thomson is well and usually remembered as a man who respected the prerogatives of Africans
and, unlike his rival Stanley, everywhere created a minimum
of unnecessary disturbance.

Thomson would probably have adopted similar tactics wherever he traveled. But, at least during the early years, he positively liked Africans, and, again in contrast to Stanley, Burton,
Baker, Speke, Rohlfs, and a number of others, regarded
them as humans rather than as some lower order of the species. He got on well with his porters, particularly in eastern
Africa; few deserted his employ and Chuma, Makatubu,
Brahim, and Beduè, the headmen of his first *safari*, willingly
engaged themselves for subsequent expeditions. Perhaps because of his youth, he seems never to have remained aloof or
to have demanded a ritual obeisance from his followers. "Whatever might be the colour of our skin," he wrote after reaching
the shores of Lake Tanganyika, "there existed no barrier between us, nor any difference but that of degree between our
respective feelings and sentiments." [12] In the beginning, too,

10. J. M. Barrie, "The Man," in Thomson, *Thomson*, 327.
11. "Report of the ... Fourth Meeting, 5th January 1885," *Proceedings of
the Royal Geographical Society*, VII (1885), 123.
12. Thomson, *To the Lakes*, I, 309–310.

his descriptions of the inhabitants of Africa were remarkably untainted by any preconceived notions of racial development. Unlike Burton, who passed through southern and central Tanganyika twenty-eight years before, Thomson's mind and eyes remained open. He refused to accept Burton's racist condemnations of the indigenous inhabitants, and approached each tribe afresh. The farther he penetrated into the interior, the more he tried to evaluate Africans and the African way of life on its own, rather than on European terms.

The Hehe, a proud warrior people of Tanganyika's southwestern plateau, provided the first major test of Thomson's character. Burton had positively abhorred the Hehe, vilifying them in his usual offhand manner. But Thomson found himself positively attracted. Burton had called them "determined pilferers"; [13] Thomson and his men left their camps unguarded and lost nothing by theft—"no one put forth his hand to touch what did not belong to him." The Hehe chiefs personified *éclat*: rarely rude, they inferred rather than imposed matters disagreeable to the expedition. *Hongo* took the polite form of presents exchanged between equals rather than the abruptness of mere tribute. Thomson approved of their low-keyed, understated approach. If the Hehe chiefs deemed his "presents" miserly, they made their displeasure known by hyperbole: for example, "the cows had stopped giving milk" or "guides were, alas, no longer available." A supplementary gift soon encouraged the milk to flow and guides to appear. "We were thus," Thomson wrote with pleasure, "gently eased of our bales to an alarming extent. But then we felt that among such noblemen of Nature's mould, it would be sheer niggardliness to be less lavish. We could but spend our wealth handsomely." [14]

During his sojourn among the Hehe, Thomson's attitudes matured greatly. He began to appreciate Africa and Africans more than before. His tolerance for the unusual increased. He found characteristic beliefs in magic more interesting than disgusting, and odd burial customs more curious than revolting. He criticized less—though he still criticized—and frequently sought reasonable, redeeming explanations for behavior that

13. Burton, *Lake Regions*, I, 239.
14. Thomson, *To the Lakes*, I, 236–237.

might otherwise have seemed repulsive to the readers of his published account. During his stay among the Hehe, and after prompting from their chief, Thomson also came to the fairly obvious but hitherto unaccepted conclusion that the typical European explorer, traveling as he generally did rapidly through the countryside, could hardly hope to form "just conceptions" of the nature of divers peoples. How, the leading Hehe chief asked Thomson, could he go back and tell his own people that he had seen Uhehe and its inhabitants if he hurried through the country, stopping never more than a day anywhere? Moreover, the intrusive nature of the white man and his caravan biased the sample. Thomson came to believe that only those whites who had taken the trouble to acquire a thorough command of a local language and who had resided at length in a particular district of the interior could speak with confidence of the indigenous way of life. In lieu of such experience—"till such justice is done"—Thomson declared self-righteously that Europeans had no right to draw dogmatic conclusions about the state or capabilities of the African mind. He had begun to realize that previous visitors had often unjustly maligned or unfairly caricatured the inhabitants of Africa. "Under the influence of fevers," he wrote, "and the thousand troubles attendant on African travelling," explorers as a class had unfairly abused Africans in print. "Few people have studied them with unprejudiced and unbiassed minds." [15]

For the remainder of his first journey, and throughout his expedition up the Ruvuma River, Thomson remained true to this precept. In comparison with those of his European contemporaries, his mind was free of obvious prejudice. This is not to say that he saw everything through proverbial rose-colored spectacles; he continued to criticize certain African modes of dress and facial decoration and tendentiously evaluated slender and dubious evidence. But he recognized that his standards of judgment were not theirs, that their life was organized differently from his own, and that no set of generalizations would do for all Africans. What he disliked, he tried to understand; what he liked, he praised. Of the people and country of

15. *Ibid.*, I, 238.

the Nyakyusa, for example, no encomium was too lavish. "The scene that opened up before me I beheld with astonishment," he wrote after entering a Nyakyusa village at the head of Lake Nyasa. "It seemed a perfect Arcadia, about which idyllic poets have sung, though few have seen it realized. Imagine a magnificent grove of bananas, laden with bunches of fruit, each of which would form a man's load, growing on a perfectly level plain, from which all weeds, garbage, and things unsightly are carefully cleared away." Neat circular huts with trimly thatched conical roofs, and walls "hanging out all round with the clay worked prettily into rounded bricks and daubed symmetrically with spots," completed the picture. The naked villagers slumbered on banana leaves in the late afternoon sun, seemingly unconscious of want and unconcerned with possible danger. The chief and his subjects received the explorer and his company with great grace; they provided food and drink freely, allowed Thomson to rest in peace, and took him on a tour of their neat and hygienic villages and cattle kraals.[16]

Of all the peoples of Africa, the Masai proved the most attractive to Thomson. Their reputation for rapacious hostility was widespread and his own initial experiences seemed to confirm the reports of earlier visitors. The Masai delighted in tormenting him as they had Gustav Fischer, his immediate predecessor. At Lake Naivasha, Fischer's farthest west, Thomson endured an "atrocious life" and unforgivable importunities: Despite his pose as a *laibon*, or high priest, and the vaunted power of his rifles, he daily let himself be exhibited and ordered about. At the behest of the Masai, he endlessly put off and on his boots, wiggled his white toes, permitted his strange skin to be stroked and his odd hair to be fingered, and disposed of an enormous quantity of beads. Yet their very power to humiliate him found favor in Thomson's, as in the eyes of many later travelers and administrators. He and they admired the proud nobility of these "true" savages. At Naivasha he met a group of elders who demonstrated a willingness to converse, a frankness, and an absence of suspicion such as the young explorer had encountered among no other Africans. Admittedly arro-

16. *Ibid.*, I, 266–268.

gant, troublesome, and overbearing, they and their fellow Masai displayed a manner and a consciousness of power sufficiently aristocratic to raise them infinitely above other Africans. To him as to later visitors, the very prideful unwillingness of the Masai to acknowledge any inferiority or give any quarter in argument or combat possessed great appeal. Then too, their physical stature and appearance, and the fact that they were nomads and seemingly "free" of constraints, was applauded by romantics like Thomson who had themselves fled from the confining cities and towns of Victorian Britain.

Thomson apotheosized the Masai. It is significant that for him these unruly men of the steppes were the best that Africa had to offer. All other Africans were compared unfavorably to the Masai, particularly—as he grew older—those of West Africa who had adopted European ways. In this sense Thomson was a Kiplingesque figure, and his glimpse of the Masai subtly but nonetheless positively made him increasingly intolerant of Africans and African behavior which did not accord with his idealized view of Masai life. Unfortunately, too, Thomson sought Darwinian explanations for the superiority of the Masai. His acquaintance with them persuaded him that peoples and races could be placed along a continuum of cultural superiority. Since in their cranial shape (he said cranial development) as in their language the Masai differed radically from the Bantu-speaking Africans with whom the explorer had previously been familiar, and since their language and appearance betokened a relationship with peoples farther north who had been classified as Hamitic—a strain "inferior" to Semitic but presumed to be better (because closer to Caucasian) than "negroid"—it made perfect, if unreflective, sense for Thomson to have accorded to the Masai a much higher position on the scale of humanity than neighboring peoples who, philologically at least, were mere "negroid" Bantu. Within this same intuitive *gestalt,* he noted speciously that the members of the four "most aristocratic" clans possessed the finest physical development among the Masai. They seemed superior to the others because of the oval shape of their heads and their more prominent elongated noses and thin lips. Only the protrusion of their cheekbones, the Mongolian shape of their eyes, their dark skins, and their frizzy hair prevented them from passing muster as "very respectable and commonplace Europeans." The Iloikop, probably because of their Negro blood, seemed by comparison, Thomson argued in a manner perfectly acceptable to the least thoughtful of his contemporaries, physically more degraded. In particular, the Njemps Iloikop, who had been forced by the loss of their cattle to turn to agriculture, had "distinctly degenerated." They could not "for a moment compete with their aristocratic carnivorous brethren." Thomson even equated simple physical shape with ethnic superiority. In his view the Njemps women had somehow lost the slender, "genteel" contours of their pastoral sisters and, in the process of becoming conscious of the soil, had acquired the poor proportions of "the negress." [17] Thus, although the young Scot had earlier viewed Africans through kindly, tolerant eyes, the Masai experience caused him to discriminate among several classes of "savage" and, it seems, to rationalize a growing feeling not only that most Africans culturally were decidedly inferior to whites but that dark-skinned people were by and large inherently incapable of rising above a preordained station of life.

It is not completely clear why Thomson, during the last ten years of his life, gradually replaced his previous public expression of affection for Africans with fairly stereotyped phrases of prejudice. Only the luster of the Masai and his individual porters remained undimmed; the capabilities of the other Africans with whom he came into contact were scorned in print and in private. In his late twenties he became in some senses less naïve and less romantic. He may also have consciously or unconsciously tried to conform to the prevalent public attitude of disdain toward matters and persons African; after all, he had to try to please a literary public and to compete for attention with the views of Stanley, Cameron, and numerous armchair critics. But it is also evident that Thomson, who admired the Masai, liked his Africans to possess primi-

17. Thomson, *Through Masai Land: A Journey of Exploration among the Snowclad Volcanic Mountains and Strange Tribes of Eastern Equatorial Africa* (London, 1883), 450.

tive virtues; "city slickers" and the somewhat Europeanized men of West Africa were, with the strong exception of the proud, gifted, Islamized, Semitic-looking, Masai-like peoples of Hausaland, repulsive to the latter-day Thomson. And the Berbers of Morocco so lacked the simplicity of the Masai that, despite their religion, they incurred his profound dislike.

West Africa shocked Thomson's sensibilities. In Freetown, Lagos, and elsewhere he met Africans who took themselves seriously and refused to acknowledge the supposed superiority of Europeans. "Young Sierra Leone is ever posing and asking you but to . . . see what the hitherto reviled 'nigger' is capable of," Thomson sneered. "And truly it is a delightful sight to behold him, with his French-cut trousers, his wealth of snowy linen, his natty cane, and his billy-cock hat placed knowingly on one side of his head, thus suggesting, by patent . . . signs, how far he considers himself to have been regenerated." [18] In a subsequent article severely critical of British colonial policy, Thomson declared that British administrative methods—"our delicacy in dealing with the rights and liberties of our 'black brethren'"—were sinking West Africa into a slough of moral and physical perdition. The result of British benevolence was that its "two centuries of intercourse with the West Coast negro have transformed him into the most villainous, vicious, and despicable being in the whole of Africa."

Thomson had begun to write like the most bigoted white settler: "We have made the mistake of attempting to govern the negroes on lines utterly unsuited to their stage of development. If you can imagine what would be the result of acting with a boy of ten as if he had the same rights and privileges of an adult—as if he was quite capable of taking a position among his elders on a footing of equality—you will have an idea what sort of offensive creature our method of rule has made the West Coast negro. And yet the illustration is weak, for the boy, though he would be spoiled and ruined body and soul and made incapable of all healthy development, has yet the making of the man in him in his own lifetime, while the barbarian negro has not the power of rising to the level of the civilised man

18. Thomson, "Up the Niger to the Central Sudan: Letters to a Friend," *Good Words*, XXVII (1886), 26.

either in his own lifetime or in the second or third generation." Finally, "the consequence of his being treated as the European's peer has been only to spoil him and retard his natural development whilst covering him with a ridiculous veneer of civilisation, which makes him the most offensive jackdaw in peacock's feathers ever seen." [19]

Like so many British administrators and settlers, Thomson abhorred what he and they termed "cheekyness"; he and they apparently distrusted and secretly feared Africans who adopted modern ways, shed their indigenous inheritance, and tried to conform to Western expectations. Thomson, once tolerant and compassionate, described Africans of the lower Niger River with scorn: "You discover that the erewhile [sic] negro has degenerated into a *nigger,* bids you 'Good morning,' and wears a lawn-tennis hat with a sunflower embroidered on it—the latest fashion on the river. The only fact which saves him from your withering contempt is the thought that he is a cannibal and likes his meat 'high,' and otherwise has a number of queer social customs." [20] The peoples of the lower Niger, and of West Africa generally, brought out the worst in Thomson. He said nothing of this sort about the Masai or the peoples of East Africa, and he would earlier have denounced any other explorer who had so unfairly cast such slurs.

By the time that Thomson returned from the Niger he had also formed a decidedly unfavorable opinion about the innate capacity of dark-skinned people. Only a few seemed to be in any sense "improveable." The vast majority, he believed (his writings, however, are inconsistent on this point), possessed no qualities or attributes which could be elevated by the civilizing influence of the West. Even his once beloved East

19. Thomson, "Downing Street *versus* Chartered Companies in Africa," *Fortnightly Review,* XLVIII (1889), 180–181. Similar sentiments, in almost identical words, are contained in Thomson, "The Results of European Intercourse with the African," *Contemporary Review,* LVII (1890), 343–347.

20. Thomson, "Up the Niger," 114. In his *Mungo Park and the Niger* (London, 1890), 323, Thomson similarly gibed: "The only circumstance which serves to maintain an air of romance about [the Niger Negro] is the knowledge we possess that he still loves his neighbour to the extent of becoming at times literally one flesh with him."

Africans—at least those of the coast—had benefited in no way from "five centuries of intercourse with various grades of civilisation . . . the natives, instead of being on a higher intellectual and moral level, are everywhere distinctly lower than the interior tribes." [21] Only his visit to Hausaland gave Thomson any hope that Africans were not totally irredeemable. In an article written for the *Journal of the Anthropological Institute of Great Britain and Ireland,* he confessed that he had "begun to form the opinion that the civilisation of the negro was an almost hopeless task. In East Africa I had seen that the influence of Arab trade and civilisation extending over some hundreds of years, and European trade and missionary effort in later times, had been alike unproductive of any genuine advance, and we have just seen that four centuries of intercourse with white men on the west coast has only had the most demoralising results." Then, "as I left behind me the low-lying coast region, and found myself near the southern boundary of . . . the Central Sudan, I observed an ever-increasing improvement in the appearance of character of the native; cannibalism disappeared, fetishism followed in its wake . . . clothes became more voluminous and decent, cleanliness the rule, while their outward more dignified bearing still further betokened a moral regeneration. Everything indicated a leavening of some higher element, an element that was clearly taking a deep hold on the negro nature and making him a new man." Elsewhere he commented: "In a hundred ways they show that they have discovered that there are other pleasures beyond living like brutes, eating what is necessary, rearing a family, and returning to the dust." [22] Thomson had found another people as fearless and self-assured as the Masai. But the crucial element in the makeup of the peoples of Hausaland, he decided, was Islam. It was the religion of the Prophet Muhammad that had transformed these peoples from savagery. Thus,

21. Thomson, "East Central Africa, and its Commercial Outlook," *The Scottish Geographical Magazine,* II (1886), 73.
22. Thomson, "Note on the African Tribes of the British Empire," *Journal of the Anthropological Institute,* XVI (1886), 184–185; Thomson, "Niger and Central Sudan Sketches," *The Scottish Geographical Magazine,* II (1886), 593–594.

Africans, if they could only be exposed to Islam, were, he had to admit, improvable.

Thomson's faith in the civilizing powers of Islam was, however, short-lived. In 1888 he embarked upon an exploration of southern Morocco that was in part intended to confirm his observations of the beneficial properties of the Muslim religion in Africa. For centuries trade routes had linked the entrepôts of southern Morocco and the historical empires of the Western and Central Sudans; Thomson therefore assumed that the peoples of Hausaland owed their comparatively high level of civilization to the impress of Moroccan Islam and Moroccan culture. But the filth of the Moroccan towns and the hostility of their inhabitants immediately shattered his preconceived notions. Bureaucrats harassed him, the servants that he had employed proved unreliable, and the different peoples of the countryside appeared far more degraded than he had anticipated. Of Marrakech, the capital of the south, Thomson found little to praise. "We saw much indeed of the 'havoc' but little of the 'splendour' of the East. . . . We were confronted at every step with evidence of a nation on a downgrade slide—of a people who had lost all earthly hopes and anticipations, who lived from hand to hand, patient waiters on God's Providence. Morocco [Marrakech] was a city grown slattern, very much out at the elbows, and utterly careless of its personal appearance." [23] Thomson saw signs of decadence everywhere. He found it impossible to believe that the Moors among whom he traveled were the descendants of men who had swept across northern Africa and had conquered most of Iberia. "It seemed incredible that the people who . . . reared such works as the Alhambra . . . are content in the present day with no higher thoughts than the unlimited indulgence of their sensual appetites." Even their religion, Thomson decided, had become a barren formula. Morocco was, he sighed, "a stagnant backwater . . . utterly irreclaimable, and bound before long to sink in the foul mud of its own making." [24]

23. Thomson, "Some Impressions of Morocco and the Moors," *The Journal of the Manchester Geographical Society,* V (1889), 109.
24. *Ibid.,* 109–110; Thomson, *Travels in the Atlas and Southern Morocco: A Narrative of Exploration* (London, 1889), 228, 435–443, 483.

Thomson, the gentle, humane, seemingly sensible explorer of the early 1880's, devoted the last years of his young life to such irresponsible fulminations and the propagation of commonplace analyses of Africa and its inhabitants. Yet liberal-thinking persons have always claimed him as one of their own. On the basis of his two most important and widely read narratives, *To the Central African Lakes and Back* and *Through Masai Land*, they assumed that Thomson, alone among his fellow explorers, respected and even liked Africans. Increasingly, during an age that has manifested concern for interracial understanding, Thomson's stature has grown. So humane an explorer, it has widely been argued, must have been refreshingly free from prejudice. And, compared to Burton, Baker, Stanley, and others, this conclusion can doubtless be supported. But by modern standards his later books and nearly all of his nonscientific articles espouse the usual late Victorian dogmatism about the inferiority of black-skinned persons. As openly as he admired a few individuals, Thomson spared no venom for Africans as a "race." He criticized their animal-like behavior, dismissed the residents of most of West Africa as pretentious peacocks "spoiled" by their exposure to English education, and thought of most Africans as rude savages. The catalogue of abuse is long, detailed, and, to a reader of his earliest narratives, surprising. As he grew older he seems to have absorbed and/or adopted the racial attitudes of his peers. Or he may simply have discarded the innocent liberality of youth for the jaundice of experience. In either case, there is no doubt that his views hardened with time; moderate expressions of disdain gave way to shrill cries of contempt. Non-concepts like "semi-civilized" abound. He substituted rhetoric for argument and pomposity for sympathy. Nowhere—not even in the narrative of his first expedition—can one find the affection that was demonstrated so consistently, albeit paternally, by Livingstone. Rarely indeed are Africans taken or described, as a group, on their merits. Usually, at least in correspondence and in print, Thomson treated them as objects to be manipulated rather than as subjects capable of acting rationally.

What, then, was Thomson's contribution to the history of tropical Africa? It is exceedingly difficult to assess his impact upon Africans. From his own testimony, and modern research among some of the peoples whose paths he crossed, it appears that he passed too rapidly and too quietly into and through the interior for his impact to have been more than ephemeral. Whereas Livingstone is a folk hero because he was almost everywhere the first European of importance; and the force of their personalities made Burton and Stanley important both at the time of their visits and afterward; Thomson was, to Africans, simply a pleasant traveler who got on with the job and left them alone. Throughout Masailand he was only a curious white man among a pack of coastal merchants; Chief Mumia in Kavirondo lived to a grand old age and remembered the visitor of his youth, but there seem to have been few others, aside from the headmen and porters of his caravans, who cherished or cherish his memory. If a history of tropical Africa from a totally indigenous and parochial point of view could be written, Thomson might deserve no more than a line or two. And those lines might mention his treaties with the Sarkin Musulmi or with fourteen putative chiefs of trans-Zambezia and—to the consternation of traditional-thinking Europeans—overlook the trail-blazing of his East African career. In Africa, Thomson is best remembered—where he is remembered at all—for his very great personal capabilities as a caravan leader; in a more restricted circle for his exploits among the Masai; and, among the geographical savants of European background, for his various discoveries, and for his earliest racial views.

As a species of the genus explorer, Thomson is difficult to assess with precision. None of his narratives and private papers include the kind of detail and minutiae that would allow a modern reader fully to appreciate the interests, if not the workings, of his mind. Livingstone and Burton especially, Stanley, Baker, and others with a slightly less absorbing intensity, and even comparatively minor figures like James Augustus Grant each distilled much more than Thomson from their African experiences. Thomson was everywhere in a hurry. Perhaps he took copious notes and later consulted them little; perceiving much, he conceivably wrote up his results too hastily. Or, intent as always upon the next adventure, he may simply have thought that an impressionistic survey would do. More likely, however, Thomson's published accounts reflect the field inquiries and observations of a traveler who jumped to conclusions rapidly, was capable of brilliant insights, but ordinarily remained content to assume and not to probe. He accepted the known and analyzed received information and his own preconceptions infrequently. Rarely given to introspection, Thomson was a man of action who could bear no leisure—even periods of enforced repose. He was foremost a traveler, not a student of divers cultures.

Thomson's energy and endurance enabled him to accomplish much more within a given length of time than perhaps any other Victorian traveler in Africa. Yet no matter how much this accent upon speed may have endeared him to his economy-minded patrons, it inhibited the ordered accumulation of geographical and scientific data. Six times he ventured into uncharted areas of Africa. He opened up new routes to Lake Nyasa and the Victoria Nyanza. He revealed the true configuration of the Konde mountains, solved the riddle of the Lukuga River and the levels of Lake Tanganyika, provided important information about Kilimanjaro and Mount Kenya, "discovered" the Rift Valley, disclosed the true nature of Lake Baringo, and noted a variety of other phenomena of interest to geographers. He described the commercial prospects of East Africa, the Central Sudan, and trans-Zambezia. He assaulted the higher peaks of the Atlas Mountains, vainly sought coal on the Upper Ruvuma and Lugenda rivers, and made treaties with different African rulers. To the advancement of science Thomson contributed geological maps and several detailed regional reports. He collected flora and shells, and obtained specimens of fauna.

Thomson thrived upon danger and subsisted upon adversity. His energy is legendary. Yet, partially because he acted during the twilight of African exploration, he made no startlingly significant discoveries. He filled in details, corrected earlier impressions, and put forward hypotheses on the basis of hearsay evidence. What he did for the most part needed doing, but he brought to the elucidation of his various tasks fortitude and intuition rather than clarity of purpose, highly developed skills of observation, or a tenacious search for truth. Pleased merely to accomplish a specific mission and to provide an overall impression spiced haphazardly with points of fact, his results may be regarded primarily as the byproducts of adventure. Furthermore, although the larger picture that he sketched advanced Europe's understanding of African geography, many portions of it were quickly superseded by the more percipient efforts of subsequent travelers. His record as an explorer betrays a want of patience and precision and reflects a single-minded, obsessional devotion to completing preordained tasks more for their own sake than for the results that they might produce.

Nothing to which Thomson turned his energies was ever fully finished: mountains were partially climbed, rivers and lakes incompletely explored, hypotheses advanced but rarely tested, peoples sketched in outline only, racial judgments made on the basis of slender evidence, and results published in part. Always in a hurry, he was goaded by an inner demon hungry for fame and adventure, but sufficiently undisciplined to fritter away many opportunities capable of advancing the explorer's reputation. Thomson lacked the vision and thoroughness of Livingstone, the depth of intellect and discursive reflection of Burton, the sheer tenacity of Speke and Rohlfs, the panache of Baker, and the entrepreneurial leadership of Stanley. But he was swift, kind, reasonably efficient, and generally successful. He possessed an intuition that only occasionally led him astray. He treated his employees fairly and eschewed violence. He faithfully served what he had decided were noble geographical and imperial ends. If he failed, he failed in terms of his own high standards of accomplishment and conduct. He failed to achieve the scientific and humanistic potential—and so means little to Africans—that seemed so promising when a mere stripling emerged from the East African interior in 1880 as a full-fledged explorer.

Bibliography   *Index*

Gardner, Brian, *The Quest for Timbuctoo* (London, 1968).

Giraud, Victor, *Les lacs de l'Afrique Équatoriale: voyage d'exploration exécuté de 1883 à 1885* (Paris, 1890).

Grant, James Augustus, *A Walk Across Africa* (Edinburgh, 1864).

―――― "On Mr H. M. Stanley's Exploration of Victoria Nyanza," *Journal of the Royal Geographical Society*, XLVI (1876), 10–33.

Gray, John Milner, "Acholi History, 1860–1901," *Uganda Journal*, XV (1951), 121–143; XVI (1952), 32–50, 132–144.

―――― "Mutesa of Buganda," *Uganda Journal*, I (1934), 22–49.

―――― "Rwot Ochama of Payera," *Uganda Journal*, XII (1948), 121–128.

―――― "Speke and Grant," *Uganda Journal*, XVII (1953), 146–160.

Gray, Richard, *A History of the Southern Sudan, 1839–1889* (New York, 1961).

Grove, E. T. N., "Customs of the Acholi," *Sudan Notes and Records*, II (1919), 157–182.

Guenther, Konrad, *Gerhard Rohlfs: Lebensbild eines Afrikaforschers* (Freiburg, 1912).

Hantzsch, Viktor, "Gerhard Rohlfs," *Allgemeine Deutsche Biographie*, LIII (Leipzig, 1907), 440–449.

Harris, Walter B., *The Land of an African Sultan: Travels in Morocco, 1887, 1888, and 1889* (London, 1889).

Head, F. B., *The Life of Bruce, The Abyssinian Traveller* (London, 1830).

Heuss, Theodor, Herbert Ganslmayr, and Heinrich Schiffers, *Gustav Nachtigal, 1869–1969* (Bad Godesberg, 1969).

Heyse, T., *Bibliographie de H. M. Stanley, 1841–1904* (Brussels, 1961).

Hird, Frank, *H. M. Stanley: The Authorized Life* (London, 1935).

Hohnel, Ludwig von (trans. and ed. Nancy Bell), *Discovery of Lakes Rudolf and Stefanie: A Narrative of Count Samuel Teleki's Exploring and Hunting Expedition in Eastern Equatorial Africa in 1887 and 1888* (London, 1894), 2v.

Ingham, Kenneth, "John Hanning Speke, A Victorian and His Inspiration," *Tanganyika Notes and Records*, 49 (1957), 301–311.

Italiaander, Rolf, *Heinrich Barth: Im Sattel durch Nord- und Zentralafrika* (Wiesbaden, 1967).

Johnston, Harry Hamilton, *The Nile Quest* (London, 1903).

Junker, Wilhelm (trans. A. H. Keane), *Travels in Africa during the Years 1882–1886* (London, 1892).

Kagwa, Apolo (trans. Ernest B. Kalibala, ed. May Mandelbaum), *The Customs of the Baganda* (New York, 1934).

Keltie, John Scott (ed.), *The Story of Emin's Rescue as Told in Stanley's Letters* (London, 1890).

―――― "What Stanley has done for the map of Africa," *Contemporary*

Anonymous, "Cameron on African Heathenism," *The Missionary Herald*, LXXVI (1880), 69–70.

Anstey, Roger T., *Britain and the Congo in the Nineteenth Century* (Oxford, 1962).

Assad, T. J., *Three Victorian Travellers. Burton, Blunt, Doughty* (London, 1964).

Ayandele, E. A., "Dr. Henry Barth as a Diplomatist and Philanthropist," *Ibadan*, XXV (February 1968), 9–14.

Baker, John Norman Leonard, "Sir Richard Burton and the Nile Sources," *English Historical Review*, LIX (1944), 48–61.

―――― "John Hanning Speke," *Geographical Journal*, CXXVIII (1962), 385–388.

Baker, J. R., "Samuel Baker's Route to the Albert Nyanza," *Geographical Journal*, CXXXI (1965), 13–20.

Baker, Samuel White, *The Albert N'yanza, Great Basin of the Nile, and Explorations of the Nile Sources* (London, 1866), 2v.

―――― *Eight Years' Wandering in Ceylon* (Philadelphia, 1874).

―――― *The Nile Tributaries of Abyssinia and the Sword Hunters of the Hamran Arabs* (New York, 1886).

―――― *Ismailïa: A Narrative of the Expedition to Central Africa for the Suppression of the Slave Trade* (London, 1895).

Barrie, James M., *An Edinburgh Eleven* (London, 1924), 101–108.

Barth, Heinrich, *Travels and Discoveries in North and Central Africa* (London, 1857–58), 5v.

―――― *Sammlung und Bearbeitung Central-Afrikanischer Vokabularien* (Berlin, 1862–1866), 3v.

Bartholomew, J. G., "Joseph Thomson," *The Scottish Geographical Magazine*, XI (1895), 524–528.

Barttelot, Walter George (ed.), *The Life of Edmund Musgrave Barttelot* (London, 1890).

Beaton, A. C., "A Chapter in Bari History," *Sudan Notes and Records*, XVII (1934), 169–200.

Beattie, John, *Bunyoro, An African Kingdom* (New York, 1960).

Bennett, Norman R., *Stanley's Despatches to the New York Herald, 1871–1872, 1874–1877* (Boston, 1970).

Benton, Philip Askell, *Notes on Some Languages of the Western Sudan* (London, 1912); republished as *The Languages and Peoples of Bornu* (London, 1968), with an introduction by A. H. M. Kirk-Greene.

Bere, R. M., "An Outline of Acholi History," *Uganda Journal*, XI (1947), 1–8.

Bovill, E. W., "Henry Barth," *Journal of the African Society*, XXV (1926), 311–320.

Bradnum, Frederick, *The Long Walks: Journeys to the Sources of the White Nile* (London, 1969).

Bridges, Roy Charles, "Speke and the Royal Geographical Society," *Uganda Journal*, XXVI (1962), 23–43.

_____ "The Royal Geographical Society and the African Exploration Fund, 1876–80," *The Geographical Journal*, CXXIX (1963), 23–35.

_____ "Explorers & East African History," *Proceedings of the East African Academy*, I (1963), 69–73.

Brodie, Fawn, *The Devil Drives: A Life of Sir Richard Burton* (London, 1967).

Brunschwig, Henri, *et al.*, *Brazza Explorateur: L'Ogooué, 1875–1879* (Paris, 1966).

Burdo, Adolphe, *Les Arabes dans l'Afrique Centrale* (Paris, 1885).

Burton, Isabel, *The Life of Captain Sir Richard F. Burton* (London, 1893), 2v.

Burton, Richard Francis, *Personal Narrative of a Pilgrimage to Mecca and El Medina* (London, 1855).

_____ *First Footsteps in East Africa* (London, 1856).

_____ "The Lake Regions of Central Equatorial Africa," *Journal of the Royal Geographical Society*, XXIX (1859), 1–454.

_____ *The Lake Regions of Central Africa* (London, 1860), 2v.

_____ *Wanderings in West Africa* (London, 1863), 2v.

_____ *Abeokuta and the Camaroon Mountains* (London, 1863), 2v.

_____ *A Mission to Gelele, King of Dahome* (London, 1864), 2v.

_____ *The Nile Basin* (London, 1864).

_____ *Zanzibar: City, Island, and Coast* (London, 1872), 2v.

_____ *Wanderings in Three Continents* (London, 1901).

_____ (Gordon Waterfield, ed.), *First Footsteps in East Africa* (London, 1966).

_____ (C. W. Newbury, ed.), *Mission to King Gelele of Dahome* (London, 1966).

_____ and Verney Lovett Cameron, *To the Gold Coast for Gold: A Personal Narrative* (London, 1883), 2v.

_____ *The Nile Basin and Captain Speke's Discovery of the Source of the Nile* (with an introduction by Robert Collins) (London, 1968).

Caillié, René, *Travels Through Central Africa to Timbuctoo and Across the Great Desert to Morocco, 1824–1828* (London, 1830), 2v.

Cairns, H. Alan C., *Prelude to Imperialism* (London, 1965).

Cambier, R., "Stanley et Emin Pacha," *Zaïre*, 3 (1949), 531–5

Cameron, Verney Lovett, *Across Africa* (London, 1877).

_____ *Our Future Highway* (London, 1880).

Capello, Hermenegildo, and Roberto Ivens, *De Angola a Conti Costa* (Lisbon, 1886), 2v.

Casati, Gaetano (trans. Mrs. J. Randolph Clay), *Ten Years in Equa toria* (London, 1891), 2v.

Castries, R. G. M. E., *Les rencontres de Stanley* (Paris, 1960).

Ceulemans, P., "Le séjour de Stanley à Zanzibar (18 mars–fin ma 1879," *Zaïre*, XI (1957), 675–685.

Chavannes, Charles de, *Avec Brazza* (Paris, 1935).

Coupland, Reginald, *Kirk on the Zambesi* (Oxford, 1928).

_____ *The Exploitation of East Africa, 1856–1890: The Slave Trade and the Scramble* (London, 1939).

_____ *Livingstone's Last Journey* (London, 1945).

Daye, P., *Stanley* (Paris, 1936).

Deschamps, Hubert, *L'Europe découvre l'Afrique* (Paris, 1967).

Du Chaillu, Paul Belloni, *A Journey to Ashango-Land and Further Penetration into Equatorial Africa* (New York, 1867).

Dunbar, A. R., "European Travellers in Bunyoro-Kitara, 1862 to 1877," *Uganda Journal*, XXIII (1959), 101–117.

_____ "Emin Pasha and Bunyoro-Kitara, 1877–1889," *Uganda Journal*, XXIV (1960), 71–83.

_____ *A History of Bunyoro-Kitara* (Nairobi, 1965).

Elton, J. Frederic (ed. H. B. Cotterill), *Travels and Researches among the Lakes and Mountains of Eastern and Central Africa* (London, 1879).

Eydoux, H. P., *Savorgnan de Brazza. Le Conquerant Pacifique* (Paris, 1932).

Farwell, Byron, *The Man Who Presumed; A Biography of Henry M. Stanley* (New York, 1957).

_____ *Burton* (London, 1963).

Fischer, Gustav A., *Das Masai-Land: Bericht über die im Auftrage der Geographischen Gesellschaft im Hamburg Ausgefuhrte Reise von Pangani bis zum Naiwascha-See* (Hamburg, 1885).

Fisher, Ruth H., *Twilight Tales of the Black Baganda* (London, 1912).

Flegel, Eduard (ed. Karl Flegel), *Vom Niger-Benüe* (Leipzig, 1890).

Foran, W. Robert, *African Odyssey: The Life of Verney Lovett-Cameron* (London, 1937).

Fosbrooke, Henry A., "Richard Thornton in East Africa," *Tanganyika Notes and Records*, 58/59 (1962), 43–63.

Fox Bourne, Henry R., *The Other Side of the Emin Pasha Relief Expedition* (London, 1891).

French-Sheldon, M., *Sultan to Sultan. Adventures among the Masai and Other Tribes of East Africa* (London, 1892).

Review, LVII (1890), 126–140.

Kersten, Otto, *Baron Carl Claus von der Decken's Reisen in Ost-Afrika in den Jahren 1859 bis 1861* (Leipzig, 1869 [I], 1871 [II]).

Kirk-Greene, Anthony H. M., "Expansion on the Benue, 1830–1900," *Journal of the Historical Society of Nigeria*, I (1958), 215–237.

_____ "Abbega and Durogu," *West African Review* (September 1956), 865–869.

_____ *Adamawa Past and Present. An Historical Approach to the Development of a Northern Cameroons Province* (London, 1958).

_____ "Barth: A Centenary Memoir," *West Africa* (1958), 1209, 1231–1232.

_____ "The British Consulate at Lake Chad," *African Affairs*, LIX (1959), 334–339.

_____ "Barth's Journey to Adamawa," in Heinrich Schiffers (ed.), *Heinrich Barth: Ein Forscher in Afrika* (Wiesbaden, 1967), 194–215.

Krapf, Johann Ludwig, *Travels, Researches and Missionary Labours during an Eighteen Years' Residence in Eastern Africa* (Boston, 1860).

Langlands, Bryan W., "Early Travellers in Uganda: 1860–1914," *Uganda Journal*, XXVI (1962), 55–71.

Lenz, Oskar, *Skizzen aus Westafrika* (Berlin, 1879).

_____ (trans. Pierre Lehautcourt), *Timbouctou: Voyage au Maroc, au Sahara et au Soudan* (Paris, 1886), 2v.

Livingstone, David, *Missionary Travels and Researches in South Africa* (London, 1857).

_____ (ed. Horace Waller), *The Last Journals* (London, 1874).

_____ and Charles, *Narrative of an Expedition to the Zambesi and Its Tributaries: And of the Discovery of Lakes Shirwa and Nyassa, 1858–1864* (New York, 1866).

Luwel, M., *Stanley* (Brussels, 1956).

_____ "Considérations sur quelques livres récents ayant trait à Henry Morton Stanley," *Bulletin des Séances, Academie Royale des Sciences d'Outre-Mer*, VIII (1962), 531–558.

Markham, Clements, "Lieutenant Cameron's Diary," *Journal of the Royal Geographical Society*, XLV (1875), 184–228.

Maurice, Albert (ed.), *H. M. Stanley: Unpublished Letters* (London, 1957).

Middleton, Dorothy, *Baker and the Nile* (London, 1949).

_____ *Victorian Lady Travellers* (London, 1964).

Mill, Hugh Robert, *The Record of the Royal Geographical Society, 1830–1930* (London, 1930).

Mollien, Gaspard, *Voyage dans l'intérieur de l'Afrique aux sources du Sénégal et de la Gambie fait en 1818* (Paris, 1820), 2v.

Moloney, Joseph A., *With Captain Stairs to Katanga* (London, 1893).

――― "The Stairs Expedition to Katanga," *The Geographical Journal*, II (1893), 238–248.

Moorehead, Alan, *The White Nile* (New York, 1960).

Mounteney-Jephson, A. J., *Emin Pasha and the Rebellion at the Equator* (London, 1890).

Mukasa, Ham, "Speke at the Court of Mutesa I," *Uganda Journal*, XXVI (1962), 97–99.

Murray, T. D., and A. S. White, *Sir Samuel Baker: A Memoir* (London, 1895).

Nachtigal, Gustav, *Sahara und Sudan. Ergebnisse Sechsjähriger Reisen in Afrika* (Berlin, 1879–1889), 3v.

Nalder, L. R., *A Tribal Survey of Mongalla Province* (New York, 1937).

New, Charles, *Life, Wanderings, and Labours in Eastern Africa* (London, 1873).

Ney, Napoleon (ed.), *Conférences et lettres de Père Savorgnan de Brazza sur ses trois explorations dans l'Ouest Africain, de 1875 à 1886* (Paris, 1887).

Oliver, Roland, "A Question about the Bachwesi," *Uganda Journal*, XVII (1953), 135–137.

――― "Six Unpublished Letters of H. M. Stanley," *Bulletin des Séances, Academie Royale des Sciences Coloniales*, III (1957), 344–358.

Park, Mungo, *Travels in the Interior Districts of Africa in the Years 1795, 1796, and 1797* (London, 1799).

Parke, Thomas Heazle, *My Personal Experiences in Equatorial Africa* (London, 1891).

[Pasha, Emin] (ed. John Milner Gray), "The Diaries of Emin Pasha— Extracts II," *Uganda Journal*, XXV (1961), 149–170.

Peters, Carl (trans. H. W. Dulcken), *New Light on Dark Africa: Being the Narrative of the German Emin Pasha Expedition* (New York, 1891).

Plewe, Ernst, "Heinrich Barth and Carl Ritter: Letters and Documents," *Erde*, XCVI (1965), 245–278.

Prothero, R. M., "Heinrich Barth and the Western Sudan," *The Geographical Journal*, CXXIV (1958), 326–339.

Pumphrey, M. E. C., "The Shilluk Tribe," *Sudan Notes and Records*, XXIV (1941), 1–45.

Ravenstein, Ernst Georg, "Verney Lovett Cameron," *The Geographical Journal*, III (1894), 429–451.

Reid, J. M., *Traveller Extraordinary: The Life of James Bruce of Kinnaird, 1730–1794* (London, 1968).

Risley, Robin C. H., "Burton, An Appreciation," *Tanganyika Notes and Records*, 49 (1957), 257–293.

Roeykens, Auguste, *Les débuts de l'oeuvre africaine de Léopold II, 1875–1879* (Brussels, 1955).

────── *Léopold II et l'Afrique, 1855–1880* (Brussels, 1958).

Rohlfs, Gerhard, *Im Auftrage Sr. Majestät des Königs von Preussen mit dem englischen Expeditionscorps in Abessinien* (Bremen, 1869).

────── *Land und Volk in Afrika* (Bremen, 1870).

────── *Adventures in Morocco and Journey through the Oases of Draa and Tafilet* (London, 1874).

────── *Quer durch Afrika. Reise vom Mittelmeer nach dem Tschad-see und zum Golf von Guinea* (Leipzig, 1874–75).

────── *Drei Monate in der Libyschen Wüste* (Cassel, 1875).

────── *Beiträge zur Entdeckung und Erforschung Afrikas* (Leipzig, 1876).

────── *Expedition zur Erforschung der Libyschen Wüste unter den Auspicien Sr. Hoheit des Khediven von Ägypten Ismail im Winter 1873–74 ausgeführt* (Cassel, 1876–1883).

────── *Kufra. Reise von Tripolis nach der Oase Kufra* (Leipzig, 1881).

────── *Neue Beiträge zur Entdeckung und Erforschung Afrikas* (Cassel, 1881).

────── *Reise durch Marokko, Übersteigung des grossen Atlas, Exploration der Oasen von Tafilet, Tuat und Tidikelt; und Reise durch die grosse Wüste über Rhadames nach Tripolis* (Norden, 1884).

────── *Angra Pequena; die erste deutsche Kolonie in Afrika* (Bielefeld, 1884).

────── *Zur Klimatologie und Hygiene Ostafrikas* (Leipzig, 1885).

────── *Von Tripolis nach Alexandrien* (Norden, 1885).

────── *Mein erster Aufenthalt in Marokko und Reise südlich vom Atlas durch die Oasen Draa und Tafilet* (Norden, 1885).

────── *Quid Novi ex Africa?* (Cassel, 1886).

Roscoe, John, *The Northern Bantu* (Cambridge, 1915).

────── *The Soul of Central Africa* (London, 1922).

Rose Troup, James, *With Stanley's Rear Column* (London, 1890).

Rotberg, Robert I., *Joseph Thomson and the Exploration of Africa* (London, 1970).

Rowley, J. V., "Notes on the Madi of Equatoria Province," *Sudan Notes and Records*, XXIII (1940), 279–294.

Schiffers, Heinrich (ed.), *Heinrich Barth, Ein Forscher in Afrika: Leben-Werk-Leistung* (Wiesbaden, 1967).

Schmidt, R., *Deutschlands Koloniale Helden und Pioniere der Kultur im Schwarzen Kontinent* (Brunswick, 1896).

Schubert, G. von, *Heinrich Barth, der Bahnbrecher der deutschen Afrikaforschung* (Berlin, 1897).

Schweinfurth, Georg, "Gerhard Rohlfs," *Westermann's Illustrierte Deutsche Monatshefte*, LXXXII (1879), 565–568.

———— (ed.) (trans. R. W. Felkin), *Emin Pasha in Central Africa* (London, 1888).

Serpa Pinto, Alexandre Alberto da Rocha de (trans. Alfred Elwes), *How I Crossed Africa* (Philadelphia, 1881), 2v.

Shepperson, George, "David Livingstone the Scot," *The Scottish Historical Review*, XXXIX (1960), 113–121.

———— (ed.), *David Livingstone and the Rovuma* (Edinburgh, 1965).

Simpson, Donald H., "J. H. Speke: A Bibliographical Survey," *Africana Newsletter*, II (1964), 22–26.

Slade, Ruth, *King Leopold's Congo* (London, 1962).

Southall, Aidan, "The Alur Legend of Sir Samuel Baker and the Mukama Kabarega," *Uganda Journal*, XV (1951), 187–190.

Speke, John Hanning, "The Upper Basin of the Nile," *Journal of the Royal Geographical Society*, XXXIII (1863), 322–327.

———— *Journal of the Discovery of the Source of the Nile* (Edinburgh, 1863).

———— *What Led to the Discovery of the Source of the Nile* (Edinburgh, 1864).

Stanley, Dorothy (ed.), *The Autobiography of Sir Henry Morton Stanley* (Boston, 1909).

Stanley, Henry Morton, *How I Found Livingstone* (London, 1872).

———— *Through the Dark Continent, or the Sources of the Nile around the Great Lakes of Equatorial Africa and Down the Livingstone River to the Atlantic Ocean* (London, 1878), 2v.

———— *The Congo and the Founding of Its Free State* (London, 1885), 2v.

———— *In Darkest Africa: Or the Quest, Rescue, and Retreat of Emin, Governor of Equatoria* (London, 1890), 2v.

"Stanley's Expedition: A Retrospect," *Fortnightly Review*, CCLXXVII (1890), 81–96.

Stanley, Richard, and Allen Neame (eds.), *The Exploration Diaries of H. M. Stanley* (London, 1961).

Stengers, Jean, "Stanley, Léopold II et l'Angleterre," *Le Flambeau*, 4 (1954), 378–386.

———— "Quelques observations sur la correspondance de Stanley," *Zaïre*, IX (1955), 899–926.

Stisted, Georgiana M., *The True Life of Captain Sir Richard F. Burton* (London, 1896).

Sutherland, W., *Alexandrine Tinne: Een Haagsch Meisje als dappere Ontdekkingsreizigster en Dochter de Liefde (Bint mtache) in Noord-Afrika* (Amsterdam, 1935).

Symons, A. J. A., *H. M. Stanley* (London, 1933).

Tate, H. R., "Two African Explorers. Part II: Joseph Thomson," *Journal of the Royal African Society*, XXXVII (1938), 449–463.

Thomson, James Baird, *Joseph Thomson, African Explorer* (London, 1896).

Thomson, Joseph, "Notes on the Route taken by the Royal Geographical Society's East African Expedition from Dar-es-Salaam to Uhehe; May 19th to August 29th, 1879," *Proceedings of the Royal Geographical Society*, II (1880), 102–122, 144.

―――― "Journey of the Society's East African Expedition," *Proceedings of the Royal Geographical Society*, II (1880), 721–742, 784.

―――― "To Usambara and Back," *Good Words*, 22 (1881), 36–43.

―――― "Toiling by Tanganyika," *Good Words*, 22 (1881), 141–144, 177–181.

―――― *To the Central African Lakes and Back: The Narrative of the Royal Geographical Society's East Central African Expedition, 1878–1880* (London, 1881), 2v.

―――― "Adventures on the Rovuma. Letters in course of an Exploration," *Good Words*, 23 (1882), 240–247, 398–406.

―――― "Notes on the Basin of the River Rovuma, East Africa," *Proceedings of the Royal Geographical Society*, IV (1882), 65–79.

―――― "On the Geographical Evolution of the Tanganyika Basin," *Report of the British Association for the Advancement of Science, 1882* (London, 1883), 622–623.

―――― *Through Masai Land. A Journey of Exploration among the Snowclad Volcanic Mountains and Strange Tribes of Eastern Equatorial Africa* (London, 1883).

―――― "Through the Masai Country to Victoria Nyanza," *Proceedings of the Royal Geographical Society*, V (1883), 544–550.

―――― "Sketch of a Trip to Sokoto by the River Niger," *The Journal of the Manchester Geographical Society*, II (1886), 1–18.

―――― "Note on the African Tribes of the British Empire," *Journal of the Anthropological Institute of Great Britain and Ireland*, XVI (1886), 182–186.

―――― "Up the Niger to the Central Sudan," *Good Words*, 27 (1886), 23–29, 109–118, 249–256, 323–330.

―――― "Niger and Central Sudan Sketches," *The Scottish Geographical Magazine*, II (1886), 577–596.

―――― "How I Crossed Masai-Land," *Scribner's Magazine*, VI (1889), 387–405.

―――― "How I Reached My Highest Point in the Atlas," *Good Words*, 30 (1889), 17–25.

―――― "Some Impressions of Morocco and the Moors," *The Journal of the Manchester Geographical Society*, V (1889), 101–118.

―――― "Explorations in the Atlas Mountains," *The Scottish Geographical Magazine*, V (1889), 169–180.

―――― "A Journey to Southern Morocco and the Atlas Mountains," *Proceedings of the Royal Geographical Society*, XI (1889), 1–17, 64.

_____ *Travels in the Atlas and Southern Morocco* (London, 1889).

_____ "To Lake Bangweolo and the Unexplored Region of British Central Africa," *The Geographical Journal*, I (1893), 97–121, 192.

_____ "The Geology of Southern Morocco and the Atlas Mountains," *The Quarterly Journal of the Geological Society of London*, LV (1899), 190–213.

Thomson, Robert S., *La fondation de l'Etat Indépendant du Congo* (Brussels, 1933).

Van Grieken, E., "H. M. Stanley au Congo, 1879–1884," *Institut Royal Colonial Belge—Bulletin*, XXV (1954), 1124–1179.

Ward, Herbert, *My Life with Stanley's Rear Guard* (London, 1890).

_____ *A Voice from the Congo* (London, 1910).

Wassermann, J., *H. M. Stanley—Explorer* (London, 1932).

Wauters, A. J., *Stanley's Emin Pasha Expedition* (London, 1890).

Welbourn, Frederick B., "Speke and Stanley at the Court of Mutesa," *Uganda Journal*, XXV (1961), 220–223.

Werner, J. R., *A Visit to Stanley's Rear-Guard, At Major Barttelot's Camp on the Aruhwimi, Congo* (London, 1889).

Bibliography

Anonymous, "Cameron on African Heathenism," *The Missionary Herald*, LXXVI (1880), 69–70.

Anstey, Roger T., *Britain and the Congo in the Nineteenth Century* (Oxford, 1962).

Assad, T. J., *Three Victorian Travellers. Burton, Blunt, Doughty* (London, 1964).

Ayandele, E. A., "Dr. Henry Barth as a Diplomatist and Philanthropist," *Ibadan*, XXV (February 1968), 9–14.

Baker, John Norman Leonard, "Sir Richard Burton and the Nile Sources," *English Historical Review*, LIX (1944), 48–61.

_____ "John Hanning Speke," *Geographical Journal*, CXXVIII (1962), 385–388.

Baker, J. R., "Samuel Baker's Route to the Albert Nyanza," *Geographical Journal*, CXXXI (1965), 13–20.

Baker, Samuel White, *The Albert N'yanza, Great Basin of the Nile, and Explorations of the Nile Sources* (London, 1866), 2v.

_____ *Eight Years' Wandering in Ceylon* (Philadelphia, 1874).

_____ *The Nile Tributaries of Abyssinia and the Sword Hunters of the Hamran Arabs* (New York, 1886).

_____ *Ismailïa: A Narrative of the Expedition to Central Africa for the Suppression of the Slave Trade* (London, 1895).

Barrie, James M., *An Edinburgh Eleven* (London, 1924), 101–108.

Barth, Heinrich, *Travels and Discoveries in North and Central Africa* (London, 1857–58), 5v.

_____ *Sammlung und Bearbeitung Central-Afrikanischer Vokabularien* (Berlin, 1862–1866), 3v.

Bartholomew, J. G., "Joseph Thomson," *The Scottish Geographical Magazine*, XI (1895), 524–528.

Barttelot, Walter George (ed.), *The Life of Edmund Musgrave Barttelot* (London, 1890).

Beaton, A. C., "A Chapter in Bari History," *Sudan Notes and Records*, XVII (1934), 169–200.

Beattie, John, *Bunyoro, An African Kingdom* (New York, 1960).

Bennett, Norman R., *Stanley's Despatches to the* New York Herald, *1871–1872, 1874–1877* (Boston, 1970).

Benton, Philip Askell, *Notes on Some Languages of the Western Sudan* (London, 1912); republished as *The Languages and Peoples of Bornu* (London, 1968), with an introduction by A. H. M. Kirk-Greene.

Bere, R. M., "An Outline of Acholi History," *Uganda Journal*, XI (1947), 1–8.

Bovill, E. W., "Henry Barth," *Journal of the African Society*, XXV (1926), 311–320.

Bradnum, Frederick, *The Long Walks: Journeys to the Sources of the White Nile* (London, 1969).

Bridges, Roy Charles, "Speke and the Royal Geographical Society," *Uganda Journal*, XXVI (1962), 23–43.

———— "The Royal Geographical Society and the African Exploration Fund, 1876–80," *The Geographical Journal*, CXXIX (1963), 23–35.

———— "Explorers & East African History," *Proceedings of the East African Academy*, I (1963), 69–73.

Brodie, Fawn, *The Devil Drives: A Life of Sir Richard Burton* (London, 1967).

Brunschwig, Henri, *et al.*, *Brazza Explorateur: L'Ogooué, 1875–1879* (Paris, 1966).

Burdo, Adolphe, *Les Arabes dans l'Afrique Centrale* (Paris, 1885).

Burton, Isabel, *The Life of Captain Sir Richard F. Burton* (London, 1893), 2v.

Burton, Richard Francis, *Personal Narrative of a Pilgrimage to Mecca and El Medina* (London, 1855).

———— *First Footsteps in East Africa* (London, 1856).

———— "The Lake Regions of Central Equatorial Africa," *Journal of the Royal Geographical Society*, XXIX (1859), 1–454.

———— *The Lake Regions of Central Africa* (London, 1860), 2v.

———— *Wanderings in West Africa* (London, 1863), 2v.

———— *Abeokuta and the Camaroon Mountains* (London, 1863), 2v.

———— *A Mission to Gelele, King of Dahome* (London, 1864), 2v.

———— *The Nile Basin* (London, 1864).

———— *Zanzibar: City, Island, and Coast* (London, 1872), 2v.

———— *Wanderings in Three Continents* (London, 1901).

———— (Gordon Waterfield, ed.), *First Footsteps in East Africa* (London, 1966).

———— (C. W. Newbury, ed.), *Mission to King Gelele of Dahome* (London, 1966).

———— and Verney Lovett Cameron, *To the Gold Coast for Gold: A Personal Narrative* (London, 1883), 2v.

———— *The Nile Basin and Captain Speke's Discovery of the Source of the Nile* (with an introduction by Robert Collins) (London, 1968).

Caillié, René, *Travels Through Central Africa to Timbuctoo and Across the Great Desert to Morocco, 1824–1828* (London, 1830), 2v.

Cairns, H. Alan C., *Prelude to Imperialism* (London, 1965).

Cambier, R., "Stanley et Emin Pacha," *Zaïre*, 3 (1949), 531–548.

Cameron, Verney Lovett, *Across Africa* (London, 1877).

_____ *Our Future Highway* (London, 1880).

Capello, Hermenegildo, and Roberto Ivens, *De Angola a Contra-Costa* (Lisbon, 1886), 2v.

Casati, Gaetano (trans. Mrs. J. Randolph Clay), *Ten Years in Equatoria* (London, 1891), 2v.

Castries, R. G. M. E., *Les rencontres de Stanley* (Paris, 1960).

Ceulemans, P., "Le séjour de Stanley à Zanzibar (18 mars–fin mai 1879," *Zaïre*, XI (1957), 675–685.

Chavannes, Charles de, *Avec Brazza* (Paris, 1935).

Coupland, Reginald, *Kirk on the Zambesi* (Oxford, 1928).

_____ *The Exploitation of East Africa, 1856–1890: The Slave Trade and the Scramble* (London, 1939).

_____ *Livingstone's Last Journey* (London, 1945).

Daye, P., *Stanley* (Paris, 1936).

Deschamps, Hubert, *L'Europe découvre l'Afrique* (Paris, 1967).

Du Chaillu, Paul Belloni, *A Journey to Ashango-Land and Further Penetration into Equatorial Africa* (New York, 1867).

Dunbar, A. R., "European Travellers in Bunyoro-Kitara, 1862 to 1877," *Uganda Journal*, XXIII (1959), 101–117.

_____ "Emin Pasha and Bunyoro-Kitara, 1877–1889," *Uganda Journal*, XXIV (1960), 71–83.

_____ *A History of Bunyoro-Kitara* (Nairobi, 1965).

Elton, J. Frederic (ed. H. B. Cotterill), *Travels and Researches among the Lakes and Mountains of Eastern and Central Africa* (London, 1879).

Eydoux, H. P., *Savorgnan de Brazza. Le Conquerant Pacifique* (Paris, 1932).

Farwell, Byron, *The Man Who Presumed; A Biography of Henry M. Stanley* (New York, 1957).

_____ *Burton* (London, 1963).

Fischer, Gustav A., *Das Masai-Land: Bericht über die im Auftrage der Geographischen Gesellschaft im Hamburg Ausgefuhrte Reise von Pangani bis zum Naiwascha-See* (Hamburg, 1885).

Fisher, Ruth H., *Twilight Tales of the Black Baganda* (London, 1912).

Flegel, Eduard (ed. Karl Flegel), *Vom Niger-Benüe* (Leipzig, 1890).

Foran, W. Robert, *African Odyssey: The Life of Verney Lovett-Cameron* (London, 1937).

Fosbrooke, Henry A., "Richard Thornton in East Africa," *Tanganyika Notes and Records,* 58/59 (1962), 43–63.

Fox Bourne, Henry R., *The Other Side of the Emin Pasha Relief Expedition* (London, 1891).

French-Sheldon, M., *Sultan to Sultan. Adventures among the Masai and Other Tribes of East Africa* (London, 1892).

Gardner, Brian, *The Quest for Timbuctoo* (London, 1968).

Giraud, Victor, *Les lacs de l'Afrique Équatoriale: voyage d'exploration exécuté de 1883 à 1885* (Paris, 1890).

Grant, James Augustus, *A Walk Across Africa* (Edinburgh, 1864).

———— "On Mr H. M. Stanley's Exploration of Victoria Nyanza," *Journal of the Royal Geographical Society*, XLVI (1876), 10–33.

Gray, John Milner, "Acholi History, 1860–1901," *Uganda Journal*, XV (1951), 121–143; XVI (1952), 32–50, 132–144.

———— "Mutesa of Buganda," *Uganda Journal*, I (1934), 22–49.

———— "Rwot Ochama of Payera," *Uganda Journal*, XII (1948), 121–128.

———— "Speke and Grant," *Uganda Journal*, XVII (1953), 146–160.

Gray, Richard, *A History of the Southern Sudan, 1839–1889* (New York, 1961).

Grove, E. T. N., "Customs of the Acholi," *Sudan Notes and Records*, II (1919), 157–182.

Guenther, Konrad, *Gerhard Rohlfs: Lebensbild eines Afrikaforschers* (Freiburg, 1912).

Hantzsch, Viktor, "Gerhard Rohlfs," *Allgemeine Deutsche Biographie*, LIII (Leipzig, 1907), 440–449.

Harris, Walter B., *The Land of an African Sultan: Travels in Morocco, 1887, 1888, and 1889* (London, 1889).

Head, F. B., *The Life of Bruce, The Abyssinian Traveller* (London, 1830).

Heuss, Theodor, Herbert Ganslmayr, and Heinrich Schiffers, *Gustav Nachtigal, 1869–1969* (Bad Godesberg, 1969).

Heyse, T., *Bibliographie de H. M. Stanley, 1841–1904* (Brussels, 1961).

Hird, Frank, *H. M. Stanley: The Authorized Life* (London, 1935).

Hohnel, Ludwig von (trans. and ed. Nancy Bell), *Discovery of Lakes Rudolf and Stefanie: A Narrative of Count Samuel Teleki's Exploring and Hunting Expedition in Eastern Equatorial Africa in 1887 and 1888* (London, 1894), 2v.

Ingham, Kenneth, "John Hanning Speke, A Victorian and His Inspiration," *Tanganyika Notes and Records*, 49 (1957), 301–311.

Italiaander, Rolf, *Heinrich Barth: Im Sattel durch Nord- und Zentralafrika* (Wiesbaden, 1967).

Johnston, Harry Hamilton, *The Nile Quest* (London, 1903).

Junker, Wilhelm (trans. A. H. Keane), *Travels in Africa during the Years 1882–1886* (London, 1892).

Kagwa, Apolo (trans. Ernest B. Kalibala, ed. May Mandelbaum), *The Customs of the Baganda* (New York, 1934).

Keltie, John Scott (ed.), *The Story of Emin's Rescue as Told in Stanley's Letters* (London, 1890).

———— "What Stanley has done for the map of Africa," *Contemporary*

Review, LVII (1890), 126–140.

Kersten, Otto, *Baron Carl Claus von der Decken's Reisen in Ost-Afrika in den Jahren 1859 bis 1861* (Leipzig, 1869 [I], 1871 [II]).

Kirk-Greene, Anthony H. M., "Expansion on the Benue, 1830–1900," *Journal of the Historical Society of Nigeria*, I (1958), 215–237.

_____ "Abbega and Durogu," *West African Review* (September 1956), 865–869.

_____ *Adamawa Past and Present. An Historical Approach to the Development of a Northern Cameroons Province* (London, 1958).

_____ "Barth: A Centenary Memoir," *West Africa* (1958), 1209, 1231–1232.

_____ "The British Consulate at Lake Chad," *African Affairs*, LIX (1959), 334–339.

_____ "Barth's Journey to Adamawa," in Heinrich Schiffers (ed.), *Heinrich Barth: Ein Forscher in Afrika* (Wiesbaden, 1967), 194–215.

Krapf, Johann Ludwig, *Travels, Researches and Missionary Labours during an Eighteen Years' Residence in Eastern Africa* (Boston, 1860).

Langlands, Bryan W., "Early Travellers in Uganda: 1860–1914," *Uganda Journal*, XXVI (1962), 55–71.

Lenz, Oskar, *Skizzen aus Westafrika* (Berlin, 1879).

_____ (trans. Pierre Lehautcourt), *Timbouctou: Voyage au Maroc, au Sahara et au Soudan* (Paris, 1886), 2v.

Livingstone, David, *Missionary Travels and Researches in South Africa* (London, 1857).

_____ (ed. Horace Waller), *The Last Journals* (London, 1874).

_____ and Charles, *Narrative of an Expedition to the Zambesi and Its Tributaries: And of the Discovery of Lakes Shirwa and Nyassa, 1858–1864* (New York, 1866).

Luwel, M., *Stanley* (Brussels, 1956).

_____ "Considérations sur quelques livres récents ayant trait à Henry Morton Stanley," *Bulletin des Séances, Academie Royale des Sciences d'Outre-Mer*, VIII (1962), 531–558.

Markham, Clements, "Lieutenant Cameron's Diary," *Journal of the Royal Geographical Society*, XLV (1875), 184–228.

Maurice, Albert (ed.), *H. M. Stanley: Unpublished Letters* (London, 1957).

Middleton, Dorothy, *Baker and the Nile* (London, 1949).

_____ *Victorian Lady Travellers* (London, 1964).

Mill, Hugh Robert, *The Record of the Royal Geographical Society, 1830–1930* (London, 1930).

Mollien, Gaspard, *Voyage dans l'intérieur de l'Afrique aux sources du Sénégal et de la Gambie fait en 1818* (Paris, 1820), 2v.

Moloney, Joseph A., *With Captain Stairs to Katanga* (London, 1893).
———— "The Stairs Expedition to Katanga," *The Geographical Journal*, II (1893), 238–248.
Moorehead, Alan, *The White Nile* (New York, 1960).
Mounteney-Jephson, A. J., *Emin Pasha and the Rebellion at the Equator* (London, 1890).
Mukasa, Ham, "Speke at the Court of Mutesa I," *Uganda Journal*, XXVI (1962), 97–99.
Murray, T. D., and A. S. White, *Sir Samuel Baker: A Memoir* (London, 1895).
Nachtigal, Gustav, *Sahara und Sudan. Ergebnisse Sechsjähriger Reisen in Afrika* (Berlin, 1879–1889), 3v.
Nalder, L. R., *A Tribal Survey of Mongalla Province* (New York, 1937).
New, Charles, *Life, Wanderings, and Labours in Eastern Africa* (London, 1873).
Ney, Napoleon (ed.), *Conférences et lettres de Père Savorgnan de Brazza sur ses trois explorations dans l'Ouest Africain, de 1875 à 1886* (Paris, 1887).
Oliver, Roland, "A Question about the Bachwesi," *Uganda Journal*, XVII (1953), 135–137.
———— "Six Unpublished Letters of H. M. Stanley," *Bulletin des Séances, Academie Royale des Sciences Coloniales*, III (1957), 344–358.
Park, Mungo, *Travels in the Interior Districts of Africa in the Years 1795, 1796, and 1797* (London, 1799).
Parke, Thomas Heazle, *My Personal Experiences in Equatorial Africa* (London, 1891).
[Pasha, Emin] (ed. John Milner Gray), "The Diaries of Emin Pasha—Extracts II," *Uganda Journal*, XXV (1961), 149–170.
Peters, Carl (trans. H. W. Dulcken), *New Light on Dark Africa: Being the Narrative of the German Emin Pasha Expedition* (New York, 1891).
Plewe, Ernst, "Heinrich Barth and Carl Ritter: Letters and Documents," *Erde*, XCVI (1965), 245–278.
Prothero, R. M., "Heinrich Barth and the Western Sudan," *The Geographical Journal*, CXXIV (1958), 326–339.
Pumphrey, M. E. C., "The Shilluk Tribe," *Sudan Notes and Records*, XXIV (1941), 1–45.
Ravenstein, Ernst Georg, "Verney Lovett Cameron," *The Geographical Journal*, III (1894), 429–451.
Reid, J. M., *Traveller Extraordinary: The Life of James Bruce of Kinnaird, 1730–1794* (London, 1968).
Risley, Robin C. H., "Burton, An Appreciation," *Tanganyika Notes and Records*, 49 (1957), 257–293.

Roeykens, Auguste, *Les débuts de l'oeuvre africaine de Léopold II, 1875–1879* (Brussels, 1955).

_____ *Léopold II et l'Afrique, 1855–1880* (Brussels, 1958).

Rohlfs, Gerhard, *Im Auftrage Sr. Majestät des Königs von Preussen mit dem englischen Expeditionscorps in Abessinien* (Bremen, 1869).

_____ *Land und Volk in Afrika* (Bremen, 1870).

_____ *Adventures in Morocco and Journey through the Oases of Draa and Tafilet* (London, 1874).

_____ *Quer durch Afrika. Reise vom Mittelmeer nach dem Tschadsee und zum Golf von Guinea* (Leipzig, 1874–75).

_____ *Drei Monate in der Libyschen Wüste* (Cassel, 1875).

_____ *Beiträge zur Entdeckung und Erforschung Afrikas* (Leipzig, 1876).

_____ *Expedition zur Erforschung der Libyschen Wüste unter den Auspicien Sr. Hoheit des Khediven von Ägypten Ismail im Winter 1873–74 ausgeführt* (Cassel, 1876–1883).

_____ *Kufra. Reise von Tripolis nach der Oase Kufra* (Leipzig, 1881).

_____ *Neue Beiträge zur Entdeckung und Erforschung Afrikas* (Cassel, 1881).

_____ *Reise durch Marokko, Übersteigung des grossen Atlas, Exploration der Oasen von Tafilet, Tuat und Tidikelt; und Reise durch die grosse Wüste über Rhadames nach Tripolis* (Norden, 1884).

_____ *Angra Pequena; die erste deutsche Kolonie in Afrika* (Bielefeld, 1884).

_____ *Zur Klimatologie und Hygiene Ostafrikas* (Leipzig, 1885).

_____ *Von Tripolis nach Alexandrien* (Norden, 1885).

_____ *Mein erster Aufenthalt in Marokko und Reise südlich vom Atlas durch die Oasen Draa und Tafilet* (Norden, 1885).

_____ *Quid Novi ex Africa?* (Cassel, 1886).

Roscoe, John, *The Northern Bantu* (Cambridge, 1915).

_____ *The Soul of Central Africa* (London, 1922).

Rose Troup, James, *With Stanley's Rear Column* (London, 1890).

Rotberg, Robert I., *Joseph Thomson and the Exploration of Africa* (London, 1970).

Rowley, J. V., "Notes on the Madi of Equatoria Province," *Sudan Notes and Records*, XXIII (1940), 279–294.

Schiffers, Heinrich (ed.), *Heinrich Barth, Ein Forscher in Afrika: Leben-Werk-Leistung* (Wiesbaden, 1967).

Schmidt, R., *Deutschlands Koloniale Helden und Pioniere der Kultur im Schwarzen Kontinent* (Brunswick, 1896).

Schubert, G. von, *Heinrich Barth, der Bahnbrecher der deutschen Afrikaforschung* (Berlin, 1897).

Schweinfurth, Georg, "Gerhard Rohlfs," *Westermann's Illustrierte Deutsche Monatshefte*, LXXXII (1879), 565–568.

―――― (ed.) (trans. R. W. Felkin), *Emin Pasha in Central Africa* (London, 1888).

Serpa Pinto, Alexandre Alberto da Rocha de (trans. Alfred Elwes), *How I Crossed Africa* (Philadelphia, 1881), 2v.

Shepperson, George, "David Livingstone the Scot," *The Scottish Historical Review*, XXXIX (1960), 113–121.

―――― (ed.), *David Livingstone and the Rovuma* (Edinburgh, 1965).

Simpson, Donald H., "J. H. Speke: A Bibliographical Survey," *Africana Newsletter,* II (1964), 22–26.

Slade, Ruth, *King Leopold's Congo* (London, 1962).

Southall, Aidan, "The Alur Legend of Sir Samuel Baker and the Mukama Kabarega," *Uganda Journal*, XV (1951), 187–190.

Speke, John Hanning, "The Upper Basin of the Nile," *Journal of the Royal Geographical Society*, XXXIII (1863), 322–327.

―――― *Journal of the Discovery of the Source of the Nile* (Edinburgh, 1863).

―――― *What Led to the Discovery of the Source of the Nile* (Edinburgh, 1864).

Stanley, Dorothy (ed.), *The Autobiography of Sir Henry Morton Stanley* (Boston, 1909).

Stanley, Henry Morton, *How I Found Livingstone* (London, 1872).

―――― *Through the Dark Continent, or the Sources of the Nile around the Great Lakes of Equatorial Africa and Down the Livingstone River to the Atlantic Ocean* (London, 1878), 2v.

―――― *The Congo and the Founding of Its Free State* (London, 1885), 2v.

―――― *In Darkest Africa: Or the Quest, Rescue, and Retreat of Emin, Governor of Equatoria* (London, 1890), 2v.

"Stanley's Expedition: A Retrospect," *Fortnightly Review,* CCLXXVII (1890), 81–96.

Stanley, Richard, and Allen Neame (eds.), *The Exploration Diaries of H. M. Stanley* (London, 1961).

Stengers, Jean, "Stanley, Léopold II et l'Angleterre," *Le Flambeau,* 4 (1954), 378–386.

―――― "Quelques observations sur la correspondance de Stanley," *Zaïre*, IX (1955), 899–926.

Stisted, Georgiana M., *The True Life of Captain Sir Richard F. Burton* (London, 1896).

Sutherland, W., *Alexandrine Tinne: Een Haagsch Meisje als dappere Ontdekkingsreizigster en Dochter de Liefde (Bint mtache) in Noord-Afrika* (Amsterdam, 1935).

Symons, A. J. A., *H. M. Stanley* (London, 1933).

Tate, H. R., "Two African Explorers. Part II: Joseph Thomson," *Journal of the Royal African Society*, XXXVII (1938), 449–463.

Thomson, James Baird, *Joseph Thomson, African Explorer* (London, 1896).

Thomson, Joseph, "Notes on the Route taken by the Royal Geographical Society's East African Expedition from Dar-es-Salaam to Uhehe; May 19th to August 29th, 1879," *Proceedings of the Royal Geographical Society,* II (1880), 102–122, 144.

_____ "Journey of the Society's East African Expedition," *Proceedings of the Royal Geographical Society,* II (1880), 721–742, 784.

_____ "To Usambara and Back," *Good Words,* 22 (1881), 36–43.

_____ "Toiling by Tanganyika," *Good Words,* 22 (1881), 141–144, 177–181.

_____ *To the Central African Lakes and Back: The Narrative of the Royal Geographical Society's East Central African Expedition, 1878–1880* (London, 1881), 2v.

_____ "Adventures on the Rovuma. Letters in course of an Exploration," *Good Words,* 23 (1882), 240–247, 398–406.

_____ "Notes on the Basin of the River Rovuma, East Africa," *Proceedings of the Royal Geographical Society,* IV (1882), 65–79.

_____ "On the Geographical Evolution of the Tanganyika Basin," *Report of the British Association for the Advancement of Science, 1882* (London, 1883), 622–623.

_____ *Through Masai Land. A Journey of Exploration among the Snowclad Volcanic Mountains and Strange Tribes of Eastern Equatorial Africa* (London, 1883).

_____ "Through the Masai Country to Victoria Nyanza," *Proceedings of the Royal Geographical Society,* V (1883), 544–550.

_____ "Sketch of a Trip to Sokoto by the River Niger," *The Journal of the Manchester Geographical Society,* II (1886), 1–18.

_____ "Note on the African Tribes of the British Empire," *Journal of the Anthropological Institute of Great Britain and Ireland,* XVI (1886), 182–186.

_____ "Up the Niger to the Central Sudan," *Good Words,* 27 (1886), 23–29, 109–118, 249–256, 323–330.

_____ "Niger and Central Sudan Sketches," *The Scottish Geographical Magazine,* II (1886), 577–596.

_____ "How I Crossed Masai-Land," *Scribner's Magazine,* VI (1889), 387–405.

_____ "How I Reached My Highest Point in the Atlas," *Good Words,* 30 (1889), 17–25.

_____ "Some Impressions of Morocco and the Moors," *The Journal of the Manchester Geographical Society,* V (1889), 101–118.

_____ "Explorations in the Atlas Mountains," *The Scottish Geographical Magazine,* V (1889), 169–180.

_____ "A Journey to Southern Morocco and the Atlas Mountains," *Proceedings of the Royal Geographical Society,* XI (1889), 1–17, 64.

———— *Travels in the Atlas and Southern Morocco* (London, 1889).

———— "To Lake Bangweolo and the Unexplored Region of British Central Africa," *The Geographical Journal*, I (1893), 97–121, 192.

———— "The Geology of Southern Morocco and the Atlas Mountains," *The Quarterly Journal of the Geological Society of London*, LV (1899), 190–213.

Thomson, Robert S., *La fondation de l'Etat Indépendant du Congo* (Brussels, 1933).

Van Grieken, E., "H. M. Stanley au Congo, 1879–1884," *Institut Royal Colonial Belge—Bulletin*, XXV (1954), 1124–1179.

Ward, Herbert, *My Life with Stanley's Rear Guard* (London, 1890).

———— *A Voice from the Congo* (London, 1910).

Wassermann, J., *H. M. Stanley—Explorer* (London, 1932).

Wauters, A. J., *Stanley's Emin Pasha Expedition* (London, 1890).

Welbourn, Frederick B., "Speke and Stanley at the Court of Mutesa," *Uganda Journal*, XXV (1961), 220–223.

Werner, J. R., *A Visit to Stanley's Rear-Guard, At Major Barttelot's Camp on the Aruhwimi, Congo* (London, 1889).

Index

Index

In this index modern geographical renderings are used for purposes of identification even where they are anachronistic.

Comoro Islands, 46
Comorro, Latuka headman, 160–161
Companhia da Zambezia, 288
Cong Alwala ("Chongi"), of Acholi-land, 132
Congo (Kinshasa), 47, 225, 226, 229, 230, 233, 234, 236, 237, 243, 244–246, 248–249, 251–252, 271, 276, 305. *See also* Congo River; Lualaba River; etc.
Congo River, 2, 48, 56, 89, 188n, 236, 240, 241, 257, 262–264, 266–269, 282–284, 285–286, 289, 298, 300
Congo-Zambezi system, and canal, 276–277, 284
Copper, 265, 275, 284, 300
Cotton, 57
Coupland, Sir Reginald, British professor, quoted, 230
Crimea, 144
Crimean War, 69, 71, 100
Crispi, Francesco, Italian foreign minister, 213
Cuanza River, 278
Cwezi, demigods, 169
Cyprus, 287
Cyrenaica, 3, 197, 219
Czillagh, Leopold von, Austrian aristocrat, 201

Dahomey, 2, 89–92, 216
Dakhla, oasis (Egypt), 199–200
Damascus, Syria, 86
Danaqla, Arab people, 167
Dar es Salaam, Tanzania, 297, 304
Darwinism, Social, 6, 144, 211, 215, 217, 311
Daym az-Zubayr, the Sudan, 152
Debono, Andrea, Maltese merchant and slave trader, 132, 159–160, 163, 167
Debra Tabor, Ethiopia, 205
Dembo, people, 152
Denham, Lt. Dixon, British explorer, 1, 4, 20, 25, 189, 192, 193, 210, 220
Denhardt, Clemens, German explorer, 206
Denhardt, Gustav, German explorer, 206
Deschamps, Prof. Hubert, cited, 4, 8
Devon, England, 142, 148
Dickens, Charles, characters used, 247–248
Dillon, W. E., British naval assistant surgeon, 258–259, 261
Dinah, fort, Congo (K), 270

Dinka, people, 152
Discovery: notion of, 19; defined, 7–8
Dondo, Angola, 271, 278
Dorugu, Barth's Hausa servant, 22, 34
Dra, Wadi, 181–182
Duku, Nigeria, 193
Dulbahantas, people, 99
Dumfriesshire, Scotland, 297, 301
Durrugu, interpreter, 195
Duveyrier, Henri, French explorer, 185, 187, 190

Eardley-Wilmot, William, British Commander, 90
Eckart, Franz, German technician, 201
Edinburgh, University of, 297, 301
Egba, Yoruba people, 88
Egypt and Egyptians, 70, 131–132, 136, 141–142, 148–149, 156, 163–164, 166–169, 170–172, 190, 196n, 197, 198–200, 204, 205, 213, 217
Elgon, Mount, 299
Embomma (Boma), Congo (K), 239
Emin Pasha (Eduard Schnitzer), Austrian administrator, 2, 171–172, 300; relief expedition and fund, 225, 226, 229, 230, 233, 234, 236, 237–238, 239–240, 247n, 252
Enfield, England, 141
Equatoria, the Sudan, 136, 141–142, 151
Erhardt, Jacob, German missionary, 100
Ethiopia, 2, 3, 69, 155, 156, 182, 190, 196–197, 204–205, 207–208, 209, 212, 214, 258
Ethnography, 134, 191–192, 246, 292, 301, 308–309; and explorers, 6, 52, 56–57, 65, 70, 76–77, 83, 85, 89–92
Eton College, 66
Exeter Hall, 228
Exploration, motives for, 2–11. *See also* under individual explorers
Explorers, as geographers, 3, 10; impact of, 4–6, 7, 9–10, 16, 20–22, 35–36, 37, 59–60, 76, 132–133, 134–135, 137, 246, 317–318, 320

Faidherbe, Louis Léon César, French governor of Senegal, 216
Faloro, Uganda, 132
Fang, people, 89
Fara'a, Hausa term, 23, 27, 33, 34
Fashoda (Malakal), the Sudan, 165

Moçambique, 42, 44
Mode Abd-Allahi, of Adamawa, 23
Moffat, Robert, nephew of Livingstone, 259, 261
Mohammed el Gatroni. *See* Muhammad al-Gatruni
Mohammed ibn Salib, Arab trader, 262
Mollien, Gaspard, French explorer, 1, 4
Mombasa, Kenya, 18, 69, 73, 124, 286, 304
Mombay, Seedy (Sidi) Mbarak. *See* Sidi Bombay
Mona Peho, chief in Angola, 277
Monrovia, Liberia, 217
Morocco, 3, 179–182, 185–186, 207, 211–212, 213, 300, 303, 305, 306, 313, 316
Moshi, Tanzania, 305
"Mountains of the Moon," 70, 78
Mruli, Bunyoro, 160
Msalima, Tanzania, 103, 113
Mseni (Unyamwezi), Tanzania, 73
Msiri, Yeke overlord of Katanga, 275, 278–279, 300
Mugema, the, chief of Busiro, 129
Muhammad Ahmad al-'Aqqad, slave trader, 157
Muhammad al-Gatruni: as Barth's servant, 34–35; as Rohlfs's servant, 190, 193–194, 197
Muhammad Besserki, of Fezzan, 190
Muhammad Shtaui, of Tripoli, 188, 209
Muhammadu Bello, Sarkin Musulmi, 27
Muhammed Ali, of Bunder Gori, 99
Muhammed 'Ali, ruler of Egypt, 70, 213
Muhammed bin Gharib, Arab slave trader, 56
Muhaya Rubambula, founder of Mwanza chiefdom, 103–104
Muhinna bin Suleiman, Taboran trader, 117, 119
Muinyi, Hassani, Arab trader, 266
Mumia, Luyia chief, 318
Munzinger, Werner, German explorer, 196
Murchison, Sir Roderick, president of the Royal Geographical Society, 45, 84, 134
Murchison Falls, 161
Murphy, Cecil, British Lieutenant, 259, 261

Murzuk, Fezzan, 189, 191
Musa Bey al-'Aqqad, slave trader, 157–158
Musa Mzuri, Taboran financier, 109, 115, 117–118, 120, 121
Muscat, Oman, 73
Muscati, with Stanley, 239
Muslim. *See* Islam
Mutesa I, *kabaka* of Buganda, 97, 106, 113, 115, 122–130, 133, 136, 170, 247, 250–251, 260–261
Mwanza, Tanzania, 102, 103–104, 122
Mwata Yamvo, chief of the Lunda, 271–273
Mwene Kula, chief in Katanga, 276
Mweru, Lake, 47

Nachtigal, Gustav, German explorer, 190, 195, 197, 200, 201, 207
Naivasha, Lake, 310
Napier, General Sir Charles James, British commander in India, 67
Napier, Sir (later Lord) Robert, British general and diplomat, 196
Natal, 259, 287
National African Company. *See* Royal Niger Company
New Orleans, Louisiana, 231, 242, 257
New York Herald, 48, 225, 227, 229
Ngami, Lake, 42, 51
Ngoni, people (Tanzania and Malawi), 46, 104, 114–115, 119, 120–121, 133, 137, 305
Ngurutuwa, Nigeria, 21
Ngwato, people (Botswana), 54
Niari River, 300
Niger River, 1, 19, 87, 177, 185, 186, 187, 188n, 194, 300, 314
Nigeria, 15–38, 87, 186, 190, 191–195, 209, 215, 219, 300, 305, 306, 313, 314–315
Nile River and sources, 17, 18, 45, 47, 48, 70, 72, 75, 78, 79, 80–85, 92–93, 97, 103, 105, 112, 123–124, 130–131, 134, 135–136, 141–142, 145, 148–150, 152–153, 154–157, 163, 167, 172, 186, 199, 200, 201, 268, 283, 284
Nilotes, people, 151. *See also* Azande; Bari; Dinka; Nuer; Shilluk; etc.
Njemps Iloikop, 312
Njivi, marsh, Congo (K), 274
Noel, Bagirmi slave with Rohlfs, 190, 193

Victoria Nile River, 153, 157, 159, 161–162. See also Nile River
Victorian Age, 5, 7, 301, 303, 311, 317; attitudes, 143–144
Vinco, Angelo, missionary in the Sudan, 149
Violence, use of by explorers, 9. See also under each explorer
Vischer, Sir Hanns, British administrator, 22
Vogel, Eduard, German explorer, 19, 21, 187, 190, 192, 193, 201

Wad al-Mak, slave trader and Debono's principal agent, 160, 162
Wadai, Chad, 19, 186, 187, 191, 193, 200, 202
Wagner, Richard, 202n
Wainwright, Jacob, and Livingstone, 49, 261n
Wales, 225; Prince of, 285
Ward, Herbert, British expeditionary, quoted, 239, 246
Weimar, Germany, 198
Welwitsch, Friedrich, Portuguese-German naturalist, 51
West Indian Naval Squadron, 257
Western Sudan, the, 2, 7, 18–19, 35–36, 184–185, 188–189, 197, 214, 215, 299–300, 316
Westernization, and explorers, 129–130, 132–133
Westminster Abbey, 225
White Nile River, 2, 80–81, 156. See also Nile River
Whydah, Dahomey, 89, 91–92
William I, Kaiser of Germany, 190 197, 204
William II, Kaiser of Germany, 190
Winterbottom, Thomas, British explorer, 4

Wissmann, Hermann von, German officer and explorer, 220
Witu, Kenya, 206
Wurno, Nigeria, 32
Wurzburg, Germany, 182

Yambuya, Congo (K), 236, 240, 241, 247n
Yao, people (Malawi and Tanzania), 107–109
Yohannes IV, Emperor of Ethiopia, 204
Yola, Nigeria, 19, 23–24, 34
Yoruba, people (Nigeria), 88, 195

Zambezi River, 42, 44–46, 54, 57, 58, 276, 284
Zambia, 3, 47, 300, 306, 318, 319
Zanzibar, 18, 45, 46, 48, 56, 57, 69, 72–73, 74, 76, 82, 84, 101, 105–106, 113, 116, 117, 131, 154, 178, 205–206, 230, 231, 232–233, 235, 248, 258–259, 266, 268, 282; Sultan of, 266, 285, 291, 298
Zanzibari guides and traders, 100, 102, 106–107, 109–113, 127
Zanzibari merchants, 70, 73
Zanzibaris, and Stanley, 232–233, 240. See also Arabs
Zaramo, people (Tanzania), 116
Zaria, Nigeria, 33
Zeila, Somalia, 69
Zella, Libya, 202
Zen en Abidin, of Timbuktu, 22
Zinder, Niger, 18–19
Zinza, people, 110, 120, 121
Zionist settlement, scheme for, 219
Zittel, Karl, German paleontologist, 199
Zulu wars, 287
Zwangendaba, Ngoni chief, 114

The Authors

NORMAN ROBERT BENNETT is associate professor of history, and research associate in the African Studies Center, Boston University. He first visited East Africa in 1959; in 1962 he was visiting lecturer at Kivukoni College, Dar es Salaam. He is the author of *Studies in East African History* (1963), and editor of *New England Merchants in Africa: A History through Documents, 1802 to 1865*, with George E. Brooks, Jr. (1965); *Reconstructing African Culture History*, with Creighton Gabel (1967); *Leadership in Eastern Africa: Six Political Biographies* (1969); and *From Zanzibar to Ujiji: The Journal of A. W. Dodgshun, 1877–1879* (1969). He is the editor of *African Historical Studies*.

ROY C. BRIDGES is a lecturer in history at the University of Aberdeen, and was a visiting professor of history at the University of Indiana. He lectured in history at Makerere University College, and has written several articles on African explorers and exploration. He contributed a biographical study of Johann Ludwig Krapf for the reissue of the *Travels* (1968), and co-edited *Nations and Empires* (1969).

ROBERT O. COLLINS is professor of history and dean of the Graduate School at the University of California, Santa Barbara. He is the author of *The Southern Sudan, 1883–1898* (1962), *King Leopold, England and the Upper Nile 1899–1909* (1968), and co-author of *Americans in Africa, 1865–1900* (1965), and *Egypt and the Sudan* (1966). He has edited numerous works, including *Problems in African History* (1968), *The Partition of Africa* (1969), and *An Arabian Diary* (1969), and has contributed essays and articles to collections and journals. He has traveled widely in the Nile Valley and East Africa and has resided in the Sudan.

ERIC HALLADAY is vice-master and senior tutor of Grey College, University of Durham, and teaches in the department of history there.

JAMES HOOKER is professor of history at Michigan State University, and the author of *Black Revolutionary: George Padmore's Path from Communism to Pan-Africanism* (1967).

ANTHONY H. M. KIRK–GREENE, spent sixteen years in Northern Nigeria, first as a district officer and latterly as professor at Ahmadu Bello University. He was also chairman of the Hausa Language Examinations Board, and has been a visiting professor in African Studies at several American universities. He is the author of a number of books on Nigeria, including *Barth's Travels in Nigeria* (1962); *Adamawa Past and Present* (1958); *The Emirates of Northern Nigeria* (1966), with S. J. Hogben; and *The Principles of Native Administration in Nigeria* (1965). He is presently senior research fellow in African Studies at St. Antony's College, Oxford.

MRS. CAROLINE OLIVER served for nine years in the British Foreign Service, and traveled extensively throughout Africa with her husband, Professor Roland Oliver of the University of London. With him she co-authored *Africa in the Days of Exploration* (1965).

ROBERT I. ROTBERG is associate professor of political science and history, The Massachusetts Institute of Technology, the editor of *The Journal of Interdisciplinary History*, and research associate, the Center for International Affairs, Harvard University. He was a Rhodes Scholar at the University of Oxford and began research in Africa in 1958. Subsequently he was a visiting professor at Makerere University College. He is the author of *Joseph Thomson and the Exploration of Africa* (1970), *The Rise of Nationalism in Central Africa: The Making of Malawi and Zambia, 1873–1964* (1965), *A Political History of Tropical Africa* (1965), and *Christian Missionaries and the Creation of Northern Rhodesia, 1882–1924* (1965), and has edited *Protest and Power in Black Africa* (1970) and George Mwase's *Strike a Blow and Die: A Narrative of Race Relations in Colonial Africa* (1967).

WOLFE W. SCHMOKEL, a native of Germany, received his academic training at the University of Maryland and Yale University. His fields of interest include the history of Liberia and German activities in Africa. He is the author of *Dream of Empire: German Colonialism, 1919–1945* (1964), and has contributed to a number of periodicals and collective works on African history. He is associate professor of history and director of graduate studies in history at the University of Vermont.